From Douglass to Duvalier

New World Diasporas

UNIVERSITY PRESS OF FLORIDA

Florida A&M University, Tallahassee
Florida Atlantic University, Boca Raton
Florida Gulf Coast University, Ft. Myers
Florida International University, Miami
Florida State University, Tallahassee
New College of Florida, Sarasota
University of Central Florida, Orlando
University of Florida, Gainesville
University of North Florida, Jacksonville
University of South Florida, Tampa
University of West Florida, Pensacola

NEW WORLD DIASPORAS
Edited by Kevin A. Yelvington

This series seeks to stimulate critical perspectives on diaspora processes in the New World. Representations of race and ethnicity, the origins and consequences of nationalism, migratory streams and the advent of transnationalism, the dialectics of homelands and diasporas, trade networks, gender relations in immigrant communities, the politics of displacement and exile, and the utilization of the past to serve the present are among the phenomena addressed by original, provocative research in disciplines such as anthropology, history, political science, and sociology.

International Editorial Board

More Than Black: Afro-Cubans in Tampa, by Susan D. Greenbaum (2002)

Carnival and the Formation of a Caribbean Transnation, by Philip W. Scher (2003)

Dominican Migration: Transnational Perspectives, edited by Ernesto Sagás and Sintia E. Molina (2004)

Salvadoran Migration to Southern California: Redefining El Hermano Lejano, by Beth Baker-Cristales (2004)

The Chrysanthemum and the Song: Music, Memory, and Identity in the South American Japanese Diaspora, by Dale A. Olsen (2004)

Andean Diaspora: The Tiwanaku Colonies and the Origins of South American Empire, by Paul S. Goldstein (2005)

Migration and Vodou, by Karen E. Richman (2005)

True-Born Maroons, by Kenneth M. Bilby (2005)

The Tears of Hispaniola: Haitian and Dominican Diaspora Memory, by Lucía M. Suárez (2006)

Dominican-Americans and the Politics of Empowerment, by Ana Aparicio (2006)

Nuer-American Passages: Globalizing Sudanese Migration, by Dianna J. Shandy (2006)

Religion and the Politics of Ethnic Identity in Bahia, Brazil, by Stephen Selka (2007)

Reconstructing Racial Identity and the African Past in the Dominican Republic, by Kimberly Eison Simmons (2009)

Haiti and the Haitian Diaspora in the Wider Caribbean, edited by Philippe Zacaïr (2010)

From Douglass to Duvalier: U.S. African Americans, Haiti, and Pan Americanism, 1870–1964, by Millery Polyné (2010; first paperback edition, 2011)

New Immigrants, New Land: A Study of Brazilians in Massachusetts, by Ana Cristina Braga Martes (2010)

Yo Soy Negro: Blackness in Peru, by Tanya Maria Golash-Boza (2011)

Trance and Modernity in the Southern Caribbean: African and Hindu Popular Religions in Trinidad and Tobago, by Keith E. McNeal (2011)

From Douglass to Duvalier

U.S. African Americans, Haiti, and Pan Americanism, 1870–1964

Millery Polyné

University Press of Florida
Gainesville/Tallahassee/Tampa/Boca Raton
Pensacola/Orlando/Miami/Jacksonville/Ft. Myers/Sarasota

First cloth printing, 2010
First paperback printing, 2011

Library of Congress Cataloging-in-Publication Data
Polyné, Millery
From Douglass to Duvalier: U.S. African Americans, Haiti and Pan
Americanism, 1870–1964 / Millery Polyné.
p. cm.—(New world diasporas)
Includes bibliographical references and index.
ISBN 978-0-8130-3472-0 (alk. paper); ISBN 978-0-8130-3763-9
1. African Americans—Relations with Haitians—History. 2. United
States—Relations—Haiti. 3. Haiti—Relations—United States.
4. Pan-Americanism—History. 5. United States—Race relations.
6. Haiti—Race relations. I. Title.
E185.61.P674 2010
303.48'27294073089969–dc22   2009051048

The University Press of Florida is the scholarly publishing agency for the
State University System of Florida, comprising Florida A&M University,
Florida Atlantic University, Florida Gulf Coast University, Florida Interna-
tional University, Florida State University, New College of Florida, Univer-
sity of Central Florida, University of Florida, University of North Florida,
University of South Florida, and University of West Florida.

University Press of Florida
15 Northwest 15th Street
Gainesville, FL 32611–2079
http://www.upf.com

For Ellison

Contents

Illustrations

Acknowledgments

I am in complete awe as I type my acknowledgments. My friend, cousin and colleague Harley F. Etienne and I often go back and forth about how "this" happened. We are two Haitian American kids from Mattapan, a largely working-class U.S. African American and Caribbean neighborhood that borders Milton, Massachusetts, a wealthy suburb, and is located a few miles south of downtown Boston. Mattapan occupies a liminal and contested space, in terms of class, geography and ethnic identity, where Pan-Caribbean and U.S. African American peoples collaborated and fused cultures yet also wrestled over limited resources. It is here where the seeds of an Afri/Haitian/American identity took root, where my hour commute to Boston Latin School (BLS) began, where, at times, I did not believe that a life beyond Blue Hill Avenue existed.

Yet, at the same time that I am overwhelmed by disbelief that this book has come to fruition, I am mindful of the amazing people who have encouraged and challenged me and who have nourished and cared for me over the years. For it was these good, bright and nurturing people who allowed me to transition beyond awe and wonder to unreserved gratitude.

But where do you start when you think about your intellectual development? Well, seventh grade at BLS sounds like a great starting point. Inez Middleton, my English literature teacher, introduced me to Shakespeare, argumentative essays and footnotes. In a failed effort to please Mrs. Middleton, I included more than sixty footnotes in a ten-page paper. I hope that her efforts to teach me to develop my own voice and arguments have translated into this monograph. To my dear mentors and history professors at Morehouse College—Augustine Konneh, Marcellus Barksdale and Alton Hornsby Jr.—thank you for being ideal models of teachers. Your memorable classes introduced me to the Haitian Revolution and U.S. African American intellectual and social history. Three incredible professors at Spelman College demonstrated a tremendous impact on my development:

Gloria Wade-Gayles, Kathleen Phillips-Lewis and Beverly Guy Sheftall. It is the quilt of a Morehouse and Spelman education that opened the doors to my consciousness.

Ann Arbor and the University of Michigan proved to be a source of joy and pain. Several brilliant scholars, administrators and graduate students impelled me to think about history, research, interdisciplinarity and identity in nuanced and uncomfortable ways. Many, many thanks to my virtuosic and gifted advisors Mamadou Diouf, Laurent Dubois, Ifeoma Nwankwo and Earl Lewis. Also, the work, teaching and counsel of Michele Mitchell, Julius Scott, Rebecca J. Scott, Kevin K. Gaines, Kelly Askew and Evans Young proved immeasurable. Much love to Beth James at the University of Michigan's Center for Afro-American and African Studies and to a number of peers who supported me and read my work during the arduous book process.

Much respect and thanks to Chantalle F. Verna, LaTissia Mitchell, Frank Guridy and Matthew J. Smith. Your insight, critique and generosity humbled me. I trust this book is better for it. Much gratitude to my dear friends and colleagues who listened, opened doors and cheered me on through the years: R. Scott Heath, Adrian Burgos, Jason Young, Geoffrey K. Ward, Stephen A. Ward, Nikki Stanton, Shawn Christian, Odis Johnson, Nathan Connolly, Shani Mott, Kidada Williams, Vanessa Agard-Jones, Samuel K. Roberts, Christina Greer, Umi Vaughn, Sherri-Ann Butterfield, Tomas Hulick Baiza, Mario Ruiz, Shaun Lopez, April Mayes, Aims McGuinness, Gina Ulysse, Candice Jenkins, Ferentz Lafargue, Tom Gugliemo, Tracy Flemming, Karen Miller, Prudence Cumberbatch, Lisa McLeod Thompson, Pervis Brown, Richard Blint, Eddy DeBriffault, Alice Backer, Jean David, Annel Cabrera and Minkah Makalani.

Several veteran scholars read parts of the manuscript and/or changed the way I approached the study of U.S. African America and Haiti. I am thankful for the guidance and inspiration of William Darity Jr., Patrick Belle-garde-Smith, Carol Anderson, Brenda G. Plummer, Alex Dupuy, Claudine Michel, Jacqueline Malone, Miriam Jimínez-Roman, Juan Flores, J. Michael Dash, Colin Palmer, François Pierre-Louis, Gerald Horne, Michel S. Laguerre, Robert Hall, Gary Okihiro, Yvonne Daniel, Felipe Smith, George White Jr., David Sheinin, Clyde Taylor, Cary Fraser, Georges Fouron, Henry Frank, Lucía Suárez, Peter Hinks, Stephen Hall, Henry Frierson and Holger Henke. I would be truly remiss if I failed to mention the individuals who took the time out to discuss their lives, Haiti and U.S. politics: Jean-Léon

Destiné, Congressman Charles Rangel, Bernard Dietrich, Annette Mac-Donald, Marie Madeline Price-Mars, Ester Dartigue, Eddy Marc-Charles and Roland Weiner. Thank you for your candor.

At the City University of New York, the College of Staten Island, I am indebted to Calvin Holder, Mike Foley, Jonathan Sassi, Catherine Lavender and the wonderful members of the History Department and staff. My home institution, New York University's Gallatin School of Individualized Study, and several members of NYU's History and Anthropology Department provided me with incredible intellectual and financial support during the writing process. Thank you to Dean Susanne Wofford, Jack Tchen, George Shulman, Ritty Lukose, Michael Dinwiddie, Jeffrey Sammons, Michael Gomez and Aisha Khan and NYU's Caribbean Working Group.

I received significant funding from a number of sources. Many thanks to these programs and institutions that believed in this project: University of Michigan Horace H. Rackham Graduate School Fellowship, New England Board of Higher Education Dissertation Fellowship—Northeastern University, PSC-CUNY Research Award, CUNY's Faculty Fellowship Publication Program and the University of Rochester's Frederick Douglass Institute for African-African American Studies Post-Doctoral Fellowship. Special recognition to several individuals who made my Rochester experience worthwhile: Frederick Harris, Cedric Johnson, Anthea Butler, Ghislaine Radegonde-Eison, Jenny Stoever, Niambi Carter, Larry Hudson, Jesse T. Moore and John Michael.

I am also grateful to all the cooperative staff at the many libraries that aided my research, including the Columbus Memorial Library, Herbert Hoover and Franklin D. Roosevelt Presidential Library, Morris Library at Southern Illinois University, National Archives, Howard University's Moorland Spingarn, Rockefeller Archive Center, Center for Research Libraries, Chicago History Museum and the Library of Congress. I am particularly indebted to the amazing staff at the Schomburg Center for Research in Black Culture. The Schomburg is my home, and Andre Elizé, Diana Lachatanere, Steven Fullwood, Aisha Al-Adawiya, Nurah-Rosalie Jeter, Cynthia Rollins and Betty Odabasian helped me immensely.

At the University Press of Florida, I would like to thank acquisitions assistant director Amy Gorelick, managing editor Gillian Hillis, project editor Jacqueline Kinghorn Brown, copy editor Barbara Drake and the UPF design and production team.

I am nothing without family and friends. Much love to my parents,

Raymond and Lorna, and my sister and nephew, Antonine and Nesta, respectively. Many, many thanks to the Polyné, Cassamajor, Etienne, Halaby, Baker, Gaffney, Marc-Charles, Knight, Edwards, Marshall and Ossé families. Thank you, Alita Anderson and Harley F. Etienne, for always being shining stars in my life. Much respect to Yohance F. Murray, Edwidge Danticat, Dale Deletis, Todd Fry, Brenda Boyd-Bell, Kenji Jasper, and Steven Allwood. Additionally, a special shout-out to Marc Cheltenham, Elliot Marshall, Woodrow M. Knight, and Omar Tarpley for giving a brother a place to lay his head while on research trips.

To my dear Bienaimé, Judy: We have been through so much. This book is dedicated to our son, but it is you who recharged my battery, provided me with a quiet space and loved me. I am forever grateful. Consider this book an apology for my funkiness. I adore you.

Note on Usage and Terminology

In this book I employ the terms "U.S. African American(s)" and "U.S. black(s)" interchangeably to refer to U.S. black citizens in the United States. Moreover, the use of the term "African American" in this monograph encompasses African-descended peoples throughout the Americas (North and South America and the Caribbean). For clarity, I also use nation of origin as a way to classify non-U.S. African Americans in the Americas (for example, Haitians, Dominicans and Cubans).

This distinction attempts to highlight two central aims. First, it challenges scholars to disrupt the "success of the logic of coloniality" in the Americas, which affirms the historical narrative of America as the sole ownership and authorship of Western Europeans. Coloniality crystallizes asymmetrical social and economic systems, displaces "economies previously existing in the would-be America," and "establish[es] 'natural' epistemic principles that legitimized the ruling out of differential economies."[1] Although the "idea" of America proves to be a European construction, the contributions of indigenous and African-descended peoples played a prominent role in the development of American (hemispheric) material, intellectual and spiritual "economies."[2]

Second, expanding the meaning of "African American" emphasizes the shared history of forced labor under racialized slavery, antiblack discriminatory practices within (post)colonial and postslavery societies, the history of intraracial migration, and the intellectual and cultural exchange of African Americans. These common experiences and interests among African Americans generally, and U.S. African Americans and Haitians more specifically, are embedded with inconsistencies, difference, and conflicts over strategy and identity.[3] Yet, these transnational and intraracial relations allow for what scholar Walter Mignolo asserts is a "decolonial paradigm of co-existence."[4] U.S. African Americans and Haitians, in particular, sought to challenge the hierarchies of power and to "change the geography of knowledge" in order to forge mutuality and cooperation within the hemisphere. The use of "African American" and "U.S. African American" complements the work of literary scholar Ifeoma K. Nwankwo by discerning "the points where here and there meet, and where the lines between the two not only cross but become blurred."[5]

Introduction

Coups, Congress and Completing the Haitian Revolution:
U.S. African Americans Respond to Aristide's "Exile"

Minutes before sunrise on February 29, 2004, in Tabarre, a suburb of Port-au-Prince, Haiti, U.S. diplomat Luis G. Moreno and several diplomatic and military officials arrived at Haitian president Jean-Bertrand Aristide's residence. According to Moreno, his presence there at daybreak demonstrated that Aristide's administration and U.S. forces in Haiti had previously scheduled this meeting in order to furtively escort the president onto a U.S. aircraft and out of the country, into political exile. Mounting reports of civilian and political acts of violence by invading Haitian paramilitary forces headquartered in the Dominican Republic threatened the life of Aristide and the tenuous strands of Haiti's political stability.[1] When asked later to recount what happened that morning, Aristide gave a version of events that remained poles apart from that presented in U.S. reports. The Haitian president vigorously asserted that U.S. forces had "kidnapped" him and his wife, attorney Mildred Trouillot-Aristide. Additionally, Aristide insisted that Washington and Haitian resistance factions had orchestrated the coup d'état to bring an end to his administration and to secure power for U.S.-backed opposition groups.

On the morning of March 1, 2004, Aristide, now exiled in the Central African Republic, made frantic calls to key U.S. African American political figures. Maxine Waters, a Democratic congresswoman representing the 35th district of California, insisted that Aristide "did not resign" and noted that the deposed president had declared: "The world must know it was a coup. I was kidnapped. I was forced out. That's what happened. I did not resign. I did not go willingly. I was forced to go."[2]

Another person who received a call from Aristide on March 1 was Randall Robinson, a paid lobbyist for the Haitian government and the former head of TransAfrica, a social-justice and human-rights advocacy organization. Robinson confidently supported the president's claims and publicly affirmed that Aristide, "a democratically elected president," had been "abducted" by the United States "in the commission of a [U.S.] American-induced coup," adding, "This is a frightening thing to contemplate."[3]

Swift public objections by the Congressional Black Caucus (CBC) and representatives of Haitian organizations in the United States commenced in the subsequent days, with public figures condemning Washington's alleged involvement in Aristide's deportation and the installation of Gérard Latortue as interim head of the provisional government. Representative Waters' passionate and resolute commitment to repairing the diplomatic nightmare, her near-quotidian press releases and the forty-hour trip taken by Randall Robinson, U.S. ambassador Sidney Williams and other key aides and sympathizers from the United States to the Central African Republic and then on to Jamaica in order to "liberate" President Aristide, demonstrated the formidable alliances that had been forged between the deposed president and leading figures within U.S. African American political and policy circles.

Operating in a post-9/11 U.S. foreign-policy framework, in which the U.S. occupation of Iraq confirmed Washington's rapid maneuvers to establish hegemonic rule, the political outcry raised by the CBC to investigate Aristide's "kidnapping" and to protect a democratically elected president in the hemisphere established an important counter-response by U.S. African American legislators against an alleged U.S. involvement in a coup.[4] In a March 16, 2004, press release, Congresswoman Waters conflated the White House's Iraq policy of eliminating Saddam Hussein with Aristide's expulsion. Waters explained:

> That's just a continuation of the Bush Administration policy of regime change and misleading the American people about everything they do. . . . They continue to lie about the lies they told to justify their invasion of Iraq, saying they never said what they said about weapons of mass destruction and Iraq's imminent threat, and they are trying to make us believe their visit to President Aristide's home at 3 a.m. on February 29, 2004, was not a forced removal. . . .[5]

A fierce opponent of the U.S. invasion of Iraq, Waters believed that deception, cloaked in the guise of advancing democracy for the benefit of

U.S. interests, cemented these two events. Yet at the same time the CBC protested the Bush administration's supposed connection to Aristide's removal; they also believed in working with Washington to protect the Haitian president. Pro-Aristide support among many U.S. African Americans countered intense opposition from the Haitian "business elite, the political middle class . . . [and] intellectuals," including a number of "human rights organizations" and global/hemispheric associations such as the Organization of American States and the United Nations, both of which defended Latortue's provisional government.[6] In spite of the disjuncture between influential, anti-Aristide Haitian voices and the boosterish approach of Aristide's Lavalas administration by U.S. African American political elites, the CBC appealed to U.S. president George W. Bush for monetary and military aid to shield Aristide from the impending threat of opposition groups and to preserve Haiti's democratically elected government. The CBC's actions reflected the complex circumstances of an influential class of U.S. African Americans who have historically chosen to work as stewards of the government and capitalist structures in order to uphold U.S. interests (such as promoting democratic government in the hemisphere and providing foreign aid), but also have challenged the ways Washington contradicted those same political ideals.

In addition, and possibly more significantly, the international uproar against Aristide's putative abduction occurred less than two months after the commemoration of Haiti's two-hundredth anniversary of its historic independence. In 2004, institutions and cities from Lewiston, Maine, to Port-au-Prince produced a litany of celebrations and academic panels honoring Haiti's revolutionary past. Concurrently, these events symbolized a shedding of the republic's tumultuous political and economic history in hopes of an auspicious future. Ron Daniels, an educator, an activist and the Peace and Freedom Party candidate for president in the 1992 election, organized the controversial "Cruising Into History" (CIH), a weeklong salute to the radical events of 1791 as well as an international planning event for Haitian economic and cultural development. Set for August 2004 (marking the month the Haitian revolution began), CIH aimed to unite people of African descent to discuss the importance of the Haitian Revolution to American and Western European histories and to create political, cultural and economic linkages between African Americans and Haitians for the advancement of Haiti. Haiti's political unrest in February 2004 shipwrecked

Daniels' history cruise, and his ambitious plans missed their mark "to uplift Haiti" and "to respectfully assist [Haitians] to finish the unfinished Haitian Revolution in the 21st century" because of their overemphasis on tourism and the fear that the event would inadvertently send a message of support to the non-Lavalas transitional government.[7]

What does it mean to "finish the unfinished Haitian Revolution"? Why did Ron Daniels understand the Haitian Revolution as being current, available and relevant to the Haitian political affairs of 2004? For U.S. African Americans, completing the Haitian Revolution signified an acknowledgment of the transformative events between 1791 and 1804 that resulted in the abolition of slavery in Saint-Domingue (modern-day Haiti) and black self-governance, yet demonstrated dissatisfaction with the ways that Haiti's legacy of authoritarianism and immense economic hardship reflected upon their domestic struggles for racial equality. Often U.S. blacks conflated the history and objectives of the Haitian Revolution, which transformed and shifted depending upon its actors, time and space, with the imagined notion of a postrevolutionary Haiti as a "city upon a hill" that, with proper guidance, could be representative of black advancement and sovereignty in the colonial and postcolonial worlds of the nineteenth and twentieth centuries.[8] This conflation manifested in a number of collaborative and Washington/U.S. African American–led political, economic and cultural projects and commissions in such realms as diplomacy, business, education and tourism.

The memory of the Haitian Revolution and the country's independence in 1804 loomed large over Aristide's departure in 2004 and, more broadly, over U.S. African American/Haitian relations. Among the lingering questions that influenced debate was whether, apart from abolishing slavery, the Haitian people had adequately fulfilled the aims of the revolution, as reflected in Daniels' call to "finish" the country's unfinished business. Randall Robinson's book *An Unbroken Agony: Haiti, From Revolution to the Kidnapping of a President* (2007) interweaves the history of Saint-Domingue and its revolution with details of events leading up to Aristide's removal. *An Unbroken Agony* exemplified a number of recent texts, interviews, speeches and online commentary in which the history of the Haitian Revolution and its bicentennial events proved the perfect instrument for U.S. African Americans and Haitians to articulate their views towards Aristide's exile and the U.S. and United Nations occupation of Haiti. "Just as Napoleon sought to restore slavery in Haiti," noted Johnnie Stevens of the International Action Center, in preparation for a rally at Brooklyn College in April 2004, "so does George Bush want to re-impose colonial rule in the world's oldest Black republic."[9]

Jean-Jacques Dessalines' declaration of Haitian sovereignty on January 1, 1804, underscored the radically transformative, thirteen-year struggle against the system of racial slavery and white supremacy. Haitian independence established the country as the first free black republic in the Americas and as the second sovereign nation in the Western hemisphere. Although frustrated Haitians and scholars of Haiti have often dismissed these historic achievements as immaterial due to decades of political and economic volatility, the Haitian Revolution and its declaration of independence have profoundly shaped U.S. African American and Haitian interactions. This influence is particularly apparent in nineteenth-century U.S. African American emigration movements and in nineteenth- and twentieth-century literary texts, educational programs, religious projects and diplomatic channels. Scholars of the Haitian Revolution and eighteenth- and nineteenth-century U.S. diplomatic and political history have noted the far-reaching effects of the Haitian Revolution on the American hemisphere: from the tightening of slave laws by the U.S. Southern plantocracy and U.S. territorial expansion (e.g., the Louisiana Purchase) to rebellious activity among enslaved peoples in the Caribbean and South America.[10]

A brief analysis of a May 1861 article written by renowned nineteenth-century abolitionist and orator Frederick Douglass, titled "A Trip to Haiti," reveals the enduring bonds forged between U.S. African Americans and Haitians since the nineteenth century. These bonds have persisted throughout the Haitian government's various political battles for diplomatic recognition, during the U.S. occupation of Haiti (1915–1934) and during long periods of political and economic volatility, as well as throughout struggles by U.S. African Americans against slavery and racial inequality during the post-emancipation period. Published in *Douglass' Monthly* one month after the start of the U.S. Civil War and one year prior to the official U.S. recognition of Haitian sovereignty, Douglass's article served two purposes. First, it attempted to reclaim or redeem Haiti for U.S. African Americans as a potential site of black potentiality and humanity within a world where "the margin of life and liberty is becoming more narrow every year."[11]

This redemptive project proved significant both hemispherically and

temporally to U.S. African American and Haitian relations. Hemispherically, "A Trip to Haiti" included the black republic, this "modern land of Canaan," within the geo-politics of black liberationist thinking, an inspiring
space that primarily the biblical Egypt and Ethiopia occupied.[12] In contrast
with these two "far off" lands, Haiti's independence, history and land proved
current, real and geographically accessible for many free and enslaved U.S.
blacks. Through oral histories and modern forms of communication such
as novels (Martin Delany's *Blake; or the Huts of America, 1859–1862*), historical texts, speeches (John B. Russwurm's Bowdoin College address "The
Condition and Prospects of Haiti," 1826) and countless newspaper articles,
Haiti's "theatre of many stirring events and heroic achievements" revealed
shared experiences of racial slavery and also imagined biological connections, with Douglass referring to Haitians affectionately as "bone of our
bone, and flesh of our flesh."

Temporally, Douglass's analysis of Haiti's revolutionary existence brought
new meaning to and pushed the limits of understanding the New World by
challenging white Westerners' "disavowal" of Haiti's modernity as well as
expanding the frontiers of liberty, freedom and republicanism in the Americas.[13] U.S. racial slavery, Douglass wrote, "stole from us those years" that
U.S. blacks might have used to expand their own knowledge and to travel.
Thus, "A Trip to Haiti" served as a way to accelerate time and to expose his
readership to new black sites, a "city set on a hill," which advanced a modern discourse largely associated with the age of European Enlightenment.
Douglass argued that "We, naturally enough, desire to see, as we doubtless
shall see, in the *free, orderly and Independent* Republic of Haiti, a refutation
of the slanders and disparagements of our race. We want to experience the
feeling of being under a Government which has been administered by a
race denounced as mentally and morally incapable of self-government."[14]

Second, Douglass's piece sought to demonstrate, particularly from a U.S.
African American perspective, that black international politics, specifically
Haiti's success or failure, possessed profound implications for U.S. social,
economic and political relations.[15] Douglass interlaced brief discussions of
U.S. vilification and dominance of Haiti with the stark realities of U.S. an-
tiblack prejudices and violence.

Both the press and the platform of the United States have long made
Haiti the bugbear and scare-crow of the cause of freedom. . . . The

fact is, white Americans find it hard to tell the truth about colored people. They see us with a dollar in their eyes . . . and for this reason they are now, as never before, looking out into the world for a place of retreat, an asylum from the apprehended storm which is about to beat pitilessly upon them.[16]

Douglass maintained firm anti-emigrationist opinions during the period of the U.S. Civil War and beyond, although he briefly flirted with the idea of U.S. African American emigration prior to and during the early stages of the War between the States. Yet due to the burgeoning interest in Haiti and escalating feelings of exasperation from the U.S. free-colored population, Douglass planned to set sail and tour "this modern land of Canaan." Therefore, as I demonstrate later in the introduction and in chapter 1, Douglass wrestled with the politics of domestic and international affairs at various moments in his life to illuminate the nuances, complexities and interconnections of a hemispheric American identity.[17] Similarly, Douglass's articulations on U.S./Haiti relations prefigures the intricate dealings that elite U.S. African Americans, like those in the Congressional Black Caucus, negotiated within and in opposition to Washington's political and economic interests in subsequent years.

It is this historical memory that threads the transnational exchange between U.S. African Americans and Haitians from the nineteenth century through the new millennium. Both groups invoke the Haitian Revolution at various moments and places as an overture to transnational exchange of ideas: to signal clearly defined boundaries of cooperation; to demonstrate universal claims of freedom, racial equality and respect and to inspire resistance to structures that oppose them; and to illuminate the fissures of a U.S. American-styled democracy that historically disempowered Africans in the Americas because of intervention and asymmetrical power relations emblematic of U.S./Haiti relations since the nineteenth century. The confluence of events—the invasion of Iraq, the bicentennial celebration of Haiti's independence and, arguably, the lingering effects of U.S. African American disenfranchisement during the 2000 election—forced U.S. blacks, particularly those who worked in the U.S. Congress as members of the Congressional Black Caucus, to shed a light on the hypocrisy and distortions of democracy in the Americas.

Black Pan Americanism: Understanding a Racialized
Hemispheric Discourse

This recent contested diplomatic episode about the overthrow of the Aristide government introduces *From Douglass to Duvalier: U.S. African Americans, Haiti and Pan Americanism, 1870–1964* and highlights the problems and promises of U.S. African American and Haitian cooperation beyond the radical abolition struggles of the Haitian Revolution. This book attempts to show how U.S. African Americans used the idealized tenets of Pan Americanism—mutual cooperation, egalitarianism and nonintervention between nation-states in the Americas—to strengthen Haiti's social, economic and political growth and stability. Additionally, *From Douglass to Duvalier* analyzes Haitians' enthusiastic and cautionary responses to U.S. African American strategies of transnational uplift within the larger framework of U.S./Haiti relations and inter-American affairs.

Many of the intellectuals, artists, journalists and activists discussed in this book, such as Frederick Douglass, Walter White, Jean-Léon Destiné, Claude Barnett and Lavinia Williams, believed firmly in the creation and inclusion of African-descended peoples in the development of organizations and in the decision-making processes of programs and policies that affected their humanity. Typically, historians deemed some of these individuals' actions, ideologies and sympathies, particularly Douglass's anti-emigrationist/anti-colonization stance, as part of the initial stages of nineteenth-century black nationalism because blackness and/or the imagined community of African-descended peoples served as a pivot on which cooperative projects for racial progress developed.[18] Inevitably, black nationalists sought to create a black nation-state, although this aim does not define Douglass's political philosophy.

However, neither black nationalism nor Pan Africanism should be used as the sole lens through which to analyze black solidarity projects and ideologies. Although individuals applied ideas such as anticolonialism and the need for technical development from these movements, Pan Americanism, in its ideal form, proved to be utilitarian for nonwhite peoples because they believed in the preservation and sovereignty of the nation-state. Moreover, Pan Americanism potentially offered a shield from and often corroborated African Americans' belief in the perpetuation and future threat of European imperialism in the Americas. In theory, blacks supported the racial and color inclusivity of Pan Americanism, and it confirmed their hope in a system of egalitarian trade and much-needed U.S. financial and technical assistance critical to Caribbean and Latin American societies suffering from the adversity of postcoloniality. Pan Americanism provided individual material and ideological benefits for U.S. African American supporters. First, it served as an axis to a network of millions of nonwhite peoples in the Americas. Second, it affirmed many U.S. blacks' loyalty to Washington's hemispheric policy and their patriotism to the United States, a government that often questioned whether or not black leadership was anticommunist, prodemocratic and/or procapitalist. For example, in 1870, Frederick Douglass's support of Republican-party politics and his promotion of U.S. expansion in the Caribbean and Latin America through trade and, in some cases, annexation allowed him to obtain high-ranking positions as assistant secretary of a fact-finding commission on annexation of the Dominican Republic and later as U.S. minister to Haiti.

Douglass proved to be a complex and contradictory figure. As a staunch abolitionist Douglass fought indefatigably for the "colored man" but stated that he was not "ashamed" of lacking race pride.[19] At the same time, Douglass often emphasized individual achievement rather than racial progress. As historian Wilson J. Moses asserts, "Douglass vacillated between an assimilationist 'melting pot' conception of American history and preachments of a multiethnic ideal."[20] The contradiction between Douglass's ideas on "individual accomplishment" and "social identity" complemented the incongruities of a U.S.-centered Pan Americanism, which, in theory, deemphasized race and color and encouraged a transnational egalitarianism, yet constantly used racial primitivism and underdevelopment to justify U.S. expansionism and imperialism.

In its idealized form, Pan Americanism offered a pathway to inclusion and reciprocity for newly sovereign yet marginalized nations of the Caribbean and Latin America within the inter-American system. But into what entity were these largely nonwhite nations being included and for what purpose? During the post-Civil War period, the United States aggressively expanded its territorial holdings and commercial markets westward and southward, solidifying itself as a formidable force in the Americas and globally and thus shaping a U.S.-centered Pan Americanism that benefited U.S. interests. Many Caribbean and Latin American peoples questioned and actively challenged a U.S.-centered inter-American movement in order to "reclaim the promise of the democratic ideal."[21]

More specifically, it is important to ask: What were some of the critiques of Pan Americanism in the nineteenth and twentieth centuries? How did African Americans, who were mostly former slaves and arguably the most muted voices in inter-American affairs challenge, support and negotiate the ideological underpinnings of Pan Americanism? Why did the hemisphere become a significant organizing tool for shaping black internationalist initiatives? These are some of the key questions that frame *From Douglass to Duvalier.*

Cuban revolutionary and poet José Martí was one of the most noteworthy nineteenth-century Latin American critics of U.S. exceptionalism and U.S. hegemonic expansion in the Americas. Martí's oft-quoted speech "Mother America," given at the First Pan American Conference in Washington, D.C., in 1889, and his essay "Our America" (1891) encapsulated the resentment and angst that many Caribbean and Latin American radical elites harbored toward the United States, a country that Martí described as a "[giant] with seven-league boots."[22] Martí's antiracist philosophy, which conflicted with the European discriminatory racial hierarchies promoted by many white Latin American elites, called for an international solidarity among Hispanophone peoples (*Nuestra América*) to build economically and culturally proficient yet interdependent nation-states. Martí articulated a Hispanic Caribbean/Latin American Pan Americanism that attempted to expunge racial/color divisions and to establish a balance of powers in the region. Placed in the context of Cuba's struggle for independence against Spain (1898), in addition to Martí's efforts to strengthen *Cubanidad* or Cuban nationalism through active recruitment of Afro-Cubans to armed service, Martí's belief that "there can be no racial animosity, because there are no races" remains admirable. Yet this perspective created a myth of a universal Cuban identity that, in some ways, silenced Afro-Cuban expressions of *Cubanidad* and Pan Americanism.[23] As historian Brenda G. Plummer argued, "Nationalism required the submersion of all alternative ethnic identities, but *Cubanidad* was distinctly white and Creole."[24]

Although this book does not focus on Cuban articulations of inter-American solidarity, it remains in dialogue with Martí's concept of *Nuestra América* (Martí's vision did not include Haiti or other predominantly black islands under British, French or Dutch control). It also sets out to move beyond this concept to capture the voices and experiences of African-descended peoples in the Americas, something that the present scholarship on Pan Americanism lacks.

U.S. blacks and Haitians have been central to the spirit of the Pan American movement because of their long history of transnational engagements. These engagements, in the form of emigration, diplomatic relations, missionary and economic cooperative projects and anti-imperialist campaigns, not only demonstrated their support of the sovereignty and interdependence of the Americas, but also revealed their unrelenting discontent with racist inequalities in the hemisphere. Specifically, I concentrate on U.S. African Americans and Haitians during the post–U.S. Civil War period and from late nineteenth-century Haiti, because their emancipation, independence, intellectual achievements, isolation (Haiti) and interactions (both imagined and real) were rooted in the transformative events of the Haitian Revolution. These elements provide a unique perspective on how race was wielded and negotiated by both groups in the re-articulations of Pan Americanism in the nineteenth and twentieth centuries.

I employ black Pan Americanism as an organizing concept to understand and examine responses, strategies and/or possible new expressions of racial solidarity movements and of political, economic and cultural development within intraracial communities. Blacks in the Americas crafted Pan Americanism to empower themselves and to insulate their way of life from metropolitan political, economic and cultural dominance, particularly from the United States. U.S. African Americans and Haitians engaged in hemispheric discourses on development by seeking to establish substantive transnational cooperative initiatives to create new possibilities for political, cultural and economic development. Black Pan Americanism is mediated and revealed by U.S. blacks and Haitians through shared perceptions of repression, national and international government policy, official publications, and interpersonal communication that emphasize an individual's or an organization's commitment to and struggles with race and nation. Black cooperative initiatives endured a complex interplay of tension and harmony indicative of their diverse political, economic and social interests.

Thus, Haitians and U.S. African Americans did not necessarily always march to the same drummer. Frederick Douglass's initial support of a possible U.S. lease of Haitian territory (1891) encountered stiff opposition by the Haitian government, particularly Haitian president Florvil Hyppolite and Anténor Firmin, a noted scholar and Haiti's minister of finance and foreign affairs.[25] Washington's hard-line approach to acquiring the Haitian bay Môle Saint-Nicolas exemplified an emerging U.S. hegemony in the Americas. By the end of the ordeal, Douglass respected Haitian sovereignty in the face of U.S aggression (see chapter 1). Haitian officials maintained their admiration for Douglass and appointed him representative to the Haitian Pavilion at the 1893 World's Fair in Chicago.[26] Manifestations of black Pan Americanism often acknowledged the benefits of an alliance, rewarded its participants through appointments, medals, honors and tributes, and/or strengthened coalitions between organizations.

The building and fortifying of relationships between the two groups—through diplomacy, education, business and cultural art forms—often involved elite U.S. African Americans and Haitians who possessed the education, the connections and, occasionally, the capital to establish transnational links necessary to jump-start Haitian development. Thus, given the available sources, primarily personal and diplomatic correspondence, commission reports and an array of U.S. African American newspapers, *From Douglass to Duvalier* is a history from above. Furthermore, the book examines these elite U.S. African American and Haitian initiatives through the imperial North/South binary of foreign relations, which reflects the northern flow of capital and asymmetrical interactions between Haiti and the United States. Although there are instances between U.S. blacks and Haitians that echo an unequal North/South division, the two groups strived for parity and sought through black Pan Americanism a more multidirectional, East/West as well as North/South framework in order to cultivate cooperative projects and challenge Western imperialism and economic dependency within inter-American affairs. Specifically, some Haitians aided Dominican opposition groups to reestablish Dominican sovereignty during the reimplementation of Spanish colonialism in the Dominican Republic between 1861 and 1865 (see the next section and chapter 1).

Haitian and U.S. African American interactions revolved around three particular issues: U.S. territorial or military aggression against Haiti, Haitian underdevelopment and internal political and economic turmoil. These discourses, which were often governed by the myth that the Haitian Revolution remained unfinished and could be completed by U.S. African Americans, demonstrated, at times, the privileging of U.S. African American perspectives on Haitian advancements in culture, health, politics and the economy. The origins of the "finishing the unfinished revolution" myth are beyond the scope of this project. Yet *From Douglass to Duvalier* intends to highlight the projects and programs of collaboration and critique that gestured, informed and, in some cases, accelerated these ideas.

Haiti possesses multiple meanings in the black diasporic imagination. The country is a source of immense pride, particularly for U.S. blacks, because of its radical liberation movement, which deposed racial slavery and European colonialism in 1804. However, while U.S. blacks in the postrevolutionary era repeatedly celebrated the heroism of Haiti's foremost leader, Toussaint L'Ouverture, they were faced with the unshakable realities of Haitian poverty, political instability and violence. In the late nineteenth century, Haitian ambassador to the United States Hannibal Price briefly discussed the ways that U.S. African Americans sought out information on Haiti but also wondered if the country was sinking into barbarism. Price wrote in *De la Réhabilitation de la Race Noire*:

> So I find that in the United States millions of men of my race are struggling vigorously to elevate themselves by their intelligence and morals in order to match the powerful civilization that surrounds them; Negroes who hastened to take place in medicine, in law, science, literature, arts, all in the highest branches of human knowledge and try so hard to win happiness and dignity. Eh! Well, I see each day some of the most distinguished of these men come to me, seeking the truth about Haiti, where they want them [U.S. blacks] to believe that the Black Republic has fallen into a shameful state of savagery.[27]

The notion that despite its impressive revolutionary past Haiti had become a failed state presented considerable challenges to many U.S. blacks seeking to counteract notions of racial incompetency. These factors bred racist images of black inferiority via popular U.S. American literature and "voodoo" films. Additionally, Washington decision-makers conflated Haitian turmoil with blackness and political ineptitude, thus rationalizing diplomatic isolation and military intervention in Haiti (1804–1862, 1915–1934). Black Pan Americanism offered U.S. African Americans a space for intraracial dialogues and cooperative initiatives centered around uplift or what scholar Candice Jenkins coined the "salvific wish." Jenkins' "salvific wish" examines a "black, largely female, and generally middle-class desire" to "protect or save black women, and black communities more generally, from narratives of sexual and familial pathology, through the embrace of conventional bourgeois propriety in the arenas of sexuality and domesticity." U.S. blacks employed a similar type of "salvific wish" to counteract disparaging narratives of Haitian politics and culture and to exhibit an "intraracial gesture toward communal protection" that shielded, as Jenkins describes, "how the black community [was] seen interracially, [and] observed and evaluated across racial lines."[28]

The legacy of U.S. African American efforts to improve the image of Haiti and shift blame solely from internal politics in Haiti and racialized notions of incompetence and violence to additional external factors, such as U.S. military and financial intervention, expands, yet remains committed to, the core of Kevin Gaines's argument about U.S. African American racial-uplift strategies in the United States. Elite U.S. African Americans understood and practiced racial uplift via an amalgamation of bourgeois ideologies of self-help, respectability and collaboration with liberal whites. They believed this strategy would weaken white supremacy more broadly and would cease U.S. intervention in Haitian affairs.[29] Although racial uplift remained dependent upon self-help ideology, U.S. African Americans' "cooperation" with whites demonstrated the interdependence of black middle-class ideology and the "dominant modes of knowledge and power relations structured by race and racism."[30] Consequently, *From Douglass to Duvalier* attempts to examine the transnational dimensions of racial uplift ideology, in which elite U.S. African Americans collaborated with whites at specific moments and used a U.S.-centered Pan Americanism and a black Pan Americanism.

Drawing on the tenets of racial uplift ideology, this book seeks to bridge development strategies expressed by Haitian and U.S. African American intellectuals, artists and entrepreneurs to the theoretical framework of Afro-Modernity. The particularities of development shift from the late nineteenth century to the middle of the twentieth century, and from discussions of education and business to those of art and tourism. Development functioned as material, technological and cultural advancement within a capitalist framework, which demonstrated Haiti as a civilized, modern nation and U.S. African Americans as central figures in Haiti's progress. In this case, development—which took the form of Haitian education reform, an increase in tourism and tourist spending, intellectual exchange, transnational trade, the growth of start-up businesses and the increasing refinement of cultural art forms—possesses a refractive quality, shining a light on modern projects in underdeveloped nations, yet also illuminating the person(s) or institutions that played a role in the former's advancement. *From Douglass to Duvalier* highlights the processes, procedures and methods that have improved the material conditions of the black republic and examines the ways that U.S. African American and Haitian intraracial initiatives sought to counteract the corrosive, racialized reading of postrevolutionary Haitian society and politics.

The convergence of these two groups often employed Western notions of modern development: democratization, mass media and mass literacy, industrialization and antitraditionalism. However, U.S. African Americans and Haitians also attempted to challenge Western discourses to create new possibilities for African-descended peoples. These counter-acts exemplified an Afro-Modernity. Afro-Modernity was "evidenced in the *normative convergence* of two or more African and African-descended peoples and social movements in response to perceived commonalities of oppression," notes Michael Hanchard.[31] The Afro-Modernity practiced by Haitians and U.S. blacks exhibited three main characteristics: the creation of an "imagined community" based upon shared beliefs of Western hegemony against African-descended peoples; the formulation of "alternative political and cultural networks across national-state boundaries"; and a clear critique of Enlightenment discourses and the "processes of modernization by the West."[32] U.S. African Americans and Haitians participated in all three processes to develop Haiti's infrastructure. Yet *From Douglass to Duvalier* highlights moments when Haitians and U.S. African Americans fully embraced Enlightenment modes and discourses, in addition to North American notions of capitalist development. As scholar Marshall Berman states, "To be modern is to live a life of paradox and contradiction."[33] U.S. African Americans and Haitians are no different from other people in the modern world. They alternately used and critiqued North American capitalist development strategies and U.S. Pan Americanism in order to improve their lives domestically and internationally.

Situating the book within an emerging field of Hemispheric American Studies, which attempts to complicate and to expand the contours of a U.S.-based American Studies, I intend to challenge U.S. exceptionalism and to emphasize the flexibility of the nation that "emerges through constant collaboration, dialogue, and dissension."[34] Furthermore, I aim to demonstrate the utility of the hemisphere to African Americans as a foundation "for their strident calls for collective action against the beneficiaries of . . . unequal relations."[35] Many educated African Americans have been well aware of the significant presence of African-descended peoples in the Americas: More than 5 million enslaved Africans endured forced settlement in the Caribbean and South America during the era of slavery, and by the end of the 1900s, an estimated 110 million Afro-Latin Americans populated the region.[36] Speaking at a meeting of the American and Foreign Anti-Slavery Society in 1853, Frederick Douglass proudly stated that more than 12 million

"Negroes" in the Americas awaited "the lifegiving and organizing power of intelligence to mould them into one body, and into a powerful nation."[37] U.S. African Americans, in particular, and Haitians, at times, believed they should take advantage of this hemispheric and demographic reality, and thus they sought to globalize the impasse that race and color discrimination caused in inter-American and world affairs.

My intellectual engagement with U.S. African American/Haitian relations and the fields of Hemispheric American Studies and American Studies has also been influenced by the important work of Léon D. Pamphile's *Haitians and African Americans: A Heritage of Tragedy and Hope* and Chris Dixon's *African America and Haiti: Emigrationism and Black Nationalism in the Nineteenth Century*. Pamphile's book provides a clear and informative overview of U.S. African American and Haitian affairs from the perspective of two centuries of "oppression" and "a common struggle for freedom."[38] Similarly, *From Douglass to Duvalier* possesses some overlap, topically and temporally. This book examines the historical interconnections of U.S. African Americans and Haitians through their shared experiences of being racially subjugated and actively campaigning for autonomy and inclusion in their respective country's national and international affairs. Yet *From Douglass to Duvalier* employs the dual theoretical lens of Pan Americanism and Afro-Modernity to more fully comprehend the structural roots and routes of these lasting engagements. Dixon's notable work examines the ways that nineteenth-century black nationalism developed through U.S. African American emigration movements to Haiti (1820s–1850s). He emphasizes the linkages between an emerging U.S. black nationalist philosophy and antiblack structural violence and prejudice in the United States. In spite of that reality, *From Douglass to Duvalier* demonstrates a different conceptual and temporal approach. It highlights the ways black nationalism in the nineteenth and early twentieth centuries proved to be both deficient and enlightening for many elite U.S. African Americans and Haitians. Both groups believed in affirming a black identity, strengthening transnational relations and developing intraracial resources, tenets that are central to modern black nationalism.[39] At the same time, these groups also employed the language of Pan Americanism to challenge U.S. military and economic aggression, to ensure inclusion in the national and hemispheric body politic and to reject notions of a mass U.S. African American emigration.

U.S. and Caribbean Roots of Nineteenth-century Pan Americanism and Its Twentieth-century Limitations

Many scholars locate the origins of Pan Americanism in the United States with the introduction of the Monroe Doctrine (1823), the policy of U.S. protection against European interventions in the Americas. In addition, scholars recognize U.S. secretary of state James G. Blaine's organization of a Pan American Conference in 1889 as a watershed moment in the development of an imagined Pan American community.[40] The Monroe Doctrine centered the United States in Caribbean and Latin American affairs, a perspective that often perpetuated violent, paternalistic and racist behaviors. Yet, while U.S. interests may have shaped the origins of Pan Americanism, Haitians have also defended their authorship of Pan American ideals.[41] During the South American wars of independence against Spanish hegemony (1810–1824), Haitian president Alexandre Pétion, more than a decade before James Monroe's hemispheric guidelines for imperial dominance, provided safe haven, arms and ammunition to Venezuelan insurgent leader Simón Bolívar. In return for aid, Bolívar promised to abolish slavery in Venezuela. For Haitians during the early nineteenth century, Pan Americanism meant the support of a radical antislavery program and the defense against European threats to recolonize independent Caribbean and Latin American states, particularly the Dominican Republic, Haiti's neighbor to the east. Spain recolonized the Dominican Republic in 1861, but Dominicans achieved their second independence four years later, thanks partly to the vociferous protests of Dominican anti-annexationists and aid from Haiti. Situating Haiti at the forefront of the formation of a Pan American community is critical because African-descended peoples have been marginalized in the discussion of inter-American affairs, which often privileges whiteness. As historian Brenda G. Plummer asserts, U.S.-centered Pan Americanism was "a way of subordinating [blackness] and other particularisms in a manner that left the nation-state intact. With the exception of Haiti, throughout the Americas that system was racially constructed as white."[42] Many independent South American states proved hesitant to adopt an antislavery policy, and if abolition did occur, Hispanophone and Lusophone governments reverted to antiblack discriminatory practices or, rather, colluded with programs of "coloniality" and socioeconomic inequality, which often echoed racial injustice in the United States.[43]

After South American independence, Bolívar remained key in further-ing an inter-American consciousness and solidifying a more cooperative paradigm for South American nations. His Pan American confederation at the Congress of Panama in 1826 proved a defining moment for a non-U.S.-centered Pan Americanism. Bolívar primarily focused on newly in-dependent Spanish-speaking states, but the absence at the conference of Haiti and Brazil, countries that possessed significant populations of black people, minimized the radical potential of such a meeting. For a program that emphasized political, economic and cultural solidarity, but failed to include African or Amerindian descendants, who constituted the hemi-sphere's most marginalized and vulnerable populations, Pan Americanism was destined to be ideologically and institutionally bankrupt. Despite hav-ing received aid from the Haitian government, Bolívar believed that Haiti had no place in his league of nations. In an 1825 letter to Francisco de Paula Santander, vice president of Colombia, which explained why certain states had been admitted to their political consortium and why Venezuela should not liberate Cuba, Bolívar asserted that "our league can maintain itself per-fectly well without embracing the extremes of the south and north and without creating another republic of Haiti [in Cuba]."[44] By 1825, a genera-tion after Haitian independence, many Latin American leaders paid heed to Bolívar's hesitation (and possibly fear) about replicating another Haiti. For them, Haiti represented a nation with no visible signposts of progress and development, largely because of a pseudoscientific notion of the inferi-ority of African-descended peoples that inundated elite and popular Latin American consciousness in the nineteenth century.[45]

During the long nineteenth century, the refusal to address the privilege of whiteness, the complexities of race and the inequities of black peoples in the Americas demonstrated the future limitations of Pan Americanism as a liberating ideology in the twentieth century. Race/color and its inter-connectedness with sociopolitical, socioeconomic and cultural phenomena (e.g., capitalism and democracy) that arrived out of modernity and racial slavery were at the center of inter-American affairs. Although blackness and the construction of solidarity movements around race proved inef-fective at particular moments (specifically when the authoritarianism of Duvalier's regime became more public), race was mobile and situational, yet integral to understanding Pan Americanism. Whether an individual or government dealt with the issues of slavery, border disputes, inter-American trade, investment and/or loans or military intervention, or sought out potential allies during international conflicts such as World Wars I and II, the beam of race illuminated the inequities of the inter-American system while offering a space to include marginalized peoples through its language of cooperation, mutual respect, peace and solidarity.[46] At various intersections of space and time, whether in Port-au-Prince and Harlem after the U.S. occupation of Haiti in 1934 or in Miami during the early years of Duvalier's presidency, articulations and manifestations of Pan Americanism changed to suit the goals of its participants.

In January 1916, during the early stages of World War I and one year after the start of U.S. occupation of Haiti, the *Baltimore Afro-American Ledger* published a revealing article on the impact of Pan Americanism on non-white peoples. Incorporating interviews with leading U.S. African American intellectuals such as Kelly Miller, a Howard University dean, Bishop John Hurst and William Pickens, a Morgan State College dean, the *Afro-American Ledger* argued that "the Negro in the United States has nothing to lose, but rather has everything to gain by Pan Americanism."[47] In the twentieth century, the movement generated interest among U.S. blacks because it potentially included millions of African descendants from Brazil, Cuba, the Dominican Republic and other Latin American countries with significant black populations, thus increasing U.S. African American support for racial equality at home and cross-cultural cooperation. Miller predicted that the "American Negro will undoubtedly be stimulated to learn the Spanish language as a medium of communication with his race brethren [in the] South."

In a more pessimistic tone, Pickens believed the United States would "do more to prejudice and degrade Latin America," and added that this was "not pure theory; it has been demonstrated in Porto Rico [sic], Cuba and other [parts] of the West Indies wherever Yankee influence has gained ascendancy." In similar fashion, Hurst also revealed his skepticism. He argued that the "Southern Republics know how hypocritical, insincere, unjust and . . . criminal is this government in its dealing with the black man."[48] Some U.S. African Americans believed that racial discrimination was an ideological virus, a transferable cancer that, if given the proper environment, would mutate and metastasize. Yet many, including Pickens, believed that an engagement with Pan Americanism would internationalize the "color question." Pickens argued in the same article that if the promotion of Pan Americanism were to be advanced, "such an event would tend to unite all the darker peoples of the Western World."

Haitians in the twentieth century were not passive actors in this cross-cultural relationship or in the development of Pan Americanism. Through their interactions with U.S. African Americans, Haitians emphasized racial solidarity. Yet when it came to relations between the Haitian and U.S. governments, especially in cases of direct U.S. military and economic interventions in Haitian affairs (the reversal of which Haitians likened to the "eagle unfasten[ing] its talons from [the] country"), Haitian officials often deemphasized race and pursued a diplomatic course that accentuated economic and intellectual cooperation in the form of agricultural expertise, U.S. aid and cultural exchange.[49] This book demonstrates Haitian agency through a myriad of examples that range from Haiti's refusal to sell Môle Saint-Nicolas to the United States as a naval station, despite Frederick Douglass's encouragement to do so, to Jean-Léon Destiné's promotion of Haitian folkloric dance both in the United States and Haiti, which implemented cultural exchange programs in the spirit of Pan Americanism.

Considering the many articulations concerning the role of Pan Americanism in shaping the social conditions of African-descended peoples in inter-American relations, it is unlikely that the egalitarianism intrinsic to the rhetoric of Pan Americanism will ever become a reality until disparaging issues of race and equality are addressed in the context of Caribbean and South American nations. But how does one generate parity when the material wealth of the United States is so much greater than that of its neighbors to the south?

The U.S. scramble for oil and other natural resources has allowed a relative bargaining chip by oil-rich nations such as Venezuela and Trinidad and Tobago. Although U.S. dominance still exists in the hemisphere, the rise of leftist Latin American states such as Cuba, Bolivia and Venezuela has renewed a sense of multilateralism and has made U.S. influence in the region uncomfortable.[50] Twenty-first-century Haiti does not possess the wealth, the resources or the power to make the United States politically or economically uncomfortable. Yet, as medical doctor and anthropologist Paul Farmer asserts, "what's at stake in Haiti" is the perpetuation of "distortions, half-truths, myths, old and new [that] leaves even people of good will and discernment puzzled as to what is really *happening* in Haiti."[51] Moreover, *From Douglass to Duvalier* intends to examine what *happened* in Haiti and in U.S. African America that resisted and advanced the "distortions [and] myths" that became critical to these two peoples' subsequent standings in inter-American affairs.

This book expands the existing literature on Haiti, which by and large concentrates on the Haitian Revolution (1791–1804), the U.S. occupation (1915–1934) and contemporary events of political, economic and medical strife.[52] It expands the frontiers of U.S. African American history and reinforces the popularity of current scholarship that emphasizes U.S. African American engagements with blacks and Latinos in the international arena. It is a history of intriguing leaders who were forced to make life-changing decisions for their countries and their race.

The monograph's temporal bookends examine the rich tapestry of anti-imperial struggle and cooperation to build and sustain development projects that demonstrated racial progress. U.S. African American and Haitian interaction is rooted in the early nineteenth century, largely after Haitian independence (1804), through U.S. African American emigration movements to Haiti upon the request of Haitian president Jean-Pierre Boyer in 1820.[53] The voices of U.S. black emigrationists are significant and convey a burgeoning black-nationalist consciousness in the nineteenth century. Yet their correspondence with Haitians, and vice versa, remains minimal, possibly owing to language barriers, the realities of failing health upon arrival in the new land and other hardships.[54] Emigrationists do not articulate the movement of U.S. expansionism and inter-American cooperation critical to this book. Thus, during the years of racial slavery in the United States, U.S. African Americans and Haitians knew little about each other's everyday lives; likewise, the political economy of Haiti had little effect on that of U.S. blacks. Subsequent to the Emancipation Proclamation, U.S. blacks gained a fuller understanding of the lived experiences of the Haitian masses. In comparison, historians have been able to unearth a more pronounced and informed interaction between the two groups after the official U.S. recognition of Haiti in 1862 and the appointment of its U.S. black diplomatic corps, which included Ebenezer Don Carlos Bassett, John Mercer Langston and Frederick Douglass.[55] The book ends during François Duvalier's presidency in 1964 when the U.S. African American community became unusually silent in response to a number of factors, including the formalization of Duvalier's dictatorship that year. This silencing was uncharacteristic of the previously active engagements between U.S African Americans and Haitians in education, business and protests against U.S. hegemony for more than a century.

Chapter 1 analyzes Frederick Douglass's responses to U.S. empire building in Santo Domingo between 1870 and 1872 and in Haiti between 1889 and 1891. As U.S. minister to Haiti and assistant secretary of U.S. president Ulysses S. Grant's commission to study the prospect of annexing the Dominican Republic, Douglass fully supported the virtues of U.S. expansion and U.S. Pan Americanism as long as these ideologies promoted effective and egalitarian development in Caribbean and Latin American nations. Douglass opposed U.S. empire if it perpetuated U.S. notions of racial domination. His ideas on these subjects shifted over time and, as I argue, proved to be linked to the progress and hardships of U.S. African American life in the U.S. South. This chapter highlights the political challenges and contradictions of Frederick Douglass, a committed abolitionist, intellectual and diplomat who fought to remain loyal to race and nation.

U.S. expansion and intervention took violent and obtrusive turns in the late nineteenth and twentieth centuries. Chapter 2 examines the latter stages of U.S. military intervention in Haiti under U.S. president Herbert Hoover and how it led to the formation of the Robert R. Moton educational commission to Haiti in 1930. The president of Tuskegee Institute, Moton suggested that both radical and conservative changes be implemented in the Haitian educational system. Through the Good Neighbor Policy, a political derivative of nineteenth-century U.S. Pan American ideals of hemispheric unity, Moton outlined a program that both enabled and challenged U.S. occupation beyond the rubric of education.

Chapter 3 investigates the role of Claude Barnett and U.S. African American business interests in the development of Haiti during the post-occupation period (1934–1957). Influenced by the economic self-help philosophy of Booker T. Washington and encouraged by the culture of inter-American cooperation under President Franklin D. Roosevelt's Good Neighbor Policy, Barnett played an important part in strengthening U.S. African American and Haitian relations. As editor in chief of the Associated Negro Press (ANP), he led an information network that exposed black readers to and educated them about Haitian political, cultural and economic affairs. This chapter argues that black Pan American entrepreneurs and intellectuals of this era truly saw no alternative to modernization other than Western capitalist development as modeled by advances in U.S. society. At the same time, capitalist entrepreneurship offered U.S. African Americans a potential way out of their marginalized economic status in the world economy.

The myriad of entrepreneurial ventures sparked by the initiatives of Haitian president Sténio Vincent during his 1934 trip to Harlem and Washington, D.C., further emphasized transnational alliances in the name of race progress and political and economic autonomy.

Chapter 4 analyzes the politics of Walter White's public relations campaign to alter Haiti's image and to increase tourism to the island nation. White's campaign paralleled U.S. policy objectives of fostering mutual cooperation and financial and technical assistance in the Caribbean and Latin America. In spite of White's accord with U.S. policies, specifically the objectives of Harry Truman's Point Four program and other inter-American projects rooted in the political ideology of U.S. Pan Americanism, White confronted U.S. hegemony of Haitian affairs, believing that an economically empowered and politically stable Haiti could profoundly affect U.S. African American advancement in Cold War America.

Chapter 5 focuses on cultural manifestations of Pan Americanism through the development of *danse folklorique Haïtienne* (Haitian folkloric dance) by the Haitian-born dance director Jean-Léon Destiné and U.S. African American dance educator Lavinia Williams. As early as the mid-1930s, the Haitian government began to support the advancement and consumption of Haitian cultural arts to increase tourism to the country. In fact, many Caribbean administrations encouraged similar investments in tourism during this time to complement industrialization and to answer the dilemmas of debt, unemployment and failing economies.[56] The work of Destiné and Williams sought to modernize Haitian dance or, rather, to discipline it, classify it and "theatricalize" it so Haiti's original art form could be exhibited on the world stage and educate audiences about Haitian history and culture. The establishment of cultural institutions and the training of Haitian dancers by a U.S. African American choreographer affirmed not only the spirit of Pan Americanism's cultural exchange programs, but also the creation of an alternative world by black dancers in which African-based art forms were celebrated and in consistent dialogue with Western culture.

Chapter 6 highlights the decline in U.S. African American and Haitian relations in response to the authoritarianism of François Duvalier's dictatorship. This nadir demonstrated competing articulations of Pan Americanism by U.S. African Americans, Haitian exiles and Duvalier supporters. Around the mid-twentieth century, U.S. blacks tended to concentrate their political efforts on more local and promising events such as the emergence of African anticolonial and independence movements in the late 1950s and early 1960s, and the budding civil rights movement in the U.S. South.

From Douglass to Duvalier attempts to push us one step further in uncovering the quest of Cuban poet and revolutionary José Martí, who sought "the truth about the United States."[57] U.S. African American congresswoman Barbara Lee, a Democrat from the 9th District in California and current chair of the CBC, continued on a similar journey in 2005 when she introduced two key pieces of legislation, the New Partnership for Haiti and the Haiti Truth acts, the latter seeking to investigate the role of George Bush's government in Aristide's second exile in 2004. Yet taking a historical look at U.S. African American and Haitian affairs within the framework of inter-American relations, the book demonstrates the articulations, implementations and critiques of Pan Americanism. Additionally, the reader will discover many instances when persistent and insidious systems of white supremacy, economic dependence, paternalism and Haitian political instability compromised the actions of these two groups. By seeking to operate through the government and within a conceptual framework of U.S. foreign policy, black Pan Americanism remained stifled, if not doomed, largely because of the racist structures of the U.S. government and the lack of an intraracial critique of how capitalism manifested in phenomena such as tourism. Black Pan Americanism served as another attempt by U.S. African Americans and Haitians to compel Washington—through transnational initiatives in the fields of business, education and diplomacy—to make good on its promises of mutual respect, cooperation, nonintervention and cultural exchange set forth so forcefully in rhetoric.

"The Spirit of the Age . . . Establish[es] a Sentiment of Universal Brotherhood"

Haiti, "Santo Domingo" and Frederick Douglass at the Intersection of the United States and Black Pan Americanism

After the bloody and transformative events of the U.S. Civil War (1861–1865), when the emancipation of enslaved U.S. blacks and the preservation of the federal government raised a relative sense of optimism for U.S. African Americans and the nation, Washington officials were optimistic about the possibilities of expanding their realm of influence and power. Former Republican senator of New York and U.S. secretary of state William H. Seward (1861–1869) led the charge for expansion because the promising growth of U.S. manufacturing and trade industries demanded new markets. As early as the late 1820s and 1830s, the White House considered annexing new territories such as Cuba.[1]

Inspired by the end of slavery and the reunification of U.S. states, renowned abolitionist and public intellectual Frederick Douglass became intrigued by the benefits of annexation for willing Caribbean and Latin American states because it integrated these nations into the fold of U.S. prosperity and hopefulness. On December 30, 1871, the *Chicago Tribune* reported that Douglass had lectured the previous evening "with characteristic force and eloquence" in support of the United States' annexation of Santo Domingo (the Dominican Republic). Addressing a predominantly white crowd at Union Park Congregational Church in Chicago, Douglass asserted that the annexation debate must be understood from a more humane and "more poetic side," in which an individual viewed the nations of the world as her homeland and the world's citizens, her compatriots. During the 1860s and 1870s, not only did U.S. expansion of telegraph lines, shipping routes, trade markets and territorial boundaries incorporate a myriad of domestic economies but, in fact, "the national economy itself became more thoroughly integrated into a world economic system."[2] During the post-U.S. Civil War era, these technological and industrial advances, as well as an emerging sense of hope and in some cases nationalism among newly freed U.S. African Americans, complemented Douglass's *weltanschauung* of interconnectivity and egalitarianism among nation-states within the global arena.

At the same time, Douglass distinguished between an intervention based upon compassion and native consent and an annexation that was "rapacious," that dreamt "only of wealth and power" and "of national domain" in the "name of manifest destiny, which [was] but another name for manifest piracy. . . ."[3] As a staunch abolitionist Douglass created a universally moral and cultural world where the physical and psychological brutalities of slavery and racism could not be justified by proslavery and polygenetic racial arguments or vicious imperialists.[4] Douglass's "moral absolutism" rejected the greed and aggressive exploits demonstrated in racial slavery, the violent expansion into sovereign Mexican territory during the 1840s and the atrocious policies of displacement toward its Amerindian population.[5] Concurrently, Douglass adamantly believed in the potential for development (industrial, technological, cultural) of Santo Domingo because it remained a sovereign, antislavery nation that independently sought the protection of the United States. Yet Douglass argued for a cooperative effort by the U.S. and the Dominican governments that would dissolve the latter's independent status. In a statement whose ethos and cadences presaged U.S. president John F. Kennedy's inaugural address in January 1961, Frederick Douglass noted ninety years earlier: "It may, indeed, be important to know what Santo Domingo can do for us, but it is vastly more important to know what we can do for Santo Domingo."[6]

How does one reconcile Douglass's support for the annexation of Santo Domingo alongside his clear protests against "rapacious" U.S. empire building? Was he an idealist, uncritical of the impact of nonviolent colonialism? Why did he advocate U.S. intervention in Santo Domingo when in 1891, as U.S. minister to Haiti, he opposed the United States' efforts to lease a coaling station, Môle Saint-Nicolas, from Santo Domingo's neighbor, the Republic of Haiti? In July 1891, Douglass resigned from his post as U.S. minister when it became unmistakably evident that the U.S. State Department wanted to obtain the coaling station against the will of the Haitian government, an aim that challenged the sovereignty of the first black r public in the Western Hemisphere.

This chapter analyzes Frederick Douglass's responses to U.S. empire-building in Santo Domingo, between 1870 and 1872, and in Haiti, between 1889 and 1891. Douglass's opinions on U.S. expansion and U.S. Pan Americanism shifted over time. U.S. Pan Americanism functioned as a North American-centered foreign policy designed to complement U.S. financial, military and political goals in the nineteenth and twentieth centuries.[7] Douglass's ideas on the intensification of U.S. interests in the Caribbean demonstrated complicity with the U.S. Pan American project. Yet this chapter also highlights the political challenges and contradictions of U.S. African American emissaries, who fought to remain loyal to race and nation. As U.S. African American rights strengthened in the U.S. South during the late 1860s and early 1870s, Douglass's support of U.S. foreign policies in the region remained unfaltering. Yet Douglass also contested the violent mode and manner of U.S. foreign policy. Subsequently, as the limits of U.S. Reconstruction solidified and as Washington's aggression against Haitian political autonomy deepened in the early 1890s, Douglass's allegiance to U.S. Pan Americanism waned. It was in this liminal space that an opportunity for black Pan Americanism, a racialized hemispheric discourse on development that sought to protect black sovereignty, materialized.

In the case of the Dominican annexation, Haitians firmly disagreed with Washington and Douglass's position, which they believed to be a potential threat to their sovereignty. Nonetheless, due to the changing racial dynamics of U.S. legislation, Douglass believed that annexation was a demonstration of transnational racial uplift that addressed material voids in the Caribbean and Latin America that had been caused by racial slavery and European colonialism. Although many Dominicans may not have considered themselves *negro* (black) or people of African descent, Douglass considered them among the "Negroes" who made up the "1,470,000" in the "Spanish Colonies."[8] Thus, his support of U.S. foreign policy initiatives was influenced by several factors in which race played an integral role: the protection and advancement of U.S. African American rights in the United States; the security of sovereign governments to rule without unsolicited U.S. intervention; and the modernization of nations that had been devastated by racial slavery and European colonialism.

Frederick Douglass's unique positions as assistant secretary to Ulysses S. Grant's commission to annex the Dominican Republic and as U.S. minister to Haiti allow for a distinct perspective on U.S. and Caribbean foreign policy from a U.S. African American envoy who believed that a just U.S. foreign policy possessed profound implications for race relations at home. One is also able to map Caribbean reactions to Washington's ever-expanding political and economic reach during the late nineteenth century.[9]

The development of U.S. empire in the nineteenth century colluded with the culture and language of racial domination. As early as the eighteenth century, "the language of technological supremacy (as against primitive 'backwardness') joined the languages of Christian and racial supremacy in the Euro-American lexicon of human hierarchy."[10] Douglass, a central voice on integrationist strategies in U.S. race relations, continued to criticize "republican politics" and its "inconsistency" during the era of slavery.[11] In the course of U.S. Reconstruction (1865–1876) and post-Reconstruction (1877–1895) Douglass sustained his condemnations of U.S. racial inequality, at the same time benefiting from and maintaining an unparalleled station as a U.S. black emissary to both the Dominican Republic and Haiti, as president of the Freedmen's Savings and Trust Company and as U.S. marshal of the District of Columbia. He frequently proved his loyalty and competency to the U.S. government in the face of continued antiblack prejudice and violence in the United States. Specifically, during the mid-1860s, racial inequality in the U.S. South was expressed through black disfranchisement; an update of the black codes; the restoration to public office of notorious Confederate politicians such as Alexander Stephens; and the emergence of white supremacist paramilitary groups like the Ku Klux Klan.

From the late 1860s through the early 1870s, Douglass observed a new society unfolding with the ratification of key legislation—the Fifteenth Amendment (1869), the Enforcement Act (1870), and the Ku Klux Klan Act (1871)—by Radical Republicans like Charles Sumner. Furthermore, the dispatch of U.S. federal troops to protect U.S. African American rights demonstrated, if only for a short time, that U.S. Radical Republican rule proved critical to U.S. black advancement.[12] A hopeful and optimistic Douglass lectured between 1872 and 1873 that the "majesty of the law has taken its stand." Douglass further noted:

> The idea that this is exclusively the white man's country—and the white man's government—has already become a superstition. The irrepressible negro[—]compelled to herd with horses[,] sheep and swine on the decks of our steam packets to travel in a Jim Crow car,

and to go to heaven in a "Jim Crow" pew—is now a member of Congress and eligible to any office of honor or profit in the land.[13]

During this critical period between 1869 and 1873, changing domestic racial politics in the United States had a profound impact on Douglass's opinions about annexation and the benefits of collaboration among nonwhite nation-states and the United States. He believed that the "sentiments of the [U.S. American] people" created a space where a "multiform, composite nationality" shaped U.S. identity, and thus "prejudice against color" would soon be eradicated.[14] Douglass's assessment of the potential for a diverse U.S. American identity that decentered whiteness converged with his attitudes on U.S. territorial expansion in the Caribbean and Latin America. He believed that the notion of a "multiform, composite nationality" included the Americas, considering the "intimate terms" [e.g., trade, proximity and history of colonialism] that the United States maintained with "the darker hued races of the world." These influential and "intimate terms" served as motives to create a cooperative, unified hemisphere, where race/color intolerance obstructed modern advancement. However, Douglass's approach still privileged the United States and its place as an authority in the hemisphere: "All signs indicate that the continent, the whole continent [and] nothing less than the continent is ultimately to belong to us. . . . Mexico, Central and South America and all the Isles of the Caribbean Sea must eventually yield to our irres[is]tible power of expansion."[15]

The zeal that President Ulysses S. Grant and U.S. businessmen exhibited toward annexation of Santo Domingo exemplified a broader movement of Washington seeking to usurp European economic control within the region. As early as the 1820s, entrepreneurs, fortune-hunters and commercial agents from the United States, often encouraged by the U.S. government, sought their riches in Mexican and Central American territories such as Nicaragua and Panama. Largely in search of isthmian canal projects and prospective trade routes, U.S representatives and independent U.S. American capitalists carved out an economic and political presence within the continental sphere.[16] Under the guise of Pan Americanism, a movement that promoted a policy of nonintervention and egalitarian commercial and political cooperation among the United States, the Caribbean and Latin America, U.S. Pan Americanism proved to be a paradox because it situated the United States as the nucleus of hemispheric relations. Rooted in the tenets of the Monroe Doctrine (1823), the aims of U.S. Pan Americanism cared less about hemispheric egalitarianism than about acquiring the "$400,000,000 annually" in trade profits from the Caribbean and Latin America. According to James G. Blaine, U.S. secretary of state (1881, 1889–1892) and a key architect of the Pan American movement, those profits bypassed the U.S. and made their way "to England, France, Germany and other countries."[17]

For many Caribbean and Latin American political leaders such as Anténor Firmin (Haiti), José Martí (Cuba), and Ramón Emeterio Betances (Puerto Rico), Pan Americanism was not a creation of the United States but reflected a poly-centered commercial and political cooperation within the Caribbean and the Americas based on a collective history of racial slavery and colonial oppression.[18] For these Caribbean intellectuals and statesmen, the drive to create a national and Pan Caribbean unity proved overwhelmingly challenging. National particularities such as vulnerability to foreign economic control in the form of reciprocal treaties, custom duties and import tariffs and frequent episodes of civil and political unrest compromised the unifying efforts of these Caribbean thinkers.[19] Despite these obstacles, Betances, a Puerto Rican leader who fought for independence, challenged the apparent differences and struggles in the Caribbean and argued during a speech in Port-au-Prince:

> . . . our past is so interwoven that I cannot paint a historical sketch of Cuba without finding traits already written in the history of Haiti. We are not allowed anymore to separate our respective lives. I repeat it; from one point to another of the large islands of the Caribbean Sea, every mind is agitated by the same question; it is the future of the Antilles. Who will be so blind as not to see it? We carry on the same fight; we struggle for the same cause, therefore we must live the same life.[20]

Douglass's ideas about inter-American relations established a middle ground between U.S. Pan Americanism and black Pan Americanism. As a U.S. African American leader, he, not unlike many U.S. African American intellectuals of his time, privileged the United States as being at the vanguard of modern development and civilization. Historian Wilson J. Moses argues that Douglass and "his contemporaries (even black nationalists) emulated the military values of Anglo-Saxon masculinity, accepted bourgeois perfectionist Christianity, and manifested their relish for standards of civilization as they understood them to exist in American society."[21] Since key figures in U.S. African American leadership centered the United States within their pantheon of civilized societies despite the scarce social and economic opportunities for blacks, many U.S. black leaders transitioned from emulating U.S. rhetoric and defending its policies to directly challenging its strategies and principles. Between 1870 and 1871, Douglass recognized the United States and its federal troops, northern occupiers of the U.S. South, as protectors of U.S. African American rights. However, Douglass's experiences as a slave and the historical legacy of bondage in African America created formidable bonds with Caribbean and Latin American nations and their leadership.[22] Despite these affinities, the language of racial hegemony inherent in U.S. Pan Americanism, as shown in U.S./Haiti relations in the early 1890s, hindered his full endorsement of U.S. Pan American initiatives.

Haiti, Santo Domingo and the United States: Historical Context to a Caribbean/U.S. Political Entanglement

In addition to the Emancipation Proclamation and the Union defeat of the Confederacy, a mosaic of "isms" saturated the sociopolitical canvas of the United States, providing some semblance of structure and order to the ruptured nation and its foreign policy goals. Nationalism, Social Darwinism, industrial capitalism, paternalism, U.S. exceptionalism and spiritualism pervaded U.S. cultural spaces after the Civil War; as a result, a new and transformative jingoism informed U.S. relations and the country's perceptions of its southern neighbors.[23] Although the U.S. Congress and most U.S. citizens focused their attention on westward expansion, domestic policymaking and mending their homeland—and European states intensified their hegemonic track in Africa, Asia and Latin America—the U.S. government orchestrated clearly defined plans to establish its economic, technological and cultural supremacy in the Americas by strengthening its import/export trade and developing its telegraphic communication systems. During the post-Civil War period, U.S. consul bureaucrats "prepared reports on commercial prospects, and naval officers scouted markets and protected merchants" in the Caribbean and Latin America.[24] The discourse of U.S. exceptionalism (i.e., technical and economic) often distinguished itself from perceptions of Caribbean and Latin American primitiveness that possessed racial, religious, linguistic and other cultural dimensions.[25]

As the United States sought to expand its markets, various regional border conflicts and political confrontations against autonomous rule in Santo Domingo entangled the Dominican Republic and Haiti. These political and territorial disputes had grave implications for U.S. and European strategic maneuvers in the Caribbean.[26] Haitian and Dominican territorial tensions originated in the early Haitian revolutionary period. Santo Domingo was a Spanish colony until it was turned over to the French in the Treaty of Basilea (1795). And, in his revolutionary quest to abolish racial slavery on the island of Hispaniola, Haitian rebel leader François Dominique Toussaint L'Ouverture declared in the constitution of 1801 that slavery was abolished and established himself as governor-general for life.

To protect the ban on slavery and the island from a reimplementation of European colonialism, the reunification of the island under Toussaint L'Ouverture and later in 1822 by Haitian president Jean Pierre Boyer proved to be pivotal moments in the Haitian political imagination regarding an inalienable right to Santo Domingo land. There are ample historical distinctions that separated the eastern part of the island from the Haitian western sphere, such as a vastly smaller population density, a swelling of multiracial inhabitants of Santo Domingo, a waning gold economy and pre-1795 border disputes between the Spanish and French. To discuss these specific points is beyond the scope of this chapter. What remains critical to understanding the evolution of nineteenth-century Haitian/Dominican relations is that these variations, along with a deeply rooted anti-Haitian sentiment that sought to erase blackness from the Dominican cultural imagination, produced what scholar Pedro San Miguel argued was a profound "psychological drama" along racial and territorial lines.[27] During Boyer's rule, the deterioration of political and economic institutions and the failure of the Haitian president to recognize the particularities of Dominican society contributed to the independence of Santo Domingo by Dominican rebels like Juan Pablo Duarte and Ramón Mella in 1844.[28]

From the mid-1840s through the 1860s, Dominican presidents like Pedro Santana and Buenaventura Báez not only encouraged free trade with the United States and other foreign governments (e.g., those of Britain and France) but also were fixated on annexing the Dominican Republic with either Spain or the United States. Santo Domingo's search for a foreign protectorate did not sit well with its neighbor to the west, who believed that because of its radical antislavery and anticolonial past, Haiti was the natural protector of racial equality and, ironically, the guardian against European political and economic aggression toward the Dominican Republic.[29]

Like the United States, Haiti had its own version of the Monroe Do trine and Pan Americanism. Under Haitian emperor Faustin Soulouque (1849–1859), Haiti invaded Santo Domingo in 1849–1850 and again in 1855 to reunite the island and to ensure that British and U.S. advances through "friendly commercial relations" and attempts to purchase potential coaling stations did not compromise Dominican and Haitian political autonomy. Scholars such as William Javier Nelson locate a tendency toward Haitian "meddling" in Dominican affairs rooted in a Haitian paranoia of European reconquests and possible reimplementation of slavery.[30] Perhaps this was the case. However, Haitian officials from the 1850s through the 1860s responded to very real strategic maneuvering by established colonial powers and their businessmen within the Caribbean and Mexico. For example, British and French threats to blockade Haitian ports because of Haitian/Dominican border battles threatened the Haitian government. Some other intimidating political and military factors included a proposed U.S./Dominican treaty by William L. Cazneau, a U.S. soldier, politician and special agent to the Dominican Republic under Franklin Pierce's and James Buchanan's administrations, to grant the United States a coaling station at Samaná Bay; Spain's re-annexation of Santo Domingo (1861–1865); and French occupation of Mexico in the early 1860s. The continuation of slavery in Spanish Cuba also threatened Haiti.[31] In November 1867, after the withdrawal of French troops from Mexico and the reestablishment of Dominican independence in 1865, Demesvar Delorme, Haitian minister of foreign affairs, warned key Haitian political figures that the United States was a formidable threat to Haitian national security and suggested that Haiti enter into negotiations with the Dominican Republic to prevent an annexation of any part of the island.[32]

Haiti was unsuccessful in preventing Spanish recolonization of Santo Domingo in 1861. Nevertheless, the black republic remained a factor in the eventual Spanish overthrow. On the same borders where Dominicans and Haitians fought and traded goods, where the state boundaries symbolized Dominican independence and Haitian efforts to protect "Hispaniola from falling prey to 'imperialists in disguise,'" many Haitians in the border commercial towns of Las Matas, San Juan and Neyba surreptitiously supplied gunpowder to Dominican rebels in exchange for livestock in the War for Restoration.[33] The United States did not directly respond to Spain's annexation of the Dominican Republic in 1861. More than likely, national concerns over issues of slavery and maintaining the Union during the U.S. Civil War delayed a response. Additionally, Washington sought to maintain neutrality so that Spain would not recognize the Confederacy.[34] Until the United States settled its domestic turmoil, the government proved to be ineffective in upholding the tenets of the Monroe Doctrine. Furthermore, Douglass did not offer any critiques of Dominican/Haitian affairs from the 1840s through the mid-1860s because his attention was focused on U.S. slavery and the Civil War.[35] However, Douglass published a critical article by James Redpath, a nineteenth-century reformer and a leading figure in the U.S. African American emigration movement to Haiti, denouncing Spain's annexation of the Dominican Republic. By 1865, Spanish control of the Dominican Republic succumbed to the pressures of Dominican rebel forces, disease, Spain's concentration on the overthrow of Benito Pablo Juárez in Mexico and U.S. informal threats to Spain's "erring policy of 1861."[36]

"Why Should Not Some Day All the Nations on the American Continent Come Together in an Annexation?"

By the late 1860s, President Ulysses S. Grant and several influential Wall Street investors, indifferent to Dominican oppositional forces during Spain's reoccupation, set their sights on annexing Santo Domingo because of its natural resources, geographic proximity and budding potential for U.S. capitalists. Again, Dominican president Buenaventura Báez, a nonconsecutive five-term president, with the support of high-ranking senators such as Jacinto de la Concha, offered direct control of the republic to the United States. On November 29, 1869, General Orville Babcock, personal secretary to President Grant, and President Báez signed two accords stating that the United States agreed to annex Santo Domingo and assumed the responsibility of its national debt of $1.5 million. The second accord confirmed that if the U.S. Senate rejected the treaty, the U.S. government could purchase Samaná Bay, a potential naval coaling station, for $2 million.[37] Yet Grant and Báez received intense political resistance from respected and authoritative figures in the U.S. Congress such as Charles Sumner, a Massachusetts senator and the chair of the Foreign Relations Committee. Sumner opposed annexation because it disenfranchised Dominicans and, in some ways, it violated international law. Instead, he called for a U.S. protectorate status for free Caribbean nations, allowing the "black race [to] predominate" in its own administration.[38]

The Senate Foreign Relations Committee rejected the treaty in March 1870 by a 5-to-2 vote but eventually conceded to Grant's proposal for a fact-finding mission to the Dominican Republic. The Haitian government was so pleased with the Committee's vote that it issued Sumner a gold medal, and a portrait of the senator was hung in the Haitian Chamber of Deputies.[39] Sumner seemed to possess the upper hand in Grant's relentless pursuit to acquire Santo Domingo, at least temporarily. In a rare moment for Frederick Douglass, a longtime admirer of Sumner's support of black racial politics, he challenged some of the senator's disparaging comments about Grant's proposal of annexation. For Douglass, acquiring the Dominican Republic was a matter of U.S. national prominence, situating the North American republic as a world power by strengthening its naval possessions. In his speech "Santo Domingo," Douglass noted that "Putting aside the eloquent and powerful opposition to that measure by one of the nation's ablest and most trusted senators. . . . [it is true that] Almost every great maritime nation in the world has some footing and foot hold in the Caribbean Sea but our own." He added that although it "may be patriotic to shut our eyes to this fact[,] I may be pardoned if I do not concur in that opinion."[40]

In January 1871, Douglass's dissatisfaction with Sumner's comments also revealed much about his full support of Republican politics:

I may be wrong, but I do not at present see any good reason for degrading Grant in the eyes of the American people. Personally, he is nothing to me, but as the President, the Republican president of the country, I am anxious if it can be done to hold him in all honor. . . .[41]

Douglass's loyalty to the Republican Party and the improvements made to U.S. blacks in the South because of Radical Republicanism remain critical to understanding Douglass's position on annexation. With the ratification of the Thirteenth, Fourteenth and Fifteenth amendments between 1865 and 1870 along with the advent of congressional support for the political rights of freedmen and women and the establishment of the Freedmen's Bureau, came a hopeful, although brief, political and social climate for U.S. African Americans. The shifting tide of unification during the post-U.S. Civil War period and the protection of U.S. blacks' rights undoubtedly offered a new perspective for Douglass's views on annexation. "Unification are [*sic*] the inspiring ideas of today," Douglass wrote. "The attempt to set up a little nation to the South of us with slavery for its cornerstone has failed and failed because of the spirit and enlightenment of the age."[42] Ebenezer D. Bassett, then U.S. minister to Haiti and a dear friend of Douglass's, understood the passing of transformative constitutional amendments as significant to potentially calming Haitian officials' anxieties over U.S. annexation of the Dominican Republic. According to scholar Christopher Teal, Bassett wrote Haitian president Nissage Saget that U.S. African Americans, "brothers and kinsmen of ourselves and of the Haitian people," were able to "exercise their ballot in the United States."[43]

In addition to the radical changes in the U.S. South due to Congressional Reconstruction, Douglass believed that his support of Republican president Grant during an important election year of 1872 was essential to continuing U.S. African American advancement.[44] Grant prevailed to the presidency in 1872, and it seemed that Douglass's vigorous political backing earned him a position as assistant secretary on Grant's presidential commission to study the prospect of Dominican annexation.

The commission included politicians such as Benjamin Wade of Ohio, a Radical Republican, Samuel G. Howe, and Andrew D. White.[45] In addition, several U.S. chemists, geologists, botanists, journalists and businessmen sailed with the commission from New York City on January 18, 1871. They arrived a week later at Samaná Bay, Dominican Republic, a strategic seaport on the northeastern part of the island. Douglass's responsibility was to "examine and report to the commission regarding the condition of the English speaking immigrants on Samaná Bay." Overall, the group's goal was to study the land and critical elements of Dominican society such as politics, education, soil potential, mineral resources, frequency of civil insurrection and public opinion regarding U.S. annexation.[46]

The commission's report of April 1871 reveals Douglass's line of questioning, provided by the lead commissioners.[47] It is unclear what the racial backgrounds of Douglass's interviewees were, although his first question to one of the unknown colonists alluded to the emigration movement of U.S. blacks to the Samaná peninsula and Haiti during the 1820s.[48] The assistant secretary received a favorable response concerning annexation to the United States, which complemented Douglass's current leanings on the subject. The unidentified colonist emphasized that the people

> ... are tired of war, and they think that under the Government of the
> United States they will have peace and prosperity. The people have

no heart for exertion under their present uncertain government, for as soon as they earn a little property, some great man puts himself at the head of a revolution, and brings on war, and one side or the other plunders the people of their property. . . . The people feel that they want a strong government to lean against for protection, and they believe that the United States would give them protection.[49]

The criticisms and frustrations of Douglass's interviewee echoed many of the aggravations of Dominican citizens who voted unanimously in favor of U.S. annexation on February 19, 1870. Yet prior to the February ballot vote, Buenaventura Báez utilized intimidation tactics against many Dominican citizens in order to coerce them to vote in favor of annexation. Báez orchestrated an intense pro-annexation propaganda within Dominican government publications such as the *Boletín Oficial*, which gave the impression that the Dominican Republic would function as an independent, self-governing body like a U.S. state—"except when in affairs in which all the states are interested, the National Congress may take action."[50] The Dominican Republic was in a unique position as a Caribbean nation aligned with the United States, reported the *Boletín Oficial*, which noted that "annexation means salvation because it will oblige Haiti to respect Dominican rights and to maintain a decent conduct and because it will persuade all Dominicans to renounce political disputes."[51]

Capitalizing on the image of Haiti as the "primitive dangerous predator that threaten[ed] to 'denationalize' Dominican civilization," Báez's propaganda perpetuated a vibrant anti-Haitian ethos among Dominican writers and intellectuals in the nineteenth century.[52] In January 1870, Haitian threats of reunification could be perceived as real by Báez because of the assassination of U.S.-supported Haitian president and Báez advocate Sylvain Salnave by followers of Nissage Saget, the leader of a northern insurrectionist faction. In September 1873, Minister Bassett reported to Hamilton Fish, U.S. secretary of state, that the Haitian war steamer *L'Union* had sailed along the northeastern coast of the island to aid Báez opponents and anti-annexationists.[53] Bassett also warned Haitian officials such as Darius Denis, minister of foreign affairs, about U.S. consequences if Haitians continued to aid Dominican rebels (anti-annexationists). The Haitian government continued to deny any involvement, but given its previous history in providing support for Dominican rebels against Spanish reoccupation and its mission to preserve a Monroe Doctrine of its own despite any significant military/economic power, it is more than likely that the Haitian government under the presidency of Nissage Saget offered help to Dominican anti-annexationists.

Bassett's reports on Haitian/Dominican relations with the United States provide a window into the work of U.S. African American diplomats who loyally protected the interests of the United States. Scholar Christopher Teal argues that although "there was no indication in any of the dispatches to Washington that Bassett may have disagreed with the annexation efforts," Bassett's "repeated warnings to Fish about the growing bitterness served as more than just reportage on popular sentiment; they appear to reveal that Bassett disagreed with such efforts."[54] However, Bassett's allegiance to the objectives of the U.S. State Department prevailed in spite of "threats" from politically minded Haitians.[55] In fact, in a memorandum dated March 9, 1871, Bassett alerted Douglass and other members of the commission of the United States' attempt to "thwart a hostile movement designed to be put on foot by the [Haitian] insurrectionists in St. Domingo."[56] During the critical moment of a U.S.-led fact-finding commission, U.S. officials proved to be intimately involved in suppressing Dominican and Haitian resistance.

If Douglass was aware of an anti-annexationist movement in the Dominican Republic and possibly the tactics of President Báez, he made no mention of it in his writings. Douglass's silence on the anti-annexation movement in the Dominican Republic demonstrated, at least, the success of Báez's suppression of the opposition or Douglass's uncritical view of Dominican public opinion and his fidelity to Washington's initiatives. It remains difficult to ascertain the true feelings of Dominican citizens interviewed for Douglass's report. Dominican opinions on annexation were a mixed bag of pro-U.S. annexation and pro-Dominican independence. By 1871, Dominican anti-annexationists seemed to be off the radar for Douglass, who strongly believed that U.S. annexation, during this time of political and social change in the United States, exemplified a march toward "knowledge" and national progress.[57]

Douglass opposed U.S. annexation during the period of U.S. slavery because he believed it further empowered the plantocracy of the slaveholders. He argued that before the ratification of the Thirteenth Amendment, U.S. expansion "meant more slavery, more ignorance and more barbarism, but that time has now gone by." Furthermore, Douglass believed that the Dominican Republic's small population and government could not survive independently in a rapidly growing world and that racism proved to be at the root of U.S. America's lack of support of annexation. Speaking at a Baltimore AME Church, Douglass asked, "Why if this nation in the past annexed with no objection Louisiana, Florida, [and] Texas" did the nation "den[y] an opportunity to Santo Domingo?"[58] Douglass's ideas aligned with the U.S. Pan American project of expansion; at the same time, he understood the Dominican government's plight as an act "to become a part of a large, strong and growing nation—only obey[ing] the grand organizing impulse of the age."[59]

In March of 1871, after Douglass returned from the Dominican Republic, he embarked upon a speaking tour promoting the benefits of annexation. His clear and intricate remarks at these events, often in church venues, interlaced a historical narrative against Western imperialism and slavery in the Americas with a belief that the Dominican Republic should be subsumed under the wing of Washington. "Spanish invaders—after enslaving and murdering in her mines and fields the native population and thus destroying the home supply of slave labor," Douglass heralded, "fixed their rapacious eyes upon the distant shores of Africa—and soon smote the heart of the world by a system of horrors such as the world had perhaps never seen before."[60] Yet at other moments within his pro-annexation lectures, he promoted, although indirectly, a U.S. exceptionalism by continuing to paint a dichotomous picture of the strong, orderly and democratic U.S. government in comparison to the "easily excited . . . revolutionary movements [of the Dominican Republic and independent Latin American governments] wholly unfavorable to industry and to the acquisition of wealth."[61]

His address in December 1871 at the Union Park Congregation Church in Chicago mentioned in this chapter's introduction, was reprinted in a number of newspapers in major cities from Boston to St. Louis. And, at the Congressional Church in Washington, D.C., Douglass asserted the centrality of the United States in Caribbean development and championed the prospect of one day unifying all nations of the Americas. "I don't see any reason why the United States should withhold needed help to another country that claims for it," Douglass asserted, "neither can I see good reason why should not some day all the nations on the American continent come together in an annexation."[62] His vision of an American continent unified the peoples of North and South America through a commitment to reason, order, moral absolutism, and Western industrial and technological development. At the same time, American peoples would be able to maintain "racial and religious differences" as long as the decentralization of cultural and ethnic peculiarities elevated the ideals of integration and egalitarianism—major tenets of Pan Americanism.[63]

By the late 1870s, it was clear that Douglass's conception of the Americas was irreconcilable with that of President Grant. Douglass remained steadfast about U.S. blacks maintaining the United States as their homeland.[64] On the other hand, in an 1878 interview with former President Grant, the *Chicago Tribune* reported that Grant strongly supported U.S. African American emigration to the Dominican Republic. Grant remarked:

> I think now, looking over the whole subject, that it would have a great gain to the United States to have annexed St. Domingo. . . . It would have a given a new home for the blacks, who were and as I hear are still oppressed in the South. If two or three hundred thousand blacks were to emigrate to St. Domingo under our Republic the Southern people would learn the crime of Ku-Kluxism, because they would see how necessary the black is to their own prosperity. We should have grown our own coffee and sugar, our own hardwoods and spices. . . . We should have made of St. Domingo a new Texas or a New California. If St. Domingo had come we should have had Hayti. A Power like ours in St. Domingo makes us masters of the Gulf of Mexico.[65]

Grant's comments came at the end of a failed U.S. Reconstruction, where the violence and segregation against U.S. blacks in the South accelerated due to the removal of U.S. federal troops. There is no evidence that Grant supported a federal policy of emigration during the early 1870s. However, in a parochial and racist fashion, Grant believed that the "Negro problem," or more appropriately, the white Southerner problem of U.S. African American freedom, at this moment of post-U.S. Reconstruction, was best served if a significant population of U.S. blacks agreed to a state-sponsored emigration movement. Douglass, however, explicitly opposed U.S. black emigration movements to Liberia and Haiti at this time and would have objected to any public policy of making the U.S. imperial "'masters' of the Gulf of Mexico." As early as September 1851, Douglass argued at the National Convention of the Liberty Party that "with the landing of the Pilgrims . . . we have had a foothold on this continent. We have grown up with you; we have watered your soil with our tears; nourished it with our blood, tilled it with our hard hands. Why should we not stay here?"[66] A decade later and on numerous occasions, Douglass repeated his anti-emigration stance. He wrote:

We are not in favor of wholesale and indiscriminate emigration to Hayti, or elsewhere; . . . the things for which men should emigrate are food, clothing, property, education, manhood, and material prosperity, and he who has these where he is, had better stay where he is and exert the power which they give him to overcome whatever of social or political oppression which may surround him.[67]

In the case of nonwhite nation-states, Douglass understood annexation as a tool for racial uplift, a moral obligation for egalitarian inclusion that addressed historical and material inequities rooted in Western slavery. Douglass believed that the weaving of countries into the fabric of the United States, a nation believed to be best suited to assist in the project of national development, symbolized threads of a larger, international unification process that included the merging of some European states and also the Confederate U.S. South with northern Union states. Douglass noted: "the English and German tongues are surrounding the Globe. . . . The Teuton now shouts over a united Germany. The long separated members of Italy have come together."[68] From Douglass's perspective, he believed that if some European groups and nations were aligning themselves, then why not countries in the Americas?

Though Douglass did not embrace violent imperial conquest, it seems clear that he proved to be woefully uninformed about the effects of an informal imperialism embedded within U.S. structural programs, reciprocal treaties and commercial accords. Caribbean and Latin American states customarily fell susceptible to the economic control of U.S. and European investors and merchants during the nineteenth and early twentieth century because of their evolution into a monocrop export culture (i.e., sugar or coffee) and the proliferation of an elite consumer/import culture that mimicked European and U.S. material tastes.[69] Also, the United States and European governments forced Caribbean and Latin American governments into inequitable contracts that penalized multilateral trade agreements.[70] The realities of capitalism and corporatism and their relationship to notions of progress challenged Douglass's universal morality. He seemed to be out of his element while discussing "banking and commerce." These industries expected "a person of moral and intellectual flexibility, [however,] his background imposed severe limitations on [his] ability to formulate a practical ethic" for industrial capitalists of his day.[71]

At ease writing about race, the abolition of slavery and social and gender inequities, Douglass advanced profoundly anticolonialist positions regarding freedom struggles in Ireland, Cuba and Mexico in the nineteenth century. As slavery still persisted in Cuba during the 1870s and Cuban rebels intensified their resistance against imperialist Spain, Douglass "ignore[d] the official neutrality of the United States" and encouraged U.S. African Americans of military age and experience to "join their fortunes with those of their suffering brethren in this hour."[72] And finally, Douglass's thoughts on Benito Pablo Juárez's "improved state of affairs" in Mexico revealed his contempt for erroneous judgments made by European Americans regarding the advancement of nonwhite nation-states. In an August 1871 essay in the *New National Era*, Douglass urged the nation to not "judg[e] them [Mexicans] from our own standpoint, making ourselves the standard, without duly taking into account the disadvantages and drawbacks under which they are laboring."[73] The "disadvantages and drawbacks" that he referred to in the essay clearly addressed the violent and deleterious effects of Spanish colonialism. In the same vein, Douglass articulated what he perceived to be the arrested development of republicanism in Latin America. According to Douglass, the United States possessed an "instinctive" understanding of republicanism among the majority of the people, "hence [their] respect for the Constitution and laws. . . . [T]his respect for the laws is one of our distinctive features, and is in fact the chief guarantee for the duration of the republic."[74] Moreover, Douglass argued that many of the South American and Caribbean countries proved deficient in their management of republican institutions. "Perhaps [there exists] a deficiency inherent to the Latin races," Douglass conjectured in a bourgeois and chauvinistic tone, which impeded the development of republicanism.[75] Yet Douglass also associated illiteracy, lack of protection of liberties, graft and lawlessness as other possible factors that contribute to the failure of creating a democratic state.

Douglass's inconsistencies, contradictions and genuine viewpoints on the question of annexation demonstrate a man wrestling with ideas of progress for nonwhite peoples within a paradox of U.S. hemispheric expansion and Latin American nation building. Douglass resolved those inconsistencies by "manipulat[ing] the rhetoric of [U.S.] American perfectionism" in order to advance the notion of racial inclusion and egalitarianism within the Pan American project.[76] In other words, Douglass articulated black Pan Americanism through his support of U.S. American values coupled with his public objections to state-sponsored racial domination, which allowed for a more just and egalitarian participation of nonwhite states in inter-

American affairs. Douglass chose to work within the mechanism of U.S. foreign policy and he remained loyal to the Republican government that made significant strides for U.S. blacks. Inevitably, Douglass believed it was impossible for the Dominican Republic to thrive on its own because "it was too small and too weak to maintain a respectable national government." And, at this particular historical moment of racial progress in the United States, he believed that there was room for any nation under the flag of the United States as long as it was their true will and it afforded the country an opportunity for substantial industrial and technological development.

As Wilson J. Moses asserted, it remains critical that scholars take "black thinkers ... seriously enough to see how they have struggled with the problems of human understanding and attempted to reconcile life's contradictions."[77] The reformer's staunch patriotism distorted the lines between "love of patria" and "love of justice" and challenged the United States' Anglo citizenry to be aware of patriotism's most important components during this post-U.S. slavery era—the need for atonement and structural transformations that perpetuated white supremacy and the effects of racial slavery.[78]

U.S. annexation of the Dominican Republic never occurred. President Grant's campaign lost its momentum after the rejection from the U.S. Senate Foreign Relations Committee. By 1873, Douglass rarely lectured on the topic. However, Douglass's speaking engagements did influence other U.S. African Americans and religious groups to endorse annexation.[79] By the middle and late 1870s, with the end of U.S. Reconstruction and the election of Republican president Rutherford B. Hayes, race relations in the U.S. South worsened. In 1876, President Hayes removed federal troops from the U.S. South and failed to reconcile the federal enforcement of the Constitution with a policy of goodwill and good faith that Southern states would protect the rights of freedmen and women.[80]

During the early to middle 1880s, domestic and international aggression against peoples of African descent intensified. In 1883, the U.S. Supreme Court repealed the Civil Rights Act of 1875, which allowed for the institutionalization of racial segregation in northern and southern states. And, in 1884–1885, the Berlin conference outlined European imperial ventures and the violent partition of the African continent. Frederick Douglass recommended John H. Smyth to President Hayes for the position of U.S. minister to Liberia in 1878. Smyth, a strong believer in U.S. African American emigration to Africa, began to fervently campaign against European colonial designs on the African continent. There is little evidence to illuminate the irony of why an anti-emigrationist (Douglass) would recommend a passionate emigrationist (Smyth). One possible answer lies in their similar views about mutual material opportunities for nonwhite societies and the United States. Smyth wrote to the U.S. State Department that Liberia's geographic location and control unlocked "a mart for many of the manufactured commodities of the United States, which would be a source of material advantage to our [Liberia] industrial classes, to the government, and would greatly aid in the stability of this republic. . . ."[81]

"To Conserve and Promote . . . Cordial Relations": Frederick Douglass at the center of U.S/Haiti Relations, 1888–1891

On June 25, 1889, Douglass accepted the position of U.S. minister to Haiti. His appointment occurred in the midst of a major political scandal involving Haitian rebel forces and U.S. businessmen and officials. In November 1888, Haitian minister to the United States Stephen Preston reported to recently elected President François Légitime that William P. Clyde, an unscrupulous steamship proprietor, had surreptitiously supplied General Florvil Hyppolite's uprising with illegal contraband, including weapons, provisions and ammunition. Compelled by a stew of political maneuvers and rumors about European economic and political privileges and concessions for recognizing Légitime's presidency, Clyde and Secretary of State James G. Blaine scrambled to impede, if not end, further European infiltration to sovereign Caribbean and Latin American markets—thus protecting the spirit of the Monroe Doctrine. By March 1889, in a bold move to protect his business interests, Clyde, with the aid of U.S. Navy Rear Admiral Bancroft Gherardi, dispatched and protected steamers transporting over one thousand cases of cartridges, "75 cases of rifles and bayonets, 1,000 pounds of powder and 17 Gatling guns for Hyppolite."[82] Several Haitian newspapers asserted that U.S. involvement in the Légitime coup demonstrated an imperial threat. Les Nouvelles reported that it was the "fixed opinion of Washington to directly enter the Haitian conflict from a powerful position and turn a profit off of the black Republican government, through partial occupation and commercial gain."[83] Although there is no evidence that President Benjamin Harrison authorized a U.S. naval officer to intercede in Hyppolite's campaign, it is obvious that Washington and U.S. businessmen played significant roles in Hyppolite's eventual removal of Légitime.

Hyppolite's election on October 7, 1889, seemed to be smooth sailing for

Clyde's schemes to obtain a Haitian subsidy and exclusive rights to ship goods and services to seven Haitian ports. U.S. merchants, alongside French and German businessmen, according to one author, played a "leading role in dictat[ing] economic policy, inasmuch as the state complied with their most important demands."[84] For example, Douglass could be a strategic ally in Clyde's plans, fervently persuading the Haitian government to accept the terms of Clyde's proposal. However, Douglass, despite his accord with promoting Haitian trade and U.S. interests, believed it to be unconscionable to advocate solely on Clyde's behalf—to turn a blind eye to other U.S. American business requests in Haiti and to indirectly undercut Haitian economic decision making. Douglass rebuffed Clyde's demands, and Clyde and his representatives deemed him an "unworthy ally." This reproachful moniker contributed to an escalating skepticism within Washington circles and U.S. print media concerning Douglass's ability to effectively serve as a U.S. diplomat who ensured and protected U.S interests in the area.[85] In an unedited version of his essay assessing Haiti/U.S. affairs, Douglass revealed his diplomatic struggle to serve "two masters," the United States and Clyde's agent E.C. Reed: "I could not see what I had said or done to make it possible for any man to make to me a proposal so plainly dishonest and scandalous," Douglass asserted shockingly. "Here was my first offense, and it stamped me at once as an unprofitable servant."[86]

Thus, the Clyde concession proved to be a significant episode in Haiti/U.S. relations that illustrated the growth and significance of the U.S. Navy and maritime trade on U.S. strategies of empire. The Clyde incident also demonstrated the jostling for supremacy between European and Anglo-American merchants in the Caribbean and Latin America, thus amplifying foreign threats of imperialism in the Americas. Although U.S. foreign policy objectives in the aftermath of the U.S. Civil War typically supported invasion and/or the appropriation of land contiguous to the United States (except for Alaska and Hawaii), Washington embarked upon an informal imperialism where inter-American affairs centered on U.S. interests and the welfare of U.S. businessmen. In some cases, Haitian leadership sought to challenge U.S. hegemony by fostering alliances based upon a shared history of tyranny. For example, President Boyer encouraged U.S. African American emigration to the republic in 1820.[87] Some Haitian diplomats such as Anténor Firmin and N. Deslandes campaigned against a policy of intervention and strived to limit the terms of U.S. expansionism in favor of Haitian multilateralism. In December 1888, Deslandes, the Haitian consul general to the United States, wrote a scathing article denouncing U.S. involvement in François Légitime's coup. "Is it not monstrous?" Deslandes exclaimed, that "the great people [U.S. patriots] who in 177[6], shook off the yoke of England, who in 1864, abolished slavery; who at the head of all nations has proclaimed the reign of law—come with men of war[,] threatening and arrogant[,] to enforce her claim by the means of bullets against a young Republic that has on its side nothing [except] its right."[88]

Deslandes' remarks directly challenged Benjamin Harrison's vision for improved U.S./Latin American relations. On September 11, 1888, Harrison accepted the Republican nomination for U.S. president. At the Republican convention, Harrison encouraged military and material strength in the United States and he sought to cultivate an amicable and respectful environment with Latin American/Caribbean states and other foreign powers without demonstrating timidity or arrogance. "Vacillation and inconsistency are as incompatible with successful diplomacy," Harrison contended, "as they are with the national dignity." To make the administration's commitment to nurturing harmonious relations apparent, the future president proposed fostering "our diplomatic and commercial relations with the Central and South American states" and supporting resolutions to the "rebuilding of the Navy, to coast defenses, and to public lands."[89]

Riding the wave of popular thought in the 1880s that necessitated the manufacturing of a fearless and proficient navy, and anticipating Mahanian theories that correlated naval dominance with national supremacy, Harrison's ideas derived from the ideals of Pan Americanism and its ideological antecedent, the Monroe Doctrine.[90] U.S. secretary of state James G. Blaine, who organized an International American Conference held in Washington on October 2, 1889, one week prior to Douglass's arrival in Haiti as minister resident and consul general, reinforced President Harrison's inter-American policy objectives. Blaine's opening speech articulated his vision for Pan Americanism. He argued:

> ... friendship and not force, the spirit of just law and not the violence of the mob should be the recognized rule of administration between American nations and in American nations. . . . It will be a greater gain when we shall be able to draw the people of all American nations into closer acquaintance with each other, an end to be facilitated by more frequent and rapid intercommunication. It will be the greatest gain when the personal and commercial relations of the American

states . . . shall be so developed and so regulated that each shall acquire the highest possible advantage from the enlightened and en-
larged intercourse of all.[91]

Hannibal Price, Haitian ambassador to the United States and a conference
participant who witnessed Blaine's aforementioned speech, authored an
extensive report on the International American Conference to Anténor
Firmin. Early in Price's report, he echoed the spirit of Blaine's Pan Americanism. At the same time, Price emphasized the need for Caribbean and
Latin American "delegates" to underscore the importance of inter-American arbitration on major political and economic issues and more egalitarian
trade relations, "as well as ways to encourage such reciprocal arrangements
from commercial ventures that could be beneficial for all by providing
greater opportunities for products of each of these states."[92]

In a November 1889 letter to Haitian president Florvil Hyppolite, Douglass's thoughts on Pan Americanism mirrored Blaine's and Price's Pan
Americanist rhetoric. The minister noted that in an effort to "conserve and
promote the cordial relations which have so long and so happily subsisted
between the United States and Haiti," it was critical to discuss the ways
in which modernization (industrial, technological, and cultural) advanced
inter-American cooperation, interdependence and racial equality.

> Happily, too, the spirit of the age powerfully assists in establishing a
> sentiment of universal brotherhood. Art, science, discovery and in-
> vention have gone forward with such speed as almost to transcend
> our ability to keep pace with them. Steam, electricity and enterprise
> are linking together all the oceans, islands, capes and continents, dis-
> closing more and more the common interests and interdependence
> of nations.[93]

Douglass's dedication and loyalty to the Republican Harrison and U.S.
foreign policy, as revealed in his support of Dominican annexation, made
him an acceptable diplomat, one who espoused U.S. Pan Americanism.
He stressed the significance of promoting U.S./Haiti commercial affairs,
praised nonviolent U.S. expansionism and attempted to ease the suspicious
and critical minds of Haitian officials wary of U.S imperialism. In spite of
Douglass's views on annexation, many Haitians did not have a problem
with Douglass's appointment as U.S. minister. Alonzo Holly, a physician
and the son of U.S. African American emigrationist James T. Holly, noted

that "Haytians hail the nomination of so lofty-minded and liberal a man as the Hon. Frederick Douglass. . . . In him we see not an 'annexationist' . . . but a gentleman who, remembering the depths of disgrace and injustice . . . will be better able to appreciate the heroic efforts of a nation whose past history influenced to no mean degree, his own career."[94]

Undoubtedly, Douglass possessed a tremendous amount of respect for the Haitian Revolution and its most famous leader, Toussaint L'Ouverture. Douglass maintained that Toussaint symbolized a "standing reply to assertion of Negro inferiority."[95] Yet the minister did not believe that it was inconsistent to promote U.S. interests in Haiti. For Douglass, encouraging friendly commercial relations served as one way to break down racial barriers and structural patterns of underdevelopment. Douglass contended: "the growing commerce and intercommunication of various nationalities, so important to the dissemination of knowledge, to the enlargement of human sympathies, and to the extinction of hurtful prejudices import no menace to the autonomy of nations, but develop opportunities for the exercise of a generous spirit of forbearance and concession, favorable to peace and fraternal relations. . . ."[96] Douglass sought a more egalitarian relationship between Haiti and the United States; this is why he adamantly objected to Clyde's proposal. It is unlikely that Douglass would have deterred or opposed transnational commercialism because of the damaging effects it posed to an already exploited Haitian economy, which endured declines in agricultural prices, competition with Brazilian coffee, foreign and elite control of wealth, crop failures and credit restrictions.[97]

President Hyppolite's response to Douglass's aforementioned missive situated U.S. African American leadership within the aims of black Pan Americanism. Admiringly, Hyppolite stated that Douglass's "reputation [was] known in the two hemispheres" and that the U.S. African American diplomat symbolized "the incarnation of the idea which Haiti is following—the moral and intellectual development of men of the African race by personal effort and national culture." The president's acknowledgment of Douglass's accomplishments as a former slave who had become an unwavering activist and an intellectual underscored the political context of Caribbean self-determination and individuality within the realm of Western colonialism. "Every nation has therefore the right to be proud of its autonomy," Hyppolite asserted, while thanking Harrison's administration "for [its] desire . . . to see Haiti participate *fully* in this tendency of the age."[98]

Hyppolite's declaration for a peoples' right to sovereignty spoke volumes as the United States set its sights on Môle Saint-Nicolas, a potential site for a U.S. naval station located in the northwestern part of Haiti. Hyppolite's assertion that Haiti was entitled to be the political and economic peer of American states proved to be an important statement during an era when U.S. dominance in the region operated as a racist paternalism.[99] At the same time, his statement may also have reflected fears and suspicions of U.S. encroachment on the Môle Saint-Nicolas.

During November 1889, an unauthorized U.S. naval warship, the *Yantic,* arrived at Môle to examine longitude coordinates to other Caribbean islands where European telegraph cables had been set.[100] As part of U.S. expansionist goals, Washington encouraged the extension of telegraph cables and modern warships. Harrison communicated in his inaugural address in March 1889 that "the necessities of our navy require convenient coaling stations and dock and harbor privileges."[101] Ideally, U.S. naval coaling stations would be situated in strategic locations throughout the Caribbean and Latin America to protect U.S. interests and to fend off European penetration. According to U.S. Navy Rear Admiral Bancroft Gherardi, "the strategical value of this Island from a naval point of view is invaluable, and this increases in direct proportion to the millions which [U.S.] American citizens are investing in the Nicaragua Canal." Gherardi further stated: "It should also be made clear to them that the United States has no desire to annex it. It would not, at the present moment, be advisable to make any effort to get possession of Mole Saint Nicolas, but I have no doubt that in the near future it can be done."[102] The State Department clearly fixed its eye on acquiring, if not exclusively leasing, Môle. The buildup of U.S. warships and arms and the spectacle of unauthorized warships floating off Haiti's coast strongly communicated ideas that violated the spirit of mutual respect and cooperation outlined in Blaine's speech at the International American Conference. Newly inaugurated and appointed Haitian executive officials balked at the idea of the United States having designs on Môle because such a scenario indirectly threatened Haitian sovereignty and could be used as fodder by hungry opposition groups seeking to dethrone Hyppolite's administration.

Douglass, whose role in and support of the acquisition of Môle Saint-Nicolas has been well documented, believed it was in both Haiti's and the United States' interests to cede Môle to the United States. However, he warned Secretary of State Blaine in December 1889 that "the presence of the 'Yankee' [*Yantic*] and of our naval officers at the Môle" justified Haitian suspicions and threats and would certainly "occasion some comment in Haitian circles."[103] The continued presence of two U.S. naval squadrons in Haiti's harbor made the most "unfortunate impression on the entire country," according to Anténor Firmin, Haiti's minister of foreign relations.[104] In April 1891, during the height of lease negotiations for the potential U.S. naval station, Firmin said that the sale or lease of the bay to any entity would be, "to the eyes of the Haitian Government, an outrage to the national sovereignty of the Republic and a flagrant violation of the first article of our Constitution."[105] In spite of the Haitian Constitution, Firmin also remarked that Haiti refused, under "the present circumstances" to "compromise . . . our existence as an independent people."[106] Tactfully, Haiti's foreign minister stated that the administration held no ill will toward the United States and that their refusal was not a result of Haitian mistrust of Washington's intentions, but it clearly demonstrated the government's unease about transferring power to the United States.[107]

During Douglass's tenure as U.S. minister to Haiti (1889–1891), he played a marginal role in political dialogues about the acquisition of Môle Saint-Nicolas. The U.S. State Department never officially empowered him to negotiate on its behalf yet it encouraged him to "cooperate" with Admiral Gherardi "in accomplishing this object[ive]."[108] As U.S. minister, Douglass should have played a central role in the negotiations but he claimed that his reputation had been "discredited" in Washington, which placed him in an "unenviable position both before the community of Port au Prince" and the Haitian government.[109] U.S. newspapers reported that the U.S. State Department contended that a white man was best suited for intense negotiations. Douglass's "honor" and pride prevented him from yielding to temptations to resign even though he maintained serious objections to Gherardi and the inappropriate way he received instructions from the U.S. State Department. Specifically, the minister quietly balked at the fact that Gherardi's appointment was not a presidential or a congressional one and that he, Douglass, received information through Gherardi and not in the familiar manner of official dispatches.

On January 28, 1891, Gherardi and Douglass met with President Hyppolite and Anténor Firmin, Haiti's minister of foreign relations.[110] According to Douglass, Gherardi executed a skillful presentation, in which he stated that the lease of Môle demonstrated "services rendered by the United States to the Hyppolite revolution."[111] Consistent with his views, Douglass approached the negotiations a bit differently but "not in opposition to"

[Gherardi's] standpoint. He emphasized black Pan American principles of friendly relations, nonintervention and cooperative development within a framework that acknowledged Haiti's revolutionary past, U.S. and European disavowals of the black Republic's accomplishments and the country's potential commercial future. For Douglass, the concession was "in the line of good neighborhood and advanced civilization, and in every way consistent with the autonomy of Haïti." Additionally, Douglass stated:

> ... that national isolation was a policy of the past; that the necessity for it in Haïti, for which there was an apology at the commencement of her existence, no longer exists; that her relation to the world and that of the world to her are not what they were when her independence was achieved; that her true policy now is to touch the world at all points that make for civilization and commerce. ... [112]

Although Douglass had a more modest role, subservient to Gherardi, his language and tone exemplified a more progressive and/or radical position—recognizing past injustices during and after the Haitian revolutionary period—within diplomatic negotiations. He encouraged Haitian multilateralism in the economy, which helped to minimize foreign dependence, as opposed to adopting the bilateral reciprocity treaties popular in the United States during the mid-nineteenth century. Those agreements barred "third parties [and] made handy instruments for conquering Latin American markets.[113]

Quickly, Firmin called into question Gherardi's notion that the Haitian government had promised Môle Saint-Nicolas. In the late 1860s, Sylvain Salnave's administration furtively negotiated sale of Môle Saint-Nicolas to the United States for taking on Haitian debt to France and defense against oppositional forces to Salnave. In this case, Gherardi presented Firmin with a copy of a Haitian pledge, but it was never formally approved by the U.S. State Department. Gherardi claimed that the Haitian officials were "morally bound" by this informal accord, but Firmin remained resolute in his stance. "Without intending to break the force of the admiral's contention," a clearly uncomfortable Douglass recognized the unsightly light of U.S. foreign politics, in which an interventionist U.S. government "covertly assist[ed] in putting down one government and setting up another."[114]

Douglass's duties in Haiti proved to be inextricably linked to the U.S. Pan American movement that sought to cultivate U.S./Caribbean and U.S./Latin American relations to the advantage of U.S. expansionism in the nineteenth century. As a principled ambassador who favored advancing U.S. trade and developing Haiti, Douglass believed Haiti had committed a grave "error" by objecting to U.S. acquisition of Môle Saint-Nicolas. However, convinced that overwhelming dissent existed among Haitians and then forced to defer to Gherardi's instructions, Douglass admittedly refused to compromise Haitian decision-makers and recoiled during the Môle negotiations, playing a self-described "humble, secondary, and subordinate" role. Douglass's value to the U.S. State Department's inter-American goals did not yield any significant revenue (outside of handling uncomplicated requests of U.S. citizens in or pertaining to Haiti), and thus he proved expendable.

The conditions, terms and lack of support by the Harrison administration undermined Douglass's authority and effectiveness in implementing U.S. Pan American objectives. Even after Douglass resigned in late July 1891 due to his declining health and controversies over the Môle affair, Secretary Blaine remained unswerving on the subject of appointing another black man, John Durham, to the diplomatic post. "What is needed is a white man of reputation and nerve," insisted Blaine to an undecided Harrison.[115] To placate U.S. African American leadership, Blaine eventually and reluctantly backed Durham for the post, a gesture that illuminates the racist tokenism common to U.S. politics. Blaine stated: "It will save you [Harrison] the annoyance of a half hundred colored men, who will quarrel over it until each is enraged as far as he can be. . . . I had hoped that a white man might be taken, but as you seem to think you are bound to appoint a colored man. . . ."[116]

As minister, Douglass remained a loyal and "good soldier," probably to a fault. He recognized the all-too-familiar position of being a "representative black man" (to borrow a phrase from Wilson Moses) whose singularity and privileged station were tenuous and impacted all U.S. blacks who journeyed after him. But, in a move that was perhaps too late for condemnations but consistent with his assessments of racial inequality in the United States, Douglass became more harshly critical of U.S. intentions in Haiti after he resigned. "White men professed to speak in the interest of black Haïti," Douglass exclaimed, adding that "I could have applauded their alacrity in upholding her dignity if I could have respected their sincerity."[117] The reformer, who had long admired the independence struggles of the Haitian Revolution and its post-emancipation efforts to build a functional government, called on the United States to deal with Haiti and Haitians as equals and to honorably live up to the ideals of Pan Americanism:

> Is the weakness of a nation a reason for our robbing it? Are we to take advantage, not only of its weakness, but of its fears? Are we to wring from it by dread of our power what we cannot obtain by appeals to its justice and reason? If this is the policy of this great nation, I own that my assailants were right when they said that I was not the man to represent the United States in Haiti. I am charged with sympathy for Haiti. I am not ashamed of that charge. . . .[118]

Douglass's blunt inquiries of U.S. ambitions in Haiti, and probably more broadly in Caribbean and Latin American affairs, exemplified the complex and unremitting concessions that U.S. African American diplomats made to effect change in nonwhite nation-states in the Caribbean and the African continent. Douglass's interpolation of the Haitian Revolution and antiblack prejudice within a decidedly U.S. Pan American movement, which masked the centrality of race and privileged local governments "that complied most completely with the U.S. agenda of market growth, strategic dominance, and racial chauvinism," exemplified the efforts of black Pan Americanists. His unashamed sympathy towards Haiti's development exhibited a connection to a burgeoning Pan Caribbean identity. Yet, the conflicts over the implementation of U.S. Pan American initiatives in Haiti rendered Douglass's ideals of inter-American affairs unsuccessful.

Conclusion

As a U.S. African American emissary and a diplomat for the U.S. government, Frederick Douglass sought to represent the interests of Washington and the virtues of marginalized blacks in the United States and the Caribbean. During the early 1870s, he supported U.S. annexation of the Dominican Republic because he believed such a move to be the will of the Dominican people and a firm step toward modern development—fashioned largely from a U.S. model of diverse export trade, democratic politics and industrial and technological advancement. Also, Douglass believed that the Radical Republican politics of the late 1860s and early 1870s demonstrated a watershed moment in U.S. African American social and political progress and that Radical Republicanism held great promise for nonwhite peoples of the Caribbean and of Latin America. In Haiti, Douglass continued to support U.S. expansion until Washington's aggression compromised Haitian sovereignty. By 1889, Haitians had lived more than eight decades as a sovereign people, and Douglass knew that Haitian leaders had made it quite clear they would not cede any land to the United States.[119] Furthermore, the lives of African and U.S. African American people profoundly changed because of the European partitioning of Africa and a return to white domination in the post-Reconstruction U.S. South. In July 1890, Douglass, who had returned to the United States from Haiti for a few months, observed a deterioration of black life in the United States. In August 1890, Douglass discussed his disappointment with the *Boston Daily Globe*. He asserted: "It was the idea of Mr. Hayes in 1877 that the time had come when the nation could safely trust the loyalty and the honor of the States lately in rebellion to submit to the requirements of the Constitution of the United States. Time has shown the contrary."[120]

Douglass's criticisms of and support for U.S. expansion in the Caribbean provide an insightful voice for U.S. African American responses to U.S. empire-building in the nineteenth century. Within a few years of Douglass's retirement as U.S. minister to Haiti and his death in 1895, the United States entered into a more intensive jingoism with Latin American and Caribbean states. In 1895, the United States moved to the brink of war with Great Britain due to conflicts over the Venezuelan/British Guiana border. And, by April 1898, Spain and the United States had declared war on each other over the fate of Cuba. The Spanish-American War of 1898 brought about repeated U.S. intervention in Cuban affairs (1898–1902, 1909–1912, 1917–1922). Additionally, the Spanish colony of Puerto Rico and the Philippines came under U.S. rule.[121] The Venezuelan calamity and the Spanish-American War proved further evidence of Washington's asserting its control in the Western Hemisphere. Douglass's denouncement of U.S. hostilities in Haiti anticipated one of the defining moments in nineteenth-century U.S. foreign policy, the War of 1898. Examined today, Douglass's views open a new window on understanding U.S. African American responses to U.S. foreign policy in the Americas. This opening may help us better understand the convergence of U.S. African American and Caribbean/Latin American relations during the late nineteenth century. In the end, Douglass's vision of U.S./Caribbean relations attempted to connect competing articulations of Pan Americanism. It was nonviolent, noninterventionist and at times

U.S. centered, but his ideas challenged the voracious manner and modes in which U.S. empire-building took shape in the 1890s.

Despite Douglass's anti-interventionist swing, U.S. imperialism intensified at the turn of the century. President Theodore Roosevelt reinvoked the tenets of the Monroe Doctrine and established the United States as a hemispheric patrolman of Caribbean and Latin American affairs due to internal political and economic instability and European aggression in the region. Between 1902 and 1934, U.S. troops occupied more than five countries in the Caribbean and Central America, including Haiti and Nicaragua. U.S. African Americans publicly objected to the U.S. onslaught on sovereign nonwhite nations. At the same time, many U.S. blacks believed that with U.S. aid (financial and intellectual), countries could implement much-needed structural and social improvements to advance the lot of African-descended peoples and to lessen the likelihood of U.S. intervention.

"To Combine the Training of the Head and the Hands"

The 1930 Robert R. Moton Education Commission in Haiti

When he addressed a distinguished group of U.S. African American educators and journalists in Port-au-Prince at the beginning of the hurricane season of July 1930, Louis C. Lhérisson believed he held the keys to improve the nation's deteriorating education infrastructure. Possessing more than 45 years of public service as a teacher, a public-instruction officer, the president of Alliance Française and as the current director of the College of Toussaint L'Ouverture, this vibrant octogenarian argued that the Haitian government needed to confront the stranglehold of economic dependency if it wanted to effectively develop Haitian schools and the minds of Haitian children. Lhérisson noted: "The general misery which has been spread throughout the country during these last ten years is aggravated by import duties which are too heavy for the impoverished tax payers."[1] Consequently, he added, this environment of suffering and depression "finds itself echoed in our schools." By 1931, the Haitian government expended less than $400,000 annually on more than 400,000 school-age children.[2] Teachers earned "laughable salaries," Lhérisson continued, while children lacked "school materials," and import duties on "school furnishings" placed an insurmountable burden on Haiti's Department of Public Instruction.[3]

The attentive educators in the audience were members of the U.S. Commission on Education in Haiti (also known as the Robert R. Moton Commission), a select group of largely U.S. African American college professors, university administrators, journalists and nongovernment officials authorized by U.S. president Herbert Hoover's administration to study and propose modifications to Haiti's public education system. The commission consisted of Robert R. Moton, president of Tuskegee Institute; Mordecai Johnson, president of Howard University; W.T.B. Williams, dean of Tuskegee Institute; Benjamin Hubert, president of Georgia State Industrial College for Colored Youth; Alphonse Henninburg, professor of Romance Languages at Tuskegee; G. Lake Imes, a Tuskegee secretary; Leo M. Favrot, a member of the Baton Rouge, Louisiana, General Education Board and the commission's only white colleague; and two members of the black press, P. L. Prattis of the Associated Negro Press and Carl Murphy of the *Baltimore Afro-American Ledger*.[4]

U.S. Americans listening to Haitians during U.S. occupation served as an ephemeral, yet significant shift in the dialogue between the two groups, which was normally dictated by John H. Russell, U.S. high commissioner in Haiti. On the other hand, Moton, as well as the other members, paid particular attention to Lhérisson's direct challenges to fifteen years of U.S. hegemony in Haiti. Many if not all of the members of the Moton Commission were familiar with the vitriol hurled at Washington's foreign policy in Haiti. By the fall of 1915, the black press in the United States had diligently publicized its opposition to U.S. imperialist ventures. Joining their efforts were prominent members of the National Association for the Advancement of Colored People (NAACP) such as James Weldon Johnson, a writer, activist and former U.S. consul to Nicaragua and Venezuela. Together the black press and leading NAACP members informed aspiring U.S. blacks and liberal white readers about the economic, social and political failures and the spoils of U.S. intervention.[5] For instance, despite Washington's objective to help diversify Haiti's agricultural production, U.S. authorities in Haiti multiplied the country's reliance on monocrop exports (e.g., coffee) at the same time that the United States profited from being Haiti's largest supplier of merchandise.[6] More than a decade under U.S. occupation, Haiti was firmly embedded in the economic margins of the hemisphere, a role characteristic of developing nations in the Caribbean and South America.

Although Lhérisson pointedly condemned U.S. control of Haitian affairs, a power that Washington similarly wielded in Cuba, Honduras, Nicaragua, Panama and the Dominican Republic by implementing racist policies of intervention, Lhérisson seemed hopeful of the outcome of the Moton Commission's pending investigation. At a time when educating the Haitian masses was inextricably linked with the fate of the Haitian economy, Lhérisson believed that Hoover's emphasis on nonintervention and military withdrawal from Haiti and Latin America, as well as "systematic intellectual exchanges" and increased commercial investment, could provide a space for more egalitarian trade agreements to ignite the Haitian economy and, in turn, ameliorate Haitian schools.[7]

Furthermore, the Moton Commission ceremony occurred within a pivotal time span, March through July 1930, a five-month period that revealed the potential for future political change and the promise of Pan Americanism. Louis Borno, a two-term president long considered a pawn of U.S. occupation forces, was not allowed by U.S. bureaucrats to seek an illegal third term. In March 1930, the William Cameron Forbes Commission, an all-white group of former U.S. ambassadors, foreign-service officers, writers and intellectuals who examined Haitian affairs more generally, recommended the abolition of the rank of U.S. high commissioner, called for the steady removal of U.S. Marines and sought to reestablish Haitian control of key administrative positions.[8] Additionally, a few well-respected Haitians like Dantès Bellegarde, a Haitian intellectual, a diplomat and an educator, articulated a renewed confidence in Hoover's leadership and its implications for strengthening Haiti/U.S. relations. On March 3, 1930, Bellegarde asserted at the Forbes Commission hearings, which assembled Haitian activists and elites to bear witness to the impact of U.S. occupation, that he "knew that [Hoover] was against the military imperialists" because of comments made by Hoover, then U.S. secretary of commerce, at the Third Commercial Pan American Conference in Washington, D.C.[9] Lhérisson remarked a few months later that Hoover possessed "a hatred for injustice" and that Haiti could "live beside the American Union, without the colossal shadow of her great neighbor causing her to disappear in the resplendent light of the Archipelago of the Antilles."[10]

Wrapping up his July 1930 speech in honor of the Moton Commission, Lhérisson concluded on three main points. First, he denounced U.S. imperialism in Haiti. Second, he encouraged an egalitarian Pan American program of "brotherhood" and "solidarity." And last, he confirmed the apprehension and possibly fear of many Haitians, particularly urban elites, that the Moton Commission would suggest to Hoover that Haiti implement a strictly industrial education agenda, indistinguishable from Booker T. Washington's model of instruction at Tuskegee Institute for newly freed and impoverished U.S. African Americans. Lhérisson, a noted Francophile, made it clear to the Moton Commission that, at least from the privileged urbanite perspective, Haitians wished to "preserve and develop" their "Latin mind" and French culture. Haitian-ness was both African and French, Lhérisson argued, as if to clarify to the education commission that a balance of academic and industrial education was the only alternative. It was no surprise that the Alliance Française had invited and sponsored the soirée honoring the education commission, sending an unambiguous message about their opinions regarding the foundations of Haitian edification. Although many Haitian elites admired the achievements of Booker T. Washington and his industrial education ideology, they remained cautious about a potential erasure of the French-influenced educational system, which operated under the auspices of the Ministry of Education and emphasized classical humanities training as well as math and sciences courses. In a move that was incongruous with the French-influenced Haitian education system, U.S. officials sought to establish Haitian instruction under the Ministry of Agriculture, thus centering agronomy and trade schools.

Indeed, Lhérisson's speech and the ceremony welcoming the Moton Commission proved to be both a contentious and a promising occasion. On the one hand, the event revealed the realities of Haiti's economic dependence on the United States and of U.S. repression and discrimination of Haitian citizens; likewise, the clash between U.S. African American educational goals and those of the French educational system illustrated the broader tensions between intraracial diplomacy and class and culture. On the other hand, the ceremony highlighted the possibilities of achieving transnational cooperation between intraracial groups and state officials within a U.S. political context of eliminating military influence in Haiti.

The program honoring the Moton Commission demonstrated the promise of black transnational initiatives in the Americas and their efforts to transcend economic and cultural barriers so as to cultivate racial progress (social and industrial development). The work of the Moton Commission established that U.S. African Americans did participate in the politics of U.S. withdrawal and worked to develop Haitian education, two issues central to the black republic's sovereignty and advancement. However, what this chapter reveals is that despite the three-week-long investigation conducted by the commission and the critical suggestions it made to improve the Haitian educational system, ultimately the group's efforts were compromised by lack of support by the Hoover administration. This compromise was largely due to the racist and obstructive behavior of the U.S. government, which provided unequal funds and transportation to the Moton Commission in comparison to the support given to the Forbes group; similarly, Washington refused to consider implementing the commission's suggestions because they did not align with U.S. interests. The failure of this educational initiative highlighted the weaknesses of U.S. Pan Americanism for blacks in the Americas, in this case, for U.S. African Americans and Haitians. These two groups confronted an ideological system that privileged whiteness and U.S. American interests in the Western Hemisphere. Additionally, U.S. Pan Americanists hindered U.S. African American efforts to be recognized as full citizens at the decision-making table. Yet despite these setbacks, the members of the Moton Commission believed that, when properly manipulated, the language and tenets of Pan Americanism—inter-American cooperation, mutual friendship and non-intervention—could serve as useful tools to address transnational initiatives of particular concern to U.S. African Americans and to the politics of the African diaspora. This manipulation functioned as part of the structural underpinnings of black Pan Americanism, a discourse that, operating within this particular educational context, emphasized a reorganized and more empowering school system during the latter stages of U.S. occupation. The foundations of this intraracial and inter-American relationship originated in the early nineteenth century (see chapter 1); however, I will discuss the roots of U.S. African American and Haitian connections during U.S. occupation so as to contextualize the significance of the Moton Commission on black efforts to work within and challenge U.S. Pan Americanism.

U.S. Occupation of Haiti as a Watershed Moment in U.S. African American and Haitian Relations

Initially, many U.S. African Americans did not respond to news of the presence of U.S. Marines on Haitian soil during the late summer of 1915. Violent opposition to Haitian president Vilbrun Guillaume Sam and the senseless murder of more than a hundred and fifty political prisoners under his administration led the government down a familiar road of political disarray. In the U.S. African American press, coverage of local news and the First World War took center stage. Historian Brenda G. Plummer noted that many U.S. blacks, except for a "handful of intellectuals who gloried in Haiti's revolutionary past," believed Haiti's political and economic problems were a "logical occurrence" of the country's backwardness and that "lurid accounts of voodoo" further intensified U.S. African American indifference to U.S. occupation.[11] Yet in a few black periodicals such as the *Baltimore Afro-American Ledger* (also known as the *Baltimore Afro-American* or, sim-

ply, the *Afro-American*) several articles in August 1915 reported the injust
of U.S. intervention. By the middle of August, a compelling three-column
political cartoon in the *Afro-American* showcased a towering, Anglo-Saxon
fatherlike Uncle Sam reprimanding a diminutive Haitian child, while
the second scene revealed a hesitant Uncle Sam standing eye to eye with
Mexican revolutionary leaders Francisco "Pancho" Villa and Venustiano
Carranza Garza. The third picture displayed a miniature and feeble Uncle
Sam cowering before the immense power of Germany and its leader Kaiser
Wilhelm II. The *Afro-American*'s political caricature clearly communicated
the racialized nature of U.S. intervention, an attitude that was reinforced
by popular and institutional beliefs about Haiti being a primitive, uncivi-
lized and militarily insubstantial black nation that needed the enlightened
leadership of the (Anglo-American) United States to administer effective
government. This egregious paternalism, as historian Mary A. Renda has
documented, "constituted a crucial part of the ideological machinery of the
occupation."[12]

In late August 1915, the *Afro-American* published remonstrative editorials lambasting Washington's program of "watchful-waitingness" with
Mexico's revolution and Germany's war. However, "when it comes to a
little, poor, poverty-stricken, black republic," the writer opined, "sailors,
soldiers and marines must be sent, the natives disarmed and the government threatened with dire punishment unless it allows this great big bully
to do what it pleases. It is a stench in the nostrils of all decent people."[13] One
journalist for the *Afro-American* claimed that the United States "had long
been desirous" of obtaining a naval station in Haiti, referring to the Môle
Saint-Nicolas affair mentioned in chapter 1.[14] Also, the reporter asserted,
the completion of the Panama Canal made Haiti an ideal site for a U.S.
military base and rendered U.S. intervention a dubious excuse for resolving
Haiti's "state of confusion."[15]

U.S. occupation may not have been a cause célèbre among the masses
of U.S. blacks in the summer of 1915, but as vivid reports of U.S. military
and economic aggression continued to appear in outlets such as the *Afro-
American,* growing numbers of U.S. African Americans began not only to
demonstrate their knowledge of international affairs but to express their
extreme displeasure with the "bullying" of Haiti. U.S. intimidation and
eventually receivership of Haitian affairs struck a chord with U.S. African
American readers, who often suffered under similar violence, discrimination and paternalism in northern and southern U.S. American communi-

ties. And by 1918 to 1919, domestic racial politics influenced U.S. African American fury toward U.S. domination in the Americas. An upsurge of U.S. African American migration to urban centers intensified competition for jobs and housing, sparking a myriad of race riots. In addition, U.S. black activists campaigned for a national anti-lynching bill, and the emergence of a radical Garveyite movement in the United States further deepened U.S. African American opposition to U.S. imperialism.[16]

Black church groups and political conventions such as the National Colored Republican Conference (1924) and the American Negro Labor Conference (1925) denounced the occupation of Haiti.[17] As mentioned earlier, James Weldon Johnson and the NAACP proved to be a formidable force, exposing the brutal confrontations between U.S. Marines and Haitian rebels, who were largely composed of peasants, property owners and rogue officers in the Haitian military. Johnson, the executive secretary of the NAACP, penned a series of articles for the *Nation* in 1920 that questioned Washington's motives in Haiti, arguing that the interests of U.S. American investors and the National City Bank of New York superseded any "humane" intentions to reconcile political disunion.[18] Johnson also helped organize in New York City a U.S. chapter of L'Union Patriotique, a Haitian organization dedicated to restoring Haitian sovereignty.[19] Many Haitian nationals and émigrés supported the work of Johnson and the NAACP. J. Joseph Adam, a Haitian immigrant living in San Francisco, California, and a member of the NAACP, commended Johnson's great effort to use his influence and to illuminate the inequities and violence amplified by U.S. occupation.[20]

The pressure from U.S. African American activists and organizations, as well Republican critics, persuaded U.S. president Warren G. Harding to form an investigative commission to study the political and economic conditions in Haiti in 1921. Initially, Harding appointed no U.S. blacks to the commission. After consistent provocation, Harding sent a token representative, Napoleon Bonaparte Marshall, as clerk to the committee. A year later, Harding's administration sponsored a trip for Moton to examine Haitian education and promote vocational instruction. Concerned about U.S control of affairs in Haiti and the Dominican Republic (the latter having yielded to U.S. intervention in 1916), Moton urged President Harding to "re-establish confidence in the minds of these *sister countries*" by taking "a firm hand" in their "economic, educational, and sanitary rehabilitation." Employing the language of "friendship," "fellowship" and "cooperation" that was central to Pan Americanism and avowed in Warren G. Harding's inaugural address on the future of U.S./European relations in the aftermath of the First World War, Moton believed those same actions of aid and mutual respect should be afforded to nonwhite nations in the Americas. Moton encouraged Harding: "whatever America does for these three Negro republics [Moton also included Liberia] it will be done in the *spirit of cooperation and not of domination*, and that there may be no encroachment on their rights and prerogatives as individual nations."[21]

The Tuskegee president did not make the voyage in 1922, but sent W.T.B. Williams, a Tuskegee dean, whose observations in the *Southern Workman* were, for the most part, evenhanded but uncritical of the occupation. Williams noted:

> The [Americans] have . . . established peace and order in the country and appear to be doing a good job in the training of a Haitian gendarmerie. . . . Americans have built hundreds of miles of good roads . . . established a fine general hospital at Port-au-Prince . . . [and] carry on considerable sanitary and health work elsewhere. The big task remaining for both Americans and Haitians is to provide adequate and effective schools, to improve agriculture so as greatly to increase production, and to organize the finances of the country upon a sound, satisfactory basis.[22]

Under the occupation, structural improvements were negligible and largely due to the repressive *corvée* system or forced labor practice, which utilized Haitian peasants on municipal construction projects. Yet although the Haitian *gourde* (currency) remained steady, as scholar Michel-Rolph Trouillot noted, U.S. occupation "briefly reduced administrative corruption [and] temporarily ended the military coups. . . ."[23] Williams' favorable impression of the achievements of the U.S. armed forces, in spite of well-documented NAACP and U.S. newspaper accounts of hundreds of Haitian deaths, considerable loss to freedoms, and increased financial reliance on the United States, may speak to the dependence of Tuskegee Institute on liberal white capital and the accomodationist roots of Booker T. Washington, founder of Tuskegee and mentor to Moton and Williams. Astutely, historian Brenda G. Plummer documented that technological and industrial development were indispensable for the rationalization of the occupation. Subsequently, no matter how impressed Williams was with the construction of roads and health facilities, "development questions could not be separated from strategic concerns" and issues of Haitian sustainability.[24] Gaining access to new markets in bucolic and remote areas (some of which required the overpowering of Haitian armed resistance) depended on the completion of roads.

By the late 1920s, U.S. African American and Haitian resistance to military and fiscal interference escalated as a result of a number of reports in Haitian and U.S. newspapers about cases of racial segregation at hotels and Catholic Church services. U.S. marines violently confronted raucous Haitian protesters, and the grim state of the Haitian economy amplified the frustrations of the urban and rural poor. Haiti's neglected class of people, typically *noir* or dark skinned, were burdened by falling coffee prices and by rising taxes on general products such as salt and matches.[25] Many scholars agree that the student strike at an agricultural school in Damien in October 1929, coupled with the protests and subsequent killing of twenty-five citizens in Aux Cayes, accelerated the public discussion of U.S. withdrawal. Sparked by layoffs at a Port-au-Prince customhouse and the complaints of "aggrieved" sugar manufacturers drained by taxes from the Haitian American Sugar Company (HASCO) in December of the same year, peasant demonstrators exhibited the "economic root of popular discontent."[26] Whether writing highbrow essays for the *Nation,* coordinating transnational political organizations like L'Union Patriotique, or organizing sociopolitical protests in which the Haitian masses stared down the barrel of a U.S. Marine's gun, Haitians and U.S. African Americans of varying socioeconomic levels crafted an anti-imperialist struggle that possessed ramifications for both groups.

During the latter stages of U.S. occupation, Napoleon Bonaparte Marshall, the nominal clerk whom Harding's administration had appointed in 1921 to help study conditions in Haiti, realized the importance of an inter-American anti-imperialist effort on behalf of Haitians. Marshall believed that such a transnational anti-imperialist program could have a profound impact on the plight of U.S. African Americans as well. Given Marshall's background as a veteran of World War I, a former supporter of Woodrow Wilson and a faithful patriot, it is unclear what circumstances led to his disgust of U.S. occupation.[27] Marshall believed that radical anti-imperial protest needed to be cooperative, transnational and intraracial. In 1929 Marshall, then president of the Save Haiti League, wrote to Jean Price-Mars, a noted Haitian statesman, ethnologist and architect of the *indigénisme* movement, explaining that the U.S. anti-imperialist movement would "mature and fructify . . . because it is precisely the movement which the American white man is opposed to . . . because I know of no assured means for the reestablishment of Haitian autonomy and sovereignty . . . [and] because the co-operation on the part of colored Americans will gain for them that universal respect, so vitally needed for their *real advancement*."[28] The former clerk identified a common foe, "the American white man," upon whom Haitians and U.S. blacks needed to focus anti-imperialist efforts. Then, Marshall noted the existence of a transnational movement between U.S. African Americans and Haitians resistant to U.S. force and united to restore Haitian independence. Marshall's position complemented the prevailing Caribbean and Latin American stance on the power and potential of a non-interventionist ideology and a program of inter-American development. Lastly, Marshall suggested that the transnational anticolonial movement would advance with the necessary collaboration of U.S. African Americans and that inevitably this relationship would lead to the "real advancement" of the Haitian people.

As I argue in chapter 1, many U.S. blacks appropriated U.S. American culture or Western paradigms as benchmarks of civilization, thus envisioning themselves at the forefront of the race. Some Haitians, like Anténor Firmin and Jean Price-Mars, noted members of the Haitian intellectual and political elite, were impressed with U.S. African American achievement in the field of education (each visited Booker T. Washington, in 1904 and 1908 respectively). As scholars, Firmin and Price-Mars paid specific attention to the intellectual and cultural advancements of Haitians. Price-Mars particularly examined the cultural production and the contributions of the black peasantry to Haitian society in his pioneering text *Ainsi Parla L'Oncle* (*So Spoke the Uncle,* 1928). Price-Mars' and Firmin's mutual interest in Booker T. Washington coincided with their research and, arguably, with the redemption of African-descended peoples as biologically inferior and their cultural products as immaterial.

Individuals like Napoleon Bonaparte Marshall and organizations like his Save Haiti League believed that U.S. African Americans and possibly nonblack American anti-imperialists were particularly able and suited to aid, if not rescue, Haitians from U.S. encroachments and instability. For the most part, they did not act in a paternalistic or authoritarian manner, although some U.S. black intellectuals demonstrated those characteristics. For example, Zora Neale Hurston's *Tell My Horse* (1938), which examines Haitian traditional or folk culture, has been critiqued for its "chauvinism" and its "superficial description of West Indian curiosities."[29] Scholar J. Michael Dash noted that the book's affirmation of U.S. intervention and its numerous "alarming and racist references" demonstrated the "[U.S] black American imagination at its least generous."[30] At the same time that some U.S. blacks struggled with their own prejudices and with "sensationalist" writings and/or alliances with the U.S. government (such as those of Moton and Douglass), many U.S. blacks such as Moton, Napoleon Bonaparte Marshall and James Weldon Johnson asserted the linkages between race, racism and imperialism, some stressing these connections more forcefully than others. Moreover, many U.S. African Americans believed that there was a common purpose: to collectively disentangle the tribulations of race and nation to produce intellectual, political and economic gains.

Having endured close to fifteen years of U.S. authoritarian rule, Haitians continued to fight. The U.S. public became increasingly disgruntled with the continuation of violence and the lack of material and economic progress in Haiti. Newly elected President Hoover, fresh from his Good Neighbor tour of Latin America at the close of 1928, in which he emphasized inter-American cooperation and nonintervention, organized the Forbes and Moton commissions to investigate the possibilities of withdrawal.

Contextualizing Hoover and Moton: The Limits
of U.S.-centered Education in Haiti

In a speech to Congress on December 7, 1929, Hoover called for a commission to be sent to Haiti to investigate the sociopolitical and socioeconomic conditions on the island. Early on, some Haitian authorities believed that this act functioned as a mere ploy to further ingrain U.S. troops in the black republic's affairs. In response to the 1929 strike and the murders in Aux Cayes, the National League of Constitutional Action in Haiti, an organization committed to protecting Haitian national rights, reported that "these troubles were magnified in official reports in order to justify the expedition of more armed forces to Haiti."[31] By February 1930, confronted with growing anti-occupation sentiment and violence, a bewildered Hoover posed two principal questions about the "Haitian problem": "How are we to withdraw from Haiti?" and "What shall we do in the meantime?"[32]

Armed with a $50,000 budget from Congress, $10,000 of which was allotted for the Moton Commission, Hoover asked Robert Russa Moton, principal of the Tuskegee Institute, to serve on the presidential commission "to exhaustively investigate and make recommendations as to the

educational system in Haiti."[33] The Moton Commission served as H
second commission; several days prior to meeting with Moton, Hoovᵤ
broke bread with William Cameron Forbes, a Massachusetts attorney and
former governor-general of the Philippines, at the White House and in-
structed him of his duties as chairman of the "first" Haitian commission.
The purpose of the Forbes Commission was to solve the "political impasse"
between John H. Russell, U.S. high commissioner in Haiti, and president
of Haiti Louis Borno and Haitian oppositional forces.[34] In addition, the
Forbes Commission sought to calm threats of violence and political coercion that might upset the relative government order that existed under U.S.
occupation.

By the time Forbes' group made its way to Haiti in March 1930, it was
clear that Moton's appointment had been an afterthought—a way to appease the discontented U.S. African American elite who believed that U.S.
black representation on the Forbes investigative committee was critical to
achieving a fair and honest assessment of Haitian conditions. In fact, Moton's role has been treated as inconsequential in various historical assessments of U.S. withdrawal from Haiti, of Hoover's Latin American policy
and of U.S. African American support of Franklin Delano Roosevelt's Good
Neighbor Policy. Historian Robert M. Spector argued that the Moton Commission's investigation was "an innocuous duty to say the least" and that
the "real activity" lay with the first commission, the Forbes Commission.[35]
Magdaline W. Shannon perhaps offered the most succinct viewpoint, stating that Hoover selected Moton as chairman of the Haitian Commission
on Education simply "because no Negroes were appointed to the Forbes
commission."[36] On March 8, 1930, the New York Age acknowledged the
secondary nature of the commission while simultaneously affirming its
great worth for Haitians. The Age reported that "the first commission may
seem the most important. . . . [However] the mapping out of an adequate
educational system to promote the making of good citizenship will have
a manifest bearing on the future of the island and its people."[37] The Age
reporter highlighted the civic benefits of learning in Haiti and its relationship to intellectual and material progress. Promoting education in Haiti
complemented a domestic movement in the United States at the turn of
the century when "race reformers promoted books as a potent tool in the
crusade to uplift, enlighten, and transform the black masses."[38] Coupled
with Anglo-American philanthropy, efforts to instruct the black masses in
the United States, Liberia, East African territories and Haiti demonstrated

a transnational scope.[39] Additionally, from a U.S. perspective, education often embodied bourgeois notions of racial uplift and a civilizing mission that sought to modernize those whom elite U.S. African Americans deemed impoverished and unsophisticated.

For U.S. African American elites involved in the business of racial uplift ideology—a set of principles that emphasized "positive black identity" and "self-affirmation through an ideology of class differentiation, self-help and interdependence"—their desire to improve the status of the race conflated "moral improvement with . . . material advancement."[40] Firmly grounded in the economic self-help philosophy of Booker T. Washington, many U.S. African Americans fully supported the economic tenets of the free market and believed that significant material accomplishment within the capitalist system challenged racial inequality in the United States and abroad.[41]

In fact, U.S.-centered modernization in the Caribbean and Latin America imposed a system of North American capitalism.[42] When Hoover entered the White House in 1929, he brought along his experience as former U.S. secretary of commerce and the ideals of the Progressive Party, which included allowing greater cooperation between government and big business, promoting international collaboration that merged self-interest with service and supporting an active government with the power to provide social welfare. Responding to the socioeconomic disparities produced by early-twentieth-century U.S. American industrialization, Progressives sought to manufacture democracy and effective government while upholding U.S. individualism and increasing domestic and foreign cooperation. Hoover biographer Joan Wilson maintained that Hoover's "cooperative individualism"—a philosophy that rewards industrious citizens, groups and nations with material rewards in expectation that U.S. domestic and foreign interests will flourish—influenced Hoover's international policy making.[43] Hoover, not unlike former U.S. executive leadership, fervently protected the economic interests of U.S. bankers and powerful bondholders who invested in Caribbean and Latin American markets. Even working-class U.S. farmers commanded the attention of Washington, particularly during the demoralizing days of the Great Depression, as evidenced in June 1930 by the passing of the Smoot-Hawley Act, which raised U.S. tariffs on agricultural products to exorbitant levels to protect domestic farmers against the competition of international trade imports.

Foreign tariffs had already left an indelible mark on the everyday lives of Haitian farmers and small business owners. Dantès Bellegarde, a foremost

Haitian intellectual and statesman who briefly taught at Atlanta University, testified before the Forbes Commission that U.S. tariffs encumbered Haitian economic mobility, "impoverishing the merchants and the small industrialists" and "making life more difficult for peasants and workers." Bellegarde argued that U.S. disregard of proposals by Haitian authorities perpetuated and intensified blight and indigence. During the interview he submitted one of his writings to the commission, noting that as early as 1918 he and other "Haitian experts, agriculturalists, agricultural engineers and lawyers" had presented a proposal to occupation authorities to restructure the farming system by establishing procedures of "small rural credit" or micro-lending to reinvigorate agriculture and empower the rural population.[44] "The [U.S.] Americans opposed this project because it was originated by Haitians," Bellegarde argued, adding that the book he was submitting detailed "the resistance met from [U.S.] American officials to serious projects for agricultural organization and for the education of the popular masses."

Hoover established the Haiti commissions to dispel this environment of disregard while simultaneously using it as an instrument of a U.S.-based outward-looking modernization strategy. The commissions' purposes were to apply a balm to internal conflicts, to secure U.S. investments and to improve Haitian infrastructure and industrial training so as to assure a consistent supply of laborers for U.S. markets. Thus, when Hoover needed an investigative body to examine general conditions in Haiti, specifically those of Haitian education, he called on Moton, who he believed best articulated the ideals of interracial cooperation in the United States.

Most members of the Moton Commission believed in agricultural and vocational methods of instruction, an outlook that complemented the pedagogical philosophy for blacks advocated by the U.S. government and most U.S. philanthropic organizations.[45] From the perspective of Washington and white Southern Republicans, Moton proved not to be an immediate threat to white supremacy in the South or to Republican politics. Moton's training in the industrial-education tradition of Booker T. Washington and his "accomodationist" leanings gave him access to influential whites and to opportunities to serve as U.S. envoy, as he intended in the 1921 President Harding study of Haitian education.

In spite of Moton's reputation as a conservative, peace-making leader, the Tuskegee president should not be dismissed as a mere clone of Booker T. Washington. Moton upheld the Tuskegee model of industrial education and interracial cooperation, yet, within the contexts of increased racial terrorism in the U.S. South, U.S. intervention in the Caribbean and Latin America and an emerging cultural (inter)nationalism stemming from the New Negro Renaissance and the more radical elements of the Garvey movement, Moton took some risks and openly criticized the federal government on several occasions. Also, he veiled his support of civil rights causes. Taking to task the philosophy of Thomas Jesse Jones, the educational director of the Phelps-Stokes Fund, and to some degree Booker T. Washington's renowned Atlanta Compromise speech, which stated that virtually nothing could be gained for Negro education by antagonizing whites and by advocating equal rights under the law, Moton insisted on equal rights for U.S. blacks in an advance copy of his speech to celebrate the Lincoln Memorial in 1922. Moton wrote:

> . . . so long as any group is denied the fullest privilege of a citizen to share both the making and the execution of the law which shapes its destiny—so long as any group does not enjoy every right and every privilege that belongs to every American citizen without regard to race, creed, or color, that task for which the immortal Lincoln gave the last full measure of devotion, that task is still unfinished. . . . Twelve million black men and women in this country are proud of their American citizenship, but they are determined that it shall mean for them no less than any other group, the largest enjoyment of opportunity and the fullest blessing of freedom.[46]

Inevitably, the Lincoln Commission censored and toned down Moton's call for full equality promised to U.S. African Americans under the Fourteenth Amendment. Moton proceeded to speak at the Lincoln Memorial celebration despite the censorship. Although largely symbolic, the commemoration of the Lincoln sculpture exemplified the sacrifices by U.S. African American reformers and educators to participate in culturally relevant events that marked both a divided United States and an emancipated people.

While Moton was sympathetic to U.S. African American protests, he sometimes masked his support for civil rights causes and organizations like the NAACP for strategic reasons. In a letter to NAACP executive secretary Walter White, Moton assured him that Tuskegee would aid in saving the life of Willie Peterson, a convict sentenced to death:

> I am sure you know Tuskegee Institute and its methods well enough to be aware that we have not been indifferent to the interests either

of Peterson or of our race as a whole. . . . Our methods, as you know, have neither paralleled nor duplicated those of your own organization, but that is no reason for assuming, as some are inclined to do, that Tuskegee Institute is remiss in its support of the cause of justice for our people in our own state. *It isn't always necessary to publish in advance one's strategy in matters of so important and delicate a nature.*[47]

Moton and other U.S. African American leaders depended on the philanthropy of whites and could ill afford to alienate white sponsors. Recognizing this dependence is critical to understanding the subtlety and fragility of U.S. black leadership and these leaders' attempts to fully integrate themselves into the domestic and international political spaces that were central to black life.

These local experiences exhibited the subtlety of Moton's struggle for equality. Race leaders who emphasized interracial cooperation and black progress so as to demonstrate the declining significance of racial inequality complemented this ideology of hemispheric collaboration and egalitarianism. It is my contention that during this highly contested period of U.S. intervention, Pan Americanism provided access for elite and aspiring U.S. African Americans who would not have publicly identified with the perceived radicalism of Pan African politics or who would not have critiqued U.S. imperialism outright. Race or blackness was not at the core of Pan Americanist philosophy, although, as Plummer argued, the privileging of whiteness was an invisible act that, nonetheless, advanced inter-American politics. The Moton Commission and its subsequent report on Haitian education exposed both the limits and the potential of this Pan American program for true cooperation.

Moton and the Education Commission to Haiti

By the mid- to late 1920s, one can clearly see Moton's innovations on Booker T. Washington's philosophies. Under his direction, the Tuskegee Institute implemented academic courses in its agricultural- and industrial-centered curriculum. And, despite popular belief, Moton believed in the benefits of an integrated training in Haiti, although he believed it should be achieved gradually. In a letter written to William Forbes a few weeks prior to the Forbes Commission's trip to Port-au-Prince in March 1930, Moton asserted that Haiti could benefit from a vocational and academic system of education:

> . . . Haiti does not differ from any other civilized country and I assume it is in the President's mind that the country should have an educational system that would supply every type of cultural and technical training to meet its need both for trained leadership and productive activity of a sort that will make the country economically independent and enable it to maintain its proper status in the family of western nations.[48]

This missive reveals that, at least by February 1930, Moton presumed that Hoover's educational aims in Haiti included achieving a balance of "cultural and technical training" to fulfill the "need[s]" of Haitians at various income and educational levels. In fact, Hoover's administration fully supported the Service Technique, the U.S.-managed agricultural school that the United States had placed under the control of the Haitian Department of Agriculture instead of the Department of Public Instruction, as many Haitians had requested. If Haitians were forced to live with the Service Technique, they believed that the revenue generated from agricultural products should fund the education department.

Washington promoted a strict agenda of industrial education in Haiti and convinced itself and, to some degree, Haitian leadership that the Moton Commission also advanced such a firm policy. Conflicting reports and rumors circulated in the U.S. executive office and among U.S. African American leadership about the Haitian people's negative perceptions of U.S. blacks and of industrial and technical training. Arthur Ruhl, a *New York Herald Tribune* employee, believed that Moton's group would be an embarrassment to the U.S. State Department and the Forbes Commission. Ruhl urged Hoover to abolish the black commission because "Contrary to what most [U.S.] Americans fancy, the Haitians are almost more touchy about [U.S.] American Negroes than our own Southerners—not because they are Negroes, for they themselves may be proud, or say they are proud, to be black, but simply because they know that Negroes occupy a subordinate social position in our country." Ruhl argued that while "Booker Washington's theory of industrial-agricultural education may suit the Negroes in the United States," and, "in theory, it might be good for the Haitian mass," the truth was that "the Haitian elite and their whole sense of cultural values, is French. They simply don't 'see' our theory at all."[49] Undersecretary of State Joseph P. Cotton conveyed his concerns to Forbes: "Dr. Moton's survey will result in the suppression of classical education and the extension of vocational and agricultural educational system."[50] Similarly, in an initial draft of the Forbes Commission's final report to Hoover, Forbes, who was optimistic about the commission's recent exploration of conditions in Haiti, contended that the U.S. State Department should only send "white men and women" who were "willing to accept the Elite on their own terms" and who were equipped to understand "their background and their aims." Forbes added that it would be "as grotesque and rudely incompetent to send to Haiti a rough and ready colored politician who is merely the product of our cotton fields or city black belt as it would to send him to Brussels or the Hague."[51]

Forbes' discriminatory views clouded his interpretation of Haitian and U.S. African American relations, which were rooted in the early-nineteenth-century emigration movements, diplomatic service, cultural expression and missionary work. The educated class of both groups was mindful of each other's history of enslavement and emancipation and their respective sociocultural institutions, such as the NAACP and Tuskegee Institute. Napoleon B. Marshall denounced the notion that inter-ethnic animosity existed. The idea became so prevalent that he addressed it in an editorial for the *New York Age* in March 1930. Marshall maintained that Haitian hostility toward U.S. African Americans revealed a propagandistic tool "sent forth by those who would perpetuate the American occupation."[52] Scholar Léon Pamphile asserted that Raoul Lizaire, *chargé d'affaires* of the Haitian Legation in Washington, D.C., reiterated the "Haitian position": that Haitians dreaded the Moton Commission's recommendations of "a program of agricultural and vocational rather than cultural education."[53] Yet Lizaire accepted an invitation from Moton to speak at Tuskegee's forty-ninth commencement exercises, which took place several weeks before the Moton Commission visited Haiti. According to the *Tuskegee Messenger*, the Haitian dignitary sang the praises of Booker T. Washington at the commencement, stating that Washington "laid the foundations for the progress of the Negro race."[54] Lizaire later laid a wreath at Washington's grave. Analogous to Louis Lhérisson's concerns about the Moton Commission, it is not out of the question that Lizaire's trepidations represented some element of the Haitian elite. However, Lizaire's tribute to Washington and his visit to the nucleus of technical training in the United States call into question Lizaire's aforementioned condemnation of the educational investigative body. It remains unclear what Lizaire and Moton discussed during the relaxing moments of Tuskegee's graduation events. It is possible that Lizaire counseled Moton on the expectations of the Haitian authorities he would soon encounter. Nonetheless, Lizaire's participation in the Tuskegee graduation ceremony revealed the complexity of the Haitian elite's perceptions of blacks in the United States and illuminated the political tightrope that the Moton-led study needed to walk if it was to receive full cooperation from Haitians. Quoting from an editorial in Richmond's *St. Luke Herald*, the *New York Age* succinctly reported that Moton must "strike upon a fine go-between in order to escape the condemnation of the ruling classes of the Negro Republic. He must, at all odds, keep the respect of the ruling black people of the island. He must watch his steps. There will probably be an effort to combine the training of the head and the hands in such a way as to serve the best interests of all classes of Haitians."[55]

Unable to schedule a joint departure with the Forbes Commission, the Moton Commission's journey to Haiti was marred and delayed by several factors: insufficient time to assemble the members; warnings from the U.S. State Department and Forbes that the group remain in the United States until after the April elections when the country would experience a more "stabilized condition"; and an inadequate mode of transportation. The latter issue, not surprisingly, mirrored the unequal treatment that Frederick Douglass received as minister to Haiti. Moton requested from Walter H. Newton, secretary to the president, a "war vessel" similar to that used by the Forbes Commission to transport them to Port-au-Prince. Deeply concerned about the secondary status afforded to the educational committee, Moton insisted that the U.S. black envoys be given "the same arrangement" as the general commission, financial as well as transportation. "As you know, there have been some rather vicious attacks on [Hoover] and myself," Moton pointed out, on Hoover "for the personnel of the Commission; that is, not having a Negro on the Commission; and on me because I accepted what some of them say was a subordinate task."[56] Moton's petition for a war vessel and an estimate of the expenses of the Forbes Commission so that his group might receive an equal amount directly challenged the prevailing domestic policy of racial segregation in the U.S. South. He refused to be treated as a second-class citizen, especially when he was officially representing the U.S. government abroad. Despite putting up a valiant effort, Moton conceded on budgetary and transportation issues. On June 10, 1930, the committee sailed to Haiti on the S.S. *Ancon* of the Panama Railroad

Steamship Line, a commercial ship that was unsatisfactory for the members' tastes.

On the committee's arrival in Haiti, June 15, 1930, the *Pittsburgh Courier* reported that a crowd of Haitians "applaud[ed]" them at the docks. One of Haiti's major daily newspapers, *Le Nouvelliste*, printed editorials and articles for several days, illustrating the racial bond shared between Haitians and U.S. African Americans and their sustained objections to U.S. military and political domination. On June 16, the day after their arrival, one writer appealed to Haitians to reaffirm their relationship to U.S. blacks: "They are our brothers, and today where we are under the yoke of white oppression . . . now more than ever we demand their help for our liberation."[57] A Haitian farmer wrote to the commission several days later: "You don't come to us as teachers, you come to our home because the black country of Haiti is your home," adding that "With you our dreams will not faint, our hope based on our common feelings will not be disappointed. . . ."[58] In another editorial, specifically addressed to the Moton Commission, the anonymous writer championed the Haitian youth, the future of the nation:

> The youth that climbs will not be handed over. She will not learn with her books to glorify the occupation and to believe that American intervention has been a kind deed. . . . The youth will learn to love Haiti, to defend her independence and to detest the interventions. . . . It is better that small peasants remain ignorant rather than knowing how to read and learn to love the foreigner who occupies his territory.[59]

As much as academic instruction possessed the power to uplift the race, for this Haitian writer, education also had the capability to distort reality among Haitian adolescents. It remains unclear if the writer was part of or emerged from the peasant class, since many *peyizan* were uneducated. Nonetheless, the writer's compelling concluding statement demonstrated one person's commitment to maintaining his/her mental and social freedom. If the commission read the editorial, it may have helped them understand and acknowledge Haitian voices within the program of racial uplift.

The commission spent twenty-four days in Haiti. During the first couple days, the commissioners were inundated with formal pleasantries befitting a U.S. delegation such as accepting greetings from the mayor of Port-au-Prince, from Provisional President Eugène Roy and from the Haitian Boy Scouts. The Haitian government even sponsored a *foutbòl* (soccer) match in their honor. As noted earlier in the chapter, the Alliance Française celebrated the commissioners at a dinner, while members of the Haitian press organized a banquet at Hotel Splendid for journalists P.L. Prattis and Carl Murphy. Dining and "listening to inspiring stories" from editors and writers of Haiti's premier publications, including Charles Moravia, editor of *Le Temps*, and George Chauvet of *Le Nouvelliste*, Murphy and Prattis hoped that their "united efforts might serve to bring the people of Haiti and the colored people of the United States closer together."[60]

During the next three weeks, the commissioners traveled extensively (except Moton who fell ill during the trip) with "efficient guides" through northern coastal towns such as Saint-Marc, Gonaïves, Plaisance, Port-de-Paix and Cap Haïtien. They researched Haitian schools, conversed with students and administrators and visited agriculturally based, U.S.-managed plants, specifically a pineapple factory maintained by the California Packing Company and a large sisal farm "operated by a group of New York stock brokers."[61] The U.S. black press detailed some of the more memorable moments primarily because of the presence of two of its noted journalists. Yet reports on the daily activities of the commission seemed to be absent from Haitian newspapers during the latter stages of the trip, possibly because no Haitian journalists accompanied the group or because the Haitian press decided to reserve judgment until the commission's report was finalized and published. President Roy confidently wrote to P.L. Prattis in July 1930 that Haitians "expect[ed] great things" from the Moton report.[62]

The commissioners had an arduous road ahead of them if they wanted to live up to Roy's expectations. Haitian schools were woefully underfunded, and educators supplemented their meager income by other means or endured without. Their wages ranged from six to ten dollars a month; as a consequence, according to Prattis, they taught "six dollars worth."[63] Haiti's educational system was fragmented into three distinct parts: the Catholic school system, the national public school system and U.S.-managed agricultural institutions, with each system controlling its own destiny. The U.S.-operated Service Technique L'Agriculture paid U.S. specialists exorbitant salaries from the Haitian treasury. In addition, many of the U.S. teachers did not speak French or Kreyòl (Haitian Creole) and taught in English. Louis Lhérisson, who was understandably annoyed by the practice of English-language instruction, commented during the Forbes hearings in March 1930 that "this process is contrary to good practice and good sense."[64] Haitian attorney Georges Leger irately noted: "We have seen professors close themselves in conference with the translator who then goes out and make[s] lectures for them."[65] Leger conveyed to Forbes that, in spite of "a number of fine buildings" and "optimistic reports," U.S.-operated rural schools were an "utter failure." A self-described "bad Catholic," Leger believed that the Catholic Church and the U.S. authorities in Haiti should have joined their efforts in "extending the system." As a result of ongoing problems, Haitians lost all confidence in George Freeman, the U.S. director of the Service Technique. By April 1930, Freeman had resigned.

In spite of the grim realities that Haitians confronted, the Moton commissioners noted while visiting a small agricultural school established by the Service Technique that it was "impossible not to notice the improvement" of Haitian schools controlled by the United States. "They are well-built, clean, and orderly buildings," the commissioners noted. "The teachers are alert, seem interested in their work and, in most cases, show the results of good training." Also, the commission praised the number of Haitian children between the ages of seven and twelve who were learning valuable trades such as "carpentry, tailoring . . . [and] tinsmithing."

Although there was an overwhelming perception that the Haitian elite preferred academic, French instruction to industrial training, several accomplished Haitians openly valued vocational education. Primarily influenced by Haitian *indigénisme*, an ideology that emphasized the value of peasant culture and African retentions in Haitian society, and/or committed to the belief that national progress was impossible without educational and structural improvements for the Haitian masses, noted Haitian intellectual Jean Price-Mars and lesser-known Maurice Dartigue worked to adapt education to the immediate conditions and needs of the community. Price-Mars' experiences as a Haitian representative to the St. Louis Exposition in 1904 and his subsequent trip to Tuskegee Institute that same year to learn and appropriate Booker T. Washington's ideas of industrial education fostered his belief in transnational relations and empowering the disenfranchised *noir* masses. In an effort to address structural inequalities at home and forge equilibrium between capital and labor, Price-Mars called for the establishment of publicity centers in New York to inform U.S. Americans and Haitians living abroad of events regarding U.S. occupation and Haitian education.[66]

Maurice Dartigue, director of rural education (1931–1941) and minister of public instruction, agriculture and labor (1941–45), firmly advocated for inter-American cooperation between Haiti and the United States. According to historian Chantalle F. Verna, a cadre of Haitian leaders underscored "intellectual cooperation" with the United States "as a viable means of addressing obstacles to the development of Haitian identity and society."[67] Dartigue, who worked as an assistant to George Freeman, believed in the pragmatism of Haiti/U.S. cooperative initiatives, in spite of the tribulations associated with the occupation. He asserted that this transnational relationship would lead to a growth in the number of skilled professionals capable of addressing the immediate and long-term issues impacting the Haitian masses. For Dartigue, industrial and agricultural education could enable the peasantry to be economically mobile, which would challenge the social and cultural marginality of the rural residents. His ideas paralleled the Washingtonian tradition at Tuskegee, which emphasized technical specialization for blacks to achieve social and economic prominence and respectability. Dartigue wrote that if given the choice between "literacy and economic proficiency, it would be wiser to develop craft work, such as making of baskets that could be sold in the United States."[68] It is possible that Dartigue might have interacted with or influenced the Moton Commission during the summer of 1930; his brief monograph *Les Problèmes de la Communauté* was published in the same year. Dartigue's argument in *Les Problèmes* is that schools produce a valuable and informed citizenry: It is "not that the pupils learn well the lessons of civics, but that the pupils become capable of observing and thinking civically so as to be able to fill their role as members of a nation."[69] The Moton Commission's report echoed the spirit of Dartigue's ideas of empowering the masses of Haitian citizens, yet it sought to push the boundaries further and believed that education facilitated the "progressive elevation of all classes of its citizenry."[70] Clearly, providing access to education functioned as an important stage in civic and economic development, yet Dartigue, a member of the privileged class, delineated between academic training for him and state authorities, and agricultural instruction for the Haitian peasantry. His understanding of the state-versus-the-masses relationship was inherently paternalistic. One author argued that elites preferred paternalistic conceptions of the state, an attitude rooted in Haitian and also Western traditions of governance, because they were responsible for shaping and granting access to state power due to their higher level of education, their "moral values" and their ability to articulate universal notions of reason and justice.[71] A couple of months after the Moton Commission returned to the United States, Dartigue embarked on his second study abroad program at Teacher's College, Columbia

University, in New York City, where he completed his master's degree in rural education.

It is important to understand that both the Haitian and U.S. African American elites advanced Western ideals of government—democracy, citizenship and republicanism—and supported mechanisms of the state, such as schools, because these fundamentals gave the appearance of an orderly, reasoned and civilized relationship between centralized authority and its citizenry. U.S. Americans' and some Haitians' comprehension and perhaps appreciation of the Moton Commission's investigative study must be understood in this context. Like the Forbes Commission, the Moton Commission was conceived and believed to address a fissure between the state and its people caused by Haitian mismanagement and underdevelopment, rather than by problems that may have been intensified by U.S. intervention. For some, Haitian ineptitude was the cause of Haiti's problems.

Among the commentators who thought this way was Joseph Fénélon Geffrard, a Haitian planter who maintained close ties with the administration of Nord Alexis (1902–1908). Although he denounced U.S. military intervention, Geffrard believed in the benefits of a Haiti/U.S. alliance and of "true Pan-Americanism . . . in order that we may be strengthened abroad and develop the innumerable riches of our country." Intolerant of the current state of Haitian affairs and Haitian leadership, Geffrard noted:

> . . . some ambitious and lazy Haitians have been instrumental in leading us to this state of things. . . . You have copied the constitutions of the most advanced countries in the world and have made out one that you have violated a hundred and twelve times. Now that the American[s] have come to wash your markets and manage your Customs, [and] clean your streets . . . you dare speak of that "scrap of paper" that you have never consulted when you want to be elected Deputies or Senators.[72]

For Geffrard, Haitian graft and corruption was the source of Haiti's decline—politically, economically and morally. "Haitian morals should be Americanized," he argued. In a similar light that illuminated the centering of U.S. supervision in Haitian affairs, although with an absence of denigration aimed at Haitian leadership, the New York Age informed its readers that the Moton Commission "must bear in mind the necessity of preparing [Haitians] to assume the duties and responsibilities of citizenship in order to make the republican form of government function as a reality, instead of being a mask for a dictatorship."[73] The *New York Age* also reiterated that "popular education based upon the American system" in Haiti might foster the everyday practice of democracy.[74] Democracy should not be the sole property of the United States to be distributed and shaped throughout the world, but many (Haitians and non-Haitians) believed the black republic to be a nation where democracy was deficient. Many U.S. blacks believed they needed to play a central role in the development of Haiti and other nations, not only to save them from the deleterious effects of imperialism but also to fulfill their role as symbols of an advanced culture. Additionally, the memory of the Haitian Revolution and its noted rebel leaders figured prominently in black Pan American initiatives; for many U.S. blacks it not only highlighted a radical antislavery movement, but also represented a belief that the spirit of the revolution and Haitian independence—characterized by racial equality, just labor rights and citizenship—could be transformed and transferred into the twentieth century with the uplift of Haitians.

At the end of the Moton Commission's trip, its members made a visit to the tombs of Haitian revolutionaries Jean-Jacques Dessalines, Henri Christophe and Alexandre Pétion. During the volatile period of U.S. occupation, the commission went out of its way to acknowledge Haiti's black radical abolitionists, symbols of Haitian sovereignty and black resistance to Western imperialism. This important gesture mirrored the ritual that Raoul Lizaire had performed several months earlier when he laid a wreath at Booker T. Washington's gravesite. The *Pittsburgh Courier* reported that Robert Moton performed the same act, placing a wreath at each revolutionary's tomb, and declared that these men "served not only the Negroes of Haiti, but the black race throughout the world by showing what Negroes might achieve."[75] This gesture by the commission affirmed the racial connection between Haitians and U.S. African Americans and served as evidence of the commission's transnational racial consciousness.

Thus, after three short weeks in Haiti, the Moton Commission returned to the United States but not without controversy. The U.S. Navy rejected Moton's request to secure a navy ship for their return, in contrast to the privileges granted to the returning Forbes Commission. During the late afternoon of July 7, 1930, Moton sent a scathing telegram to President Hoover, outlining his embarrassment about the discrepancy between the two commissions' travel accommodations. "Your commission is inconvenienced and about to be humiliated in the matter of transportation to the United States," Moton wrote, adding:

> ... We have been trying for the last 10 days through regular diplomatic channels to secure these promised accommodations without success. The best we are offered is a mine sweeping tug [S.S. *Ancon*] ... inadequate for our party [and] uncomfortable and unsuited to the dignity of our mission. I feel that the people of Haiti as well as the colored people of the United States will regard this as a humiliation.[76]

When the U.S. State Department failed to bestow the official naval vessel, the U.S. black press quickly attacked the Hoover administration, stating that the handling of the commission's return signified the administration's "Negro-phobic attitude."[77]

Upon the Moton Commission's arrival, Prattis published a series of articles criticizing U.S. intervention and U.S. authorities. His appraisal of U.S. foreign policy in the Americas echoed the condemnations of several South American nations that denounced a U.S.-style Pan Americanism that sanctioned military, political and economic intrusion in non-U.S. affairs. The *New York Times* reported that the Argentine press, *La Prensa*, condemned Hoover's administration and the Forbes Commission for excessively focusing on Haiti's "internal problems" instead of the "evacuation of foreign military forces." For *La Prensa*, the commissions' visits to Haiti proved that the "United States is continuing its intensive activities in the territories it has illegitimately dominated without bringing its new activities into accord with its promise to re-establish right," noted the *New York Times*.[78] Argentina and other autonomous Latin American countries believed their independence could be compromised if U.S. occupation was not properly addressed. Prattis' ideas complemented those of *La Prensa* but also specifically addressed the impact of North American hegemony on African-descended peoples, an issue of race and color typically ignored by Latin American elites who privileged national identity.[79] Prattis' criticisms rendered him and some members of the Moton Commission, particularly Mordecai Johnson, unconfident about how effectively the group could support Haitian development and autonomy:

> We sensed that the Haitians were expecting us to do something, however nebulous, for them. . . . [T]here is a large group of hard-to-put-

your-hand-on-Americans in Haiti and a few in America who have cut the pattern of the spirit of America in Haiti. That spirit condemns. It is a spirit of which I would be utterly ashamed if I were not a Negro. It is an ugly, arrogant, contumacious force. What is that spirit? It is the attitude which was assumed at the beginning of the occupation by the average American marine toward some 'niggers' whose country had been invaded and taken under control.[80]

Although on its surface U.S. Pan Americanism emphasized international cooperation and "mutual helpfulness," the movement, rooted as it was in the imperial paternalism of the Monroe Doctrine and nineteenth-century U.S. expansion, treated southern nations of the Western Hemisphere as its backyard, centered U.S. capitalism and perpetuated the malignancy of racism. Moton, Prattis and other members of the commission supported this notion of "mutual cooperation," but, as Douglass argued, they abhorred the "rapacious" manner in which U.S. relations with nonwhite nations took shape. The Moton Commission believed in the potential of transnational cooperative initiatives and the importance of U.S. African American participation in the work of U.S. foreign policy as it pertained to people of African descent, not only because it benefited themselves and/or their institutions, but also because it provided a sense of agency to confront the problems particular to the black world.

For example, in late July 1930, Moton sent Hoover's secretary, Walter Newton, a memo stating that the work of the Hoover commissions would "fail" if the U.S. State Department forced Haitian president Eugène Roy "to endorse the nomination of Mr. [Carl] Colvin," an assistant to George Freeman, the former director of the Service Technique.[81] Ernest Chauvet, the editor of Le Nouvelliste, considered a radical and a "thoroughly bad influence in Haiti" by William R. Castle, U.S. undersecretary of state and chief of the Latin American division, appealed to Moton to change Hoover's recommendation. Hoover's nomination of Colvin proved to be a divisive moment, for it signified a cementing of U.S. control in Haitian affairs and a disregard of Haitianization of key state positions recommended by the Forbes Commission. Since Hoover had made the nomination while Moton's educational commission conducted its study in Haiti, Moton believed it placed his group in a very prickly position with Haitian authorities. Soon, Moton's suggestion that Hoover reconsider the nomination of Colvin stamped him as a troublemaker who had been "taken in by the radicals down there," noted Castle, who added that Moton was "certainly going outside of his regular work to communicate with people in Haiti on quite other phases of the Government's difficulties. . . ."[82] Colvin's nomination was directly connected to the overall objectives of the Moton Commission, since his group examined the functionality and efficiency of Haiti's educational system. Although Moton did not disagree with the existence of the Service Technique, he believed that Colvin's nomination and his association with Freeman was an "affront" to himself and compromised Haiti/U.S. diplomatic affairs. The lack of support from the U.S. State Department demonstrated its indifference to the Moton Commission's propositions if the group opposed U.S. plans for withdrawal and education. The conflicts faced by U.S. African American representatives of Washington, such as Douglass and Moton, highlighted the political impediments to substantive and even minor changes to U.S. affairs in Haiti.

The tense relationship between Hoover's administration and the Moton Commission continued and culminated with the submission of the group's final report. When Moton presented it to the U.S. State Department in October 1930, the U.S. government considered the proposal flawed and an embarrassment to past and present U.S. educational achievements. In January 1931, Assistant Secretary of State Francis White noted that if Moton refused to correct the unspecified "inaccuracies," he would recommend that the State Department continue to publish the report and "point out" the mistakes and "make a statement that the United States Government is not going to contribute to the support of education in Haiti."[83] It remains unclear what those "inaccuracies" were or if they existed at all. Yet U.S. State Department officials expressed their displeasure and casually shelved Moton's proposal, particularly because of its numerous criticisms against U.S. foreign policy and financial management.

Officially titled "The Report of the United States Commission on Education in Haiti," the Moton Commission Report contains sixty-one recommendations on topics ranging from the administration of the national schools and the Service Technique to the management of Haitian finances. Many of the report's suggestions sought to empower Haitian education officials, such as the secretary of state for public instruction, and to equip the educational community with the appropriate native personnel and funds so as to immediately begin the *désoccupation* process. Furthermore, the report highlighted the need to ensure Haiti's financial and political progress. Some of the significant recommendations for national schools and finance included:

Moton Commission's Educational Suggestions

Appointing the Secretary of State for Public Instruction as chairman of state educational council with powers to adopt regulations for general administration of all schools, and to recommend the educational budget to the Legislative Assembly.

Providing the Secretary of State for Public Instruction with an adequate staff of assistants, one each in the fields of primary, secondary and superior education.

Creating local school boards in districts or in communes for the encouragement of local interests in public education.

Providing a permanent joint commission composed of the two governments; one of the Americans should be of Negro descent that shall formulate plans for the articulation of the activities of the Service Technique with the National School system.

Place the Service Technique under the Department of Public Instruction instead of the Department of Agriculture.

Moton Commission's Financial Suggestions

Establishing higher salaries for teachers.

Applying the national debt payment as a capital investment in carrying out the recommendations made in this report.

Asking the U.S. to undertake payment of American personnel's salaries now engaged or to be engaged in Haiti without further charge upon the Haitian treasury.

Enlisting the interest of private philanthropy by the U.S. government in the above undertakings "in the manner and spirit that have already contributed so effectively to the progress of the Negro in the US."

Providing a long-term loan to Haiti at a low interest rate.[84]

The Moton Commission's proposal to improve Haitian education was undoubtedly bold and ambitious. The tone of its educational and financial suggestions implied the U.S. government's culpability in the decline of the Haitian educational system, but also specified the economic responsibility that the U.S. needed to assume to ensure Haitian educational and economic progress. The Moton Commission was opposed to the budgetary allowances of the U.S.-managed Service Technique, to the high salaries of U.S. officials and to the subsumption of the Technique under the Department of Agriculture instead of the Department of Public Instruction; likewise, the report commented that U.S. complicity remained excessive and unfair. Albert Crouze, an Anglo-American who lived in Haiti for a number of years and periodically provided intelligence to the White House on Haitian affairs, reported Haitian grievances that U.S. officials under Freeman's administration earned $750 per month while Haitian assistants, "who [do] all the work receive $50" each.[85] Moreover, the Moton Commission wrote that bifurcating the country's agricultural and academic schools, in addition to adding U.S. expenditures up to 65 percent for the "creation and maintenance of a wholly new and separate system," in spite of the existence of an "established system that has proved its worth in the development of the Republic," was "[in]consistent with our national sense of justice and equity."[86]

The Moton Commission asked the U.S. government to provide the country with low-interest loans, to influence U.S. philanthropic organizations to donate funds and to stop depleting the Haitian treasury by paying U.S. officials out of its own coffers. By making these recommendations, the commission contested the derogatory and violent elements of U.S. Pan Americanism and pushed forward the notion that American nations that supported such an ideological program for inter-American cooperation should also be equipped with creative solutions to repair and to empower countries that it had adversely affected. The Moton Commission Report asserted that the superior and hegemonic role that the U.S. had undertaken in Haiti "made it difficult to secure Haitian cooperation and a constructive policy or program." The report's authors argued:

> Had there been less of a disposition to deal with the island as a conquered territory and more to help a *sister* state in distress . . . less of enforced control and more of *helpful cooperation* . . . less of a desire to demonstrate efficiency and more to help others to the efficient direction of their own affairs . . . the U.S. might to-day have greater reason to be proud of her intervention in the affairs of a struggling neighbor.[87]

The report's choice of words highlighted not only the subjugated status of blacks in Haiti but also the shared experiences of racial violence and second-class citizenship, as well as the strong self-determinist ethos, ingrained in U.S. African American life.

Had they been implemented, the Moton Commission Report's main propositions would likely have made significant strides in combating Haitian dependency and improving the Haitian educational system. Yet despite their soundness, Francis White recommended that several suggestions be immediately dismissed, on the grounds that if the secretary (probably Secretary of State Henry Stimson) were to be asked in a press conference why the United States refused to adhere to the educational commission's financial recommendations, he could "well point out that this was the Commission's recommendation . . . [and] not necessarily [that] of this Government, and that as this is contrary to our previous practice in such matters, it would not be practicable. . . ."[88] White's advice to U.S. State Department officials revealed the limits of U.S. foreign policy and U.S. Pan Americanism because it implied that transformative reconstruction of a country's institutions during a multiyear forced occupation proved not to be a worthy precedent and ceased to be pragmatic.

Seven months after the commission submitted its final report, the U.S. government quietly published it in April 1931. G. Lake Imes, secretary to the Moton Commission, consistently pressed Hoover's secretary, Walter Newton, about the lack of recognition the Commission received: "Has it occurred to you," he wrote, "that up to this time the President has not made any acknowledgement to the United States Commission on Education in Haiti, for services which they rendered in making the investigation and filing their report? This is perhaps an oversight."[89] The president's silence was not an oversight but a calculated response to Moton's associations with Haitian "radicals" and the report's major criticisms of U.S. management of Haitian educational affairs. The Moton Commission Report was, inevitably, ignored. Interestingly, four years prior, during the Mississippi Flood of 1927, Moton had submitted a report to Hoover supporting the claims made by dispossessed blacks that U.S. National Guardsmen were discriminatory in their relief efforts. That report also was censored and disregarded by the U.S. government. One week after Imes sent his letter to Hoover's secretary, the U.S. government conveyed a letter of gratitude to the members of the commission.

Conclusion

U.S. African American Pan Americanists often assisted in modernizing projects as part of their own program of racial uplift. Education, the form of either institutional development or individual instruction, fostered the practical and intellectual development of a number of nations, from Cuba to Kenya and from the Philippines to South Africa. However, U.S. understanding of progress remained self-centered. Haitian Pan Americanists welcomed the economic and intellectual investment from the United States that advanced national programs of infrastructural development. In December 1930, one month after the Haitian presidential election, President Sténio Vincent confirmed that Haiti welcomed U.S. "experience and capital," but denounced the "adventurer, speculator of the promoter type."[90] Some members of the Haitian urban elite questioned the application of industrial training to their particular situation because they believed that this style of U.S. American pedagogy, often perceived as being specific to the plight of newly freed U.S. African Americans, belittled Haitians who were products of self-emancipation. Yet, similar to U.S. blacks, they challenged the aggressive, paternalistic tactics of U.S. authorities that denigrated Haitian sovereignty.

The Moton Commission Report affirmed the political direction of Vincent's administration by promoting Haitianization and *désoccupation*, yet maintaining favorable relations with U.S. capitalists as a means to address Haitian economic marginality. The report balanced harsh criticism with praise of and empathy for U.S. programs and ideas, a juggling act typical of U.S. African American leadership, which was constantly negotiating and renegotiating racial and national allegiances in the international political arena. The idealistic tenets of Pan Americanism—transnational cooperation within intellectual, cultural and economic realms, and nonintervention—allowed for such mobility and exchange to take place between both groups because it emphasized preserving the capitalist nation-state, an idea with which the Moton Commission was in full accord. The spirit of inter-American affairs also publicly decentralized race or blackness (although whiteness was indirectly privileged), a perspective that complemented the less public racial persona of Moton and other officials of Tuskegee Institute and Howard University, leaders who did not subscribe to Pan Africanism or the overtly racial politics of Marcus Garvey. This is not to say race was immaterial to the commission; references to the Haitian Revolution and its significance to black progress exemplified the purpose of transnational racial uplift. As black Pan Americanists, they understood that the universal, unifying themes of cooperation and friendship could be used to call into question U.S. foreign policy in Haiti, a symbolic nation in the U.S. African American imagination.

As Moton picked and chose his battles, support for the U.S. educational commission in Haiti proved dubious and nominal from its inception. Hoover's administration did not believe that Haitians would accept the commission's leadership; the commission received second-class accommodations on their travels; and the U.S. ignored their suggestions for improvement. Contrary to the aims of the U.S. government, the members of the Moton Commission believed in a long-term interracial and transnational commitment to Haitian education. The commission affirmed that at different historical and highly contested moments of struggle, particularly against Western imperialism, African-descended peoples demonstrated their "obligations and responsibilities to each other."[91] The implied U.S. African American social contract with Haitians took shape in many forms for many years. As President Sténio Vincent assumed power and reiterated his support of economic initiatives between Haiti and the United States, blacks in the United States again led the charge in shaping Haiti's future with entrepreneurial projects. These efforts crafted another space, particularly for U.S. blacks, to strike a balance between self-improvement and the work of international racial progress.

"We Cast in Our Lot with the Policy of Good Neighborliness"

Claude Barnett, Haiti and the Business of Race

By 1934, U.S. military occupation in Haiti had ended, and Haitians and U.S. African Americans seemed hopeful of the black republic's future. In April that year, Haitian president Sténio Vincent paid a special visit to several sites in Harlem while on a goodwill trip to the United States to discuss with President Franklin Roosevelt the future of Haiti/U.S. relations. During his quick visits to the Dunbar National Bank, the Harlem Young Men's Christian Association (YMCA) and the Paul Laurence Dunbar Apartments, the latter a nonprofit cooperative community located between 149th and 150th streets and Seventh Avenue, Vincent exuded a spirit of racial solidarity and cooperation, reported the *New York Age*. At a luncheon in his honor at the YMCA, the Haitian president remarked that he "envisioned a great opportunity for progress for the two groups in Haiti and the United States" and encouraged U.S. blacks to explore "the tremendous agricultural advantages, especially in the production of coffee and cotton" that his country offered.[1] Arturo Schomburg, an Afro-Puerto Rican scholar and bibliophile who provided the opening remarks at the luncheon about the history of Haitian independence, appropriately noted that the "eyes of the world, and especially of the Negro in this country, are on President Vincent and his nation."[2]

Indeed, the U.S. African American gaze remained fixed on the business potential of Haiti. The postoccupation period presented an opportune time to speculate despite the economic hardships that typified Depression-era politics. President Vincent's call for investment and financial collaboration met with positive responses from U.S. African American businessmen willing to shape an ambiguous plan into concrete action. On May 23, 1934, A. L. Holsey, the director of the National Negro Business League, wrote to

Claude Barnett, the founder of the Associated Negro Press (ANP), arguably one of the most important news-gathering organizations of black life in the Americas from the 1920s to the 1950s, about U.S. African American delegates' plans to meet with Haitian officials "in a semi-official conference for a thorough discussion of the possibilities" of establishing a Haitian Afro-American Chamber of Commerce, based in New York City.[3] Intrigued, Barnett responded that "certainly nothing could be more desirable than the establishment of an *entente cordial* [cordial understanding] between our Haytian brethren and our [U.S.] American group."[4] Another business-man who responded to Vincent's call was Léon F. Desportes, the general manager of Utilites d'Haiti, a bus company and Haitian import business. In August 1934, Desportes attempted to sell shares of his Harlem-based com-pany to U.S. African American investors. Seeking the social and business connections of Barnett in October of the same year, Desportes aspired to build up "strong economic ties for the mutual advancement of both groups" by having U.S. blacks and Haitians manufacture and purchase products from one another.[5] Within the same month, the newly formed Haitian Afro-American Chamber of Commerce assembled some of the leading U.S. African American engineers, businessmen, educators, manufacturers, veterinarians and nautical experts for a short, self-financed fact-finding trip to Haiti to meet with President Vincent and Haitians of good standing who were willing to enter into an "*entente cordiale*" with their black "breth-ren" from the United States.

Throughout the timeline of U.S. African American and Haitian interac-tions and cooperation, the Haitian Afro-American Chamber of Commerce served as a stepping stone for commercial projects between the two groups. Like many capitalist enterprises, some of these joint ventures failed and others flourished. I am less interested in the success or failure of these small ventures than I am in the political ideas and calculations that fostered the need to articulate, create and publicize transnational commercial ventures and in the politics and social conditions that informed their implementa-tion. It is within this historical, sociopolitical and socioeconomic moment, that of post-U.S. occupation Haiti (1934–1957), that I examine the benefits and limitations of black Pan Americanism on the effectiveness of U.S. Af-rican American and Haitian leadership to create a racialized hemispheric solidarity.

As a businessman and the architect of a global black news network, Claude Barnett played a key role in promoting U.S./Haiti entrepreneurial initiatives for more than thirty years. As early as 1929, when Barnett successfully recruited Clamart Ricourt, a Haitian attorney and the editor of *Petit Capois*, as a foreign correspondent for the ANP, Barnett sought to inform U.S. African American readership on Haitian affairs and to advocate for the advancement of Haitian society. Ricourt believed journalism and his affiliation with the ANP to be part of an "evangelistic mission" of racial pride and progress for African-descended peoples. Additionally, Ricourt considered the reporting of important events, such as the violent clashes between northern occupiers and indigenous rebel forces and the U.S. control of Haitian customhouses, to be part of his duty to the ANP's black constituents, whom he described warmly as "my people in America." Reflecting on a moment that encapsulated many Haitians' fury with U.S. military and financial intervention and the exasperation of African-descended peoples under the yoke of Western colonialism, Ricourt noted optimistically that "the day will come when the Ethiopian race will be at the head of all nations."[6] This rallying cry for black self-government and self-determination took place at a pivotal moment in both U.S. imperial intervention and in Haiti's *indigénisme* movement. *Indigénisme* was a racial and cultural response to Washington's intervention and embraced the perceived roots of an *authentique négritude* (authentic blackness) and indigenous values in the face of the racist paternalism that defined U.S. occupation. Ricourt's assertion demonstrated his deeply held belief in the importance of black cooperative efforts in times of anti-imperialist struggle.

Barnett responded to Ricourt by affirming his desire to inform U.S. African American readership about Haitian politics and culture. "It is our hope," Barnett asserted, "that such information widely distributed may be of benefit in creating the right sort of public opinion as regards our brethren there. The effort is not a commercial one, but one purely of service."[7] Coming from a graduate of Tuskegee Institute who had "virtually sat at the feet of Booker T. Washington" (arguably the leading figure in African American economic self-determination ideology), Barnett's promises that his intentions were void of financial interests should be taken with a grain of salt. Barnett's offer of "service," which I interpret as an attempt to communicate an innocent, openhanded benevolence toward racial progress, should not be divorced from the individual and cooperative business activities (e.g., savings programs, small-craft enterprises, personal service businesses, mutual-aid societies and manufacturing companies) that have fostered the survival and development of black communities for centuries.

The U.S. African American tradition of commercial ventures has largely developed for the purpose of individual mobility and collective advancement directly linked with the local, national and international arenas. It is in this vein that I situate Barnett's ANP information network and U.S. African American and Haitian capitalist ventures. Highlighting intraracial and transnational business efforts during the postoccupation period (1934–1957) demonstrated a commitment by Haitians and U.S. blacks to a program of international racial uplift. These capitalist ventures complemented Washington's and Port-au-Prince's foreign policy objectives of inter-American cooperation. Yet given the racist and paternalistic history embedded in U.S./Caribbean and U.S./Latin American relations, we also should interpret U.S. African American and Haitian enterprises as representing direct challenges to U.S. intervention in Haitian affairs and to the duplicity of a Washington-centered Pan American project of collaboration. Thus, we need to ask how did Barnett and other U.S. African American professionals reconcile the conflicting ways that their plans for transnational racial uplift both reflected and challenged U.S. power politics? As firm capitalists, Barnett and others espoused the language of development as the only immediate option for creating a competitive Haitian society within inter-American and global affairs.[8] Haiti's industrial and financial accomplishments provided a symbolic space for African-descended peoples, particularly U.S. blacks, to articulate the economic, cultural and intellectual possibilities of an independent black state.

In this chapter I examine the role of Claude Barnett and emerging U.S. African American business interests in the development of Haiti from the end of U.S. occupation to the early stages of François Duvalier's presidency. This period underscores U.S.-style inter-American programs that sought to spread U.S. democracy, to maintain political order in the Western Hemisphere and to promote the Good Neighbor Policy, a paradoxical foreign policy that emphasized maintaining effective, cordial relations with Latin American and Caribbean nations while implementing "gunboat diplomacy, military occupation and dollar diplomacy" whenever these practices served Washington's interests.[9] Politically minded and entrepreneurial U.S. African Americans and Haitians proved to be deeply influenced by this government-backed (U.S. and Latin American) modernization project, which intended to foster good trade relations, cultural exchange and the promise of fair and equal treatment to nonwhite nation-states in the Americas. In spite of the promises of Pan Americanism, U.S. African American and Hai-

tian business enterprises revealed the ways in which capitalist ventur_
came a strategy for achieving racial progress and individual gain v...
inter-American affairs.

Many of these development plans were compromised by Haiti's legacy of
depending economically on foreign states, as well as by disputes between
U.S. African Americans and Haitians, by lack of capital investment and
by internal politics in Haiti that were shaped by weak institutions. However, U.S. African American and Haitian cooperation aimed to build a new
economic solidarity that strengthened commercial activity through trade,
Haitian tourism and the promotion of a more stable and democratic Haiti.
For many U.S. African Americans and Haitians, the goal of creating a new
image of Haiti could serve as an influential model for future black international initiatives and provide a shining example of a successful and autonomous black state.

Claude Barnett and the ANP were pivotal to this discussion because
both served as consistent links between several disparate individuals,
events and movements between U.S. blacks and Haitians over a period of
three decades. Using an analogy from current technology, I like to think of
Barnett as a router, an electronic device that forwards information along
networks using prescribed units of information to determine the ideal path
for the data.[10] Rather than examine Barnett as a centerpiece, it is more
useful to understand him and the ANP as integral components or linch-
pins of a larger system of African diasporic politics and resistance, one
that was founded on the ideological platform of racial progress and supported by sundry institutions (e.g., education, entrepreneurship, religious,
et cetera). Like a myriad of other graduates of Tuskegee and black colleges
and universities in the U.S. South, Barnett was trained to use his skills not
only for personal gain but also for the betterment of his community—local, national and international. As students and later as race men and race
women, these college-educated citizens became tools or devices of alternative systems and institutions centered on the advancement of African-descended peoples.[11] Barnett's establishment of the ANP proved critical in the
documentation of black life in the United States and beyond, particularly in
Liberia and Haiti. Through the dedication and industriousness of its black
correspondents in the United States and abroad, the ANP forwarded information not only to its own readers but also to other U.S. black newspapers
such as the *Chicago Defender* and the *Pittsburgh Courier*. Barnett was connected to a number of news networks, but for the purposes of this research,

I examine Barnett's efforts to link Haitians/Haitian affairs and U.S. black politics, a process that aimed to situate U.S. African American investors and skilled workers at the center of Haitian development plans during the postoccupation period. Finally, regarding this metaphorical router who distributed information and connected individuals over certain distances, I examine how Barnett, unlike a computer's router, often carefully filtered information about both Haiti and U.S African America in order to paint an optimistic, rich and vibrant picture of African-descended peoples' forward march through modernity.

Claude Barnett, the Associated Negro Press and Reporting the Business of Race

Claude Barnett was born on September 16, 1890, in Sanford, Florida. A child of domestic workers, he was raised in Chicago but returned to the U.S. South to attend Tuskegee Institute in 1904.[12] As a young college student, Barnett was deeply influenced by Booker T. Washington's philosophy of economic self-help and vocational training. "It was there," at Tuskegee, Barnett remembered, "where I . . . drank in the magic of his [Booker T. Washington] strength, his vision, [and] his matchless wisdom."[13] Washington's emphasis on black empowerment in the United States and abroad, through industrial training and economic development, helped produce a class of black leadership particularly in the United States and the Caribbean that proved critical to black progress in the early twentieth century.[14]

As part of that growing black leadership, Barnett returned to Chicago in 1906 and became a civil servant, employed as a postal worker for the next six years. From 1916 to 1918 he operated several businesses, including an advertising agency and a business selling photographs of famous U.S. African Americans, and he also helped organize the Kashmir Chemical Company, manufacturer of Nile Queen cosmetics. Barnett capitalized on the marginalized black consumer market that was eager to take advantage of material services. In 1918, Barnett sold advertisements for the *Chicago Defender* to earn money for a trip to California and back. From this experience, he founded the ANP in March 1919 on the South Side of Chicago.

The ANP operated as a mail service that provided member U.S. black newspapers such as the *Chicago Defender* and the *Pittsburgh Courier* with political and cultural news from and pertaining to U.S. African Americans and African-descended peoples.[15] Member newspapers were free to edit or "ignore" the articles it received weekly from the ANP. According to scholar Linda J. Evans, "ANP articles did not necessarily appear in identical form from city to city, and newspapers often failed to include a credit line when they printed stories or columns provided by the ANP."[16] For the most part, the ANP adopted a moderate approach to reporting U.S. black affairs in order to appeal to numerous publications. The ANP typically covered stories about black achievement, black church news and conventions, U.S. African American political figures and U.S. national news, such as Roosevelt's New Deal policies, that affected the lives of black communities. During its early years, the ANP maintained its business primarily through selling memberships. Generally, these fees covered many of the ANP's operating costs.

The ANP's accessibility allowed it to become a major social force in the education of U.S. blacks. The U.S. black press spoke to all literate classes of people, and, arguably, those readers, in turn, informed the illiterate. The U.S. African American press proved to be at the center of a global information network and, as historian Penny Von Eschen has argued, it was essential to the making of the politics of the African diaspora.[17] The abuse and misuse of blacks in the world wars, the Pan African congresses of 1919 and 1927, New Negro interests in Africa and the Caribbean, the Marcus Garvey movement and the Italian invasion of Ethiopia proved to be watershed moments in developing the international interests of the ANP and the U.S. black press. The significance of these events and movements provided a space where a global awareness, sparked by racism and imperialism in the black world, was cultivated. As a result, many African-descended peoples deemed it necessary to create political, social and economic alliances to protect and improve their rights and race relations.

U.S. publications and networks such as Marcus Garvey's *Negro World*, T. Thomas Fortune's *New York Age*, the NAACP's *Crisis* and Barnett's ANP informed hundreds of thousands of people about diasporic affairs, as did Haitian periodicals such as *Le Nouvelliste, Le Matin, Le Temps* and *Haïti-Journal*. Both U.S. African Americans and Haitians developed strong traditions of print journalism rooted in the nineteenth century despite immense economic and political aggression by whites. The effectiveness of newspapers and journals as a means of mass communication contributed to a culture of learning and intellectual exchange that crossed class and domestic borders. Some influential U.S. African Americans such as William Pickens, field secretary for the NAACP, believed that the U.S. black press functioned as one of the few vehicles that could reveal the truth about the state of U.S.

African America and about other marginalized groups in the U.S. Pickens asserted: "If such a minority [racial, political or religious] does not express itself through organs of its own, it will not be expressed. The Associated Negro Press, therefore, belongs in interest, to every colored person of the country. It is our only hope of shoveling ourselves out from under the avalanche of lies that are annually let loose upon us."[18] Thus, the U.S. black press contributed to the authoritative process of self-making.[19] Finally, as increasing numbers of U.S. African Americans became interested in the global politics of black life and wanted the "truth" about domestic and international affairs, the U.S. black press responded with more coverage.

Prior to the 1930s, most newspapers reported international news by cutting articles out of mainstream U.S. newspapers and rewriting them for readers. However, international journalism changed in the 1930s and 1940s due to increased interest by the U.S. African American press and its customers.[20] Determined to acquire exclusive reports that documented African diasporic affairs, more U.S. African American-based papers began to pay for foreign correspondents and for the travel expenses of U.S. reporters. This proved to be an infrequent and expensive feat for many struggling newspaper companies. Nonetheless, Barnett's ANP was one of the first news services to seek out foreign correspondents and to send U.S. black journalists abroad. It remains unclear how Barnett obtained the services of foreign correspondents in Haiti, such as Clamart Ricourt. Yet during the U.S. occupation of Haiti, Haitian and U.S. African American leadership and organizations such as the NAACP and L'Union Patriotique made the issue of Haitian sovereignty and intraracial cooperation one of immediate precedence.

Economic Self-Help Ideology and the Business of Race

From the beginning of U.S. occupation, U.S. investors deemed Haiti "an island of opportunity."[21] Feeling confident about U.S. intervention in Haitian affairs, U.S. white investors capitalized on business ventures that focused on building Haitian infrastructure: banking, agriculture, roads and railroads. After the occupation, white U.S. businesspeople maintained their financial interests in Haiti, yet U.S. African Americans desired to play a larger role in creating transnational business initiatives. Claude Barnett and the ANP published and often orchestrated such business ventures in Haiti with other black entrepreneurs. Barnett's entrepreneurial spirit, his considerable experience in Republican politics and his work with then-Secretary of Commerce Herbert Hoover during the 1920s, when Barnett advised the department on the hiring of blacks in order to promote U.S. black businesses, provided a strong foundation for Barnett's international financial interests.[22] Thus, born from the economic self-help ideology of the Tuskegee Institute and influenced by the self-determination spirit within a U.S. African American lived experience, Barnett exemplified and advanced the business of racial progress.

U.S. African American self-determination and self-help have been powerful social philosophies since their introduction after racial slavery in the United States and the Americas. Primarily noteworthy during the period of Reconstruction and post-Reconstruction with the advent of Booker T. Washington and black colleges in the South, U.S. African American self-determination has been largely discussed within the parameters of legal segregation and racial inequality in the United States. Yet historian Juliet E. K. Walker's pioneering work on the history of U.S. black business documented enslaved and free commercial life that had maintained local and international dimensions since the seventeenth century. Usually having few resources and little capital, African-descended peoples have managed to save and to create sole proprietorships and cooperative endeavors, from "African-slave secret burial societies established in the 1600s and continuing with free-African mutual aid societies founded in the 1700s."[23]

During the nineteenth century, emigration movements and import-export trading opportunities, primarily with Sierra Leone, Liberia and Haiti, fostered U.S. black business activity. Walker asserted that George McGill, a Baltimore entrepreneur who had purchased his freedom and that of a number of his relatives, organized the Maryland Haytian Company in 1819 "to charter ships for emigration to Haiti."[24] Before the U.S. Civil War, some prosperous Louisiana black planters set up viable plantations in Haiti. And, in the 1920s, Jamaican-born black nationalist Marcus Garvey, whose Black Star shipping line, owned by the Universal Negro Improvement Association (UNIA), not only hauled commercial goods to the Caribbean and Latin America, but also "provided passenger service between New York and various foreign ports, including . . . Bermuda, for $75; Port-au-Prince, Haiti, $90; [and] Colon, Panama, $100."[25] Domestic and international enterprise not only proved critical to U.S. African American survival but also highlighted the long tradition of U.S. commercial ventures in spite of anti-black prejudices, violence and a lack of government support.

The achievements of graduates from Tuskegee, Hampton, Fisk and other predominantly U.S. African American colleges created a class of educated and business-minded "New Negroes," who believed they were situated at the vanguard of society and were distinguishable from the black masses in and out of the United States.[26] In the *Tuskegee Messenger*, George E. Haynes described the New Negro as someone who was striving to emerge from "the restrictions and injustices of the past. . . . He is growing conscious of his own worth as an individual and race conscious of his value as a group."[27] Addressing the topic of U.S. African American personal and economic worth during his annual New Year's message at Tuskegee in 1925, President Robert R. Moton reminded audience members to be proud of their accomplishments:

> We should, and do, rejoice that in spite of the difficulties, in spite of injustice here and there, in spite of discrimination, no where in the world has the Negro made such wonderful progress, along so many lines and on such a large scale as right here in America. There is no need today for discouragement; rather there is every reason for hopefulness from whatever angle we may view our situation.[28]

Moton's comment that "no where in the world has the Negro made such wonderful progress" illustrates a sentiment felt by many U.S. blacks who perceived themselves at the center of racial uplift in the black world. U.S. African American achievements in building educational institutions, in science, in business and in art, coupled with the indispensable role they had played in developing the United States, nurtured the belief among many black middle-class citizens that they were the leaders and the messengers of the modern world. One is able to understand more fully these ideas of intraracial leadership and cooperation during the U.S. occupation of Haiti.

U.S. African Americans and Haitians Respond to the Executive Accord of August 1933: A Context to Transnational Ventures

Barnett's engagement with the politics of U.S. intervention in Haitian affairs (1915–1934) helped develop his interest in foreign reporting. In 1930,

Barnett sent ANP journalist Percival Prattis to Haiti to report on Robert R. Moton's presidential commission to study educational development. Prattis' participation in the activities of the Moton educational commission put the ANP in touch with contacts, both Haitian and U.S. American, who were willing to be future correspondents for the ANP. Restoring Haitian economic and political autonomy became front-page news and proved to be of the utmost importance to U.S. African American intellectuals who actively objected to U.S. imperialism.[29] Specifically, U.S. African American remonstrations against the Executive Accord of August 1933, an agreement that assured the U.S. government's control of the Haitian budget, internal revenue, reserve funds and customs, provides a context to understand challenges to U.S. economic hegemony and the subsequent rush of U.S. African American interest in investment during the postoccupation period.

In 1927, participants in the Fourth Pan African Congress in New York City called for economic and political reform in Haiti. Representatives from the Pan African Congress demanded that "the American Receiver General of Customs be replaced by equitable agreement" and that "the attempt of [U.S.] American capital to dominate the industry and monopolize the land of Haiti be decisively checked and turned into such channels as will encourage industry and agriculture for the benefit of the Haitian people."[30] Dissatisfied with U.S. manipulation of Haitian economic affairs, the members of the Pan African Congress wanted to develop Haiti's economy through trade and the creation of businesses. Building industry and the "reorganization of commerce in order to aid the masses rather than a few" were two main Pan African goals during the interwar period.[31]

Protests against the Executive Accord of August 1933 underscored the ways that the U.S. black press and leaders examined the fine points of U.S. occupation, as well as the Haitianization of the administration. Issued on August 7, 1933, the accord stated that U.S. command would cease when "all outstanding bonds were liquidated" by U.S. bankers.[32] Additionally, it provided for the transfer of control of the Haitian Garde d'Haiti (Haitian military police) and the withdrawal of the U.S. Marines. The NAACP, the American Civil Liberties Union and a number of Haitian senators condemned U.S. financial control in statements published in the mainstream and the U.S. black press and also during the 1933 Pan-American Conference in Montevideo, Uruguay. In December 1933, an ANP journalist reporting on the Montevideo summit argued:

The nations of Europe owe the United States billions of dollars, but our government does not try to impose a financial dictatorship on Great Britain or France or Germany or Russia. But because it can do so with no injury to itself . . . it will usurp the sovereignty of a small nation like Haiti and defend the seizure with a lot of talk about debts and treaties. . . .[33]

Executive Secretary of the NAACP Walter White communicated with Haitian statesmen Jean Price-Mars and Dantès Bellegarde and pressured them to remain firm in their opposition to the August 1933 accord.[34] Bellegarde stood steadfast against foreign manipulation of Haitian finances. The ANP reported in a November 1933 press release that Dantès Bellegarde, Haitian minister to the United States, had resigned because of the "setting up of an American [U.S.] financial dictatorship."[35] One month later, Eugene Davidson, Washington correspondent for the ANP, detailed the arrival of Bellegarde's replacement, Albert Blanchet, who had previously served as Haiti's minister of foreign affairs (1932–1933) and who had also signed the Executive Accord of August 1933. Mordecai Johnson, president of Howard University, invited Blanchet to his historic black institution to discuss current Haitian affairs. The new Haitian minister to the United States argued that the August 1933 agreement "unquestionably . . . further cement[ed] the friendship between our two countries."[36] U.S. African American readers of ANP-member newspapers may have been shocked or at least a bit confused by Blanchet's comments, given the anti-U.S. receivership stance by U.S. African American leadership. Yet it is possible that many U.S. blacks were reticent to publicly criticize or to question Blanchet's comments because of his optimism about Haitian control of the armed forces and plans for U.S. military withdrawal in 1934 and because of his confidence of future Haitian and African American collaborations.

The U.S. government remained under the impression that the Executive Accord of August 1933 had received general approval in Haiti aside from opposition from a few adversaries of President Vincent. Undersecretary of State Phillips informed President Roosevelt that Vincent believed that Dantès Bellegarde had solicited the ACLU to criticize Washington. Phillips carefully advised Roosevelt that the U.S. government's hands were tied by ironclad treaties and commitments to U.S. investors that had been issued at the beginning of the occupation. "Except for this obligation," Phillips conveyed to Roosevelt, "we would, of course, be only too glad to discontinue forthwith our connection with Haiti's financial administration."[37]

President Vincent explicitly expressed his displeasure with U.S. financial receivership, invoking the tenets of Roosevelt's Good Neighbor Policy to highlight the hypocrisy in U.S. foreign affairs. According to one ANP writer, Vincent's objections were "couched in the politest, friendliest, diplomatic language." Yet a letter from the Haitian president to Roosevelt on November 16, 1933, challenged the legitimacy of earlier treaty agreements. Vincent argued:

> . . . although they [the financial provisions of the Executive Accord of August 1933] are in conformity with the stipulations of the protocol of 1919 and of the loan contract of 1922 . . . these previous agreements themselves . . . infringe [upon] the essential attributes of the sovereignty of a friendly nation. Is this disparagement of a member of the great Pan-American family, after all, really necessary? It is permissible for . . . the Government of the United States wishing to give a new proof of its desire henceforth to be a good neighbor of all the American States, will be able to renounce a useless financial control in Haiti by a spontaneous act which would be the most eloquent affirmation of a common will towards friendship, towards better understanding, towards inter-American economic cooperation and collaboration . . . of the nations of the three Americas.[38]

Vincent's remarks firmly positioned Haiti within the Pan American family. At the same time, they exemplified the fragility of Haiti's membership within this inter-American alliance and exposed the Haitian administration's powerlessness to police the integrity of Pan Americanism.

Many politically minded U.S. African Americans insisted that Hoover and Franklin D. Roosevelt organize an effective exit strategy in Haiti and, of course, address racial inequities at home "with great frankness if they expected Negro votes" and if they wanted nonwhite peoples to take seriously U.S. Pan Americanism.[39] Barnett continued to criticize the Wilsonian racist paternalism that characterized U.S. involvement in Caribbean and Central American affairs, although his commentary was indirectly broadcast and filtered through the coverage of Haitian affairs within the ANP.

During Hoover's presidency, the United States confronted extreme economic depression at home and cautiously rethought its costly imperialist

ventures in the Caribbean and Latin America. Transitioning from direct
U.S. control in government ministries and the armed forces to native rule,
Hoover and then Roosevelt advocated for U.S. military withdrawal from
Haiti. By September 1934, the U.S. military had departed the island, but U.S.
banks and bondholders still managed Haitian finances. In spite of economic
dependency, there remained an air of hopefulness as troops exited Haitian
ports. During the first week of September 1934, President Vincent conveyed to the U.S. president his belief that U.S. withdrawal would usher in a
"reign of moral peace throughout this hemisphere by a sound application
of international justice and mutual respect."[40] In spite of Vincent's public
dispute with Washington's continuing management of Haitian finances—a
fiscal control that would last until 1941—the Haitian president accepted the
August 1933 accord and recognized Haitianization of the Garde d'Haiti as a
political victory, which advanced his image as the second great liberator of
Haiti among many elite Haitians and, initially, among U.S. African Americans.[41]

The Haitian Afro-American Chamber of Commerce and
the Commission to Examine the Future of Haitian and U.S. African
American Enterprise during the Post-occupation Period

If the post-World War II period in Haiti was an era of projects, the 1930s
was a decade of commissions examining the problems affecting and the
possibilities of improving Haiti's infrastructure. Three U.S.-led investigative commissions in four years, the Hoover-organized Forbes and Moton
commissions in 1930, followed by the Haitian Afro-American Chamber of
Commerce Commission in 1934, highlighted U.S. attempts to study and
become architects of Haitian affairs.

On August 17, 1934, the Haitian Afro-American Chamber of Commerce
Commission sailed from New York City to Port-au-Prince.[42] On board
were Chairman Willis N. Huggins, an educator; Joshua Cockburn, a nautical expert; A. A. Alexander, a civil engineer; A. A. Austin, a realtor; Charles
Govan, an entrepreneur and an engineer; Dr. O. M. Waller Jr., a veterinarian; and Mrs. Ferrol V. Smoot, an ANP representative. Arriving in Haiti
five days later, the commission soon met with city and national officials
and Haitian businessmen, including the mayor of Port-au-Prince, Frederic
Duvigneaud, and Chief of Police Eugène Dégand. Members of the Haitian
Afro-American Chamber of Commerce Commission also participated in

a ceremony similar to that performed by the Moton committee in 1930, commemorating Haiti's triumvirate revolutionaries Toussaint L'Ouverture, Jean-Jacques Dessalines and Henri Christophe by laying wreaths on their statues.[43]

The following morning, August 23, 1934, President Sténio Vincent and Léon Laleau, secretary of state for foreign affairs, greeted the commission at an official opening reception. The president assured the group that "the necessary records and channels of information of the City and National Government" were at their disposal. In a stirring response in French to Vincent's address, Chairman Huggins, a former history professor at Alabama A&M University, conveyed the historical continuity of Haiti as a racialized symbol of freedom, progress, anti-imperialism and economic opportunity. Huggins declared:

> The careers of L'Ouverture, Dessalines and Christophe represent a re-birth in the new world, of the spirit of the ancient Ethiopian kings . . . and [of] the earlier builders of empires in West Africa; of Theodore II and Menelik II in Abyssinia (modern Ethiopia). . . . The citadel of Christophe at Milo [sic], three thousand feet above the sea, is but a flash of the black man's urge for massive building as shown in certain ruins in the Nile Valley, the West Coast and the Zymbabwe [sic] in South Africa.[44]

Haiti's resonance in the U.S. African American imagination as a site of racial symbolism and economic opportunity is not paradoxical but consistent with the idealized historical narrative of U.S. black history in the nineteenth century, which was often used to demonstrate human agency and the positive contributions made by African-descended peoples to the pre-modern and modern worlds.[45] Demonstrating achievement in the black diasporic world continued to be a significant activity as the Haitian government tried to reshape its image and rejuvenate its economy during the post–U.S.-occupation era. The interconnectedness of material wealth, architectural mastery, ancient notions of empire building and revolutionary resistance to colonial oppression seemed to serve as a blueprint to racial progress for the Haitian Afro-American Commission and substantiated African-descended peoples' participation in the evolution of modernity. In spite of Huggins's praise and his comparisons of Haiti to the great civilizations of Egypt and Ethiopia, the Haitian Afro-American Chamber of Commerce Commission understood that Haiti and U.S. African America endured grave financial problems during the Great Depression of the early 1930s and particularly during the post-U.S. military intervention in Haiti. "The world is in the throes of cataclysmic social and economic changes," argued Dr. Huggins in the commission's official report, " . . . yet it finds time to cast an eye and strain an ear to see and hear what you [Haiti] are doing and what you may do in the future."[46]

The economic recession affecting international trade and agricultural prices worldwide during the 1930s clearly worried the commission. There was some unease that Haiti's economic future possessed larger implications for black self-government in the colonial international arena and for U.S. African American advancement. As scholar Michel-Rolph Trouillot has pointed out, Haiti had "the dubious honor of being one of the few solvent countries in the world" during this time; thus, to effectively challenge the effects of the global financial crisis, U.S. African Americans and Haitians relied on mutual cooperation that took on local and transnational forms.[47] Chairman Huggins noted that the "road back to prosperity . . . can be traversed if the nations will summon and use faithful and efficient trusteeship; develop competent workers; and use the higher way of maintaining social order." Ideas of race and nation, of Pan African and Pan American politics, were not mutually exclusive but continued to play off one another for those individuals who believed in the power of black self-empowerment and in the moral obligations governments owed to one another.

During their weeklong study, members of the Haitian Afro-American Chamber of Commerce Commission visited President Vincent's plantations in Léogâne and Geffrard and inspected the teacher and agricultural training school in Damien and the Artibonite department of Haiti, which Huggins observed as a "vast underdeveloped area which awaits settlers from [U.S.] America who with patience, money and brains can make that valley blossom like a rose."[48] Huggins's imagery does conjure up the language of empire-building reminiscent of European New World settlement and U.S. westward expansion. Yet the spirit of this transnational relationship lacked the violent and racist paternalism that informed European and Anglo-American development.

Commission member Joshua Cockburn, a Harlem real-estate broker originally from the Bahamas and a former captain of the S.S. *Yarmouth*, the first ship of the UNIA's Black Star Line, possessed extensive nautical experience and examined the utility of Haitian ports.[49] Realizing that the key to boosting commercial relations between Haitians and U.S. African

Americans was fostering an excellent shipping industry, Cockburn noted that Haiti possessed several valuable and operative ports at Cap Haïtien, Port-de-Paix, Saint-Marc, Jacmel and Miragoâne; however, shipping rates were as much as three times higher than those at other ports in the world. These exorbitant rates created an extreme "burden" on goods produced by Haitian peasants, a group that Cockburn noted "must . . . overcome the handicaps of tariffs" in order to effectively contend in the international marketplace.[50] A Haitian farmer from Port-de-Paix articulated the planters' need for a reliable shipping line, stating that growers had "lost considerably on account of this main factor [of] transportation. . . . As soon as the people will know that they can depend on a regular line, all the Republic will be planting bananas regardless of the island's fitness."[51] Cockburn's investigation into the adverse effects of shipping rates on Haitian enterprise and his inquiries about Haiti's principal exports to the United States (coffee, sugar, bananas, logwood, sisal and rum) revealed that trade relations between Haiti and the United States were "badly unbalanced." For example, from 1931 to 1932, Haiti produced nearly 46 million pounds of coffee, and U.S. companies purchased just 965,982 pounds; however, since the 1820s U.S. merchants had controlled a significant market share of Haiti's imports, supplying nearly 45 percent by 1821.[52] The commission's nautical expert argued that the United States needed to purchase more Haitian products to ease the Haitian government's dependence on U.S. merchandise. Furthermore, he suggested, U.S. African Americans and Haitians should establish and "man" a steamship corporation, organize a mutual savings bank and "immediately . . . co-operate with Haitians for the development of the banana [and coffee] industry."[53]

Four principal investigators on the Haitian Afro-American Chamber of Commerce Commission offered poignant educational, commercial and scientific advice regarding Haiti's dilemma of modern development. However, for the most part, the ideas presented in the commission's official report lacked the specificity and detailed problem-solving strategies needed to create meaningful action at the next level of this transnational program of racial uplift. Charles Govan, a former engineer for the Black Star Line and the manager of a Harlem transportation and warehouse business, encouraged Haitians to implement a laundry service and to incorporate modern machinery to multiply the production of tobacco, soap, rum and leather goods. Huggins offhandedly suggested that retired U.S. school teachers, "both black and white . . . go down there and help during this transition period, in the spirit that the 'Yankee School Marm' went into the deep South to aid the blacks during Reconstruction."[54] Veterinarian and Cornell University graduate O. M. Waller Jr. recommended that Haitians look into an aggressive scientific poultry-raising program that would improve sanitary methods and produce a "better market fowl and greater laying hens" for the world market.[55] Clearly, the U.S. African American Commission possessed a myriad of working ideas for Haiti's future, but noticeably absent from the official report issued nearly one year after the group's visit were concrete plans for fundraising, repaying debt, obtaining licenses, finding potential distributors and deciding on strategies to settle potential grievances. Moreover, the *Official Report of the Haitian Afro-American Chamber of Commerce's Commission to Study the Commercial, Agricultural and Industrial Possibilities of the Haitian Republic,* as the 1935 document was titled, featured few Haitian voices like that of the Haitian planter in Port-de-Paix that could adequately inform and guide the strategic planning of this transnational business relationship. Therefore, although Haitian officials articulated their initial excitement and support for U.S. African American economic ventures when the commission visited Haiti in 1934, the commission's final report expressed a particularly U.S. African American, nonrepresentative perspective on Haitian development.

When members of the commission returned to New York City in September 1934, they were greeted with "a monster reception by persons interested in their findings," including Charles E. Mitchell, the former minister to Liberia. These black capitalists were clearly optimistic about the possibilities of building a successful transnational network of business enterprises that would promote U.S. African American and Haitian interests and lead to industrial development in Haiti and black urban areas in the United States. The welcoming party members asserted that they "cast in [their] lot with the policy of Good Neighborliness" inaugurated by the "illustrious leader of the [U.S.] American people," Franklin D. Roosevelt.[56]

Several organizations emerged within a few years of the Haitian Afro-American Chamber of Commerce Commission's trip to Haiti. Often these companies maintained identical staff, were offshoots of one another and had their offices just a few blocks from one another in Harlem.[57] In July 1935, Alvin C. Gary, secretary of Haitian Afro-American, Inc. (HAAI), and director of Utilites d'Haiti, wrote that the time was "ripe" for skilled black technicians and engineers to handle technical aspects of importing goods and services to Haiti. Serving also as an organizer of the Haitian American

Appliance Company (HAAC), Gary told Barnett that the HAAC did not want to "limit the scope" of the organization to Haiti but intended to include Ethiopia and Liberia in the "economic picture."[58] Gary further noted that Haitians provided so much support that the Haitian business community published a magazine titled *Goodwill* written in French, English, Spanish, German and Italian. Founded on December 14, 1934, in Port-au-Prince, *Goodwill* claimed to be a "mouth piece of Commercial and Economic development." In 1935, Ludovic Rosemond organized a "Goodwill commission" of Haitian merchants, who spent several months in the United States studying modern business methods and commercial possibilities between Haiti and the United States.[59] U.S. African American entrepreneurs affiliated with the Haitian Afro-American Chamber of Commerce believed that their work fulfilled two missions: first, to expand capitalist ventures abroad to realize the promise of modern industrial and technical development in the black world, and, second, to demonstrate that they were active supporters of and participants in U.S. foreign policy.

Yet to fulfill the promise of Haitian modernization, U.S. black entrepreneurs first had to comply with their contracts with Haitian business owners in Port-au-Prince. In October 1935, Utilites d'Haiti General Manager Léon Desportes, whose businesses maintained offices in Harlem and Port-au-Prince, sought arbitration from the Haitian Afro-American Chamber of Commerce on a dispute involving Charles Govan, one of five principal investigators on the commission to study commercial prospects in Haiti.[60] Govan had contracted to operate six omnibuses in Port-au-Prince; however, only three were in service as of June 16, 1935. Henri Rosemond, a Haitian writer living in the United States who had organized the commission's meeting with the Haitian business community during their Pan American trip in August 1934, reported this violation. In addition, Govan had failed to deliver the necessary "financial reports of the business" to the Port-au-Prince branch every three months as previously agreed. It is unclear if there was any willful, malicious intent on Charles Govan's part to dishonor the contract made with Utilites d'Haiti or if he did so because his funds had quickly dried up. Nevertheless, written just one year after the commission's return from Haiti, Desportes' letter to the Haitian Afro-American Chamber highlighted problems of mismanagement and lack of communication and revealed that joint U.S. African American/Haitian business ventures embarked on unstable ground.

In the mid-1930s, there existed a couple of encouraging examples of the influence of the Haitian Afro-American Chamber of Commerce. For instance, early on it seemed that the chamber of commerce possessed no major influence outside Harlem and Haiti, the two keys centers of the black Atlantic. However, in February 1935, Alfred Rochester Green, a member of the Liberian Research Society in Los Angeles, was able to write that the U.S. State Department was now arguing for a more "favorable balance of trade between the two republics."[61] Among the business successes that can be attributed to the chamber's efforts was the founding of the Haitian Coffee and Products Trading Company in 1935 by Major R. R. Wright, the president of the U.S. black-owned Citizens and Southern Bank and Trust Company, in Philadelphia, Pennsylvania. Apparently influenced by Joshua Cockburn's glowing report about opportunities in Haiti, the wealthy banker bought a sizeable amount of Haitian coffee to be distributed in the United States.[62] In April 1937, Wright ventured to Haiti on a self-proclaimed "Good Neighbor Tour" with five influential and well-to-do U.S. African American businessmen and attorneys, including C. C. Spaulding, the president of the North Carolina Mutual Life Insurance Company of Durham, North Carolina, and Elder L. Michaux, a radio evangelist. The U.S. State Department made note of Wright's trip, and although it typically encouraged commercial relations between U.S. and Haitian citizens, Washington officials conveyed a tone of amusement about the "very vague and general talk" by the potential U.S. African American investors who "have given no indication of being prepared to make such investment." "Major Wright may have increased his order for coffee," noted George A. Gordon to Sumner Welles, assistant secretary of state; however, he went on to say, "President Vincent has indicated that although he has been trying all week to elicit some definite suggestions or proposition from these visitors, he has completely failed to do so, and in rather plaintively humorous vein[,] he has further indicated that this was just what he expected."[63]

The tenuous strands of Haitian and U.S. African American relations sustained by the Haitian Afro-American Chamber of Commerce slowly eroded due to ambiguous plans, breach of contracts and a lack of adequate credit and start-up capital due to U.S. economic Depression-era politics that maintained international effects. Several Latin American nations defaulted on loans during this time, and South American exports to Europe and the United States declined in the early 1930s.[64] The timidity of U.S. African American investors such as Wright must be placed in that economic context. By 1934 and 1935, U.S. aid to Haiti had decreased, and the country faced increased competition from French colonies in Africa and Asia, which soured negotiations for renewable French credit loans.[65] The quality of Haitian coffee suffered because Haitian farmers lacked the capital to improve methods and production. Furthermore, the depreciation of Haitian currency and the fact that many nations refused to issue loans to Haiti if the U.S. government did not express direct interest demonstrated a severe risk to any potential investor.[66] Lastly, President Vincent's dismissive remarks about U.S. African American commitments did not take into account the early rumors and reports of Haitians being killed on the Dominican/Haitian border. This bloody reality horrified U.S. African American sympathizers on a human-rights level, at the same time that it drew pause from potential investors concerned about the potential loss of agricultural labor.[67]

"Indissolubly Bound" Yet Out of Business: Haitian/U.S. African American Critiques and the Realities of Pan Americanism

The Haitian Afro-American Chamber of Commerce existed for less than five years. Yet correspondence between Haitians and U.S. blacks and efforts to improve Haiti vigorously continued after its dissolution, with a shift in focus from intraracial institutional building to politics and tourism. New issues that commanded the two groups' attention included the 1937 massacre of thousands of Haitians authorized by Dominican president Rafael Trujillo (estimates of casualties range from 1,000 to 35,000); the politics of World War II; Haiti's political stability and color politics; and the possibilities of Haiti capitalizing on an emerging cultural tourist industry. However, as the U.S. government virtually ignored the Haitian slaughter and the politics of World War II exacerbated racial inequities and antiblack prejudices in the United States and abroad, forcing U.S. blacks to organize for victory at home and overseas, some U.S. African Americans, particularly Barnett, became increasingly critical of Roosevelt's Good Neighbor Policy. Despite these changes in the United States, the Haitian government, under the leadership of President Élie Lescot, continued to be faithful to an inter-American policy that provided minimal gains for Haiti.

During a harrowing week of violence in October 1937, Dominican armed forces murdered thousands of Haitians with Trujillo's consent.[68] Outrage over the massacre, which was rooted in a complex history of border and labor disputes as well as nineteenth-century fears of an Africanized Dominican Republic, was quickly defused by Washington officials, who claimed that the U.S. government lacked "authority" to interfere with this territorial and local conflict. In November 1937, President Vincent formally asked Roosevelt for U.S. assistance, in conjunction with aid from Cuba and Mexico, regarding the horrific situation along the Haitian/Dominican frontier. Representing the "American Negroes who are very deeply concerned with the grave situation . . . in Haiti and San Domingo," Walter White contacted U.S. Secretary of State Cordell Hull to suggest that U.S. African American writer James Weldon Johnson head a U.S. delegation to investigate the borderland carnage.[69]

By and large, black Pan Americanists requested official state and federal affiliation and/or affixed their transnational initiatives to federally recognized policies. These acts may have complemented elite aspirations and/or provided a sense of self-importance and "notoriety," as White was known to seek.[70] At the same time, the moderate and radical actions of U.S. African American activists/intellectuals remained critical to advancing an anticolonial, antiracist and antiviolent agenda. Some scholars have inferred that during the second Italian invasion of Ethiopia (1935–1936), U.S. African American fervor (which included minimal "military and humanitarian relief") against the incursion may have influenced Washington's "moral embargo" on materials needed by Italy.[71] White and a number of "moderate and conservative [U.S. African American] voices" tried to set up a meeting with President Roosevelt to discuss the Italian invasion, but the meeting never occurred. Similarly, White's attempts to create a delegation to examine how the United States could alleviate Haitian suffering never took shape because of Washington's inaction. Whenever black Pan Americanists held onto the notion that their initiatives should partner with U.S. government structures, the limitations of U.S. African American and Haitian cooperation proved glaringly apparent. Pan Americanism seemed even more elusive and insufficient to address the international concerns of black America. Yet after the despot Trujillo agreed to compensate Haiti without ever having acknowledged wrongdoing, the U.S. State Department's stance became self-congratulatory and a dubious victory for Pan Americanism in bringing about peace in the Caribbean states.[72]

The Haitian government under Élie Lescot backed away from U.S. criticism and overwhelmingly tried to foster a more beneficial relationship with the United States. In December 1941, President Lescot stated to Edward J. Sparks, chargé d'affaires of the U.S. Legation, that his government declared war against Japan, Germany and Italy. The extension of Germany's commercial dominance in Latin America and the Caribbean only rivaled that of the United States. As Brenda Plummer has noted, hemispheric programs of "economic assistance" such as Nelson Rockefeller's Institute of Inter-American Affairs helped to "effect the removal of German influence."[73] Haiti's declaration of war was a surprising gesture from a militarily insignificant republic, which demonstrated the lengths to which Lescot would go to prove his allegiance to the United States, its global ideals and the potential transfer of U.S. monetary aid. Although his offer was declined, Lescot volunteered the military assistance of 50,000 Haitian citizens for armed and agricultural service in order "to free our Hemisphere from the intolerable danger of f[l]oundering under totalitarian barbarism."[74] By 1942, Lescot's administration had its eye on reaping the benefits of its grand gesture of support for the United States during World War II. He believed that by "orientat[ing]" Haitian society to the goods, resources and technical knowledge of the United States, these benefits would ensure a burgeoning economy and help the nation capitalize on post-World War II modernization efforts. Lescot noted:

> While Haiti is today indissolubly bound to the United States in the war, it is after the war, after our victory, through your happy initiative, ... that my Country, within the protecting shadow of yours, ... will be able to enjoy genuine economic stability and thus make definite strides toward progress. We are preparing modestly . . . but steadily, for this post-war period.[75]

Convinced that Haiti could succeed if it maintained close ties with Washington, Lescot interpreted Pan Americanism as demonstrating faithful support for a war that possessed minimal implications in Haitian affairs, a position that might enable Haiti to profit from consistent U.S. aid and technical knowledge.

In some respects, noted U.S. African American historian Rayford W. Logan mirrored Lescot's pro-U.S. investment stance. During Haiti's nineteen-year-long occupation, Logan vehemently denounced U.S. intervention. However, during the postoccupation period, Logan projected a "mild" manner and "upbeat timbre" toward Haiti/U.S. relations.[76] In April 1942, while on a trip in Port-au-Prince, Logan wrote optimistically about some of the changes and minor improvements that the black republic had undergone since U.S. occupation. He noted how, in spite of some of these advances, U.S. capital investment remained critical to Haitian development. Logan's ideas, jotted down in his travel diary, illustrate his move toward an intensified yet regulated U.S. involvement in Haitian affairs. He wrote:

> Port-au-Prince is still poor and black . . . [yet] the streets in the business and residential sections are kept scrupulously clean. . . . [S]ome buildings have been repaired or painted . . . but there are still too many shacks along the waterfront. . . . Italians and Syrians run most of the retail stores; Haitian women are still working as laundresses for Chinese owners. . . . Cuba, Haiti and Liberia are all to a certain extent under the control of American capital and the American government. Since this is true, why not accept this control as a fact and use it to raise the standard of living? . . . [T]he control seems inevitable; more and more the 'backward' nations are unable to lift themselves by their own bootstraps. But the control should be international.[77]

Logan was a member of the advisory committee of Nelson Rockefeller's Office of the Coordinator of Inter-American Affairs (CIAA), also called the Institute of Inter-American Affairs (IIAA), a U.S. Pan Americanist organization that complemented Roosevelt's Good Neighbor Policy. In this official capacity, Logan advocated strong U.S. investment in Latin America but argued that sustained U.S. investment did not mean that the country condoned despotism, class stratification or graft in the Americas. In fact, Logan submitted a "very confidential preliminary report" to Rockefeller advocating a "Good Neighbor New Deal" that included "a willingness for [U.S.] American people to pay higher prices for sugar and rubber, etc. so that Latin American workers could enjoy higher wages."[78] Logan never received an answer from Rockefeller, and he later wondered if his recommendations had been considered "silly or superb." Concurrently, Logan worked diligently on a book that examined the history of African-descended peoples in Latin America and how they contributed to "hemispheric solidarity." Logan biographer Kenneth R. Janken documented his aspirations to create a "Latin American institute" at a historically black college in the United States. Moreover, Logan hoped to become U.S. minister to Haiti one day.[79] Thus, it is important to understand Logan's support of inter-American programs as a way to advance his personal and intellectual goals. In addition, Logan's black Pan Americanist plan, which, in this instance, sought to increase the wages of Caribbean and Latin American laborers by forcing higher prices on U.S. and European consumers, attempted to improve the lives of millions of black peoples in Latin America and the Caribbean who were being "ignored or discriminated against" within inter-American affairs.[80]

Logan clearly challenged the CIAA to lobby for more financial and intellectual aid to Haiti to build up its infrastructure. Yet the events of World War II captured the political, social and economic energy of many U.S. African American intellectuals who empathized with the vulnerability of Haitian affairs. An emerging anticolonial movement in the United States and sub-Saharan Africa, whose focus included domestic issues connected to World War II, played center stage in U.S. African America. And, although U.S. blacks faced antiblack prejudice within the military and defense industries, they made crucial contributions to the war effort by purchasing war bonds, serving in the military and volunteering.[81]

At the same time, during the early period of World War II (1939–1944), Washington provided some aid to Haiti as it experienced severe unemployment and "agricultural decline." The U.S. government paid special attention to Haiti and other countries in the Caribbean and Latin America, particularly as these nations related to "strategic security and efficient wartime production."[82] Washington officials from the U.S. Department of Agriculture (USDA) and the Civilian Conservation Corps (CCC), a New Deal work-relief program for young men, traveled to Haiti to assist local Haitian agronomists with increasing sugar and coffee production, reforesting the land and meeting the country's irrigation needs. In 1939, CCC director Robert Fechner spent five days in the country assessing Haiti's agricultural-based economy. Also in 1939, the Haitian government requested a two-year extension of the work contract of Thomas A. Fennell, a USDA agricultural expert who advised Haiti's comprehensive public works program.[83]

By 1941, Haiti had become the site of a massive campaign to increase the production of rubber and sisal for the U.S. war effort. With financial backing from the Export-Import Bank of Washington, Haiti and U.S. officials organized the Société Haïtienne-Américaine de Développement Agricole (SHADA), an agricultural program primarily set up to increase the production of rubber for the World War II effort. SHADA maintained six divisions or working plantations and over 60,000 employees throughout western and northern Haiti.[84] In effect, the United States established a monopoly on rubber and sisal exports in Haiti and displaced a significant population of independent Haitian farmers. Lescot worked hard to maintain those connections with the U.S. agricultural elite and organizations that provided necessary jobs and income. For Lescot, concrete institutional building exemplified the promise of Pan Americanism. However, a number of problems led to SHADA's demise. Environmental disasters such as drought proved significant. In addition, astronomical food prices due to food shortages, the emergence of anti-U.S. protest because of Haitian displacement and advancements in the production of synthetic rubber caused Washington and U.S. rubber companies to abandon their contract with the Haitian government, an act that "accentuated the chronic problems of poverty and underdevelopment."[85] Ultimately, the SHADA debacle accelerated the end of Lescot's presidency.

Within the realm of black Pan Americanism, Lescot's hemispheric aims did not figure in U.S. African American commercial relations, as was the case with Sténio Vincent. As previously mentioned, U.S. blacks' concentration on racial politics at home and on internationalist anticolonial efforts in sub-Saharan Africa highlighted a brief shift away from Haiti between 1939 and 1945.[86] However, Barnett's ANP did disseminate several favorable articles about Lescot, a former Haitian minister to the United States and a one-time "familiar figure in the Negro picture in Washington" who frequently attended "local [U] street movie houses" and "fraternity dances."[87]

Yet Claude Barnett's interest in and commitment to reporting the news about Haiti and communicating with Haitians remained consistent. During the golden days of U.S. African American print journalism, Barnett strived to keep blacks in the Americas informed of immediate political, economic and racial issues. With the advent of the Second World War and the growth of Pan Africanism, the international left and anticolonial movements in Asia and Africa, Barnett's ANP worked tirelessly to provide international news for burgeoning U.S. black newspaper companies and their readers. Acquiring and maintaining international correspondents was important to the reporting process, but a lack of funds and ongoing political instability in developing nations made it difficult for the ANP to do so.[88] Despite the challenges, Barnett remained steadfast about acquiring news from Haiti and fostering cordial relationships in the spirit of black Pan Americanism.

Within this racialized view of hemispheric cooperation, Barnett expressed his disappointment with how U.S.-based inter-American organizations failed to address the realities of racism in the United States. In September 1943, Nelson Rockefeller's CIAA and the National Press Club of Washington sponsored a visit to the United States for Haitian journalists and other newspaper representatives, including Roussan A. Camille of the

Haïti-Journal, Ulrick A. Duvivier of *Le Nouvelliste* and Louis A. Mercier of *La Lanterne.* Showcasing the country's war industries and industrial development, the CIAA organized a tour of General Electric, the Ford Motor Company, the Carnegie Steel Company and the Great Lakes Naval Training Station.[89] Annoyed that these journalists were not introduced to U.S. African American communities, Barnett wrote to Louis A. Mercier offering his regret "that visitors who come to the United States from our *sister countries of South America* find themselves so shielded from the prevailing racial attitudes in the United States." Frustrated, Barnett noted:

> . . . They are never given an opportunity to meet the Negro element in our population nor a chance to observe the great contribution which the black citizens of the United States are making to the war and to the life of the country. . . . Even with as fair a chairman as is Nelson Rockefeller of the Office of Coordinator of Inter-American Affairs, the visitors from Brazil, Columbia [*sic*] and other South American countries are permitted to gain their impressions from the most lowly of the Negro people or from hasty glimpses as they are conveyed about the country. . . . This is unfortunate for a country which boasts of its democracy when in truth we are the least democratic country in the Western Hemisphere when it comes to racial matters.[90]

The above excerpt illustrates Barnett's criticism of U.S. Pan Americanism, which privileged largely white U.S. corporations and communities and turned a blind eye to racial inequality in the United States and to the achievements of a respectable class of U.S. blacks. By showing their Haitian guests these "modern" facilities, the CIAA communicated an example of U.S. American progress. Furthermore, Barnett's statements reveal his displeasure with the type of U.S. blacks presented to Haitians and in what manner the guests visited U.S. African American communities. Barnett maintained bourgeois ideals on race and racial uplift and, in this case, wanted the international community to see the best that U.S. African America had to offer, or at least a balanced exposure between the middle class and the working poor. Barnett believed that the office of the CIAA distorted the reality of racial injustice in the United States during World War II, which proved to be problematic because making civil rights and racial inequality international issues helped garner worldwide support.

To maintain and strengthen alliances between Haitians and U.S. African Americans, Barnett often served as an intermediary between the two groups, organizing tours to Haiti, scouting new business deals and arranging job opportunities for U.S. African Americans in Haiti. In 1947 Barnett spoke to SHADA representatives on behalf of James P. Johnson, a young black forester. In 1946, Dr. Joseph Buteau, vice president of the Haitian Red Cross, asked Barnett to help him gain backing for his organization from U.S. blacks. Although Barnett steered Buteau towards "National Red Cross channels," stating that U.S. African American masses needed to know more about the issues affecting Haiti before they could lend a hand there, the ANP chief helped organize a tour of Haiti for upstanding U.S. blacks from Chicago, and Buteau operated as their main Haitian contact.[91]

For a short while, Buteau remained a source of information for the ANP. He reported to the news service on the 1946 political revolution in Haiti, where Dumarsais Estimé's *noiriste* platform, a system of dark-skin rule in Haiti, defeated *mulâtre* (light-skinned) power. This event shifted the focus of previous ANP reports from U.S./Haiti economic and political relations to Haitian color politics. In February 1946, an ANP release on Haiti opened, "We want a black president."[92] Barnett asked Buteau several questions about Estimé's color and its effect on Haitian society. Buteau grossly downplayed Haiti's color politics, explaining, "We [Haitians] do not have to give it [the question of complexion] a too wide importance. It is only a political platform used often in the course of the history of this country, but it is not a reality of the Haitian life. . . ."[93] To a degree, some Haitians have not consciously contemplated color issues among their families and fellow citizens, often deferring to national identity (being Haitian). Yet the conflict between the *mulâtre* elite and *noirs* is deeply ingrained in Haitian society and traces its roots to the Haitian independence movement of the eighteenth and nineteenth centuries.[94]

The color politics of Haiti resonated well with Barnett and U.S. African Americans because the issue of light vs. dark complexions has also played an integral role in the politics of U.S. black leadership and racial purity, and access to resources. Examining the issue in the context of a racialized economic self-help ideology, historian Kevin Gaines argued that a racially mixed U.S. aristocracy "tended to be socially exclusive and lukewarm toward the self-help ethos of material advancement that motivated the rise of ambitious and often darker-complexioned, former slaves and their descendants."[95] Many newly educated and upwardly mobile U.S. blacks whose "claims to status were based not on the older credentials of freedom, wealth, or family background, but on education and race-conscious uplift activities" believed that mulattoes dominated leadership positions, threatened the advancement of dark-skinned peoples and demeaned them in social settings.[96] A dark-complexioned man himself, Barnett seemed to favor the ascendancy of a dark-skinned leader in Haiti. To the ANP editor, such an ascent testified to the abilities of a dark-complexioned population, which often represented the historically marginalized black masses. President Estimé's privileging of the black middle class and the indigenous culture of the Haitian masses for the purposes of promoting a national identity and Haitian arts sparked a wave of cultural nationalism in the 1940s. The post-1946 era in Haiti exemplified the growth of tourism, when many middle-class and elite U.S. Americans and Europeans consumed Haiti's folk culture.

Back in Business . . . For Now: Tourism and U.S. African American Ventures in Haiti during the 1950s

With the Haitian government giving more support to the arts, the advent of the Bicentennaire Exposition, which celebrated the 200th anniversary of the founding of Port-au-Prince, and an increase in U.S. American and European tourists to the island, Haitians and U.S African Americans in the mid-twentieth century believed the time was opportune to foster better relationships and benefit from overseas currency and investment. Tourists, regardless of race, brought foreign capital to the island. Like NAACP Executive Secretary Walter White, who is discussed in chapter 4, Barnett promoted tourism in Haiti and the Caribbean. At the same time, Haitians like Jean F. Brierre, a poet and undersecretary of tourism, understood that both groups could learn more about the other's political and social struggles. In September 1950, Jean Brierre wrote an encouraging letter to Barnett stating his intent to always do his best "to better relationships between colored people of the U.S.A. and Haiti. We have lived too long and far away from each other and I want any Haitian to know about your great struggle in the States."[97]

In addition to developing tourism, Barnett and others believed that Haiti demonstrated a wealth of business opportunities. U.S. African American businessmen viewed development and investment as the keys to achieving progress and ensuring political stability. Yet, the midcentury transition of presidential power in Haiti was mired in political and military conflict. In 1950, when the Estimé regime fell to Paul Magloire, a former colonel in the Haitian army, Barnett revealed his disappointment about the change in government. In spite of his frustration with yet another contentious Haitian regime change, Barnett sent President Magloire a hopeful and supportive letter that highlighted the interconnectivity of Haitian affairs with U.S. African American racial politics and perceptions of African-descended peoples.[98] Thus, as a means to develop Haiti, Barnett and other U.S. African Americans began another wave of entrepreneurial ventures in Haiti.

In March 1950, Barnett wrote in an ANP press release that Haiti desired "Negro business people with capital and know how which assures their competence to operate worthwhile business projects."[99] As Sténio Vincent had done twenty years before, President Magloire encouraged U.S. African American investment. Chester K. Gillespie, a U.S. African American attorney who vacationed in Haiti for two weeks in February 1951, spoke with Magloire about the available business opportunities on the island. In a March 9 letter to Barnett, Gillespie expressed great confidence that U.S. blacks "would have the complete and anxious cooperation of the government," a collaboration that exemplified this movement of intraracial and transnational racial uplift projects.[100]

During his April 1950 Founder's Day speech at Tuskegee Institute, Barnett highlighted the potential success of self-determination and international racial cooperation. His speech "Lifting Your Horizons" describes the work of James O. Plinton, a Tuskegee graduate, pilot and president of the Haitian American Cleaning Company. Plinton's commercial venture was one of the few successful businesses to emerge from this intraracial and transnational alliance. After failing to launch an aviation line in Liberia, Plinton set his sights on nations in the Caribbean and Latin America. In 1945, he and a partner from the Virgin Islands organized and franchised Latin American Airways, Inc., with the help of U.S. African American millionaire Major R. R. Wright, an investor in the Haitian Afro-American Chamber of Commerce. Soon, Plinton acquired full control of daily airline operations in Ecuador, whose government recruited him to reorganize their "shaky commercial airline industry." Unfortunately, Plinton's time in Ecuador proved ephemeral. Plinton asserted that "politics and race" forced him to leave the country and start anew. He accepted an offer from Haitian president Estimé to help organize and operate the Haitian National Airways. The Haitian National Airways never materialized, but from 1947 to 1949, Plinton overcame adversity and started another small airline business, Quisqueya, which carried passengers, mail and cargo to a number of Caribbean islands.

By 1949, Plinton was seeking his fortune "on the ground" as well as in the air. The Caribbean proved to be a trendy destination for middle- and upper-middle-class U.S. Americans and Europeans due to Europe's postwar troubles and slow reconstruction efforts. And, similar to other U.S. African American entrepreneurs, intellectuals and artists, Plinton maintained a strong connection with Haiti, the Caribbean's only independent black nation. He wanted to capitalize on Haiti's emerging tourist industry, which was luring visitors to the well-publicized Bicentennial Exposition (1949) and piggybacking on the growing popularity of Haitian folkloric dance and painting; likewise, Plinton wished to contribute to the country's development. In 1949, he installed and operated the first modern laundry service in Haiti. He owned five branches in Haiti, employed more than fifty of its citizens and often piloted his plane to its various coasts to receive the laundry of incoming cruise ships.[101]

During a radio interview with Etta Moten Barnett, Claude Barnett's wife and a well-known U.S. African American actress, concert singer and Chicago radio host, Plinton told the largely U.S. black audience that they "don't just want to be another citizen [in Haiti] . . . if they [U.S. African Americans] feel the areas of development are filled they are quite wrong. . . . There are areas that need aid with finance as a secondary effort"; however, making a social "contribution" was most important.[102] Plinton encouraged U.S. African American investment in Haiti, but, according to him, investors needed to understand the centrality of racial solidarity and its social value. Claude Barnett underscored Plinton's sentiment as he finished his Founder's Day speech to the Tuskegee students, faculty and alumni. Barnett explained, "There is money, if that is important, there is opportunity, to demonstrate racial pride waiting for the right man in every trade. . . . As Dr. [Booker T.] Washington and Dr. Moton used to tell us, and as Dr. Patterson insists today, opportunity is everywhere, if you just prepare for it, plan for it, and lift your horizons."[103]

Indeed, having capital benefited U.S. African Americans and allowed them to help develop the interests of others. Yet Barnett's personal and economic investments in Haiti appear to have affected his assessment of U.S.-centered modernization projects there. Barnett wrote to his Haitian friend Paul Chetien in 1951: "I shall always be on the lookout for someone with adequate capital; however, if an especially good prospect opens up I hope you . . . will advise me to seek support for it."[104] Intrigued by Haiti's proximity to the United States, its potential to attract tourists and its historical significance as the first free black republic in the Western Hemisphere, Barnett and other black entrepreneurs lacked a critical framework to assess Haitian economic development projects. Despite this failing, they remained quite vocal and condemnatory when it came to addressing racial issues in the global arena. For Barnett, developing Haiti's infrastructure, at all costs, would aid Haiti's progress. The journey towards industrial and technological development, believed to be effective strategies to break down racial barriers, allowed developing nations and groups, like Haiti and U.S. African America, to deal with the United States and European nations on equal terms. However, many of the business schemes privileged skilled migrants and activities in urban centers and thus lacked any meaningful focus on the rural, agricultural sector, which both empowered and exploited the Haitian masses.

Between 1946 and 1956, Haiti became a nation of "projects" sponsored by foreign organizations.[105] Programs and economic missions sponsored by UNESCO, the World Health Organization, SHADA, the United Nations (UN), the Institute of Inter-American Affairs and other entities perpetuated the illusion of progress, as Michel-Rolph Trouillot has argued. An ANP press release dated April 1951 reveals an increase in credit to $14 million from the Export-Import Bank of Washington to develop the Artibonite region of Haiti. Following its established middle-of-the-road approach, the ANP emphasized the effectiveness of Pan American technical and financial programs to deal with the problem of "an expanding population on shrinking land resources."[106] Barnett directly expressed faith in U.S.-centered assistance programs to maintain a level of confidence in private investment. In May 1952, Barnett proposed to New York attorney Blackwell Smith that a maritime program be organized to register ships coming through the northern Caribbean region. "Close to the United States, anti-Communist, in high favor with our Government, with no [sea] program at present, [Haiti] would seem to be made to order for such an effort," wrote Barnett.[107] Smith was uninterested in the project, but Barnett continued to push the issue, stating that the United States had a "large voice in keeping [Haiti] straight."[108]

The United States had played a substantial role in Haitian political and economic affairs since the advent of U.S. occupation. The country's presence in Haiti symbolized U.S. influence in the Caribbean and Latin America at large, and with the onset of Cold War politics, Haitian leadership often fell in line with anticommunist rhetoric, a strategy that often ensured access to various levels of U.S. foreign aid. Magloire's administration presented itself as firmly anticommunist and welcomed U.S. aid for modernist projects. A. J. Wakefield, U.S. representative for the Point Four Program, noted to Barnett that Magloire "left no doubt that he looks to a technical assistance program—an integrated UN and Point Four program to assist him in the task of economic development and social advance."[109] Inter-American programs such as Point Four, a U.S.-sponsored agenda that provided technical and financial assistance to developing nations including those in Latin America and the Caribbean, remained influential in Haiti despite the three regime changes in the 1940s and early 1950s. In contrast, Rayford Logan proved to be a bit more critical of the Point Four Program. Continuing a theme he had explored in his 1942 diary, Logan argued that Caribbean and Latin American citizens must be paid a livable wage to be able to "buy in the world market." Otherwise, Logan continued, "Point Four will indeed mean making imperialism more profitable than it has been in the past."[110]

The prospect of developing the Artibonite Valley, the growth of tourism and what Trouillot described as the era of "government displays, of picture postcard projects" convinced Barnett and other U.S. African American businessmen that Haiti could provide economic leadership among African-descended peoples during this era of modernization. In March 1951, Barnett commented that Haiti could, in fact, "contribute considerable leadership" to this renaissance of black self-determination. For example, in May of the same year I.J.K. Wells, the director of *Color* magazine, sought out the leadership of President Magloire to hire a U.S. African American engineer to help develop the Artibonite Valley. Wells suggested A. A. Alexander, a U.S. African American engineer based in Des Moines, Iowa, who had traveled to Haiti in 1934 with the Haitian Afro-American Chamber of Commerce. Alexander owned and operated the American Caribbean Company, which performed work in Puerto Rico and Venezuela.[111] Wells' appeal to Magloire highlighted his commitment to a racial solidarity that maintained biological and sociohistorical components:

> If a Negro engineer capable, respected and honorable should build this project for Haiti, it will bring to the Haitian people the love of Negro people throughout the world and certainly high respect from all other races who recognize that Haiti believes in itself and its own

extremely well qualified people. In making this appeal, may I say to you that there is no racial prejudice in me whatsoever and I do not therefore ask for consideration out of animosity or jealousy, but for the reason above given. Mr. Alexander has white associates; therefore, giving the contract to him means you are recognizing both races. May I say, however, that measured for its pure, cold political worth to Haiti, this will mean a great deal toward binding to Haiti the good will of Negro people of this country. In the long run, your own blood in this country will support Haiti long after profit-takers, not kin to you, have forgotten Haiti and gone on about their business.[112]

Race and racial solidarity became central to discussions of Haitian industrial development in the 1950s. Although race was central to Wells' assessment as well, Wells was still operating within the particularities of a hemispheric framework. Black Pan American rhetoric offered Wells a window to concretize his "goodwill" entrepreneurial venture. Wells, who did not want to seem discriminatory, clearly wanted to send a message to U.S. whites that blacks in Haiti and the United States were indeed independent and capable of actualizing technological and industrial projects. Here, U.S. black capitalists utilize race and the business of race as a networking tool across borders for the benefit of both sides. Wells' initiative complemented the atmosphere of U.S. black self-help and racial cooperation in the Americas during this period and situated Haiti as a site for racially symbolic statements.

Recalling the strong anticolonial movements that flourished during the 1940s and 1950s among African-descended peoples and the efforts to modernize black nations through material development, Barnett believed that a new spirit of growth and progress had surfaced. "Not only in Haiti is this spirit of development arising. . . . Darker peoples all over the world from Liberia and Ethiopia and Africa in general, . . . are feeling a new sense of self-determination," wrote Barnett in 1951.[113] Barnett and the ANP continued to spotlight encouraging or optimistic aspects of black life in the African diaspora. In July 1952, James Plinton proudly wrote to Barnett about his assembly of "top-notch" U.S. African American tennis players in Haiti. Plinton stated that it was a "marvelous success" and that "another great round has been won in this fight to regain the *mutual respect* between Afro-America and Haiti for true brotherhood."[114] Barnett promoted the screening in the Haitian capital of several short films about U.S.

Fig. 3.1. Claude Barnett pays homage to a bust of Toussaint L'Ouverture, Haiti, 1952. (Photo courtesy of the Chicago History Museum.)

African American life, including *The Negro in Business and Industry, The Negro in National Affairs* and *The Negro in Sports*.[115] Subsidized by Chesterfield Cigarettes, these films show clips of notable figures such as Frederick D. Patterson, president of Tuskegee Institute, Illinois congressman William Dawson and Olympic medalist Jesse Owens, the narrator, smoking cigarettes and extolling the achievements of U.S. blacks in public arenas. Propagandistic cinema was a tool of a U.S. African American transnational racial uplift program that sought to influence and inspire Haitians in finance, politics and professional sports in the same way the history of the Haitian Revolution inspired blacks from the United States.

Fig. 3.2. Jacques Leger presents Claude Barnett with the Haitian National Order of Honor and Merit Award, Haiti, 1955. (Photo courtesy of the Chicago History Museum.)

Hurricane Hazel devastated Haiti's cacao and coffee crops in 1954, pushing the country's struggling economy into dire straits. Hesitant about scaring off U.S. and European tourists, Barnett cautioned Denys Bellande of the Haitian Information Service against reporting the harrowing news of suffering Haitian masses while many of the elite "celebrate and face life gaily." Barnett suggested that Bellande could not afford "to paint distress so glaringly . . . so as not to destroy the picture of sunshine and glamour we wish people to think of when they turn to Haiti."[116] To help tourism succeed in Haiti, Barnett tried to maintain the public perception of Haiti as the picture of unruffled stability.

Despite impressions that the country was progressing in the 1950s, the derisory health and living conditions of the Haitian masses exemplified a struggling and fragile economy. The population growth and migration to the capital from 1930 to 1950 placed significant strains on the urban housing sector. A 1950 census revealed that 100,000 units failed to meet fundamental needs of inhabitants.[117] Fewer than 30 percent of households in Port-au-Prince possessed electricity. Overcrowding and unsanitary housing produced high numbers of tuberculosis fatalities (300 to 350 deaths per 100,000). By 1950, there were 1.7 million cases of yaws, a bacterial skin and bone disease, although a massive eradication program reduced that number to fewer than 100 cases by 1969.[118] The scarce ratio of hospital beds to members of the population, a meager 0.7 beds per 1,000 citizens, proved one of the lowest in the Americas. Additionally, the annual loss of medical practitioners who departed for better opportunities in the United States, France, Canada and the Congo demonstrated health and economic systems in crisis.

An advocate for the national bourgeoisie, President Magloire continued to oppress the urban poor and their advocates. He imprisoned dissidents such as Daniel Fignolé, leader of the Mouvement Ouvrier Paysan (MOP), a populist-leaning organization that supported the rights of peasants and the laboring urban poor. Barnett and the ANP did not adequately report on or highlight these stories about Haiti. This failing demonstrated the limitations of Barnett's probusiness outlooks and possibly his fear of scaring off potential investors. Black Pan Americanists' commitment to bourgeois frameworks of respectability, the positive public display of black leadership, in addition to a loyalty to the biological and somatic essence of race, offered no room in which to overtly condemn foreign black leadership.[119] Considering the vast reach of European colonialism during the period, few independent black nations possessed black heads of state or were subjected to criticism from the U.S. black press.[120]

Barnett, the End of the Magloire Administration and the Limits of Pan Americanism

From 1955 to the onset of Duvalier's presidency in September 1957, the circle of friendship between U.S. African Americans and Haitians began to contract.[121] In a letter to Mauclair Zéphirin, Haitian ambassador to the United States, Barnett critiqued Haiti's role and lack of participation in international affairs. The 1955 Bandung Conference in Indonesia was a pivotal moment in Pan African politics because, as Brenda Plummer argued, it "reinforced a new cultural consciousness that seemed to arise on the pyre of colonialism."[122] For Barnett, "the lines [were] being drawn" between the Caucasian world and the "darker peoples" of the earth. And Haiti, as a sovereign state, needed to take the lead in racial and political affairs in the Western Hemisphere. Barnett argued: "It may not be enough to think alone of Pan American or even inter-American status. . . . The Yellow and Brown races are looking about for statesmen and programs which will let them out of bondage."[123] The ANP editor challenged the Haitian government's relationship with U.S. Pan Americanism and its effectiveness at addressing colonialism and racism. For the Haitian government, U.S. Pan Americanism and its twentieth-century ideological byproducts—Roosevelt's Good Neighbor Policy, Rockefeller's CIAA and the hemispheric components of Truman's Point Four programs—demonstrated the notions of nonintervention, cultural exchange and necessary aid packages. During the mid-1950s, the Haitian government focused on strengthening these Washington ties; thus the notion of "taking the lead" on black international politics by Haitian government representatives operated at the margins of their foreign policy.

Maintaining the appearance of progress became extremely difficult as Haiti edged closer to the Duvalier presidency. Haiti's external debt was at its highest in history. Outbursts by radical peasant organizations such as the MOP's protests threatened Magloire's administration. Towards the latter months of 1956, Magloire decided to extend his presidency. As a result, a labor and business strike ensued in December 1956 causing political and social unrest. Magloire resigned on December 12, 1956.

Barnett continually sought accurate information regarding the chaotic end of Magloire's administration. There were five provisional governments in Haiti from December 1956 to August 1957 and nineteen presidential candidates. Naturally, Barnett requested information on Haitian affairs from his contacts in Haiti such as Emmanuel Racine, Denys Bellande and Mauclair Zéphirin, a former Haitian foreign minister (1954–1955). The political confusion of the time and the "instability of the system to maintain or reform itself" caused Barnett's contacts to primarily focus on state matters and to ignore his requests.[124] Moreover, Barnett's emphasis on reporting positive stories of Haitian affairs offered little room for manipulation by Racine and Bellande. In December 1956, Barnett wrote to Zéphirin stating that U.S. blacks fervently wanted "to know what is transpiring in Haiti. There has been nothing from your office nor from Racine."[125] Subsequently, Barnett warned that Haiti's stability "must not be questioned," adding that particularly "when Cuba and Dominica [probably the Dominican Republic] are showing signs of erupting, Haiti should remain the area where people feel free to go. There are thousands who need to become acquainted with Haiti and this is a good time to achieve that end."[126] Without accurate information, foreign business interests were being compromised, and the uncertainty of Haitian politics and its economy threatened Barnett's race-based diasporic agenda. During this politically and economically volatile time, progress was measured by stability and was evidenced in the maintenance of democracy, the accumulation of wealth and the ability to withstand imperialist encroachments by so-called developed nations. Haiti suffered from a brand of politics, according to Barnett, that was susceptible to "graft and looting of the country's finances. This halts real progress."[127]

Eager to stay abreast of the situation in Haiti, Barnett sought out familiar friends such as dancer Lavinia Williams and businessman James Plinton. Addressing the issue of the general strike, Barnett again centered tourism as the economic bloodline of the Haitian economy. The strike would deal a "death blow" to tourism, wrote Barnett, who wondered how it would "benefit . . . the personal fortunes" of Haitian merchants.[128] In June 1957, Lavinia Williams responded to Barnett, assuring him that "Haiti has been through a real crisis, but it seems to me all is fine again. I hope so, for the good of the country."[129] Likewise, Etta Moten, Barnett's wife, inquired about the state of Haitian affairs among her associates, particularly Lucienne Estimé, a leader in the Haitian orphanage movement and the spouse of President Dumarsais Estimé. Lucienne Estimé confirmed the relative calm that the country experienced when the provisional government of Haitian general Léon Cantave stepped down and Daniel Fignolé's short-lived administration was deposed.[130] From May to October 1957, General Antonio Kébreau established a totalitarian government under the auspices of the Military Council of Government.

Still bent on shaping positive news stories about Haiti, Barnett and the ANP ignored the installation of Kébreau's totalitarian government. With the news of pending elections coupled with the encouraging comments from Lucienne Estimé and Lavinia Williams, Barnett remained optimistic about demonstrating Haitian democracy and political stability. From 1956 to 1957, Haiti experienced a "crisis of hegemony" among its "traditional power groups": the *mulâtre* elite, the black middle class and the Haitian Legislature. This "crisis," coupled with a political landscape that continuously marginalized the Haitian peasantry from political affairs and with a decrease in power of the Haitian bourgeoisie, helped François Duvalier ascend to the presidency in September 1957.

Duvalier's *noiriste* rhetoric appears to have placed him in good esteem with Barnett for a short time. In November 1957, Maurice A. Casseus, official interpreter of the Haitian Presidential Palace, told Barnett that President Duvalier was "prepared to play the part" of former president Dumarsais Estimé, best known for his *noiriste* agenda. For the most part, Barnett, as well as other U.S. African Americans such as Katherine Dunham, admired the politics of Estimé. Haiti's cultural popularity had thrived under his leadership, and Dunham compared him to revolutionary leader Toussaint L'Ouverture because of his ability to lead and care for the Haitian peasantry.[131] Similarly, Barnett's admiration of Estimé swayed him to accept Duvalier's administration. Barnett confidently wrote to Duvalier in November 1957: "The fact that you are made in the mold of and ascribe to the policies of our late friend President Dumarsais Estimé, makes us [U.S. African Americans] believe that under your regime things will develop to the advantage of the people farthest down."[132] Duvalier never officially responded to Barnett, and during his rule the Haitian peasantry did not prosper. Duvalier and Estimé did possess some similarities, namely their belief that the black petty bourgeoisie should be the primary representative of the masses and thus they would become leaders of the nation's "cultural and moral regeneration."[133]

Conclusion

Influenced by the economic self-help philosophy of Booker T. Washington and serving as editor in chief of the ANP, Barnett headed an information network that educated U.S. black readers on Haitian political, cultural and economic affairs. As part of an aspiring U.S. African American class, Barnett was among many who believed that capitalist development was best suited for racial advancement. Thus, he fought to organize and introduce U.S. African American investors to willing Haitians in order to encourage political and economic solidarity; to promote racial progress and Haitian tourism; and to ensure democratic and stable government in Haiti. In conjunction with the vision of Sténio Vincent and U.S. African American and Haitian entrepreneurs, Barnett's plans to improve Haitian society and to help advance U.S. African American business ventures by reporting Haitian affairs in the ANP, developing commercial advocacy organizations, increasing U.S. tourism to Haiti and promoting industrial and technological development exhibited a black Pan Americanist agenda of intraracial and inter-American cooperation.

Barnett and the ANP played significant roles in the business of race. As the largest and longest established U.S. black news service, the ANP helped inform a substantial U.S. African American population about the politics of the African diaspora. At its peak, "nearly two hundred papers, or 95 percent of black [U.S.] American newspapers" subscribed to the ANP service.[134] Like Walter White and other journalists and intellectuals, Barnett believed that U.S. African American and Haitian relations should be nurtured because Haiti's history of revolutionary struggle and sovereign status as a black nation possessed budding promise on issues such as racial injustice, Western imperialism in the Caribbean and continental Africa and black self-rule.

Yet the privileging of the Haitian Revolution and Haitian independence in the U.S. African American imagination in many ways obscured what scholar Robert Fatton Jr. argues is the "authoritarian habitus" rooted in the "material foundation" of the Haitian state.[135] The "complicated repertoire of practices, attitudes and behaviors" that had been inherited from French hegemony in Saint-Domingue and replicated in post-independence Haiti produced a "pattern of exclusion" and authoritarianism, remnants of which linger in twenty-first-century Haiti. Haiti's "authoritarian habitus" does not mean that the country is incapable of economic, political and social advances. However, these patterns require cooperative and internal initiatives that acknowledge Haiti's history and that foster institutions, such as vibrant community organizations, that challenge the longstanding forces of racial hierarchies and economic and ecological degradation. While existing community groups lack meaningful impact at the state level and often suffer from poor funding, yet, as Fatton notes, "these networks defy the ugly realities of squalor and violence" by providing "responsive, accountable power."[136]

With the exception of James Plinton's cleaning-service enterprise, most of the transnational business projects launched during this time failed to go beyond the realm of ideas, partly due to lack of sufficient capital. Nevertheless, these efforts embodied the black Pan American and Pan African spirit that flourished during the World War II and postwar periods. As Juliet E. K. Walker has argued, "There is a propensity in American culture to view the social and economic condition of blacks as one of failure, as opposed to acknowledging that the government has failed blacks."[137] Undoubtedly, black businesses failed, but it is critical to understand fully how racism, a legacy of economic dependence, foreign interests and internal problems contributed to the collapse of commercial projects that sought to undermine hegemonic power structures.

Unfortunately, Barnett lacked foresight and the means to critique the effects of tourism and U.S. Pan American projects such as SHADA. Many U.S. projects offered benefits at a surface level and adversely affected the lives of the Haitian rural peasantry, a population significantly ignored in the strategic planning of Haitian/U.S. African American business enterprises. However, Barnett and the ANP privileged those stories that sought to demonstrate the ascendancy of the black world and to encourage potential U.S. black investors. "We [U.S. blacks and Haitians] are beginning to awaken them [U.S. blacks]," wrote Barnett to Haitian secretary of state Luc E. Fouche, noting that "They can form an important part of the stream of visitors who go to Haiti, and our hope would be that some would wish to invest and make their homes there. It is a land especially attractive to people of color."[138] It was in this vein of collaboration, cultural exchange and investment that Barnett labored to help Haitian society.

4

"What Happens in Haiti Has Repercussions Which Far Transcend Haiti Itself"

Walter White, Haiti and the Public Relations Campaign, 1947–1955

Sightseeing . . . shopping for incredible bargains . . . dancing . . . swimming . . . lazing . . . looking . . . filling your eyes with the beauty of Haiti's tropical and mountain foliage, moonlight on the sea, palms and pines. . . . All this awaits you—only four short hours from Miami.

Haiti Tourist Information Bureau, 1953

Haiti is really a heaven land . . . where it's always spring—warm sun and cool trade winds . . . tropical flowers and Alpine mountain views . . . the best food west of Paris, by the way . . . a new International Casino . . . sailing, spear-fishing . . . trips into history by burro-back, or Cadillac. Make your reservations early.

Haiti Tourist Information Bureau, 1953

On September 20, 1947, NAACP Executive Secretary Walter White wrote to Joseph D. Charles, Haitian ambassador to the United States, outlining his recommendations to transform Haiti's public image. According to White's memorandum, U.S. perceptions of Haiti as a "poverty-stricken, illiterate, hopelessly backward country whose people are little removed from the jungle and practically all of whom practice voodoo" posed significant challenges to strengthening Haiti/U.S. relations and, inevitably, to the Caribbean nation's advancement as well.[1] White asserted that Haiti needed a calculated overhaul of key facets of its image—political, economic and cultural. Once his plans were implemented and carried out and their results publicized throughout the international arena, Haiti's public relations (PR) campaign would prove essential to Haiti's subsequent progress and improved role in inter-American affairs. Since Haiti's independence from European colonial powers in 1804, the black republic had remained a symbol of African American resistance and potentiality for self-government;

thus, Haiti's progress exemplified the achievements of African-descended peoples in the realms of self-government and economic and social development. With the aid of the Haitian government, his future wife Poppy Cannon and private and public support, Walter White served as one of the leading U.S. African American figures who contested the dominant racialized readings of Haiti by presenting to the world a more refined and positive image of the black republic.

In this chapter, I contend that Walter White's PR campaign paralleled U.S. policy objectives of mutual cooperation and financial and technical assistance in the Caribbean and Latin America. In spite of the secretary's accord with U.S. policies, specifically the objectives of Harry Truman's Point Four Program and other inter-American projects rooted in the political ideology of U.S. Pan Americanism, White confronted U.S. hegemony of Haitian affairs, believing that an economically empowered and politically stable Haiti could profoundly affect U.S. African American advancement in Cold War America. However, despite his optimism and determination, White's and Haitian officials' focus on developing tourism as a main springboard of the public relations campaign proved ineffective to the advancement and training of the Haitian masses. The goals of the public relations campaign were inspired and ultimately compromised by a program of racial uplift, foreign ownership and underdevelopment in Haiti.

Scholars of U.S/Latin American relations have typically interpreted U.S. Pan Americanism as an imperial project that intended to expand U.S. political and economic influence in the region.[2] Absent from most of the scholarly literature on Pan Americanism have been the voices of U.S. African Americans, Afro-Caribbeans and Afro-Latin Americans, who both criticized and praised U.S. policies. Likewise, discussions of Pan Americanism have largely ignored the joint programs embarked upon by U.S. African Americans, Afro-Caribbeans and Afro-Latin Americans. Including these alternate perspectives of the discussion of U.S. Pan Americanism, particularly those perspectives that surfaced amid widespread struggles against U.S. intervention in the Americas, antiblack prejudices and the dilution of black radical leadership, reveals the centrality of race and racial equality in the landscape of inter-American affairs. Within the larger context of the NAACP's focus on independence struggles in Africa and Asia and also U.S. African American civil rights, White emphasized the futility of hemispheric unity and the failure of Pan American programs if the United States did not confront the systemic racism against blacks at home and abroad.

Acting on his beliefs and in full collaboration with the Haitian govern ment, White launched an inter-American PR campaign that spotlighted the promise of the republic of Haiti, a nation that had embodied black pride and radical anti-imperialism in the U.S. African American consciousness since the nineteenth century.[3]

Walter White's Public Relations Campaign, 1947–1955

The first record of White discussing plans to change U.S. perceptions of Haiti and to assist the country's economic and cultural development is a letter dated August 22, 1947.[4] Writing to his close friend William Hastie, governor of the U.S. Virgin Islands, White commented on the natural beauty of Haiti and the Virgin Islands and on their potential to become an economically sound, industrial nation-state and territory, respectively. White's statements in June 1950 to Haitian president Magloire exemplified his early goals for Haiti. He and the NAACP wished for "enlightened and unselfish investment capital to flow through Haiti," adding that "We want to see the economic, educational, health and the cultural status of the most impoverished Haitian raised to a more affluent and permanent level."[5] At the inception of the PR campaign, the secretary formulated a humanitarian and capitalist agenda in which tourism advertisements, positive and cultur- ally empathetic publicity and acts of Haitian/U.S. American cooperation would attract foreign tourists and investment to Haitian shores. In turn, White and the Haitian government believed that educating outsiders about Haitian culture and society would increase cash flow to the island, benefit- ting the Haitian economy, its masses and its infrastructure.

The PR campaign developed in several stages. First, White discussed his concerns with Haitian president Dumarsais Estimé and with members of the PR firm Frank H. Berend & Associates in 1947. This firm devised a preliminary plan to raise large amounts of capital to publicize Haitian tour- ism and to sway popular opinion by direct monetary contributions, events, tourist parties, lotteries and sport shows. Berend & Associates' initial ideas demonstrated genuine intent to change Haiti's image. Yet, according to White, their plans to organize a "better understanding between Haiti and the United States" lacked substance. Many of the proposed events fulfilled a solely profit-driven agenda that lacked the practicality, cultural sensitivity and intelligence the secretary demanded to counterbalance the infusion of capital. One particular event called for the expansion of the Haitian lottery to an international scale. Other suggested fund-raising events included a Madison Square Garden Haiti Night, an annual dinner at the Waldorf-Astoria for the Friends of Haiti, a cruise featuring top entertainers from the United States and a program that would attempt to dispel disparaging U.S. opinions of *vodou*. According to the firm's memo, this opinion shift could be accomplished "by bringing Voodoo into the open and making it what it actually is—a deep, religious fervor."[6] Unimpressed with the firm's superficial ideas, White later rejected Berend & Associates' proposal.

The second stage of the campaign dates to September 1947, when White wrote to Ambassador Charles with his own proposal suggesting that a formal institution be created to protect Haiti's interests. White called for collaboration of Haitian experts and an interracial committee of U.S. specialists to oversee and counsel Haitians on affairs such as finance, education, agriculture, forestry, literature and tourism. Organizing a joint Haiti/U.S. advocacy committee proved a protracted experience. White's appeals for a Conference of Progressives, his continued battles with W.E.B. Du Bois concerning the direction of the NAACP and his consultation of the 1948 UN General Assembly in Paris regarding human rights violations and the systematic disempowerment of African-descended peoples probably shifted White's attention away from coordinating a Haiti/United States commission in 1947 and 1948.[7] By June 1949, on the heels of one of Haiti's largest national celebrations and tourist attractions, the Bicentennaire Exposition Internationale, White reintroduced the idea of creating a Haitian-American advisory board based in the United States, in collaboration with the Peter Hilton Advertising Agency.

The Haitian-American Advisory Board for the Economic Development of Haiti, as it was named, sought to organize "new enterprises in Haiti on a basis which would protect the interests of Haiti and its people." White believed that "there [was] a reservoir of ability and goodwill in the United States, which could actualize such an institution."[8] As a tireless defender of integration and U.S.-style democracy, as long as democratic theory remained consistent with practice, White understood that the United States and an interracial body of U.S. American specialists were particularly equipped to help realize Haiti's technological and financial development. Many U.S. African American integrationists, social scientists and policymakers looked to the United States as a model and a center for economic development for less developed nations. In fact, White was often criticized by the U.S. African American Left, particularly by W.E.B. Du Bois, for his political allegiance to President Truman and his calculated conformity to Washington's politics on U.S. domestic and foreign policy during the early Cold War period. As an elite-driven integrationist and activist, White completely recognized the power that Washington wielded and the authority that U.S. investors maintained on an international scale; that was why he advocated for the Haitian-American advisory board to be located in the United States. Given U.S. influence in global affairs, White believed that the United States possessed the power to effect change in the periphery of the African diaspora, a view that many U.S. black intellectuals have held since the nineteenth century.[9]

In spite of White's political alignment with liberal white elites such as Eleanor Roosevelt and Nelson A. Rockefeller in the late 1940s, he remained wary of foreign and exclusively profit-driven motives in Haiti, such as inappropriate business schemes by U.S. venture capitalists and politicians. In his proposal to establish the Haitian-American advisory board, White warned against the possibility of U.S. investors entering into such a group strictly to benefit themselves. The secretary argued: "In view of the fact that the basic motive of the founders of the corporation would be to assist Haiti and not commercial, the ultimate profits of the corporation should not accrue to the benefit of individuals."[10] Just as White believed in the political and economic might of U.S. capitalists and elected officials, he also understood how power and profit corrupt. White's political and economic interests in Haiti stemmed from his anti-imperialist activism during U.S. occupation of Haiti (1915–1934), when gross abuses of Haitian sovereignty by the U.S. military (such as the United States taking control of the Haitian treasury) and physical violence against the Haitian masses became common institutional practices.[11] White's memories of U.S. exploits in Haiti may have informed his compassionate mission for this transnational advisory board. He stated in his subsequent 1949 proposal to President Estimé that the organization would be "run as a business and would have a grasp of business technique but its motivation would be humanitarian" and its eventual earnings devoted to the Haitian people and the economy.[12]

There is little evidence that the board existed beyond its proposal stage, perhaps because of White's failing health, "late-in-life future plans and intra-association [NAACP] bickering," which caused him to take a leave of absence.[13] These issues were compounded by personal and professional matters that diverted his attention from the execution of the Haitian-American advisory board in 1948 and 1949, which included the controversy about White's romantic affair with and subsequent marriage to Poppy Cannon, a white woman, and criticism leveled against White by a number of NAACP board members, including Arthur Spingarn and Channing Tobias, a YMCA official who questioned White's "energy" to the mission of the NAACP.[14] In addition, when White decided to return as executive secretary of the NAACP, the acting secretary, Roy Wilkins, stubbornly objected to accepting a "subordinate position in the NAACP hierarchy," which may have briefly shifted White's priorities.

By 1950, as White reassumed leadership at the NAACP, it became clear to the board of directors that White functioned as only the "titular head" of the organization. Walter White biographer Kenneth R. Janken asserts that White aspired to "ease into a semiretirement" and sought to choose new ventures at his leisure.[15] The vigor that White imparted to the Haitian PR campaign in 1947 and 1948 resurfaced in the early 1950s. On September 16, 1950, Poppy and Walter White held a conference at their home in West Redding, Connecticut, where leading U.S. figures such as Eleanor Roosevelt, Ralph Bunche, federal judge Julius Waties Waring and various U.S. state officials contemplated improving Haiti's image. Although Janken maintains that the event "took on the flavor" of a day of rest and relaxation rather than that of an "earnest policy-proposing gathering," I argue that this event did provide the necessary momentum to execute White and Cannon's program of uplift through positive publicity.[16]

Additionally, what remained apparent was that the Haitian cause of economic and social development was gaining support among elite U.S. sympathizers. Noteworthy political and business figures such as Eleanor Roosevelt, Mary McLeod Bethune, an educator, a civil rights activist and the founder of Bethune-Cookman College, and Samuel Pryor, vice president of Pan American Airways, served as sponsors for events and advocated for change in Haiti. The Haitian government awarded Bethune the Haitian Order of Honor and Merit in 1949 for her work with Haitian orphans. Haiti's ability to garner public support from notable U.S. Americans and the publicity efforts of the NAACP helped create an air of excitement and anticipation about the country's tourist attractions, national events and cultural productions. To maintain momentum, White proposed that films be produced about Haiti that would encourage investment, foster appreciation for indigenous arts and crafts, promote native foods and increase sales of Barbancourt Haitian rum in U.S. stores.[17]

As early as the 1930s, Haiti had encouraged international relations with the express purpose of enlarging its tourist industry. Haitian art and folk-loric dance entertained audiences in galleries and on the international stage with the aid of art educators Selden Rodman and DeWitt Peters and dancers such as Jean-Léon Destiné, Katherine Dunham and Lavinia Williams. In 1944, Peters established the Centre D'Art in Port-au-Prince, where Haitian artists painted, sculpted and developed their crafts, many of which depicted *vodou* culture, peasant life and the historical moments of the Haitian Revolution.[18]

In addition to promoting consumption of Haitian goods and services, White recommended holding a conference on Pan American education at the University of Haiti, in Port-au-Prince. The purpose of the conference would be "to analyze, improve and unify educational systems for the Americas in the democratic processes." Suggesting that supporters seek financial aid from the Rockefeller and Rosenwald foundations, two philanthropic institutions that were in full support of the aims of U.S. foreign policy, White believed that such a vision "would affirmatively place Haiti in the foreground of intellectual leadership and should be far more effective than mere denials of Haiti's intellectual backwardness."[19]

The suggestions and changes outlined in White's proposal would remain irrelevant if he and the Haitian government failed to raise implementation funds. As it turned out, Haiti's agriculture-based economy was unable to generate enough profits to collaborate in a multiyear publicity blitz with participating U.S. corporations, namely the Peter Hilton PR firm. Although Haiti's cash-crop division expanded, the value of exports between 1951 and 1955 was less than that achieved under U.S. occupation, particularly in the profitable span of 1924 to 1928.[20] Michel-Rolph Trouillot attributed the decline of exports to an increase in domestic consumption of agricultural goods due to the Haitian peasantry's exponential population growth between 1930 and 1950 and migration of peasants to urban centers.[21] Also, beginning in the 1940s, "ecological degradation" played a significant role in the systematic decline of the agricultural economy. White's memorandum to Ambassador Charles made it clear that he understood Haiti did not possess the capital to invest in "expensive propaganda" or to attract U.S. or international investors. At the same time, upon White's suggestion, the Haitian government entered into a contract with the Peter Hilton agency. As early as July 1950, an "embarrass[ed]" White had to intervene and petition the Magloire administration to pay its debts. "The reputation of Haiti itself would not be enhanced in the [U.S.] American business world," wrote

White, "should the word get around that it is not a responsible government with which to deal."[22]

Haiti struggled to distance itself from a colonial legacy during the post-U.S. occupation period. As one author notes, capitalist centers are "inherently inward-looking (even if expansionist): they exercise primary control over a definite territory and derive their momentum from the dynamics of coercion and consent within that space."[23] Marginalized countries were perpetually caught within a web of conflict and tension between the control of the state and the control "inherent in [foreign] dependency."[24] Despite having achieved independence, Haiti still bore the burdens of imperialism and economic dependency from its nineteenth-century past when British, French and German foreign traders in Haiti "favored the foreign merchants in the race for the Treasury's riches."[25] During the late nineteenth and early twentieth century Haiti relied more and more on foreign governments and traders and began to use foreign-trade taxes extracted from the Haitian peasantry to pay off its debt. The Haitian state's dependence skyrocketed, and, according to one 1892 committee of inquiry, "all the funds generated by the export duties on coffee, cacao, and logwood were committed to ensure the service of the loans whose origin had been the immoderate expenditures of the administration."[26]

At the onset of U.S. military intervention (1915–1934), the United States intensified Haiti's financial problems in two major ways: by augmenting the coffee export industry and by "raising the share of the value of imports and exports sucked up by the state through custom duties."[27] In 1947, President Dumarsais Estimé responded to the economic pressures of North American imperialism when the United States reminded the government of an expected loan payment authorized in 1922, while under U.S. occupation. Estimé, confronting the endless and insurmountable obstacles of financial debt and lack of control of fiscal operation, strongly advocated for "financial emancipation" from the U.S. government. The president publicly stated:

> Your [U.S.] government, born of a revolution which proclaimed for individual freedom from servitude and from fears and [from] nations a universal democracy, that is to say for the right of nations to dispose of themselves, your government then, cannot fail to strive for what each good Haitian in his heart desires—*financial emancipation*. In short the problem is placed upon us to ascertain if we can be

in a position to give to this country the proper working equipment for draining, irrigation, reforestation; a careful planned agricultural program so that not one centimeter of soil may remain unproductive; an industrial plan that will assure the manufacture . . . of certain raw materials, to the end that we may become less dependent upon the foreigner for certain products of prime necessity. . . .[28]

Entrenched in Estimé's plea to the United States to forgive Haitian debt, or at least to provide some relief of payments, lay the expectations and frustrations of the Haitian citizenry at home and abroad toward U.S. foreign policy. In 1946, the New York branch of L'Union Patriotique Haïtienne, a national civil rights and independence organization organized during U.S. occupation, sent a memorandum to the U.S. State Department challenging Washington's stranglehold on the Haitian economy. L'Union Patriotique located its homeland's economic hardship in the matrix of an imperial legacy and the political ideology of the Good Neighbor Policy. The organization argued:

. . . that each country [Haiti and the United States] in its own way is the other's largest customer, and that the dependence of the Haitian economy on the United States makes it a matter of life or death to the Haitian people as to whether the relationship between the two nations is friendly or otherwise. Haiti accepts the principle of the Good Neighbor Policy as the foundation of her national and foreign policy and hopes that the United States will reciprocate her desires and wishes.[29]

L'Union Patriotique's statement should be understood in the context of U.S. pressure on Haitian officials to modify their constitution to enable the United States to gain a stronger foothold in the Haitian economy. President Estimé sought to protect the government on issues such as foreign ownership and non-Haitian involvement in commercial activities; however, as Plummer asserts, the Haitian legislature "compromised on most of these matters" by consenting to expand non-Haitian rights to own real estate and by permitting foreigners to "control investments through Haitian managers."[30] Thus, Haitians in the United States and within the nation articulated a challenge to Washington to deal with the black republic on a fairer and more egalitarian stage, similar to the actions and statements made by

White and other U.S. African Americans within this black Pan American space. Yet the asymmetrical economic relations between the Haitian and U.S. governments typically led to a Haitian compromise.

In a letter to President Truman, White boldly exposed the United States' generous lending practices to nonblack nations. He argued that "some of these loans have been to countries which clearly indicated that they had neither the ability nor the intention to repay such loans."[31] Declaring that such actions could be construed as examples of "Yanqui imperialism" and racial bigotry, White called for an increase in U.S. aid to Haiti. The secretary's actions and his support of Haiti did not go unnoticed by Haitians living in the United States. As early as 1944, Haitians applauded White's efforts to help their native land and to promote an authentic inter-American cooperation. Henri Rosemond, a journalist who worked closely with the Haitian Afro-American Chamber of Commerce Commission in 1934 and served as executive secretary of the Etoiles du Tropique Club (Tropical Stars Club), a Haitian cultural organization in Brooklyn, New York, praised White's diligent work "for the development of the Good Neighbor Policy, and a Cordial Entente in the Americas especially between the Republic of Haiti and the United States of America."[32] Rosemond also made White an honorary member of the Etoiles du Tropique Club. The reshaping of Pan American ideology by U.S. African Americans and Haitians to deal with race and to denounce the perpetuation of economic imperial legacies, in addition to Haiti's own historic problems exacerbated by a culture of economic dependency and U.S. intervention, carved out a black Pan American space by the 1940s and 1950s for this public relations campaign to be justified and supported by the Haitian government.

The Haitian government fully supported White's PR campaign in 1949. After obtaining the support of Estimé, whose *noiriste* administration intensified Haitian color politics and "ideological polarization," the "efforts and projected outcomes of the campaign" held Ambassador Charles' "best attention."[33] Charles worked in close collaboration with the Peter Hilton Advertising Agency, of which Poppy Cannon, White's wife, was an employee. Charles demanded that the Hilton Agency be more specific in its reports to Haitian tourist offices in Port-au-Prince and in New York and that it be more strategic in its approach to potential tourists:

You have written that an average of 50 to 60 inquiries on the advantages touristically and commercially of Haiti are received every day by the [Hilton] firm. But no precise statistics, daily, weekly or monthly are given, no exact number received from each state of the Union listed. . . . Such a statistical table would give a clearer idea of the intensity and result of the propaganda campaign. . . . It is not sufficient to receive numerous requests for information on Haiti, but it is necessary that the brochures, bulletins, pamphlets, and the replies which are made be of a nature to influence . . . the traveler to eventually [choose] a voyage to Haiti.[34]

Over the next few years, the PR campaign executed a tactical publicity blitz by effectively using U.S. television, radio and print media sources such as the *New York Times, Reader's Digest, Ebony* and *Jet* to build its cultural tourist industry.[35] One 1956 *Jet* article titled "Beauty in Haiti" showcased and exoticized Haitian women so as to lure tourists to experience the "island beauties."[36] The French Riviera and other European destinations, according to White, would be inactive due to the structural and economic devastation of World War II. Moreover, White noted during the early years of a U.S.-led European recovery plan and anticommunist agenda that "the unrest resulting in riots and revolutions in Europe, the fantastic cost of living because of inflation, and the anti-U.S. propaganda spread particularly by Russia in Italy, France and other parts of Europe" would decrease U.S. and European tourism to these places again.[37] As a result, Haiti was "ideally suited" to attract U.S. travelers of the "right type" with U.S. currency. According to White, the "right type" of tourists abstained from gambling, maintained good moral standing and possessed the "right type of attitude towards race."

Haitian tourism prospered during the presidencies of Estimé and Magloire (1946–1956). Middle-class liberal white visitors and elite U.S. African Americans and Haitians embraced Haitian history and indigenous art, music and dance. The erection of new buildings, hotels, roads, casinos and highways attracted more vacationers. Additionally, a $4 million loan from the Export-Import Bank of Washington allowed for irrigation and agricultural projects in the Artibonite Valley to take root. The completion of these projects created the illusion of progress.[38] The Estimé administration spent millions preparing for its bicentennial exposition in 1949 and 1950, despite Haiti's struggling economy and critiques from Haitians, particularly journalist Henri Rosemond.[39] Back in the States, White enthusiastically reported on Haiti's progress in an April 1950 press release: "Less than a year ago many of the people, especially in the rural areas which make up most of this excitingly beautiful country, seemed to be clothed chiefly in patched garments—immaculately clean but nevertheless rags. Today one almost never sees such badges of poverty but instead inexpensive but whole garments even on women and men working in the fields."[40] In a significant gesture of support for Truman's foreign aid in Latin America and the Caribbean, White attributed Haiti's ephemeral gains to the "wisdom of the Point Four Program," an agenda that made financial assistance a priority in U.S. foreign policy by 1950.[41]

The secretary's backing of Truman, despite the administration's abysmal record on civil rights, proved to be a deliberate move by White and certain members of the NAACP because their support would preserve the elite connections of this historic civil rights organization. Direct pressures and the threat of being isolated from Washington's decisions on civil and human rights compromised U.S. African American leadership during the Cold War. Biographer Janken astutely asserted: "The foreign and domestic cold war made White's emphasis on lobbying obsolete because government officials were demanding conformity as the price of access."[42] For White, "the price of access" made evident his unwillingness to sacrifice privileged relationships with key U.S. officials in order that domestic and international programs, organizations and financial and technical assistance were fulfilled.

Despite the secretary's credit to Truman's Point Four Program, he also acknowledged Estimé's leadership in the material progress of Haiti. In a letter to then Colonel Paul Magloire, which expressed his disappointment with the ousting of Estimé by Magloire's army (1950), White stated that "within the past two years [the Estimé administration] transformed the reputation of Haiti being a poor country inhabited by uneducated people to its true status as one of the most charming places in the world."[43] And in lieu of the chaotic shift in executive power in Haiti, White remained gravely concerned with preserving Haiti's perceived progress because as White aptly stated to Magloire in May 1950 "what happens in Haiti has repercussions which far transcend Haiti itself."[44]

After Estimé's presidency, authoritarian and military leadership was reestablished in Haiti. Having led state repression of the Haitian Left since Estimé's rule, Magloire's conservative government sympathized with the Haitian bourgeoisie, dismantled much of the *noiriste* and "black consciousness" gains of the Haitian masses and black middle class, and was heralded by Washington as an anticommunist protector of U.S. interests.[45] Further-more, Magloire's continuous abuses of Haitian opponents and adversarial print media such as the Peasant Worker Movement (MOP), the Popular Socialist Party, *La Nation* and *La Réveil* caught the attention of White, who threatened to reveal Haitian government repression.[46] White's 1951 warn-ing to Magloire and Ernest Chauvet, a Haitian representative to the United Nations, demonstrated a potentially bold move by the secretary. White be-lieved he possessed the upper hand because of his elite connections with U.S. investors, philanthropic foundations and policymakers. However, he also had much to lose if Haiti presented itself as totalitarian and susceptible to graft.

White's word of caution to Magloire proved to be empty or at least compromised, yet again, by his political and personal investment in the black republic. Government repression continued at the same time that of-ficial Haitian reports boasted of improvements in the tourist industry and other infrastructural undertakings under Magloire's five-year development plan:

> The laying with asphalt of the national highways . . . is progressing nicely while simultaneously in the main cities of the country the as-phalting of the streets is carried on satisfactorily. . . . Several of our best hotels are expanding and new beach sites are being laid out. . . . As a matter of fact the number of tourists visiting our country has jumped from 8,404 in 1949 to 13,582 in 1950, while 1951 has brought on a new increase of 30% on the 1950 figure. According to the forecast of the governmental tourist bureau the increase for 1952 will be consider-ably higher.[47]

Haiti's projected increase in tourist arrivals and its anticipated cut into the $19 billion in tourist revenue in the Caribbean market demonstrated a windfall for Haitian tourism.[48] Tourist visits to Puerto Rico and Haiti doubled and quintupled respectively between 1949 and 1954, while Cuba's share of the Caribbean market declined in those years.[49] Thus, with the promise of an emerging tourist industry in Haiti, White seemed optimistic and for a time turned a blind eye to Magloire's politics of repression.

Information from Harry Truman's office also revealed the advancements of Point Four projects in Haiti. George M. Elsey, assistant to the director of the Office of Mutual Security, an executive office of the president, wrote to White in October 1952 confirming:

In addition to control operations through clinics and mobile units, a public health education program in sanitation, nurse training, and construction of water supply systems [are] being carried on throughout the country. . . . Haitian and American technicians are operating extension offices which help farmers to modernize methods of crop and livestock production. Agricultural technicians are also assisting to organize '4–H' type clubs and cooperatives. Improved seed for crops, fruit and reforestation seedlings are also distributed. . . .[50]

Positive updates between 1950 and 1952 served as balms over White's angry wounds about Magloire's coup d'état and Haitian state abuses. In addition, it remained unlikely that White would publicly chastise Magloire's administration when White's own wife, Poppy, served as an official publicity agent of the Haitian government. Highly publicized news of Haitian material progress obscured the reality that Haiti remained overly dependent on its agricultural exports and that industrialization remained elusive. Minimal agriculture increases in the country's GNP did occur in 1951 and 1952, but Haitian agricultural output actually declined. The optimistic and ubiquitously upbeat publicity demonstrating the development of Haitian infrastructure and agricultural sectors covered up the truth that "agricultural yields had slowly regressed to nineteenth century levels" due to an increase in the peasant population, migration to the urban centers and environmental degradation.[51]

Despite setbacks in agriculture and industry, the PR campaign became even stronger under Magloire's watch. In 1951, the establishment of the Haiti Tourist Information Bureau (HTIB), led by Gérard de Catalogne, in New York City's Rockefeller Plaza, exemplified the profound impact that White's campaign had on Haitian tourism. This organization served as a source of news, photographs, editorials and posters pertaining to Haitian politics, culture, tourism and opportunities for trade in the black republic. Hollywood attempted to profit from Haiti's popularity by beginning talks about premiering the movie *Lydia Bailey* in Haiti. In April 1952, Guy Laraque, an official with the tourism bureau in Haiti, proudly stated in a letter to Catalogne that "Haiti is happening to become one of the greatest tourist centers of the Caribbean," adding that last year's tourist season had been "excellent, all the hotels were filled, the visitors were satisfied."[52] Five months later, Haitian secretary of state Mauclair Zéphirin happily expressed his gratitude to White and his wife Poppy Cannon after a recent visit:

. . . His Excellency is pleased to note the continuous efforts that you exert in favor of Haiti, with the aid of Mme. White [Poppy Cannon]. Your commentary on the radio has captured the broad range of the [U.S.] American public and is a certain sign of the success of your propaganda in favor of our country who count you as one of its dearest friends.[53]

Tourist arrivals continued to improve until the early days of François Duvalier's regime, "from a total of 17,708 in 1951 to 65,766 in 1956."[54]

In conjunction with the existing Haiti Tourist Bureau, established in 1928, and the U.S.-based Haiti Tourist Information Bureau, Cannon's objective was "to convince potential investors" (more than likely U.S. investors) to provide capital to the new Magloire regime.[55] Her responsibilities, an obvious extension of White's work, encompassed five facets—governmental and political affairs, economic affairs, tourism, public relations and advertising—which were to be performed in union with Magloire's five-year economic development plan, devised in 1951. One of the plan's main projects was damming Haiti's biggest river, the central Artibonite, to irrigate some 120,000 acres of land. Additional projects included building agricultural schools, establishing a farmer's bank and constructing some 300 miles of paved road. However, much of Haiti's aid from U.S. and UN assistance programs, $5,959,000 and $637,800 respectively in the early 1950s, including matched funds by Haiti ($8.2 million), did not pay for "reconstruction of the infrastructure" but rather was allotted to pay Haiti's external debt.[56] Given these financial obstacles, White proudly declared to Secretary of State John Dulles in 1953: "If ever there was an 'operation bootstrap,' what Haiti is doing merits such a description."[57]

Although Haiti's paltry funds were not solely used for reconstruction efforts, Cannon effectively promoted Magloire's economic development plan to "potential investors," the media and U.S. representatives to attract capital to the country. In September 1951, she asserted to Haitian minister of state Luc E. Fouche that she had received a number of inquiries from investors on the basis of the secretary's word in the *New York Herald Tribune* that corruption within the Haitian government had ceased. Cannon reported:

One of the inquirers is interested in ascertaining by means of a geologic survey whether there may not be manganese and other materials in Haiti. Another is interested in cane products which would be converted into industrial alcohol. A third has expressed interest in investment in hotel and other accommodations which would increase the tourist trade.[58]

Without a doubt, Cannon's efforts were essential to the success of her PR campaign. She emphasized "good pictures" of Haiti's progress, encouraged human interest stories and prepared material to be published, viewed and heard in media sources, both those centered on U.S. African American life and those written for mainstream Anglo-America. She even suggested gourmet food products, such as fine salt from Gonaïves, for epicurean travelers to try and advised that historical markers be created to indicate monuments of significance as tourist sites.[59] Haiti needed to diversify its economy, and Cannon's suggestions sought to implement various sources of income. In many ways, White and Cannon believed that an infusion of capital into the black republic would be pivotal to reconstructing the nation's identity in the eyes of non-Haitians.

Examining tourism as a development strategy of White's and Cannon's PR campaigns facilitates the dialogue between modernization and economic dependency of Haiti from U.S. occupation through the Magloire regime. Modernization theory or theories on marginal capitalist societies highlight the limitations of tourism as a development strategy. Modernization theory originated during the post-World War II era and was perceived by many social scientists as a means of merging various disciplines to empirically comprehend political, social and economic development. Scholar Michael Latham argued that these theorists and their policy-making allies advanced "liberal social values, economic organization and democratic political structures" to developing nations, at the same time permitting the United States to arrest the spread of Communism.[60] Members of the Council on African Affairs (CAA) favored these liberal tenets of modernization. According to historian Penny Von Eschen, Paul Robeson and Max Yergan supported postwar economic restructuring and argued for the need to find "new markets" in order to circumvent a global economic failure. Yergan argued: "Raising the living standard . . . to a new and higher level is an indispensable condition for gaining economic security in the post-war world."[61] Walter White's position on the modernization of Haiti and tourism as means to raise the living standard was consistent with CAA ideology during the postwar period.

The emergence of Haiti's tourist industry did not necessarily help the country's pursuit of financial emancipation and economic independence.

Tourism placed a tremendous strain on the country's human resources and local infrastructures such as electrical and water supplies and sewage disposal systems. Haitians endured many economic disadvantages: low levels of income; unequal distribution of income and wealth; high levels of unemployment and underemployment; a heavy dependence on agriculture; and high levels of foreign ownership of manufacturing and service industries such as the Standard Fruit Company and the Haitian-American Sugar Mill Company.[62] An examination of the Haitian tourist guides produced in the 1950s reveals the disproportionate amount of alien ownership of products and institutions established for the tourist economy. U.S.-owned Delta Airlines and Pan American Airways and KLM Royal Dutch Airlines offered daily and weekly flights. Avis Rent A Car System, LLC, provided the bulk of car rental services. RCA Communications and All America Cables and Radio owned and operated a considerable volume of direct-radio facilities in Port-au-Prince. With the exception of Barbancourt rum and Haitian-produced handcrafts, travelers were encouraged to purchase duty-free, non-Haitian products such as perfumes, jewelry, clothing and glassware at the Free Port Shopping Center, in Port-au-Prince.[63] Modernization theory, which often emphasized emulating Western modes of industrial and technological development, underscored the potential of tourism as a form of modernization that "transfers capital, technology, expertise and 'modern' values from the West to less developed countries (LDC)."[64] For the most part, the Haitian government and elite U.S. African Americans accepted this form of development because they believed that the tourism industry possessed a compound effect that linked tourism development with business and job creation. Some working-class Haitians and former peasants who moved to urban centers benefited minimally from tourism, particularly in the service industry, where they served as taxi drivers and waiters, and in the handicrafts industry. However, overcrowding in the cities placed a grave strain on available resources.[65]

Strengthening inter-American ties between Haitian and U.S. leadership proved essential to the PR campaign's plans of ensuring the spread of democracy in Haiti, encouraging capitalist development and opening an avenue that would enable Haiti to apply for more U.S. aid. After making a trip to Haiti in 1953, White communicated to Paul Magloire that the NAACP pledged "to continue to help in your struggle to provide a more abundant life for Haiti's people and to strengthen democracy in the Western Hemisphere."[66] White and Cannon pushed vigorously for the U.S. State epartment to accept Magloire as an official visitor to the White House. If Magloire were accepted, he could press the United States for Point Four aid, a U.S. program that made foreign aid a "permanent element of national policy."[67]

In 1951, White and Cannon worked to bring Magloire to the United States. Coupled with the fact they desired to attract U.S. investors and to lobby for more Point Four aid, their reasoning also addressed race and Communism. White believed that Magloire's trip provided a small but significant step in challenging prevailing images of racial discrimination and racial violence against U.S. blacks by U.S. communists. The U.S. government supported programs during the Cold War that attempted to respond to or rather offset international readings of U.S. white supremacy by sending refined artists and musicians to Eastern Europe, Asia and Africa.[68] Washington believed that the presence of these cultural ambassadors would promote the notion of U.S. democratic ideals of racial tolerance. White emphasized: "At this time when the United States is being bitterly assailed among the colored peoples of the world who constitute two-thirds of the world's population an invitation to President Magloire would have both deep significance and value in demonstrating to the enemies of America that many of the stories about race prejudice in this country are not accurate."[69] Voiced at a time when racial discrimination and segregation of blacks prevailed in the United States and the NAACP's legal and economic efforts to combat racial violence and discrimination had become more pronounced, White's blatantly inaccurate statements about U.S. race relations may startle readers today. However, placed in the context of Washington's "new arrangement" concerning U.S. black activists, the secretary's softened stance on racial injustices and its international connections reinforced the power of Cold War politics and the vulnerability of its black opponents and sympathizers. Inevitably, the secretary's statements and opinions on race in this transnational context were consistent with his ideas about the PR campaign. They attempted to develop and reshape notions of race and/or blackness so as to fit an ideal U.S. representation of race and racial attitudes.

Albert Mangones, a Haitian architect and a cousin of Jacques Roumain, noted Haitian writer and founder of the Haitian Communist Party, indirectly challenged the aforementioned anticommunist spirit of the secretary's claim as early as July 1948. Angered by the U.S. embassy's influence on the architect's access to his own visa due to his "personal politics," Mangones declared that if a society that supported "effective measures against illiteracy, effective struggle against the appalling poverty of our masses, effective guarantee of individual freedom . . . effective universal suffrage, effective liberation from foreign control [and] effective struggle against foreign monopolies and imperialism" be regarded as "communist, anarchist or un-american . . . [then] I am still for it."[70] Mangones concluded that if he were "to be subjected [to] Jim Crow practice as well as the Lincoln tradition, the sanctity of the profit motive as well as the People's generosity, the Truman doctrine as well as Roosevelt's Four Freedoms—then I would choose not to go to such a new America. . . ."[71] Mangones' statement, carefully read by White and the NAACP, exemplified the disconnect between Haitian laborers and professionals sympathetic to socialist ideology and U.S. African American supporters of democratic capitalism. It highlighted the rupture that the threat of communism caused to transnational race relations among blacks. Socialist politics in Haiti and other nations in the Americas largely deteriorated during the Cold War period because of U.S. political and economic influence and well-funded U.S. dissemination of democratic and capitalistic ideals. Haitian dependence on democratic and capitalist centers and White's campaign functioned as important factors in weakening the Haitian communist movement.

Upon Magloire's arrival in the States, White and Cannon arranged public meetings for him in New York City. In addition, Columbia and Howard universities bestowed honorary degrees on the Haitian president, as did Fisk University in Tennessee. Cannon attempted to arrange meetings with top officials of the Ford Foundation, such as Paul Hoffman, Dr. Robert Hutchins and Chester Davis. U.S. philanthropic organizations during the interwar and postwar periods mimicked and supported the goals of U.S. foreign policy.[72] Reaching out to the Ford and Rockefeller foundations was a way to strengthen relations between the Haitian government and U.S. foundations, which could provide developmental capital to Haiti. With U.S. funds, foreign investors benefiting from financial relations and cultural exchange proved imminent. Conversely, the idea of creating a Haitian-American Economic Resources Board composed of Haitians and U.S. Americans of distinction resurfaced as a way to affirm the place of Haitian officials at the decision-making table. On January 5, 1955, President Magloire arrived in the United States and on January 27 he gave an address before a joint session of the Senate and the House of Representatives.[73] A symbol of ultimate exposure and publicity in the United States, *Time* magazine put Magloire on its cover and told readers that "by the standards of 1954 model

Fig. 4.1. *Left to right:* Fisk University president Charles S. Johnson and George Redd, dean of the College of Higher Studies, honor Haitian president Paul Magloire with an honorary doctorate, Nashville, Tennessee, February 3, 1955. (Photo reproduced courtesy of Bettmann/CORBIS.)

materialism the world's first black republic should perhaps still be reckoned an [un]sanitary, barefoot failure. But by less pragmatic standards, it must be counted a heart warming success—gentle, peaceable, individualistic, persevering and utterly free."[74] *Time*'s article lacked trumpeting words of praise; nonetheless, White and Cannon were pleased at Haiti's exposure on a grand scale. Subsequently after returning to Haiti, Magloire wrote White in February 1955 thanking the secretary for his long-term work for Haiti and declared that "excellent relations . . . exist between *brothers* of the same race living in the United States and in Haiti."[75]

Conclusion

The fanfare that surrounded President Magloire's arrival in the United States in 1955 marked the pinnacle of White's PR campaign. From the winter of 1955 until 1956, the rumblings of another political disruption were heard throughout Haiti as Duvalierist forces established claims on the presidency, threatening to disrupt the tourist industry. On the evening of March 21, 1955, Walter White, a diligent and indefatigable supporter of Haiti, collapsed from a fatal heart attack in his New York home. White's death marked the official end of his Haitian PR campaign. Claude Barnett's ANP service issued a press release about a week later remembering White and his fond memories of Haiti: "The great improvement which had been going on in Haiti had impressed Walter. Right in the Hotel Choucoune, the addition[al] wings with their ultra-modern air-cooled rooms, the new swimming pool surrounded by tropical fruit trees and flowers, the superior service, all were things about which he commented . . . [Moreover,] he was glad to see the increased flow of tourists."[76]

White's Haitian PR campaign can best be characterized as a U.S. African American- and Haitian-rooted black Pan American project whose center was rooted in racial progress for Haiti and U.S. blacks. Although it increased tourism and spurred U.S. interest in agricultural and industrial investment, it failed to counter the country's economic decline. White's campaign sought to introduce new economic and industrial growth into an overly dependent rural economy. In the minds of liberal modernization reformers, it was necessary for less developed countries to undergo a transition from an agricultural economy to an industrial one in order for the modernization process to occur. Tourism could provide that spark, reformers believed. It created jobs, afforded access to foreign (U.S.) currency, led to improvements in local infrastructure and established external economies. Rooted in a legacy of memory and black cultural production of the Haitian Revolution, White's PR crusade exposed tourists to Haitian history, culture and politics. Haiti served as the premier vacation spot for many U.S. Americans and Europeans during the late 1940s through the mid-1950s, the golden age of Haitian tourism.[77] However, tourism strained the country's already overburdened human resources and local infrastructures, making life even harder for poor Haitians. As a result of the state's emphasis on developing the tourist industry, it became overly dependent on foreign visitation while lacking the financial infrastructure and the political stability needed to support it. Most of the scanty funds that Estimé and Magloire acquired failed to complete infrastructural projects.[78]

The secretary's campaign often coincided with larger U.S foreign policy objectives—modernizing less-developed countries in the Caribbean and Latin America to promote the spread of democracy and capitalism so as to ensure U.S. influence. Then again, White sincerely worked for a new economic independence for the Haitian government, but the Haitian government's efforts, along with those of the NAACP, fell victim to Haiti's history and legacy of imperialism, intervention and underdevelopment.

The politics of the Cold War fostered an environment of fear and threatened U.S. African American radical leadership. Thus, U.S. African American integrationists had little choice but to support U.S. aims. White was no exception to this pattern. He was prodemocracy and procapitalist—a Pan Americanist who supported Roosevelt's Good Neighbor Policy at the same time that he defended nonwhite anti-imperialist struggles throughout the developing world.

Haiti remained a mythic country in White's imagination because its people had defeated European imperialism in the nineteenth century and persevered during U.S occupation. White believed that Haiti was a symbol, a trope of Afro-Modernity suffering under a system of economic dependency and, at times, a racist U.S. foreign policy perpetuated by its self-interests.[79] Indeed, the secretary's work, in collaboration with the Haitian state, to develop Haiti's economy and change its image corroborated a larger global process or political program to attack the effects of white supremacy. Thus, by aiding in the modernization of Haiti and fighting racism and economic inequality on all fronts, Haitians and U.S. blacks struggled to realize the tenets of Pan Africanism and Pan Americanism in order to produce a black Pan Americanism that specifically addressed American hemispheric issues.[80] Race mattered, and U.S. African American leaders, particularly, used this issue to challenge U.S.-style Pan Americanism and related foreign-policy objectives.

In 1941, White asked the question that many U.S. African Americans had struggled with since the American Revolution but more recently at the beginning of World War II: How could U.S. blacks defend democracy and U.S. ideals when they continually confronted antiblack prejudice? Fully aware of U.S. modernization efforts in Latin America and the Caribbean, White asserted to Nelson Rockefeller that the "continuation of the stereotypes of the Negro not only creates resentment in Latin America but is a matter of infinite irritation to American Negroes who are being asked to defend democracy."[81] Racial discrimination, the secretary asserted, operated as a threat to U.S. friendship and the Good Neighbor Policy. To combat racial prejudice and honor the tenets of inter-American cooperation, White recommended implementing several ideas and programs that would help the United States regain the trust of Latin American and Caribbean nations. He suggested that the Institute of Inter-American Affairs create an exchange program for U.S. African American students and professors with their counterparts in Latin America to discuss race and hemispheric solidarity. He also suggested that the institute arrange tours throughout Latin America by U.S. African American singers and musicians such as Marian Anderson, Paul Robeson and Duke Ellington. Furthermore, he recommended that the institute send a small commission of U.S. whites and blacks to ascertain "the extent of the hostility to the United States which has been created by race prejudice" so that they may "correct and overcome these misconceptions and prejudices" brewing in Latin America and the Caribbean.[82]

After 1945, both Haitians and U.S. blacks committed themselves not to the past but to the future. They redefined "America" not solely as the United States, but as the countries in the Western Hemisphere that needed one another to achieve real democracy and modernity at that moment of war and post-world war transition. Pan Americanism demonstrated that this movement was not just a political ideology organized around U.S. influence in the region, but, as Haitian ambassador Joseph Charles affirmed, it was "a belief made from faith and common love . . . to prepare the unity of the world. For this unity is the safe guard not only for our civilization, liberty and peace, but again it guarantees the human races very survival."[83]

5

"To Carry the Dance of the People Beyond"

Jean-Léon Destiné, Lavinia Williams
and *Danse Folklorique Haïtienne*

Developing effective cultural relations proved to be an important element in the Pan American project. U.S. African Americans, Caribbeans, Latinos and a few U.S. government officials understood that building and improving cultural programs and promoting the exchange of ideas (economic, technical and artistic) across boundaries might "break down some of the racial barriers" in the United States and in the international arena.[1] During the early 1940s, as described in the previous chapter, Walter White and the NAACP conveyed serious concerns to Nelson Rockefeller and others about the long-term "success" of the Good Neighbor Policy if the United States failed to address the issue of "color prejudice" and neglected to highlight some of the contributions that nonwhite citizens had made to inter-American affairs. Robert G. Caldwell, a cultural relations official in the U.S. government, agreed with White. Caldwell affirmed that the United States could not "overlook . . . the fairly complex racial question of Latin American peoples."[2] Several intellectual and educational programs were implemented at the state and federal levels but few critically addressed race, racism and imperialism in the Americas.[3]

At the local level, U.S. African Americans, Caribbeans and a few liberal whites in the United States believed that it was important to inform the U.S. American public about two main issues in the context of inter-American affairs: first, that there existed significant populations of African-descended peoples in Latin America and the Caribbean; and second, that their struggles and achievements proved important to the success of Pan Americanism and of race relations in the United States. In March 1942, Frank R. Crosswaith, chairman of the Negro Labor Committee, wrote to Walter White about a ten-week lecture series on "The Negro in the Western

Hemisphere" being offered by Ruediger Bilden, an anthropology professor at Fisk University and a research fellow at the Rockefeller Foundation.
The Harlem Labor Center on 125th Street sponsored the three-dollar-a-seat
Bilden lectures.[4] In Chicago, the Pan American Good Neighbor Forum, an
interracial and nonsectarian organization approved by Rockefeller's Coordinator of Inter-American Affairs (CIAA) office, which advocated the improvement of inter-American relations, also held several talks on "the relations of Negroes in the entire hemisphere."[5] These lectures and information
sessions rarely affected U.S. foreign policy in the Americas or the political
affairs of Caribbean and Latin American nations, but they informed many
individuals about the history and central roles black people and cultural
relations played in the development of Pan Americanism.

The cooperation between the Haitian government and Walter White in
the development of Haitian tourism served as one example of the significance of cross-cultural relations in inter-American affairs. Yet if the Haitian tourist industry in the 1950s prospered, what attracted middle- and
upper-class travelers? Notions of a "primitive" and "mysterious" Haiti intrigued many tourists. Haiti symbolized the Africa of the West, without
the long voyage, and maintained some semblance of U.S. influence. As
scholars Gérarde Magloire and Kevin Yelvington assert: "In the anthropological imagination of Haiti with its legacy of colonial and neocolonial
ethnography, itself a cousin to travel narratives, 'Africa,' 'Vodou' and 'Race,'
among others, have remained key images in the representation of Haiti
as a whole."[6] This "anthropological imagination" intersects with popular
ideas, and the images of "Africa," "Vodou" and "Race" become "synecdo-
ches, standing for 'African savagery' as part of a larger colonial discourse
on the religions of 'primitive' people regarded as fetishistic, superstitious,
cannibalistic. . . ."[7] Dance, in particular, Haitian folkloric dance, among
other cultural art forms, served as the vehicle through which many tourists authenticated their racist and paternalistic beliefs. Yet ethnographers
and Haitian and U.S. African American choreographers of Haitian folkloric
dance utilized this art form and shaped it to affirm their connections to an
African past and a history of racial slavery in the Americas. As part of an
ideological movement to study indigenous traditions such as *indigénisme*
and *négritude*, Haitian folkloric dance served two additional purposes.
First, it constructed a perception of an authentic Haitian cultural identity
that attempted to force the Haitian aristocracy to recognize the sacred and
secular contributions of the black masses to the formation of the nation and

include them in the economic and political decision-making of the state. Additionally, Haitian folkloric dance advanced the notion that the *peyizan* or black peasantry had created a cultural art form valuable enough to be praised locally and cherished internationally.[8] As the world began to recognize and appreciate Haitian art forms, Haitian folkloric dance operated as a vehicle to articulate Haiti's right to participate in inter-American and global affairs. In some ways, Haitian and U.S. African American dancers attempted to create community outside the world of policy. Yet the orbit of influence for Pan Americanism and its manifestations (e.g., the Good Neighbor Policy and the Alliance for Progress) proved vast, particularly when the political, cultural and economic relations of inter-American affairs informed cultural and intellectual exchange programs and U.S.-based scholarships. It is within this cross-cultural and cooperative framework that I examine the work of Jean-Léon Destiné and Lavinia Williams, two noted dancers/choreographers of Haitian folkloric dance.

During the week of April 7, 1951, the Haiti Tourist Information Bureau (HTIB) and the City of New York sponsored a series of cultural events celebrating "Haiti Week of New York." The festivities not only served as a platform to display the finest in Haitian culture but also functioned as an "appeal for collaboration" with the U.S. government and its citizens to fully participate in the economic revitalization of the Haitian republic.[9] Key to the bureau's "appeal" was building a sound tourist industry in Haiti that encouraged "[U.S.] Americans from New York and other states of this great Sister Republic [to] get better and better acquainted with this Tourist Paradise that Haiti represents. . . ."[10] The HTIB's reference to the United States as a "Sister Republic" echoed the tone of Franklin Roosevelt's Good Neighbor Policy, a U.S.-centered foreign policy that promoted nonintervention and cooperative economic and cultural programs in the Americas. Although there are ample critiques of asymmetrical hemispheric relations between the United States, Haiti and other Latin American countries, the Haitian government still courted collaborative financial ventures with the United States to alleviate the country's struggling economy.[11]

Haiti Week proved a critical moment in the development of Haitian tourism. Haitian cultural festivities in New York City were organized on the heels of significant political transition and economic depression in Haiti, particularly Magloire's coup d'état against President Estimé in May 1950. Furthermore, operating within a politically charged environment of the Cold War, in which the absence of sociopolitical freedoms in the United

States due to the threat of communism often pushed radical activists and intellectuals to call attention to the "cultural realm," "Haiti Week" also can be understood as a stage on which progressives could champion the notions of material and cultural advancement.[12] Reports and advertisements in the HTIB's official publication, *News of Haiti*, trumpeted Haiti's modern technological projects, such as the construction of new roads and buildings, which offered the illusion of progress.[13] Material advancement in Haiti accentuated the "illusions of pleasure" for the middle-class North American traveler despite the aftereffects of the 19-year-long U.S. occupation of Haiti, which had offered minimal structural improvement and held the country in arrears to U.S. investors. Celebrated Haitian and U.S. African American artists, dancers and literary figures such as Jean-Léon Destiné, Katherine Dunham and Jean Brierre participated in Haiti Week programs, sending the clear message that the arts were Haiti's most valuable resource.

This chapter focuses on the development of *danse folklorique Haïtienne* (Haitian folkloric dance) by Jean-Léon Destiné and Lavinia Williams and how they employed their art to entertain and educate audiences about Haitian culture, while using folkloric dance as a discipline with which to train Haitian dancers in the 1940s and 1950s. From the mid-1930s through the 1950s, the advancement and consumption of Haitian cultural arts gained the government's full support as a means to develop its fledgling tourist industry. In fact, many Caribbean administrations encouraged tourism during this time to complement industrialization and to answer the dilemmas of debt, unemployment and failing economies.[14] The emerging popularity of Haitian dance, as well as that of Haitian painting and music, attracted curious tourists and artists and helped reinvigorate Haitian cultural production and consumption. Paradoxically, this emphasis on the folkloric perpetuated elitist notions and racist images of Haitian culture as exotic and primitive.

The challenge for Haitian artists to escape "the trivialization of [their] culture as either exotic or demonic" in the minds of foreigners remains overwhelming.[15] Influenced by racist travel narratives and zombie films such as *White Zombie* (1932) and *I Walked with a Zombie* (1943), which proliferated in the U.S. American landscape during U.S. occupation (1915–1934) and postoccupation (1934–1957), many tourists were intrigued by notions of a "primitive" and "mysterious" Haiti. Foreign tourists typically held bigoted views about the *vodou* religion and its sacred dances, perceptions that Destiné and Williams were never completely successful in overcoming. Nevertheless, within this transnational cooperative space, Destiné's and Williams' innovations and transmission of Haitian dance did educate dancers and their audiences about Haitian and West African-based cultural heritage(s). Their pioneering efforts attracted tourists to the island and demonstrated that the arts could enhance and create new possibilities for the modern project of economic and cultural development.[16]

I argue that the work of Destiné and Williams sought to codify Haitian dance—to discipline it, classify it and theatricalize it—as a means to exhibit Haiti's art form and its cultural ambassadors on the world stage and to educate their audiences about Haitian history and culture. During the "golden age" of Haitian tourism, from the late 1940s to 1956, Destiné and Williams transformed the pedagogy of Haitian folkloric dance by establishing national institutions in Haiti that imparted technical discipline to this folk art form by incorporating floor stretches, body conditioning, ballet training and classes in choreography to the dancers' regimes.[17] Destiné and Williams created troupes of polished, well-conditioned, professional dancers, who, in contrast with folkloric dancers, presented a more "cultivated" and agreeable image to middle-class liberal vacationers from the United States and Europe. More importantly, the establishment of cultural institutions and the training of Haitian dancers affirmed the creation of an alternative world by black dancers in which African-based art forms were celebrated and in consistent dialogue with Western culture.

The influence of Katherine Dunham, world renowned choreographer, anthropologist and activist, on the study and appreciation of Haitian dance and *vodou* specifically, and on Caribbean dance more broadly, is key to understanding the intersections of identity, movement, ethnography and performance in the African American diaspora.[18] Dunham mentored both Destiné and Williams, among countless others, but I focus on Destiné and Williams in this chapter because I deem their extensive work in building institutions of dance in Haiti as critical to understanding the cultural dimensions of black Pan Americanism. During this golden age of tourism, Cold War politics, anticolonialism and continued racist readings of Haitian culture, dance schools and training created, shaped and circulated discourses on intraracial cultural connectivity. They also demonstrated transnational cooperative initiatives that could potentially generate new knowledge, capital and exchanges for Haitians and U.S. African Americans, as well as for other blacks in the Americas.

Fig. 5.1. Dancers perform in choreographer Lavinia Williams' "Les Racines D'Haiti, Ceremonie du Bois Caïman," at Hotel Oloffson, Port-au-Prince, date unknown. (Photo courtesy of the Lavinia Williams Photograph Collection, n.d. Box 11, Photographs and Prints Division, Schomburg Center for Research in Black Culture, New York Public Library, Astor, Lenox and Tilden foundations.)

Haitian folkloric dance and Haitian visual arts, particularly painting, were arguably the most prominent and popular art forms that were show-cased to the international public. During the presidencies of Estimé and Magloire (1946–1956), Haitian art forms prospered, not exclusively due to state support but to other factors that promoted interest in indigenous *vo-*

dou rituals and peasant culture as well. These influential factors included cultural exchange programs, foreign interest and *noiriste* politics, which circulated black nationalist thought within Haitian society. While the visual arts certainly played a key role in this cultural flowering, this chapter concentrates on Haitian folkloric dance in particular because of its international exposure and acclaim, its choreographers, the magnitude of its audiences, its participatory elements and the frequency of its performances, as well as folk dance's symbiotic relationships with the *vodou* religion and the growth of tourist entertainment structures such as hotels, clubs and theatre venues. Dance performances occurred in school auditoriums, theatres, open-air sites and nightclubs, entertaining small and large audiences on a nightly basis.[19] The popularity of folkloric dance shows in theatre settings motivated several hotels in Haiti to host performances similar to Broadway musicals. *Vodou*-inspired dances became *en vogue*, so much so that hotels and nightspots such as Hôtel Ibo Lele and its Shango Nightclub appropriated the names of *vodou* divinities. Secular *danse folklorique* functioned as a more visible and tangible manifestation of sacred *vodou* ritual, the latter having troubled presidents Vincent and Lescot in the 1930s and '40s. The air of hopefulness that followed the end of U.S. intervention had also ushered in state-sponsored repression of sacred *vodou*, which Vincent and Lescot considered to have a politically and culturally regressive effect on the state and on the (re)formation of Haitian national identity. Despite these qualms, the state deemed folkloric dance, bled of its sacred elements, a viable cultural commodity to attract tourism. Because of these factors, folkloric dance, arguably more than Haitian painting, deserves particular attention in regard to its influence on the growth of Haitian tourism, national development and cultural nationalism.

"We Now Have an Artist": Jean-Léon Destiné at the Intersection of Folkloric Dance and *Vodou*

In September 1935, some conservative elements of Haitian society, particularly Haitian elites and print media sources such as *Le Matin*, applauded President Vincent's legislation against *les pratiques superstitieuses* or superstitious practices. Revisions in the penal code that same year stated that popular dances or Haitian folkloric dance, void of any sacred rituals or the sacrifice of livestock in submission to deities, were legal, despite dance's inextricable connections with *vodou*.[20] Scholar Kate Ramsey asserted that these legislative changes were spurred by the development of cultural nationalism during the U.S. occupation period, which "mark[ed] the moment when it became politically desirable . . . for the state to distinguish popular dance from prohibited ritual."[21] Popular dance became evidence of a national culture or identity and of Haitian cultural progress, while religious rituals perpetuated notions of Haitian "primitivism" and cultural "inferiority."

Since the late 1930s, the Catholic Church in Haiti had promoted an anti-superstitious campaign with the support of the state. Intrusions by Haitian police and Catholic clergyman on *ounfò* (temples) and other sites where Haitians were suspected of participating in *vodou* ceremonies disrupted worship and instilled fear in the practicing Haitian peasantry. Jean-Léon Destiné, who was educated in Catholic churches and schools in Saint-Marc, possessed firsthand knowledge of the Church's power over the Haitian aristocracy and the middle class. Coming from a middle-class family of "modest means," Destiné explained in a 2002 interview that the Catholic Church "told us [Haitians] it [*vodou* worship] was a sin [and that] you're going to hell. All of us . . . accepted it."[22] In Haitian social politics there existed a stark conflict between Christianity and *vodou*. Within the Haitian elite, Christianity operated in an antithetical way to the complex philosophical and religious beliefs of *vodou*, the religion of the Haitian masses. The latter was perceived as backward and contradictory to Catholic theology. On the other hand, the Haitian peasantry and certain *indigéniste* scholars such as Jean Price-Mars, who critically advanced the cultural production of the Haitian masses, deemed *vodou* as being symbiotic with Catholicism and also African-based. As Michel-Rolph Trouillot asserts, the elite and the peasantry "to different degrees . . . shared religious beliefs rooted in the same African-dominated cosmology and took part in similar rituals."[23] This theological division along the lines of class was clearly noted by both Destiné and Katherine Dunham as they navigated the waters of folkloric culture and the illegal sacred rituals of *vodou*. Destiné stated: "folksongs to them [the Haitian elite] were *vodou* songs—which is stupid! The minute there is drumming they think it's *vodou*."[24] Dunham, a U.S. African American dancer and an anthropologist, noted on her initial research trip to Haiti in May 1935 how President Vincent "paid deference to 'folklore' for the sake of the growing interest of tourists in the island, but an air of secrecy clothed all the serious ceremonies. . . ."[25] The Haitian government, according to Dunham, frowned upon "investigations" that unearthed the schism

between "the thin upper crust of the Haitian elite . . . [and] the black peasants, who really were by numbers and by historical content and character
and humanness . . . the *true* Haitian people."[26] The remarks by Destiné and
Dunham highlighted how class divisions, particularly ruptures triggered by
elitist cultural denigration of *vodou* belief systems and *vodou*-inspired art
forms, operated at the intersection of *danse folklorique* and *vodou*.

The issues of cultural authenticity and its putative accurate represen-
tation(s) of Haitian society and its citizens can also be situated at this intersection. At this crossroad, the privileging of the Haitian peasantry or
folk culture as the architects of an authentic Haitian cultural past displaced
elite contributions to Haitian identity and alluded to folk contributions to
a Haitian future. Favoring the peasantry limited the extent to which Haiti's
national identity could be (re)constructed.[27] The state, indirectly, situated
the peasantry at the center of national identity with the official negation of
"primitive" rituals and *les pratiques superstitieuses*. The "primitive" implies
the original, or as Marianna Torgovnick asserts, a necessary stage of development through which humankind has passed.[28] Vincent's 1935 legislation
coupled with the major impact of Jean Price-Mars' seminal text *Ainsi Parla
L'Oncle* (*So Spoke the Uncle*, 1928) on black consciousness and the value of
the Haitian peasantry reintroduced the centrality of the Haitian masses to
the current and future development of Haitian national identity.

Destiné's recollections of these class and legal conflicts and their connections to Haitian national identity can be traced to an incident involving
Lina Fussman-Mathon, a pioneering Haitian folkloric dance artist, pianist
and composer, a small group of young Haitian male singers/dancers and
the Haitian police.[29] One Saturday night, Fussman-Mathon brought four
boys including Destiné to a *vodou* ceremony in the rural section of Port-
au-Prince to expose them to the indigenous rituals and dances of the Haitian peasantry. Fussman-Mathon deemed the experience critical for their
training because her dance and singing troupe had been formally invited to
perform at the National Folk Festival in Washington, D.C., and she wanted
her performers' movements to reflect those of authentic Haitian folk dance.
According to Destiné, this trip was his initial introduction to *vodou* culture,
and apparently he never revealed to his parents the nature of the outing.
Destiné trembled when he arrived at the ceremony because he believed that
he and the group were committing sins against the Catholic Church. During the ceremony members of the Haitian police force arrested the group
of observers and participants. Destiné recalled the police reprimanding the

dancers, yelling, "Don't *you* know *you* are not supposed to be here?" Once they had been brought to the police station, Fussman-Mathon phoned government officials to explain that her dancers had been preparing for the folk festival in Washington, D.C. The group was soon released from police custody but with a strict warning.[30] Most likely, the dancers had been freed due to several factors: president-elect Élie Lescot supported the Washington folk festival; the troupe was training to represent Haiti in the United States; and officers bowed to the influence of Fussman-Mathon and the boys' middle-class families. Yet, as this incident illustrates, the state's mission to craft a modern image for Haiti clashed with the promotion of Haitian folklore, particularly dance, and its dependence on so-called primitive elements of the *vodou* religion.

Fussman-Mathon's folkloric troupe participated in the National Folk Festival held in Constitution Hall, Washington, D.C., in May 1941. Considered an example of Pan Americanism at its best, the festival encouraged hemispheric cultural exchange and understanding.[31] Destiné remarked that Haiti was one of the few countries at the festival that represented African culture. To his surprise "there were no Cubans and no Brazilians" performing at the event. Brazil and Cuba, he asserted, were "the two strong African influenced countries that could compete with Haiti and now we [the Haitian folkloric troupe] were the only real one that would bring Africa!"[32] Destiné's excitement about the troupe's representation of a West African-derived cultural past fused with Haitian elements may have been a product of many years of reflection on his part. However, it addresses various angles of cultural perception and authenticity. From Destiné's reading of the event, the dancers performed Haitian songs and dances inextricably linked with West African traditions, memories and philosophies. Their creative involvement in the folk festival also afforded them the opportunity to travel and to obtain some level of notoriety and possibly access to monetary or cultural resources.

The Haitian state believed that the troupe's participation figured into a larger Pan American project that could potentially reap the benefits of increased tourist activity and positive exposure for the nation. The reconciliation of these two views manifested itself in inter-American programs and Haiti's *nouvelle cooperation*, which explored ways to expand and strengthen relations between Haiti and the United States.[33]

The folkloric troupe's performance received enthusiastic reviews from the U.S. press, and according to Destiné the dancers frequently sent newspaper clippings back to Haiti. Destiné claimed that the Haitian people "couldn't believe" the overwhelming positive response that U.S. American audiences gave to the dancers' renditions of *vodou*-influenced choreography: "You wouldn't dare do those things in public [in Haiti] . . . and Washington was loving it." The troupe's exposure and acclaim planted the seed in Destiné's mind that he might have a future in dance in the United States. Given the contentious relationship between folkloric dance and *vodou* and its conflict with the Catholic Church, Destiné asserted that "there was no future in dance" in Haiti.

Before the troupe left the United States, President-elect Lescot hosted a reception for Fussman-Mathon's company. During the event, lead drummer André Janvier, one of three Haitian drummers who accompanied the group, decided to address Haitian and U.S. officials about the role that *vodou* and Haitian folklore played in his life. Destiné paraphrased Janvier's speech:

> Mr. President, Mr. Diplomatique. I am a peasant. Since I was little I was told that my great, great parents came from Africa, the place called Dahomey. I never knew that one day, the way they [the elite] treat me in Haiti, I [would] feel like a second class citizen. Here I am in Washington, D.C., and I am received like an artist. I want, Mr. President, please give me a token, whatever it is, so when I go back home I'll show everybody this is what *vodou* did for me.[34]

Stirred by the speech, Lescot gave Janvier a medallion, an act that symbolized the legitimization of folkloric dance by the Haitian state. Yet, one month later, Lescot supported the Church's anti-superstitious campaign in the Haitian countryside.[35]

When the troupe returned to Haiti, Destiné was forced to think about how he would make a living. He had learned typography at the Haitian newspaper *Le Nouvelliste* during the summer of 1941 and later returned to the United States on a print-media scholarship by the Rockefeller Foundation.[36] Philanthropic organizations such as the Ford and Rockefeller foundations often tailored their grants and giving to the goals of U.S. foreign policy. In this case, Roosevelt's Good Neighbor Policy and the ideals of Pan Americanism encouraged technical development and international exchange in the Americas. Destiné's Rockefeller grant was an example of such inter-American exchange. It was during his two-year stay in the United

States that Destiné made initial contact with the world's leading dancers and choreographers such as Martha Graham, Katherine Dunham, Pearl Primus and Asadata Dafora, a Sierre Leonean dancer, to learn the technical aspects of modern dance.[37]

Haitian officials and cultural elites heard about Destiné's performances in the United States and were impressed by his ability to garner support and interest in Haitian folkloric dance. Haiti's cultural officials asked Destiné to perform in Haiti, stating that the government would only invite "the elite and the educated, not the masses. This is art, and you will be able to attract tourists." The boy who had once been rounded up in a nighttime raid now served as his country's cultural ambassador. Friends, Haitian politicians and officials communicated to him that the government needed to send him back to the United States "to make people realize that we [Haitians] have an artist."[38] By the late 1940s and early 1950s, Haitian officials concentrated on exporting culture and attracting tourists' foreign capital because these efforts demonstrated Haiti's cultural advancement and produced modest gains in the service economy. At the same time, the ripple effects of tourism placed a significant strain on the country's infrastructure, increasing the need for more electricity, a central water supply and a sewage disposal system.

Destiné returned to the United States in 1946, intent on entertaining and educating U.S. audiences about Haitian folkloric dance. Changing U.S. perceptions of African-descended peoples remained a critical task during the World War II period, when racial discrimination and hegemonic colonial governments still reigned in Africa and the Caribbean. Haiti was a contested space where blackness and indigenous cultural expression battled the prevailing images and stigmas of black primitiveness and inferiority.[39] Haitian educational institutions such as the Bureau d'Ethnologie, in Port-au-Prince, attempted to counteract beliefs in black inferiority, particularly concerning the rural black masses of Haiti. While working at Le Nouvelliste, Destiné attended classes at the Bureau d'Ethnologie to learn more about vodou, Haitian folklore and how the Haitian masses retained aspects of West African traditions. Studying under Jean Price-Mars, Destiné remembered that Price-Mars's text Ainsi Parla L'Oncle became "the first book that started to open our eyes to tell us that we are not of European descent." This book highlighted the syncretic nature of Haitian life, blending African and European elements, which propelled many in the Haitian elite to ask: "Who are we—Frenchmen or African?" Destiné believed that Haitians were rooted in a West African cultural heritage, even though many of the Haitian elite renounced such claims.

According to Destiné, some U.S. African Americans during the interwar and post-World War II periods refused to be associated with African culture; in addition, their knowledge of Haiti was quite limited.[40] At the same time, U.S. African American intellectuals and artists like Katherine Dunham, Langston Hughes and Paul Robeson proved essential in providing an alternative racial and ideological framework for many U.S. blacks. Additionally, these individuals introduced Destiné's talents to a wider audience. Dunham invited Destiné to become a guest artist in her Broadway production *Bal Nègre* (1946). This production maintained a successful two-year run throughout the United States and Mexico. Langston Hughes invited the dancer to sing and perform at parties in New York City. When the New York City Opera produced William Grant Still's *Troubled Island,* a tragic opera about the reign and death of Haitian Emperor Jean-Jacques Dessalines, Hughes alerted Still to Destiné's dancing skills. In addition, Destiné and Paul Robeson, a U.S. African American political activist, communist and entertainer, forged an amicable relationship in the late 1940s.[41] By 1948, Destiné had formed his own dance company and was performing to sold-out audiences in theatres, concert halls and supper clubs throughout the United States. He even starred in the prize-winning film *Witch Doctor,* which premiered at the Sutton Art Theatre in New York City.[42] The dancer's widespread popularity enabled him to entertain and educate U.S. audiences about Haitian folkloric dance and Haitian progress and also helped him continue to establish relationships with U.S. African American intellectuals and artists.

Always seeking a moment to educate others about the indigenous aspects of Haitian folk culture, Destiné introduced dancer and critic Ted Shawn to Haitian folkloric dance and brought him to several *vodou* ceremonies in December 1949. In May 1950, Shawn argued that Haitian dance demonstrated a "rich and varied" style. And as a result of having viewed Haitian dance in its "raw material state," coupled with his exposure to Destiné's finished performances, Shawn was surprised at how Destiné maintained the "ecstatic, frenzied and spontaneous" nature of Haitian *vodou* dance and created set routines with a sense of "reality."[43] Shawn noted that prior to Destiné's historic achievement, "[Haitian] choreography—group dance as planned, architectural work of art . . . was unheard of."

For some dance critics, Haitian dance did not equate to modern dance. Terms such as "ecstatic" and "spontaneous" symbolized primitive notions of the art form. Some critics suggested that Destiné's participation, influence and fame in Haitian folkloric dance somehow modernized the unmodernizable aspects of Haitian dance. Ted Shawn's statements in *Dance Magazine* elaborated this point; he noted that Destiné "has taken material which in the hands of other Negro choreographers has always had a touch of Broadway and a slight pandering to the cheap and sensational taste; and without losing any of the dynamic quality of utter sincerity and dignity of great art."[44] To this particular critic, Destiné exemplified the authentic, yet polished Haitian performer.

In 1949, the Haitian government asked Destiné to organize a national dance troupe to perform at the celebration of the two-hundredth anniversary of the founding of Port-au-Prince.[45] La Troupe Folklorique Nationale served as the best publicity for Haiti. Under the leadership of President Dumarsais Estimé, the Bicentennaire Exposition Internationale showcased Haiti's excellence and advancement in cultural arts. Painters, dancers and musicians played an essential role in inter-American cultural diplomacy and also communicated Haiti's attractiveness to tourists.[46] U.S. African American educator and race leader Mary McLeod Bethune's invitation to a presidential ceremony at the Bicentennaire exhibited Haitian/U.S. African American linkages to a common struggle. At a "very dignified" ball at the royal palace, President Estimé honored Bethune for her tireless work to improve Haitian education and the lives of Haiti's orphans.[47] The ceremony's organizers called on Destiné, now considered a Haitian cultural ambassador, to perform his heralded "Slave Dance." This routine interpreted the evolution of enslaved African descendants from the moment of bondage to their physical and psychological emancipation. At the moment of rebellion, Destiné struggled onstage with the chains that imprisoned him and eventually broke free, after which he energetically danced throughout the ballroom to demonstrate the emergence of a revolution and the beginning of a free black republic.

Bethune seemed to interpret the dancer's breaking of the chains as an action with a very modern relevance. When Destiné severed the links, Bethune walked over to the fallen chain, picked it up, struggled with it and broke it again.[48] This was a significant and symbolic gesture given that it was performed in front of Haitian and international dignitaries in 1949, when racial discriminatory practices, racial violence and social and economic inequality plagued Bethune's United States. Bethune's immediate and spontaneous response to Destiné's "Slave Dance" revealed the depths of U.S. African American hardships and echoed the transnational political and cultural engagements between both groups in the postoccupation era.

It became clear during the Haitian Bicentennaire that Destiné had an agenda to promote indigenous Haitian culture and history. President Estimé promoted a *noiriste* government and society, in which color (dark skin) was privileged over qualifications and the lighter skin of the *mulâtre* elite, and in which folk culture was celebrated. Destiné combined folk art forms with dance band arrangements and European instrumentation to create *vodou-jazz*. The mixture appears to have been a deliberate artistic choice by Destiné during this *noiriste* period, when it was as fashionable to emphasize native or folk rhythms as it was to incorporate the big band arrangements and Cuban elements that so appealed to tourists. Destiné's musical group consisted of traditional drummers such as Ti-Roro, Ti-Marcel and Alphonse Cimber and the popular *vodou-jazz* band Jazz des Jeunes, which embodied *noiriste* ideology and often challenged the cultural legitimacy of other Haitian dance bands that did not espouse "folkloric" or indigenous popular music.[49] Thus, Destiné's artistic vision complemented the Haitian cultural roots of the peasantry and consequently entertained audiences by communicating an art experience that offered cultural awareness of Haitian life. His success was among the components that helped bring notoriety and European and American capital to an emerging tourist industry in Haiti.

Lavinia Williams and the Technical Training of Haitian Dancers

Destiné's and Lavinia Williams' participation in the cultural events of Haiti Week in the spring of 1951 set the stage for Williams' thirty-year-long relationship with the black republic. During these festivities, Papa Augustin, a Haitian drummer and a cultural consultant to Katherine Dunham's dance company, invited Jean Brierre, poet and director general of the Haitian State Tourist Office, to Lavinia Williams' dance school in Brooklyn. After watching Williams' dance technique and her approach to modern dance, Brierre remarked that "this [was] the kind of basic technique that I want my people to learn." Within two years, Alphonse Cimber, who was Haiti's Master of Drums, the president of the Haitian-American Society and Destiné's drummer, mentioned to Williams that the Haitian government planned to invite a foreign dance teacher to improve the technical skill of Haitian dancers. Subsequently, with the help of Haitian cultural officials, the Haitian government invited Williams to become a national dance instructor for six months. Excited, Williams wrote to Haiti's minister of propaganda Roger Savain in December 1952: "It has always been one of my fondest ambitions to be given the chance to call upon my dance knowledge, and varied dance background, and present this knowledge to the people of Haiti."[50]

The Haitian government's offer to Williams begs that the question be asked: Why did Haitian officials seek a non-Haitian to teach dance in Haiti when there were qualified nationals for the position? After all, Destiné had led La Troupe Folklorique Nationale for a number of years and had trained many Haitian dancers, both male and female. Likewise, Viviane Gauthier was a well-trained Haitian dancer during this time.[51] I contend that the Haitian government sought out classically and formally trained modern dancers to bring "technical" and "disciplined" training to Haitian performers. During this period of intensifying Haiti's exposure through tourism and cultural exchange, the Haitian Office of Tourism believed that Lavinia Williams also brought prominence and possibly access to U.S. cultural resources. In April 1957, the *Haiti Sun* reported: "Haitian artists, until a few years [ago], knew nothing about modern dances, tap dancing or ballet. Now there are hundreds of young people assisted by a French teacher, and several Haitian and American teachers, who are being trained in other forms of the dance."[52] Williams' dance pedigree, which included several years' experience performing with Eugene Von Grona's American Negro Ballet (1937–1939), in Agnes de Mille's production of *Obeah* (1940), with Katherine Dunham's company (1941–1945) and in Noble Sissle's USO tour of *Shuffle Along* (1945–1946), proved instrumental to her earning the national instructor position and significant to the perception that Haiti—at least, culturally—continued to move forward.[53]

Born in Philadelphia, Williams' first memories of dance were joyful and painful. She recalled how she gyrated on top of a box at home to impress her family. During the degrading years of Jim Crow segregation, she had to enter through the back door of a segregated Virginia dance school to take ballet lessons.[54] Studying ballet in the 1930s, Williams encountered racial discrimination as a young U.S. African American woman in a white ballet world. In an interview with Annette McDonald she stated that "being brought up in [the United States] you were told you were not supposed to be a ballet dancer because you're black and your behind is too big, and your feet are flat. . . . I could never get a job in America as [a] black ballet dancer because they took away that part of me, [they] took away my ballet technique and made it modern or acrobatic."[55] Although Williams finally found work performing in Eugene Von Grona's American Negro Ballet, at Harlem's Lafayette Theatre, her reminiscences highlight the prejudices that black dancers encountered with respect to the black female body and the U.S. African American approach to dance. African-descended dancers could not escape the primitive trope in the dance world, which, in the minds of some blacks' notions of the primitive, did not necessarily carry a negative connotation. It was often characterized as a source of origin or basic. Yet ideas about the primitive within the larger North American society and elite dance circles racialized and made inferior notions of primitive dance, images that blacks believed they had to continually counteract. A glance through a 1939 program for the American Negro Ballet, for example, reveals how literature of the time perpetuated the stereotype that black dance was inherent, simple and primitive:

> The stirring imagination of the Negro and his innate understanding of the fundamental values have left deep, permanent impressions on the arts. In the dance, however, this talent has been confined chiefly to dance-hall jazz and African rituals. . . . These limited dance forms— while reflecting man's elemental character—have provided no outlet for the deeper and more intellectual resources of the race. In his search for expression the Negro has made several attempts to enter the serious dance but he has been handicapped by economic conditions and the lack of artistic opportunity.[56]

Although the quoted material attributes the marginalization of U.S. black dancers to "economic conditions and the lack of artistic opportunity," the writer also considers "dance-hall jazz and African rituals" to be "limited forms" of dance and not "serious dance," thus reinforcing hierarchies of cultural forms and the primitive nature of African-descended peoples. Such beliefs weren't confined to anonymous program writers. U.S. African American intellectuals and activists such as James Weldon Johnson also believed that black folk art was primitive, to a certain degree. Johnson praised the American Negro Ballet Company for "defying the traditions that would limit the Negro's art to native or instinctive art. . . ."[57]

After performing with the American Negro Ballet from 1937 to 1939,

Williams joined Agnes de Mille's production of *Obeah* in August 1940. During this production Williams acquired an interest in the culture and art of the Caribbean. The Caribbean, Williams asserted, was "the missing link to Africa" and was a root that many U.S. blacks ignored. Williams' strong technical abilities and her interest in Caribbean cultures enabled the dancer to make a smooth transition to Katherine Dunham's company in 1941. According to Williams, Dunham asked de Mille for five students and after a few months Dunham assigned Williams as a student instructor in the company.

Williams' experience in the Dunham Company profoundly influenced her understanding of dance and the ethnology of dance in countries with people of African descent. To prepare for and understand the Dunham technique, Williams noted the importance of understanding an ethnic group's art as a way to better comprehend a people's identity. Participating in a culture and obtaining a so-called authentic knowledge of why people danced were central to the Dunham method and to Williams' evolving understanding of dance. In her journal, Williams wrote: "beginners should be well acquainted with the history of primitive peoples ... [and should] make a careful study of authentic rhythms in song and dance and of their native costumes and customs."[58] Additionally, Williams noted the significance of culture and movement as opposed to imitating it; this was vital to creating a better dance form, to producing a superior theatrical production and to teaching students how to improve human relations. Dunham's school and her dance company institutionalized this ethnological technique and aimed to provide a well-rounded education for its students. In January 1946, Dunham wrote to Williams about expanding the Dunham School in New York City to include theatrical and academic courses such as acting, elementary French and general anthropology. Dunham wanted to give students "every chance to become equipped for the human race...."[59] After five and a half years of working with Dunham, touring with the company throughout the United States and Canada and participating in such films as *Cabin in the Sky* and *Stormy Weather*, Williams parted ways with Dunham. Williams toured Europe in Noble Sissle's USO production of *Shuffle Along* and when she returned from Europe, she opened a dance studio in her home in Brooklyn with the money she had earned on the tour.

Williams' upbringing in the Christian church facilitated her transition to *vodou* religion and other Caribbean faiths. Williams recalled her grandmother being blessed with healing powers and also watching people in church catch "the holy ghost." She maintained that she was drawn to the "Holy Rollers [and] the Sanctified people."[60] These experiences, Williams noted, prepared her to learn about and participate in *vodou* and to recognize differences between *vodou* worship and Christian worship. Williams discussed being possessed (the disciplining of the body) by *vodou lwas* (divinities) three times. In an interview, she remembered her possession experience to be one of elation and clarity:

> You are at the peak in your mental approach to who you are, and the cycle goes up—and you come to terms with yourself, mentally, physically, everything. It's like a happy meeting with yourself. But in the U.S. when you get to the height, somebody's going to come and say 'a heathen' [and] bring you smelling salts because sometimes they pass out.[61]

Williams' early Christian experiences gave her a foundation to embrace *vodou* culture in Haiti. In addition, her participation and possession in *vodou* rituals carved out a space where she continued to learn and to develop folkloric dance and where she realized the significance of being free of restraint or social judgment.

Discriminatory opinions from friends surfaced when Williams decided to accept the teaching position in Haiti. Some of her friends commented: "Well, you want to go to the West Indies, that's like taking coals to Newcastle. They [West Indians] already know how to shake."[62] Common racial and ethnic stereotypes about African-descended peoples and their "intuitive" knowledge of dance persisted within U.S. cultural spaces, as revealed in the 1939 program notes for the American Negro Ballet and in Destiné's early perceptions about U.S. African Americans. Williams, as well as other dancers and participants in *vodou* and folkloric dance, emphasized the tremendous amount of training and practice involved in dance performance. Her response to such misinformed assertions underscored that "it's not shaking that's important; . . . there is a discipline to knowing how to shake; that is important." Furthermore, Williams argued, "I know when I analyze the shoulder movements, for instance, it is like mathematics. Everything is according to music. The African and West Indian beat is so technical, that you can't just get up and do anything."[63] Thus, Williams' formal training, her association with Dunham's company and her extensive international travel shaped her into an ideal candidate for Haitian officials.

On April 23, 1953, Williams arrived in Haiti with her two daughters and was met by a committee of Haitian delegates, including Emerante de Pradines, a popular Haitian singer.[64] Her technical responsibilities included giving dance instruction at the Lycée des Jeune Filles, training several teachers from the Bureau of Sports, offering physical culture classes and body conditioning exercises to the members of La Troupe Folklorique Nationale and acting as a special instructor to the troupe. Claude Barnett reported for the ANP that Williams' "technical skill" facilitated the development of Haitian potential in the field of dance. Barnett asserted:

> What Miss Williams has done, of course, is to establish a systematic pattern for developing the Haitian potential for basic African dances, a potential that has long been a part of the island's culture, by applying technical skill; a sort of blending of the cultures of the two countries in one art form. . . . The ballet, voodoo dancing, the Latin rhythms and acrobatic dancing, as developed to a high degree on the American stage, have all been fused into what has come to be regarded as the Afro-Haitian dance.[65]

The Haitian government and U.S. African American leaders like Barnett maintained that Haitian dance needed technical training to advance, to attract tourists and to modernize aspects of Haitian culture.

During this era of post-World War II development, the social, political and economic aspects of Caribbean and Latin American societies were entrenched in a language of modernization. Modernization was often defined by a nation's ability to move progressively forward in technological and industrial development. It also encompassed cultural arenas, particularly dance and art in the Caribbean. *Vodou*-inspired folkloric dance, rooted in the cultural memory and modern experiences of racial slavery and New World cultural syncretism, underwent a calculated transformation by black dancers and choreographers during this time. The transformation required that Haitian folkloric dance be classified, disciplined and packaged so it could be shared with the modern world via formal dance instruction, African-based cultural awareness programs and tourist entertainment. Rex Nettleford, a noted Jamaican dance scholar, encouraged the "systematisation" of dance knowledge and history to build a "sound technique." Nettleford's ideas about disciplining Caribbean dance articulated the transmission of an Afro-modern consciousness made possible through sharing of cultural information, history and talents among African-descended peoples in the Americas.[66]

In November 1954, Williams founded the Haitian Academy of Folklore and Classic Dance (HAFCD), a manifestation of the classification of Haitian dance. The Academy married modern dance, classic ballet and secular Haitian dance to create an innovative Haitian folkloric dance tradition. Williams sought to "carry [the] 'dance of the people' beyond its present 'accepted' stage and develop it so that it can be interpreted, classified and appreciated by all students of the dance and art lovers in general."[67] HAFCD offered courses in ballet, choreography and folkloric dance, each of which served a particular function in developing the modern Haitian dancer. Ballet, as stated in Williams' text *Haiti Dance*, operated as dance's classic foundation, a universal language that conveyed a "mastery of body mechanics to increase the grammar and vocabulary of the dance for individual students."[68] Training Haitian choreographers, well versed in the techniques and methods of Martha Graham and Louis Horst and the "movement and exercises from . . . Katherine Dunham, Michael Kidd, Helen Tamaris [and] Kyra Nijinsky," created new designs and modifications to sacred dance. Finally, studying folkloric dance enabled students to understand the forms and functions of *vodou*-dance and song and revealed the relation between Haitian dance and the country's history.

For Williams and associated Haitian officials, the new dance synthesis was not simply a matter of incorporating European forms and exercises into Haitian dance in order to legitimize it or the cultural modernity of Haiti. Like the Bureau d'Ethnologie, which used European scholarly practices to investigate local culture, the HAFCD served as an educational institution whose objective established the significance and promoted the historical and cultural traditions of the Haitian masses. Nevertheless, the transformation of Haitian sacred culture demonstrated the malleability and fluidity of culture whose existence was being threatened by Haitian anti-superstitious laws. Subsequently, the Academy created culturally astute dancers or, rather, ambassadors for Haiti. Régine Mont-Rosier, an advanced ballet student at the Academy, became one of Haiti's cultural ambassadors during the late 1950s when she earned a scholarship to the Ballet Arts at Carnegie Hall in New York City. Mont-Rosier's significant press in Haiti demonstrated Williams' success as an instructor and heralded Haiti's potential to produce another great artist like Destiné.[69]

Williams' technical training and her relative fame as an American dancer proved a perfect match for Haiti, which sought to generate interest in its cultural art forms to increase tourism and better its international im-

5.2. Lavinia Williams *(left)* instructs young Régine Mont-Rosier in ballet, Haiti, 1959. (Photo courtesy of the Lavinia Williams Photograph Collection, 1959 Box 8, Photographs and Prints Division, Schomburg Center for Research in Black Culture, New York Public Library, Astor, Lenox and Tilden foundations.)

age. With the full support of the Haitian government, Williams became a central figure in tourist and socially elite circles. She served as mistress of ceremonies at the Open Air Theatre Verdure, narrating the secular dances to vacationers. Williams broadcast her radio program *Glimpses of Haiti* three nights a week to expose tourists to and educate them about the richness of Haitian history and culture.[70] The national and international popularity of Haitian folkloric dance, coupled with the growing reputation of Haitian "primitive" art, created a sense of national pride among many Haitians, including some Haitian elite, who typically shunned the cultural production of the masses. According to Magloire and Yelvington, "folklore had been made to serve nationalist movements," and, similar to the ways it was utilized in the texts of Jean Price-Mars during the violent years of U.S. occupation, folklore was being resurrected to complement the perception of President Magloire's *noirisme* and to build nationalist fervor in favor of the government's modernist projects.[71] Williams' training in ballet bridged gaps between participating elites, the black middle class and the masses. Although Williams explained that she initially had received the most resistance from Haitian elites, who claimed that "ballet belonged to [them]" or that their child was forbidden to dance folklore, these dance institutions allowed children of various social classes to interact in later years and introduced the Haitian masses to ballet as well as to the secular *danse folklorique*.

It is clear that Williams envisioned Haiti as a potential center of black cultural production in which "people could come from all over the world for study, and for rhythmical inspiration." In July 1954, Williams asserted that with the cooperation of the Haitian government and its people, "not only will a new group of tourists be coming to Haiti, but they can help us to realize an establishment which may some day incorporate not only dancing, but music, painting, drama, opera, and all of the other related subjects to help found a University of 'Beaux Arts of Haiti.'"[72] Institution building, the production of a dance philosophy and scholarly research in dance, and social and economic development through cultural exchange, tourism and an effective promotion of racial and cultural identity manifested her black Pan American ideals. Borrowing from her understanding of the Dunham technique, she decided that students must study the history and the background of Haitian folk dances to be able to identify various rhythms and to understand the meaning of the dances in relation to Haitian culture and religion. The *Haiti Sun* reported that Williams not only "develop[ed] choirs and cultivat[ed] the voices of the young Haitians, but she also gave them an appreciation and a pride for their national art."[73]

Lavinia Williams spent the next several decades in Haiti and other countries of the Caribbean, teaching, dancing and embracing Haitian culture. Indeed, it was a source of spiritual inspiration and creative fulfillment to work with Caribbean choreographers and to help systematize national dances in countries such as the Bahamas, Jamaica and Guyana. She worked within this profoundly American and black hemispheric space because she believed that its history of New World slavery provided a window into the creativity of African-descended peoples and possible linkages to a constructed homeland—Africa. When she heard the drumbeats in Haiti, what she deemed the "heartbeat in the bosom of Mother Africa . . . that mediates you from the unknown to the known," she knew that this was where she belonged.[74] Her dance pedagogy sought to bring recognition to Haiti's shores and also to complement the work of the Bureau d'Ethnologie by educating many Haitian dancers about the form and function of Haitian folkloric dance so as to enrich these artists' understanding and appreciation of Haitian and West African culture. She claimed that renowned dancer Isadora Duncan accomplished a similar type of work: "she discovered modern dance and went all through Europe and Russia, and she sort of said that there's another way of doing things. And I've said the same thing with my black people."[75]

Conclusion

Dance for Destiné and Williams was indeed a form of entertainment. However, these dancers' art possessed larger social and political implications that meant considerably more to them and Haitians than did pure amusement. By advancing *vodou*-inspired Haitian culture, these dancers made bold statements against an incredibly class-conscious Haitian society that ignored and demeaned art forms with peasant origins. These artists understood that creativity could be used as currency and could help advance Haitian national identity and the Haitian economy and possibly develop cultural pride and consciousness in the African diaspora. The popularity and evolving representation of Haitian folkloric arts operated as a means to address challenges to modern development in Haiti. Thus, it is important to situate the development of folkloric dance within the framework of Pan American cultural relations. Destiné and Williams secured international

grants and performed at cultural events to foster a greater cultural understanding of and cooperation with African-based secular and sacred dance
forms.

Destiné's and Williams' engagements with modern cultural forms, which
centered on the historical and cultural experiences of African-descended
peoples, pushed the boundaries of Western modernism and rationality and
challenged how black cultural expression figures into that construction.
The growth of industrial capitalism and technological development during
the first half of the twentieth century defined the modern world and the potentiality of modern man. However, the development of modern dance and
art, particularly of *vodou*-inspired Haitian folkloric dance and U.S. African
American modern dance, attempted to incorporate and expand the narrow
understanding of modernity so as to include other modes of development,
movements and historical experiences. The activities of these Afro-modern
dancers were significant because they used the realities of antiblack and
antipeasantry prejudices to advance a black internationalist consciousness
and served as a means to develop Haiti through tourism and cultural redemption during the postoccupation period. The fusion of dynamic folk
customs and modern ingredients was not contradictory; rather, it affirmed
the culturally redemptive histories and experiences of African-descended
peoples with Western dance forms, institutions and discourses in order to
produce new ideas, organizations and conversations.[76] Indeed, the legacy
of Destiné and Williams at midcentury complements the work of a number
of black artists and intellectuals who struggled to affirm the humanity and
memory of black peoples through art and institution-building.

Reclaiming indigenous practices and traditions such as *vodou* and dance
by intellectuals and cultural artists inspired the cultural politics of a Haitian
country doctor who had a profound impact on the future development and
image of Haiti. Influenced by the *indigéniste* writings of Jean Price-Mars,
François Duvalier ascended to the executive office by obtaining the support
of *noiristes* left over from the Estimé and Magloire regimes. The rediscov-
ery of the cultural routes and roots intrinsic in the *indigéniste* movement
"opened the political field for the proponents of 'legitimacy,'" typically supporters of the right of dark-skin leadership and control. Thus, as Michel-
Rolph Trouillot asserts, the "political symbolism" and subsequent chain
of events and ideas that led to a succession of dark-skin leaders feasted on
"analogies rather than on logic." Trouillot contended that many Haitians,
including political remnants from Estimé's administration, believed that "if

the reevaluation of the black race was legitimate, if the reevaluation of national culture and the restoration of national dignity was legitimate, then *noirisme* was legitimate. And if *noirisme* was legitimate, then Duvalier was legitimate."[77] Duvalier used this unsound political platform to establish one of the most notorious authoritarian governments in the hemisphere.

6

"The Moody Republic and the Men in Her Life"

François Duvalier, U.S. African Americans and Haitian Exiles, 1957–1964

The Haitian state has always been authoritarian: from Dessalines to the two Duvaliers.

Michel-Rolph Trouillot

Dr. Duvalier cannot be trusted; he is cynical and his philosophy is a sort of nihilism more tragic than existentialism.

Camille Lhérisson

The Republic of Haiti is a beautiful woman waiting to be wooed. Unfortunately, her political behavior tends to scare away potential sweethearts, and on this fact alone rests the tale of the republic's chronic economic woes.

Lancelot O. Evans

Camille Lhérisson was vexed. The former secretary of state of public health and education under Paul Magloire's administration and a current political exile residing in New York City, Lhérisson voiced his great displeasure in the *New York Age* regarding the Friends of Haiti, a U.S.-based philanthropic organization that continued to support Haitian political and aid organizations in spite of the abuses carried out under François Duvalier's authoritarian regime. As secretary general of the Democratic League of Haiti (DLH), Lhérisson argued that any help from the Friends group would be fruitless "until an atmosphere of democracy and human liberty was restored to the Republic."[1] The DLH was part of a constellation of anti-Duvalierist political factions that had emerged in key sites of Haitian migration including the Bahamas, the Dominican Republic, Miami and New York City. These factions included Jeune Haïti, Combat and the Alliance Patriotique Haïtienne, which, along with the DLH, denounced the proliferation of state violence against Duvalier's political opponents, largely consisting of Haitian elites. In January 1959, Lhérisson warned close advisors to the Haitian president and *New York Age* readers not to be fooled by Duvalier's "new found love for the United States." He warned that "unspeakable tortures and humiliations" were still being inflicted upon the elderly, women and children by the *cagoulars*, the "infamous night prowling secret police."[2] Furthermore, Lhérisson demanded that Duvalier clean up Haiti's "financial mess," an economic crisis that Lhérisson failed to mention stemmed from the economic legacies of Estimé's and Magloire's administrations.[3] Nonetheless, Lhérisson cautioned Washington to "think carefully before making any further decisions to prop up a regime which is due to fall momentarily." Clearly, anti-Duvalier organizations believed that the potential $6 million "grant-in-aid" offered by the Eisenhower administration coupled with support from local nonpolitical groups perpetuated what scholar Michel-Rolph Trouillot identifies in this chapter's epigraph: a Haitian authoritarianism firmly rooted in the country's post-independence period.[4]

In spite of persistent efforts by Haitian exile groups to advance their cause through U.S. print media sources, responses to the Duvalier regime from the U.S. African American press and from business and intellectual cliques remained varied. There were several cases when U.S. blacks initially defended Duvalier's government as democratic and just, arguing that the president's forces shielded the nation-state from a "counter-offensive against anti-Duvalier factions abroad."[5] The ANP's Claude Barnett continued to encourage U.S. African American tourism during the early years of Duvalier's presidency. Additionally, in July 1959, the *Chicago Defender* deflected anti-Duvalier criticism and contended that despite being "overburdened with administrative responsibilities and harassed by political plots . . . from all impartial accounts, [Duvalier's] administration generates the brightest hope for the future of Haiti."[6] U.S. African American support of Haitian presidents had remained fairly consistent since the nineteenth century, when U.S. blacks backed whoever managed to wield executive control. At the other end of the spectrum, some members of the U.S. black press were among the first to "raise the red flag" on state tyranny in Haiti.[7] Thus, U.S. African American responses to Duvalier's regime were in flux between 1957 and 1961; then opinion became unusually silent after Duvalier assumed an illegal second term in 1961 and formalized his dictatorship in 1964.

The advent of François Duvalier's autocracy produced divergent ideas among U.S. African Americans, Haitian exiles and the Duvalierist state about the best way to communicate and implement national and hemispheric change. Many U.S. blacks expressed their support for black Pan Americanism by criticizing the lack of U.S. aid for countries like Haiti. In addition, some U.S. African Americans denounced the intervention and insurgency initiated by Haitian exiles against Duvalier. For Haitian exiles, black Pan American ideals could only materialize with full U.S. African American support of an anti-Duvalier government. Furthermore, Haitian exiles attempted to promote nonracialized Haiti/U.S. relations at the federal level by emphasizing Duvalier's forceful removal and the severance of Washington's financial assistance programs. To attract foreign aid, Duvalier and pro-Duvalier supporters conveyed inter-American unity by demonstrating the Haitian government's allegiance to U.S. foreign policy objectives such as anticommunism. Yet when U.S. aid or foreign policy proved insufficient and ineffective, Duvalier, despite lacking the economic power, attempted to redefine U.S.-centered Pan Americanism by emphasizing national self-determination, communist influences and the creation of non-U.S. multilateral alliances. These were politically touchy subjects for Washington, which wanted to steer weak countries away from communist threats.[8] Varied articulations on Pan Americanism and how it could be used to improve the black republic inevitably triggered a fissure in U.S. African American and Haitian relations. Concurrently, the rupture of U.S. African American and Haitian initiatives was also aggravated by new political and ideological movements that had been influenced by the racial politics of World War II and the post-World War II period, specifically the upsurge in political activism during the U.S. civil rights movement, continental Pan Africanism and anticolonial movements. These noteworthy and admirable sociopolitical movements for change eclipsed the antidemocratic and violent politics of the Duvalier regime and forged a relative silence on the development of intraracial Pan American relations from 1961 to 1964 and after Duvalier's declaration of despotic rule. This period offered U.S. African Americans an opportunity to expand and develop the frontiers of black Pan Americanism and programs of transnational racial uplift so that it could firmly establish a language of antiblack authoritarianism. However, the overwhelming silence from U.S. blacks, with few exceptions, underscored the shortcomings and frailties of identity politics and racialized solidarity movements that can be rendered ineffective by uncritical loyalties to blackness and repressive black leadership.

Within the pro-Duvalier and reticent politics dichotomy that defined U.S. African American relations with Haiti between 1957 and 1964, émigrés like Lhérisson went on the offensive exposing acts of state terrorism, graft and lawlessness. To take advantage of the politically contentious moment of the Cold War in the Americas, when the United States often decided to provide financial and/or military support (overt or covert) to Caribbean and Latin American nations according to how far a country dissociated itself from Fidel Castro's socialist politics, Lhérisson linked Duvalier's aggressive civil officers, the *cagoulars* or the *tonton-makout*, with the Soviet NKVD (Narodny Komissariat Vnutrennikh Del), a repressive police force under Joseph Stalin.[9] The politically charged efforts of the Democratic League of Haiti to establish the Duvalier government as "authoritarian," procommunist and "nihilistic" to U.S. African Americans and the larger public helps frame this concluding chapter on U.S. African American and Haitian relations during the François Duvalier presidency. It demonstrated the tension and control over Haitian affairs and the country's image exerted by several actors and institutions—François Duvalier, the U.S. African American press and elites, Haitian exiles and the U.S. government—that have not been previously discussed as a group in the realm of inter-American affairs. Given that Duvalier came to power in the divisive era of the Cold War, it is critical to examine how these various individuals and political enterprises articulated competing visions of black Pan Americanism and U.S. Pan Americanism in order to aid the ongoing modernizing project of Haiti's economic, political and social infrastructure. The calls for modernization, specifically an adherence to constitutional law and U.S.-style development programs, took place despite the resurgence of U.S. hegemony in Caribbean and Latin American affairs, evidenced by covert military intervention in Guatemala in 1954, by the U.S.-sponsored Bay of Pigs invasion in Cuba in 1961 and by U.S. occupation of the Dominican Republic in 1965.

For example, Lancelot Evans, a journalist for the *New York Age*, believed that Haitian rebel groups in the United States did not possess a comprehensive vision for democratic reform and thus impeded the potential for effective progress. In 1959, Evans penned several articles about Haitian political and economic instability and the impact of Haitian exiles on the black republic's advancement. Invited as a guest of the Haitian government in 1958,

Evans argued that Haitian political and economic stability offered Haiti its best chances for success. He asserted that the work of a "moody group" of elite Haitian exiles "waiting for a chance to grab power through force instead of by orderly constitutional process" hampered stable development.[10] Some Haitian exiles protested Evans' pro-Duvalier stance, and in May 1959, the *New York Age* published one of these confrontations between Evans and a Haitian émigré. The unidentified Haitian asserted that "if he had the money to buy guns he would be able to muster a strong invasion force to overthrow Duvalier." Evans responded in a way that challenged the Haitian gentleman to appeal to Duvalier's call for national unity and to combat disease and poverty. According to Evans, the Haitian replied: "Duvalier really doesn't mean a word of what he says. . . . Mr. Evans, if you knew Haitians as well as I do, you would learn never to take their words seriously."[11] In an attempt to demonstrate support for a democratically elected government and to advocate for a sovereign black nation in the hemisphere, Evans promoted the idea in the *Age* that Haitian exiles had no interest in advancing Haitian progress but rather were more interested in "toppling" the Duvalier regime for self-serving purposes.

If Evans condemned some Haitian exiles as obstructionist and self-serving, he was equally critical of Haiti itself. His anthropomorphization of Haiti as a "beautiful woman waiting to be wooed," quoted in this chapter's epigraph, articulated his frustrations with Haitian development within the framework of a transnational courtship, a political and economic bond between nation-states that emphasized the ideology of inter-American cooperation. In effect, it implied a privileging of the U.S. government and venture capitalists as ideal "sweethearts" to aid in the project of technical development and democratization.

Energized by the crumbling of the walls of empire in Africa during the late 1950s and early 1960s, U.S. African American capitalists such as Evans and Barnett assumed the "vocabulary of modernization with no critique of power relations. . . ."[12] Since Haiti possessed a long history of autonomy and a rich network of relations with U.S. blacks, the projects of economic investment and promoting business- and structural-development opportunities often eclipsed critiques of internal Haitian political and financial decisions, especially when it came to making critical assessments of Duvalier's regime after 1957. These interwoven anticolonial events, the development of modernization theory and the unique historical memory of Haiti as emblematic of antislavery/anticolonial and black independence distinguished Haiti at this particular moment of the late 1940s through the mid-1950s.

With reports of Duvalier's repression swirling in the mainstream U.S. press between 1958 and 1971, it eventually proved difficult for many U.S. African Americans to continue to ignore a destructive reading of Haitian affairs, particularly in the context of their own march toward civil rights and the radical anticolonialist politics emerging from newly independent African nations. Lhérisson's use of the term "nihilism" in the chapter's epigraph is significant because news stories, works of fiction and television broadcasts have largely characterized Duvalier's time in power (1957–1971) as über-violent, maniacal and irrational. In 1963, NBC broadcast journalist David Brinkley interviewed Duvalier, along with some former government aides and several Haitian exiles, on his television program *David Brinkley's Journal.* Oddly, it was Duvalier's publicity director, Herbert Morrison, a white man and former Hollywood press agent, who took center stage in the two-part television segment. Morrison claimed that Duvalier's office contained a "voodoo altar" that featured two dolls, one of former president Eisenhower "in effigy" and another of ex-secretary of state John Foster Dulles. Eisenhower's voodoo doll had its heart area "circled in pins," and Dulles's "pins" were arranged around his pancreas, Morrison said.[13]

Duvalier's reputation took another blow when the U.S. State Department's Office of Medical Services completed a secondhand psychiatric evaluation of the Haitian president, arguing that he suffered from a "paranoid personality" that "approached psychotic proportions at times."[14] According to the report, a rational North American "observer," in contrast to a *vodou*-influenced national, would find Duvalier "sicker" than most heads of state. The unpublished evaluation argued that Haitians in general were a "paranoid" group because of the ubiquitous "animism" on the island; the report asserted that even the "veneer of education does not necessarily change such a core belief pattern." Although the state department's medical evaluation was circulated only among members of executive and military circles, its influence was indirectly felt by the general public. The report's characterizations of Haitians and their government reveal a sordid legacy rooted in the ideology of nineteenth-century scientific racism and the post-Haitian Revolutionary period.[15]

In fact, a cloud of sensationalism has continued to hover over Duvalier's fourteen-year-long rule, making it difficult to clearly ascertain Duvalier's impact on the Haitian nation-state, its diasporic citizens and the U.S. African American population that has played a pivotal role in Haitian autonomy since U.S. military occupation in 1915. Of course, the astounding accounts of government repression and violence that took place during Duvalier's reign do not mean that such descriptions lack validity or truth. My point is that such pervasive reports of magic, darkness, oppressive activity and lunacy allowed for a misguided and shortsighted perception of the Haitian *realpolitik*. Francophone literature scholar J. Michael Dash asserts that "the belief that Haiti had simply lapsed into savagery in the 1960s . . . acquired great currency."[16] Graham Greene's popular novel *The Comedians* (1966), a fictional account of Haiti under Duvalier rule, minimizes Haiti to a land of obscurity, barbarity and *vodou* drumming. *The Comedians* follows in the literary tradition of Joseph Conrad's *Heart of Darkness*, in which the African continent symbolizes a stagnant and primitive world as well as an entryway to the fundamental nature of humankind. Haiti under Duvalier epitomized Greene's and Conrad's notions of "primitive" Africa. Dash argues that "Haiti, like Africa, had been fixed 'textually' since the nineteenth century as a literary 'sign,' inexhaustively suggestive of mystery and carnality."[17]

Popular interpretations and mainstream news reports of Duvalier's Haiti directly challenged black Pan American notions of uplift and development. With some exceptions, U.S. African American print media and intellectual circles deemphasized the prominent role that Haiti had typically played regarding issues of black self-government and the potential for blacks to shape their economic and political destinies. In contrast with earlier decades, fewer U.S. blacks visited Haiti and reported news concerning Haitian politics during the late 1950s through the 1960s. Minimal reports on Haitian affairs by U.S. African Americans, the destabilization and formalization of Duvalier's authoritarian state and the minimal critique of Duvalierism by U.S. blacks indicate a shift in their international political focus and a failure among U.S. African American intellectuals to address human rights issues when faced with intraracial violence abroad.

"The Nation Was the State. The State Was Duvalier": U.S. African Americans and Haitian Exiles at the Intersection of Duvalierism

Haitian Exiles, Cold War Politics in the Americas
and Duvalier's Authoritarianism

"With God's help . . . we are determined that no selfish human being nor malevolent and despoiling world forces will conquer and destroy [Haiti's] national will."[18] With these words, Duvalier opened his speech on October 22, 1958, outlining the Duvalierist revolution of economic and ideological reform. Following the aftermath of the failed July 1958 invasion led by Alix "Sonson" Pasquet, a Haitian exile in the United States and a former military commander, Duvalier's populist speech articulated his belief in his divine power to lead, protect and enrich the nation.

Pasquet's eight-man invasion team, consisting of five U.S. nationals and three Haitians, had drifted into the coastal village of Montrouis and managed to subdue state army barracks and to capture an ammunition depot.[19] Duvalier forces quickly suppressed the incident and blamed the attack on the influence of former president Magloire, now residing in New York City, and on former presidential candidate Louis Déjoie, president of the Democratic League of Haiti. Despite the 1958 state victory, a *New York Times* article reported the angst of a high-ranking Haitian official: "We do not care where they [Magloire and Déjoie] go, Europe or even Russia, just so they get out of the United States where they can cause our Government so much harm with their plotting."[20] Duvalier declared to his audience that anarchy from abroad and home had "thwarted" him from providing "the peace and security" that he had "hoped to give . . . during this first year of [his] administration." He claimed that invading oppositional exile groups, coupled with the political and economic corruption inherited from the Magloire administration, had caused the current social and financial upheaval. Thus, in order to "marshal all honest souls . . . for the freedom and for the welfare of our country," Duvalier maintained that it was his celestial right, "whenever circumstances warrant . . . to act openly against false friends as well as against the avowed enemies of our country."[21] Duvalier's address established the tone of his administration that order would be instituted through him personally and that Haitian opposition would meet with severe repercussions.

The story of Roland Weiner offers another example of the breadth of Duvalier's state power. A Haitian engineer, Weiner came from a wealthy family of mixed ancestry, Haitian and German, in Port-au-Prince. The Weiner family managed a successful rum distillery and a coffee export company. An avid skin diver and spear fisher who owned a modest cabin cruiser, Weiner recalled the day in 1959 when several Cuban men approached him and claimed they were interested in his hobbies and wanted to use his boat, which was located off the coast of La Gonâve. According to Weiner, when the Cuban men met up with him early one morning, they hijacked the boat and attempted to sail to Cuba to volunteer for Castro's revolution.[22]

The Haitian Coast Guard intercepted Weiner's boat and arrested everyone. Fortunately for Weiner, his brother-in-law had attended school with Duvalier and had connections with the regime (although Weiner claimed to be an anti-Duvalierist). Soon he was released from prison. Fearful that Duvalier's civilian force could possibly arrest him again because of his connection with the Cuban volunteers, Weiner acquired a visa and moved to Chicago.[23]

In reference to Duvalier's police force and the community of fear, distrust and corruption in Haiti, Weiner asserted that "anybody . . . if they didn't like you . . . went and said that you were plotting against Duvalier."[24] Weiner commented that the Haitian professional class (doctors, lawyers, engineers) "all left Haiti like the plague during the Duvalier era."[25] Weiner's story is significant not only because it reveals the pervasiveness of Duvalier's unrestrained civilian force, who could and did punish at will, but also because it demonstrates the impact of the Cuban Revolution on Haitian exiles and on U.S. foreign policy in the Americas. Although Weiner admitted that he did not advance an overtly political stance, the possibility of his being linked with pro-Castro exiles proved precarious.

Fidel Castro's formalization of a socialist regime and its potential influence on Haitian society offered politically ambitious Haitian émigrés a chance to benefit from U.S. Pan Americanism by attracting support from an anticommunist U.S. government. Communist influence proved negligible in Haiti and posed a minimal threat of ousting Duvalier's administration. Yet Haitian exiles like Clement S. Benoit, a former consul to the Bahamas and a leader of the Bahamian-based Haitian Revolutionary Party, claimed that the "Red doctrine" was "rife" in Haiti.[26] U.S. fears of communist infiltration in Haiti garnered significant press in the United States. Adolf A. Berle, a Kennedy advisor and former New Dealer, reported that communists had secured positions in Duvalier's administration and that a group of Guineans had been seen on the streets of Havana. The general assumption, Berle stated, was that "their destination was Haiti."[27] Guinea, the first independent Francophone state (1958), possessed strong anti-imperialist and anticapitalist leadership in President Sekou Touré. With the propagation of socialist doctrine in various parts of the world, Western capitalist powers such as France believed that communism had influenced the Guinean independence movement, particularly since Touré lobbied the Soviet Union for economic assistance. Additionally, the United States worked to encourage Touré to reject communist advances by the Soviets. Journalist Al Burt claimed that communist literature had been circulated to Haitian youth and peasants and that Duvalier "flirted with Czechoslovakia and Poland and Russia . . . as a further warning to the United States that it had better reopen its checkbook."[28] One author noted that early in Duvalier's presidency, "the Cuban democrat Carlos Prío Socarrás offered to pay him for the use of Haiti as a Castroite base."[29]

Caribbean and Latin American countries used the Cuban Revolution to bolster their political loyalties and to mimic Washington's foreign policy agendas for the region. Many financially strapped but independent Caribbean and Latin American states such as Haiti looked to the United States for monetary aid to continue on their paths to industrial and technological development.[30] In return for U.S. assistance, these states indirectly pledged to resist the spread of communism and to promote democratic principles. At the same time, the failed CIA invasion of Cuba in April 1961 conveyed a message to Caribbean and Latin American leadership that nation-states were susceptible to U.S. military intervention if countries promoted or turned a blind eye to activity by communist supporters. Duvalier's allegiance to this informal inter-American contract was no exception; however, he often threatened to do business with socialist nations in order to acquire a portion of the nearly $77 million that the Kennedy administration allotted in annual funds for military aid in Latin America.[31] In July 1964, Director of Caribbean Affairs Kennedy Crockett held a tense meeting with Rene Chalmers, Haitian minister of foreign affairs, about the "growth of Communism in Haiti if Duvalier does not receive active U.S. support, including aid."[32] Chalmers insinuated that the Haitian government might "be forced to establish diplomatic relations or expand trade with one or more Soviet Bloc nations." These hints of flirting with socialism coupled with exaggerated claims of a burgeoning communist influence in Haiti served as fodder for the emerging Haitian exile community, particularly in the United States.

The Duvalierist state amassed a myriad of enemies during his regime, including a number of anti-Duvalier groups who advocated vague democratic reforms but primarily fought to remove the president. Many of Duvalier's political opponents, who chose or were forced to leave the country, sought asylum and opportunities in metropolitan centers of the United States such as New York, Chicago and Miami. The metropole offered the "attraction" of capitalism and financial gain for all.[33] On June 8, 1958, a U.S. newspaper reported that technically trained Haitians were "dissatisfied with conditions at home and [were] eager to take jobs in other countries."[34] The *Chicago Tribune* observed in 1965 that "the exodus of doctors, lawyers, teachers, business men and young people is depleting the small upper class which normally runs the country."[35] From 1950 to 1970, nearly 8 percent of Haiti's population immigrated to the United States, Canada, the Bahamas and Francophone Africa and Europe. Fleeing largely because of the formation and strengthening of Duvalier's totalitarian regime, many of these Haitians were educated and technically skilled citizens who sought freedom, safety and economic opportunities. As a result of this massive exodus, Haiti experienced a sizeable "brain drain" during that period from which it, unfortunately, has yet to recover.[36]

Many of the principal social and economic institutions that the bourgeoisie and the Haitian aristocracy benefited from or supported were severely compromised under Duvalier's rule. The 1960–1961 student strikes threatened the power of the Duvalierist state. As a result, the Université d'Haiti was closed, and the Université d'Etat formed under the auspices of the state. Also, between 1960 and 1962, conflict between the Catholic Church and the president heightened. Duvalier's replacement of foreign bishops with Haitian ones demonstrated the state's dominion over the Church. Historian David Nicholls argued that Duvalier's *noiriste* critique of the Church and the Francophile elite shows that the president did not want to be responsible for supporting "ecclesiastical colonialism."[37] Yet Duvalier replaced a foreign colonialism of religious proportions with a state despotism, which drove many Haitians away from the island.

Duvalier understood himself to be not only the leader of the state and overseer of state power but also the embodiment of the state. Yet the state is not an independent variable whose objectives can be "reduced to the intentions of its current rulers."[38] Rather, the role of the state must be invested in "social relations." Therefore, although Duvalier maintained and wielded a great deal of power, at different moments he negotiated that authority with various Haitian classes and embraced, in particular, the black petty bourgeoisie and the peasantry through propagandistic mass rallies, songs and cultural programs. One author notes a *meringue* song, "Duvalier nan Bataille" (Duvalier in Battle) by Ensemble Raphaël Nérette, which praises the state's 1958 victory:

Duvalier yap barou mitraille ou pas couri	Duvalier, under machine gun fire, You didn't run
Cé Bon Dieu qui voyer'ou ici comme president	God sent you here as president
Duvalier yap barou canno ou pas mouri	Duvalier, they gave you cannon, you didn't die
Cé Bon Dieu qui voyer'ou ici	God sent you here
Comme gnou Sauveur	As a savior
Duvalier ou metter en militaire pou'r commande	Duvalier, you command the military[39]

The effectiveness of the Duvalier revolution lay in the leader's ability to convince the peasantry that they, as valuable citizens, made "patriotic sacrifices" and constructed Duvalier as savior of the nation.[40]

Ethnomusicologist Gage Averill had noted that a formidable *noiriste* musical movement defended the Duvalier administration in the "songs and slogans of the day."[41] Another song performed by Ensemble Raphaël Nérette, titled "Dr. François Duvalier," written by Jean Legros, exemplifies how popular music advanced the principles of Duvalier's authoritarian government and spread the message that Duvalier had the power to "save Haiti":

Duvalier bon papa	Duvalier, good Father
Duvalier bon chef d'Etat	Duvalier, good Chief of State
Cé bon Dieu qui mété ou la	It's God who puts you here
Pou vine sauvé Haïti	In order to save Haiti
Haïti ap régénéré	Haiti is regenerating
Grâce à Docteur Duvalier	Thanks to Doctor Duvalier
Toute rue an asphaltée....	Every road will be paved in asphalt....[42]

The terror inspired by state-sponsored violence, coupled with the administration's savvy focus on cultural politics, assured the endurance of the Duvalier regime. Government-sponsored carnivals and the *koudyay*, festive street celebrations held by powerful political leaders, steered the proletariat's attention from social and economic ills to "the populist passions of the masses with pro-Duvalier, anti-elite displays."[43] Drinks, fare and music at these strategic events attracted and demonstrated support for the political ideals of the National Palace. When Duvalier declared himself "president for life," the *Chicago Defender* reported that thousands of Haitian peasants were "trucked" into Port-au-Prince to attend ceremonies where cups of *bouillon,* a hearty Haitian soup, were handed out. Among some Haitians, Duvalier's new moniker became "Bouillon Doc."[44] Events such as these sought to mobilize the Haitian masses under the nebulous cultural construct of the nation.[45] The ambiguity of Duvalier's nationalist ideology enabled him "to speak to the nation as 'brother' without ever defining the terms of this brotherhood."[46] It provided a space in which the administration's actions, whether violent, cultural or economic, could be understood as "necessary" functions of the state to preserve order and control. Scholar David Nicholls argued that Duvalier's populist rhetoric "may have led to a new consciousness on the part of the masses."[47]

Noiriste politics became an effective tool to garner grassroots and popular support. *Noirisme* confirmed two main principles: that dark-skinned Haitians should wield state power and that "the black petty bourgeoisie is the natural representative of the masses."[48] Duvalier privileged the black middle class and considered it best suited to lead the masses and to shape the Haitian "soul."[49] As amorphous and obscure a concept as it is, Duvalier failed to define the Haitian soul. Yet it seems that on Pan American Day, April 14, 1963, Duvalier argued that Haiti's true consciousness and will stemmed from the radical abolitionist period of the late eighteenth century, which culminated in Haitian independence in 1804.[50] The revolutionary spirit of the Haitian Revolution affirmed the humanity of enslaved African descendants and pushed forward the progress of African-descended peoples in spite of Western oppression. The president stated that the Haitian Revolution set the mold of a "true" representative democracy that upheld the "principles of self-determination and non-intervention" in the Americas. Duvalier's reference to the Haitian Revolution within the context of Pan American Day is significant for two reasons: first, because it situates Haiti as a founder of an anti-imperialist, mutually cooperative inter-American ideology, which has been historically compromised by the U.S. government; and second, because Duvalier believed he was fathering a new nation, forging a fresh identity in the tradition of Toussaint L'Ouverture, in which the "responsibility to encourage and promote the economy by putting the country back to work on a practical and productive basis" echoed L'Ouverture's militarized labor reforms.[51] Duvalier believed it was up to the Haitian state to refashion the Haitian soul.

In opposition to Duvalier's nationalist speech on Pan American Day, which emphasized nonintervention and self-determination, Haitian exiles in New York responded with a nationalist press conference a month later on the symbolic day of La Fête du Drapeau (Haitian Flag Day), May 18, 1963. Ironically, in the office of the Carnegie Endowment for International Peace in New York, Hermann L. Desir, representative of the League of Haitian Patriots (LHP) and former Haitian consul, stated that the LHP acted as a "spokesman for and coordinator of several smaller exile groups throughout the Caribbean area and the United States." Claiming to have "2,000 to 3,000 men presently under league command"—from New York to Jamaica to Venezuela—Albert Chassagne, a medical technician at St. Vincent's Hospital, said that the LHP possessed a "good chance" of ousting Duvalier.[52] In 1966, the New York-based anti-Duvalier group Alliance Patriotique Haïtienne expressed in broad terms that their goals included removing the "tyrant Duvalier; proclaim[ing] its solidarity with democrats at home . . . [and forging] unity between political leaders and workers' organizations. . . ."[53] Clearly, many Haitian exiles wanted Duvalier gone, yet they did not offer a clear political/economic platform on which to build their case.

Although Haitian exiles garnered some early victories, the Haitian government's military and political influence proved formidable against attacks. According to Robert M. Sayre of the U.S. National Security Council, Duvalier's forces "round[ed] up all relatives of any exiles from grandmothers to babies in arms. . . . [Duvalier] has told his household staff, if he goes, he will go like Hitler and level Port-au-Prince." Furthermore, in an effort to defeat rebel forces on the southern coast, armed with M-1 rifles that proceeded to give Duvalier's military a "bloody nose in their first encounter," the Haitian government requested authorization from the U.S. State Department for thirty T-28 aircraft.[54] Sayre was under the impression that the White House would overrule a sale; however, in 1965, Haitian consul Rudolph Baboun and four men from Miami, Opalocka, West Palm Beach and Hollywood, Florida, were indicted on charges of piloting "two World War II T-28 fighter planes to Haiti" for $10,000 each.[55]

By 1965, Haitian exiles had failed to expel Duvalier seven times. Often Haitian expatriate reactions, both political and armed, to the troubled state of affairs were made outside of historical, political and economic contexts. Typically from the bourgeoisie or the elite, Haitian exiles refused to believe that their social classes had played any part in creating the poverty and political and economic discord of the country. The "chorus of protest" against the Haitian elite, rooted in the post-Haitian independence period and articulated in Haitian and U.S. (U.S. African American and Anglo American) literature, such as Jean Price-Mars's *La Vocation de L'Élite* (1919) and Langston Hughes's novella *Popo and Fifina* (1932), brought to the forefront gross inequities embedded in the Haitian class structure. U.S. African American dancer Katherine Dunham expressed immense frustration toward the elite and "complaining" expatriates. An aggravated Dunham wrote: "This is *your* monster! You have created it, live with it, don't be afraid to die if you feel it pulling you and yours into the dark ages!"[56] Dunham, whose activism and institution-building work in East St. Louis during the civil rights era is well known, could testify to young U.S. African American protests against racial violence and segregation in the U.S. South.[57] Thus, in the Haitian context she exemplified a Lockean belief that resisting unjust state power is the citizen's right. Yet Dunham also warned Haitian elites and opposition groups that their politics and privileges in Haitian society figured prominently in the architecture of inequality and disorder.

It is important to understand that Haitian exiles responded to a specific political emergency after having witnessed the brutality of the Duvalier government and the consolidation of his totalitarian administration. Grand and modest protests were needed to defy the regime and open up dialogue in North America and Haiti about human-rights issues and democratic change. When innocent people were arrested and tortured for associating with an anti-Duvalierist or even for simply refusing to sell a pro-Duvalier newspaper, as was the case with bookstore owner Madeline Sylvain Bourchereau, the objections and dissent voiced by Haitian exiles proved valuable in challenging social and political injustices.[58] The picketing of the Haitian ambassador's residence by members of the Democratic League of Haiti in New York City did little to arrest state atrocities in Haiti; however, it informed neighbors and drew local media attention to anti-Duvalierists' political displeasure and to Washington's support, although waning, of an "unpopular dictatorship."

Yet each foreign attack and threats from Washington to discontinue aid appear to have fortified Duvalier's regime and to provoke deeper criticism of Pan Americanism by the Haitian government. The *New York Times* reported in October 1962 that in the face of significant decrease in U.S. aid (except for a remaining $1 million earmarked for an antimalaria campaign), Duvalier attempted to rally the Haitian masses to "self-finance" their destiny. "Construct your roads with me in joy," Duvalier announced at a construction site near Port-au-Prince.[59] In an earlier speech that year, titled "Paix et Pain Pour Survivre" (Peace and Bread for Survival), Duvalier scoffed at Haiti's position under the "optics of world interdependence and continental solidarity." According to Duvalier, Pan Americanism was deficient because the United States gave little aid. Duvalier argued: "We will not surrender this country to slavery in order to supply our arid soils with water, with roads to foster civilization and progress. . . . [Therefore,] the country and the people will have to do away with deceitful and delusive notions of *mutual assistance*."[60] The *New York Times* reported in October 1962 that an excise tax on consumer goods and a "forced payroll and business levy in the form of 'liberation bonds'" had been implemented.[61] In addition, tollbooths were erected on roads and bridges to raise funds. Some Haitian officials denounced the United States and the role it may have played in attempts to overthrow the administration, highlighting Duvalier's aforementioned critiques of Washington. Historian and journalist Elizabeth Abbott noted that Jacques Fourcand, Duvalier's personal physician, called the United States a "'nation of sluts' who raped black girls in Alabama and loosed police dogs on them."[62] Fourcand warned that "if Haitians joined [U.S.] Americans to plot against Duvalier . . . blood will flow in Haiti as never before. The land will burn from north to south, from east to west. . . . The dead will be buried under a mountain of ashes because of serving the foreigner."[63] The Duvalierist state labored arduously to minimize foreign or domestic resistance. By intimidating Haitians at home, Duvalier hoped to thwart opposition abroad.

The Haitian diaspora in the United States played a functional role in Haiti's transnational political field. Speaking as immigrants and concerned Haitian citizens, the exiles' protest expanded national political discourse, challenged the authoritarianism of the Duvalierist state and transformed the exiles themselves into mobile transnational actors. Anthropologist Michel S. Laguerre broadly defined the transnational political field as "an open arena in which elected and nonelected individuals, with or without the explicit knowledge of the state, and sometimes acting against official state policies, engage in formal and informal political practices for the purpose of influencing the everyday policies and politics of another state."[64] Haitian exiles in the United States, the Bahamas and the Dominican Republic undoubtedly took advantage of U.S. liberties to organize and to develop political and intellectual activities geared to removing Duvalier.

Scholars such as Averill and Laguerre view the emergence and protest of the Haitian diaspora as the "antidote to Duvalierism" and the insurer of democracy in Haiti. However, Trouillot and other scholars are more critical of the role of the Haitian diaspora in pressuring the totalitarian system. Trouillot asserts that "the possibility for the middle-classes of establishing themselves in Africa (the Congo and Senegal), in Europe and especially in North America (Canada and the United States) underburdened the political arena, adding to the [Haitian] state's margins for maneuver."[65] Both assessments provide constructive insight into the impact of the Haitian diaspora on affairs in Haiti. Haitian exiles were needed to disseminate news about the Duvalierist state, to articulate an interventionist vision of inter-American affairs (calling for U.S. military aid in ousting Duvalier) and to challenge a prevailing U.S. African American silence on Duvalier's regime. At the same time, exiles lacked a coherent and specific vision for Haiti's future beyond expelling Duvalier. Given this limitation, I hesitate to affirm that replacing an autocrat with politically ambitious Haitian émigrés would have ensured a democratic and transformative Haiti in the 1960s.

"Naturally [We Would] Be Partial to Haiti, But [We] Get No Information from the Haitian Government": Critiques of U.S. Aid and the Nadir of U.S. African American and Haitian Relations

As stated in the opening paragraphs of this chapter, it is critical to understand how U.S. African Americans looked upon Haitian exiles as obstacles to progress in Haiti. It became difficult and uncommon for U.S. blacks to criticize the Duvalierist state when Haitian exiles were linked with unconstitutional invasions and lacked a clear vision for change. Alongside the critiques of anti-Duvalierist Haitian émigrés, many U.S. blacks attributed the black republic's ongoing economic hardships and political instability to a racist premise of U.S. foreign assistance.

Foreign aid, particularly from the United States and international aid organizations such as the International Monetary Fund, financed minor structural-improvement projects in Haiti, such as building new roads to Jacmel and developing the Port-au-Prince wharf. And yet, foreign aid also reinforced Duvalier's dominance by "passive acceptance and outright e dorsement."[66] In October 1959, Duvalier thanked U.S. president Dwig Eisenhower for the $6 million relief grant the state had received the prior year but argued that it remained insufficient. Still facing a $2.5 million state deficit, Duvalier said the government was "obliged to cut government spending drastically in many areas," including public works, education, health services and salaries for government employees. According to Duvalier, the budget cuts fueled "political unrest," and supplemental aid was critical to maintain order and democratic ideals. By 1960, in an effort to "achieve a sustained increase in national income and employment" and to finance structural projects to "fight underdevelopment," the Haitian government sought between $25 million and $30 million from the United States.[67] To receive these funds, Duvalier understood that he had to win the confidence of the U.S. State Department by convincing Eisenhower that he would rein in graft within his administration: "The monetary aid that is being extended to Haiti definitely is not and will not be misappropriated," he insisted in a letter to Eisenhower, adding that "Haiti cannot afford the extravagance of personal greed in government sponsored projects." Henceforth, he contended, "no person in the Haitian government will have access to these funds."[68] Duvalier claimed that although, "theoretically," the Department of Finance would distribute these funds, he would allow independent organizations like the International Cooperation Administration to administer U.S. aid. To some degree, this promise may have put Washington at ease. The reality at home revealed that Duvalier rejected the notion that decision-making on behalf of the republic occurred outside the executive office. His intolerant attitude toward an "organizational division of labor" assured "incompetence and inefficiency" and solidified corruption among Haitian functionaries.[69]

It remains unclear how much money the United States loaned to Haiti during Duvalier's presidency; some estimate that it averaged $12.5 million annually.[70] By 1961 to 1962, U.S. aid had temporarily ceased due to opposition to the public nature of Duvalier's brutal dictatorship. However, it is well known that Washington backed the Haitian leader during the first few years of his presidency in an effort to placate the Haitian chief executive and to win key Haitian votes within international policy institutions such as the Organization of American States and the United Nations. One unidentified Haitian businessman asserted that the "thinking people of Haiti all know that Duvalier was put in power by the United States and buttressed there with millions of dollars in aid during the first years of his regime. We think that since the United States now has unbuttressed him, it should go a little further and pull him down. Only the United States can do it."[71] As early as 1954, George Humphrey, secretary of the U.S. Treasury, advocated to Eisenhower that the United States "should . . . stop talking so much about democracy and make it clear that we are quite willing to support dictatorships of the right if their policies are pro-American."[72]

During the Cold War, U.S. financial and intellectual support of Haiti, articulated through the ideology of U.S. Pan Americanism, attempted to curb the spread of communism and to pacify assaults on North American influence in Haitian affairs. Although valid, this perspective tends to obscure how Duvalier used Pan Americanism against the United States to challenge U.S. economic dominance and to bolster his power as president. Duvalier referred to the tenets of Pan Americanism to foster more equitable economic trade agreements and to request reforms in current loan agreements with the United States. In June 1959, for example, Duvalier asked for assistance from Eisenhower to barter Haitian bauxite for U.S. American wheat. Duvalier's proposal of a five-year contract with the U.S. Commodity Corporation could have provided a necessary jolt to the Haitian economy, supplying jobs and increasing government profits.[73] Rather than commit to a five-year contract, the two leaders signed a one-year agreement three months later due to the legal ramifications against antimonopoly programs in the United States. Washington claimed that it had satisfied its bauxite requirements for the year. In July 1960, Duvalier penned another "goodwill" request to Eisenhower to facilitate a "5 year moratorium" from U.S. private creditors to ease Haiti's financial obstacles.[74] Despite the Haitian government's impressive record of paying its creditors, the United States ignored Duvalier's financial appeal; however, the request shows the bold lengths to which the Haitian president would go to solve his country's economic crises and how significant the language of Pan American language was to his outreach strategies.

Duvalier continued with these methods after John F. Kennedy was elected in 1960. Duvalier called on the new president in October 1961 to pay heed to the impact of declining coffee prices on Caribbean and Latin American nations. Since 1959, world market coffee prices had declined 25 percent. Echoing demands made at the Punta del Este conference in Uruguay in August 1961, which petitioned for the "stabilization of . . . prices of basic products in the Latin American economy," Duvalier asserted that it was "essential that efforts be made to prevent the hemispheric philosophy of coexistence through economic and social mutual assistance . . . from being jeopardized."[75] Although the Kennedy administration pumped $20 billion in economic aid to Caribbean and Latin American states through its ambitious Alliance for Progress program in 1961, of which the Punta del Este charter articulated the objectives of the Alliance, Haiti and Uruguay were the only two countries in the region that endured substantial decreases in their per-capita gross national products.[76]

For an elite few in the U.S. African American community and the U.S. black press, the grave predicament of Haitian economic and political affairs, often judged in relation to the amount of aid and economic stability that sovereign nonblack nations sustained, has historically provoked dissent. Eural Grant Jackson, a U.S. African American employee of the New York Public Schools, recognized Haiti's negative press and its periphery status among other Latin American states. Just a few months after Duvalier's election, Jackson argued that Haiti's political and economic woes after 1934 did not reveal Haiti's incompetence or "incapability of economic rehabilitation, but that probably we [the United States] failed to perform our supposed mission adequately while we were there."[77] The author shifted the responsibility of Haiti's instability to the United States but admitted that U.S. aid and technical assistance would prove beneficial if administered "in the true spirit of Pan-Americanism and equality." Jackson trusted that the United States, as a leading developed nation, could effectively support ailing nations in the Americas. However, he warned that U.S. blacks were "wary of U.S. help" considering its legacy of paternalism and imperialism in the Americas. To Jackson, Haiti's problems tested Washington's theories and practices of Pan Americanism. He defended the position that the United States should not aid Haiti "in the sense of the outmoded 'white man's burden'"—only advantageous to U.S. foreign policy—but in the spirit of "objective reciprocity." Thus, he offered a black Pan Americanist perspective that sought to empower a symbolically rich nation in the U.S. African American imagination, as well as to contest the idea that Haiti's declining state of affairs was the cause of a racialized ineptitude rather than its being partly rooted in U.S. imperialism during the Wilson and Harding administrations.[78]

The U.S. African American press reported Haiti's dissatisfaction with the United States' total aid package in 1961, which amounted to $14 million.

Three years later, in April 1964, the Inter-American Development Bank (IDB), a multilateral financing and economic development institution for the Americas, in which the United States wields the most capital and voting power, credited nearly $3 million to Haiti to develop its water systems. This loan possessed political implications since it signified a move away from the hard line under Kennedy and the "resumption of foreign assistance" to Haiti in order to encourage Haitian resistance to Cuba's socialist regime.[79] The *Chicago Defender* printed a critical response to the IDB's loan, calling it a "straw in the wind" and openly challenging President Lyndon B. Johnson's "War on Poverty" program.[80] "Haiti should come within the purview of this crusade," argued the *Defender*.[81] Under the 1964 U.S. Economic Opportunity Act, some government-sponsored organizations such as Head Start, the Community Action Program and Job Corps promoted rights and opportunities on behalf of the poor. The *Defender* advocated on behalf of Haitians and included them in their national and racial boundaries. The newspaper's statements exemplified transnational racial solidarity; in addition, the periodical challenged the United States on how it allocated funds to thwart the spread of communism. The *Chicago Defender*'s opinion piece vehemently centered its critique of Washington on the issues of race, inter-American relations and global communism:

> . . . [U.S.] American critics of the Caribbean republic seem to enjoy pointing to Haiti's poverty as conclusive evidence of her inability to be a self-sustaining nation. But Uncle Sam hasn't been as generous to Haiti as he has been to other countries far removed from this Western Hemisphere. The United States has poured close to five billion dollars in Asia and continues to pour money into Laos at the rate of a million dollars a day. These vast sums are expended in what appears to be a futile attempt to halt the onward march of Communism in East Asia. It would be far more profitable for the United States to relieve an economically depressed country right on its door-step and keep it from being transformed into another Cuba than to fight Communism in far Laos. . . . Uncle Sam can afford it. Why wait?[82]

Many U.S. African Americans showed support for U.S. efforts against communism. In spite of that, they also questioned the U.S. government's monetary and ideological dedication to the development and security of the Americas. Some U.S. blacks even questioned the putative evil of communism, arguing that state rights proved more detrimental to U.S. African

Americans and the modern United States than did communism.[83] U.S. African American points of view were indeed varied, but what remained consistent during the unforgiving days of the civil rights movement, anticolonial struggles and Cold War suppression was an economic and racial solidarity within the vein of black Pan Americanism that challenged U.S. hegemony and advocated for U.S. monetary support for developing black nations.

The *Defender's* support for substantial U.S. aid to Haiti should not be conflated with defending Duvalier. After 1961, U.S. African American support for Duvalier weakened due to his administration's well-known exploits. Yet some U.S. blacks faced the difficult dilemma of reconciling needed assistance and international collaboration with Haitians with publicly denouncing a black head of state who was piloting a historically symbolic nation of the African diaspora. A few U.S. African Americans vehemently argued that the "U.S. government can ill afford to associate itself with any regime that comes to power by foul . . . or suppresses the civil rights of the people under the guise of national security."[84] However, U.S. black newspaper accounts and press releases typically avoided making direct indictments.[85]

In comparison, the mainstream white American press deliberately drew attention to Haiti's poverty and the authoritarianism and violence of Duvalier's regime. Often reports on Haiti's affairs lacked historical context (particularly the elision of the nineteen-year U.S intervention), and the country frequently was linked with racist propaganda about voodoo rituals. Roch L. Mirabeau argued in the *Nation* in 1963 that "after the withdrawal of the Marines, there was nothing to prevent Haitian leaders from building on the *solid* foundation left by occupation forces."[86] The failure of U.S development during its occupation (discussed in chapter 2), the legacy of economic marginalization and SHADA's agricultural disaster during the post-U.S. occupation period surely propelled Haiti into its less-developed-nation status.

Former U.S. Marine Corps officer and noted writer Robert D. Heinl Jr. perpetuated sensationalist accounts regarding a Duvalier representative who had visited the tomb of John F. Kennedy: "His errand, on direct orders from 'Papa Doc' was to secure a bit of earth, [and] a breath of air from the graveside" in order to imprison the "soul" of Kennedy and "control the State Department's decisions regarding Haiti."[87] Arguably, the lurid tales of soul possession and megalomania that predominated the mainstream press in the late 1950s and early 1960s angered and embarrassed U.S. African American leadership, which, at the turn of the century through the Harlem Renaissance, had challenged these debasing images to assert civic rights and blacks' respectability in U.S. society. One *Chicago Defender* writer fervently contested these "headline-hunting" accounts of "ingrained racism" and defended the African origins of Haitian *vodou*.[88]

As early as July 1957, prior to the Duvalier regime, Haitian writer Jules Blanchet deemed the work of the U.S. press "yellow journalism—devoid of feeling, heart and magnanimity." Blanchet's open letter to the editors of *Time* magazine and the *New York Herald Tribune* asserted that the U.S. press focused on Caribbean/Latin American issues only when "violent popular agitations, insurrections and civil war burst out."[89] Blanchet downplayed the Haitian government's problems and limitations by contrasting them with the racist and brutal treatment of U.S. African Americans by southern U.S. whites in the form of lynchings, white intimidation at poll booths and racial inequality. Blanchet asserted:

> We do not pretend to world leadership. We understand our capabilities, and that knowledge saves us from many disappoint[ments]. We have no atomic industry. . . . We do not have 180,000,000 inhabitants . . . but we know what humanism is, we are no hidebound Ku Klux Klan adherents, and in this year of grace 1957, we are not lynchers. We have a concept of man which transcends his color.[90]

Blanchet's statement critiqued white supremacy and the abuses of technology; it also expressed his *négritude*. It alluded to the particularities of race (blackness) and nation but also addressed notions of the universal. Scholar Manthia Diawara argues: "When the particular is successful, its central themes begin to illuminate other struggles and creative projects."[91] Blanchet's reference to the struggles of U.S. African Americans to challenge exploitation and affirm one's humanity exemplified the breadth of *négritude*. However, Haitians, like other African-descended peoples, lacked the resources and control to widely disseminate these ideas of *négritude* and new meanings and critiques of freedom, love, blackness, modernization and civilization. Therefore, they relied on "Euromodernisms such as Marxism or Christianity to define their Négritude for them."[92] Without the means to widely distribute those new meanings, the literature and news of the day portraying black inferiority and governmental incompetence continued to define ideas of Haiti for the mainstream white press.

As stated in chapter 3, Claude Barnett sought to counteract these dominant images and descriptions of Haitian affairs during the early years of Duvalier's presidency. Barnett, who attended Ghanaian President Kwame Nkrumah's inauguration in March 1957, understood that the growth of continental Pan Africanism was connected to the need to boost people's knowledge and appreciation of the "Africa of the West," Haiti. In a letter to Duvalier, Barnett asserted that U.S. black masses knew "too little about the Pearl of the Antilles" and that more "colored people" needed to visit Haiti because it was "one country where the races can mix with ease and where Negroes can feel really free."[93] During the Duvalier regime, Barnett continued to encourage tourism. He suggested to different individuals and Haitian groups that U.S. vice president Richard Nixon be invited to visit the island. "The spotlight of publicity would follow him," wrote Barnett, adding that Nixon's visit "would be one of the greatest possible stimulants to encourage other people to go."[94]

In tandem with a few reports in the *Baltimore Afro-American* and the *Amsterdam (NY) News* and one letter from Emmanuel Racine, an Associated Negro Press Haitian correspondent, Barnett vigorously worked to create an alternative narrative that disrupted the longstanding reality of Haitian authoritarianism and violence.[95] In March 1958, Racine compared life under Duvalier's regime to life under the Ku Klux Klan. Racine explained to Barnett that "over 100 [Haitian citizens] are 'under woods' [in hiding] . . . and if the private police put a hand on them, they will endure all kind of tortures. We [Haitians] have a small KKK."[96] Racine's references to the KKK, the white supremacist group that has its origins in the post-Reconstruction United States, is particularly revealing considering that Duvalier's paramilitary force, the *tonton makouts*, did not discriminate or brutalize Haitians based on color or class. Duvalierism's violence was "limitless."[97] Duvalier's suppression of free speech and his antipathy toward adversarial groups, particularly the press, illustrated the extent of state power. In 1958, Duvalier forces attacked several "press rooms," including that of the *Haiti Miroir*. Additionally, members of Duvalier's brutal armed paramilitary group incarcerated "three newsmen . . . for writing and publishing articles 'disrespectful' of the army."[98] Despite Duvalier's boundless control of the state and his suppression of anti-Duvalierist critique, Barnett, who preferred to highlight optimistic viewpoints on Haitian affairs, chose not to chastise Duvalier's administration and remained in an editorial holding pattern until he heard from the Haitian head of state.

By 1958, Barnett had lost contact with Emmanuel Racine but continued to write letters to him. In September 1958, he commented that a few "[U.S.] colored reporters" had given in to Haitian "sensation mongering" and said that he did not trust the validity of their information. Similarly, he asked Kurt Fisher, a German collector of Haitian art and historical documents, for current information about Haitian affairs but was dissatisfied with Fisher's accounts. Barnett tried to gather information from Haitians living in New York and Chicago in the early 1960s but revealed in another letter to Racine that "everyone here [Haitians in the United States] . . . seems afraid to talk. Some of them are indignant but I assume they have relatives there [in Haiti] and don't want the long arm to reach out after them."[99] The newspaper articles chronicling the political struggles of Haitian exiles in the *New York Age,* as well as those in the *New York Times,* seemed to have been ignored by Barnett.

In another effort to obtain official news from Haiti and disseminate positive stories about the country, Barnett pressed for better communication between the two groups and ensured U.S. African American loyalty to Haitians. On May 2, 1963, Barnett noted:

> The newspapers stories appearing in the United States' papers are certainly not to Haiti's advantage. . . . I think one error which the Haitian Administration has made is that they have not paid attention to the Negro newspapers. These papers representing Negro people would naturally be partial to Haiti but they get no information from the Haitian government.[100]

Barnett's claims that the Haitian government should purposefully utilize U.S. African American print media coupled with his assertion that the U.S. black press would "naturally be partial to Haiti" typified a commitment by the ANP to advocate for Haiti's progress and development. It signified an inter-American solidarity where race, during the politically charged moment of civil rights, black nationalism and continental Pan Africanism, was being pushed more to the center of U.S. African American/Haitian relations. Yet due to the lack of communication between the Haitian government and the ANP, Barnett admitted that his influence was limited. It remains unclear why communication between Duvalier's administration and members of the U.S. African American press, particularly Barnett, an influential member of the press corps, never materialized. Although there were some minor exceptions, such as Lancelot Evans, Duvalier never utilized the U.S. black press as had past Haitian presidents.[101] For the most part, Duvalier addressed the U.S. African American experience—particularly racial segregation—only when it proved to be in the state's interest or if the Haitian government was in a "fight with U.S. administrations."[102]

Like other U.S. African American journalists such as Lancelot O. Evans, Barnett seemed to give Duvalier's leadership the benefit of the doubt. Despite negative reports about Duvalier, Barnett preferred to communicate directly with Duvalier rather than print secondhand reports. On May 9, 1964, the same year Duvalier declared himself President for Life, Barnett wrote to the Haitian president claiming that the ANP possessed a number of Haitian citizens as "friends . . . but the view from the United States makes it difficult to know which of our friends may be enjoying your favor."[103] Also, in an attempt to obtain firsthand information, he stated: "There have been times when your image in the minds of people in this country and especially in the regard of Negro Americans might have been greatly changed, but we have not known the truth of various reports."[104] Barnett remains an important figure in the transnational politics of the African diaspora, and I contend that his continued efforts to support Haitian affairs and Duvalier stemmed from his deep sense of racial solidarity and his belief that Haiti could survive and thrive with the leadership of a black president. Yet Barnett missed a real opportunity to complicate and critique Haitian leadership and its relationship to the United States because he failed to reconcile black despotic rule with a program of transnational racial uplift.

Conclusion

"My dear Claude, we are proud to be Negroes," wrote Eric F. Etienne, an interpreter at the Palais National in Port-au-Prince. It was April 1968, but Barnett had died in August 1967.[105] Duvalier's office had not heard of the passing of one of its strongest advocates. The letter was a clear indication that communication between key U.S. African American figures and the Haitian government had dissipated. Etienne was under the impression that the ANP functioned as a positive vehicle to disseminate news regarding the "Duvalier revolution." However, that ship had sailed. The period launched with Duvalier's self-proclamation as President for Life in 1964 through his death in 1971 should be considered the nadir of U.S. African American and Haitian relations. When he declared himself dictator, the U.S. black press barely issued a critique. The *Baltimore Afro-American* reported:

Aside from Duvalier's own desires, some Haitians point to two other factions behind keeping him in office for life. One is a group of officials in government who do not wish to lose their special privileges. The other involves the voodoo priests who have wide influence.[106]

In this case, the *Afro-American* adopted the racist language more prevalent in the white press. It might have reflected U.S. African American frustrations at Haitian authoritarianism and the limitations of black Pan Americanism during the height of the civil rights struggle and continental Pan Africanism. The relative silence within U.S. African American political, media and business circles was apparent. With the exception of Duvalier's book honoring the life of Martin Luther King Jr. after his death in 1968, the four days of national mourning after King's assassination and the naming of a Port-au-Prince street after the civil rights leader, discussions on Haitian politics were minimal. Duvalier's commemoration of King proved to be an empty gesture given the Haitian leader's record on human rights, the continued indigence of the peasantry and his use of the tragedy as an opportunity to advance *noiriste* politics.[107]

Initially, U.S. African Americans supported Duvalier because of the history of racial solidarity with the country and the perception of Duvalier's being a champion of the peasantry. During the moment of anti-imperialist struggles and civil rights conflicts, domestic and abroad, racial unity served as a practical political program and affirmed the U.S. black presence in racial progress. The invasion of Haitian exiles and the elitism that they historically demonstrated in Haiti factored into U.S. African American perceptions. Although some U.S. blacks, such as writer Rosa Guy, noted their satisfaction with Haitian expatriates' education and Haiti's ability to send them to developing countries in Africa, many exiles were characterized as power hungry and serving as obstacles to true democracy.[108] At the same time, the escalation of the southern civil rights movement and Cold War threats refocused U.S. African Americans' attention on national issues of racial discrimination and racial violence. The Cold War period stifled many of the more revolutionary constituents of the U.S. civil rights movement who maintained ideological bonds with African, Latin American and Caribbean anti-imperialist movements. On the one hand, some U.S. black activists navigated the international and national pressures that characterized the Cold War period. On the other hand, as historian Penny Von Eschen asserts: "Although civil rights leaders such as Martin Luther King and Bayard Rustin were personally interested in anticolonialism, it was not a programmatic part of the civil rights movement."[109] The intensification of the southern civil rights movement and the undermining of radical, anti-imperialist and socialist thought during the Cold War surely impacted and refocused U.S. African America's international agenda. This shift should not be taken to mean that more radical U.S. blacks forgot or were oblivious to African diasporic politics—the protests of the CIA-sponsored murder of Patrice Lumumba and support of Fidel Castro's regime prove otherwise—but it suggests that U.S. African Americans were forced to negotiate and at times stifle their political affiliations and beliefs at specific moments. Duvalier's repression and antidemocratic politics lost out to the more positive stories of African independence in the U.S. black press. After Duvalier's death in 1971, momentum built up again between the two groups. U.S. African American politicians and ambassadors such as Congresswoman Shirley Chisholm (NY) and Andrew Young condemned the human-rights violations against Duvalier's successor, his nineteen-year-old son Jean-Claude (Baby Doc) Duvalier.[110] Advancements in the U.S. civil rights movement, fuller understandings of postcolonial Africa and of the problems/limitations of African leadership and a more acceptable anti-Vietnam War ethos in the United States proved to be among the factors that provided a space in which to critique Haitian leadership. However, U.S. African American and Haitian cooperation would not be the same until years to come.

Notes

Note on Usage and Terminology

1. Mignolo, *Idea of Latin America,* 47–48.

2. Ibid., 22. For more on the invention of the Americas by Europeans, see Edmundo O'Gorman, *La Invención de América;* Jorge Cañizares-Esguerra, *How to Write the History of the New World: Histories, Epistemologies, and Identities in the Eighteenth-century Atlantic World* (Palo Alto, Calif.: Stanford University Press, 2001); Enrique Dussel, *The Invention of the Americas: Eclipse of "the Other" and the Myth of Modernity* (New York: Continuum Publishing Company, 1995); Anibal Quijano and Immanuel Wallerstein, "Americanity as a Concept; Or the Americas in the Modern World-System," *ISSA* 1, no. 134 (1992): 549–556.

3. Refer to Brent Edwards, *The Practice of Diaspora: Literature, Translation, and the Rise of Black Internationalism* (Cambridge, Mass.: Harvard University Press, 2003), 13–14; Nwankwo, *Black Cosmopolitanism,* 18.

4. Mignolo, *Idea of Latin America,* 106–107.

5. Nwankwo, *Black Cosmopolitanism,* 17.

Introduction

1. For more on Jean-Bertrand Aristide's presidency and his 2004 departure, refer to these important texts: Dupuy, *Prophet and Power;* Hallward, *Damming the Flood;* Deibert, *Notes from the Last Testament;* Aristede, Aristede, Chomsky, Farmer and Goodman, *Getting Haiti Right This Time;* Fatton, *Haiti's Predatory Republic.*

2. Waters, "Congresswoman Maxine Waters' Statement on Kidnapping of Haitian President Aristide," press release, March 1, 2004, http://www.house.gov/waters/

3. Goodman, "Randall Robinson: Aristide Says 'Tell the World It Is a Coup,'" interview with Randall Robinson, Democracynow.org, March 1, 2004. Refer also to Randall Robinson, *An Unbroken Agony.*

4. Rangel, phone interview with Millery Polyné, November 8, 2006. Randall Robinson and many members of the Congressional Black Caucus, including Maxine Waters and Charles Rangel, emphatically believe that the United States forced Aristide out of the executive office. As Robinson asserts, it is difficult to prove if the event was the result of

a "conspiracy" by the U.S. government; thus, I can neither confirm nor deny that such a kidnapping took place. Furthermore, investigating this issue is beyond the scope of my book. Refer also to Laguerre, "Homeland Political Crisis, the Virtual Diasporic Public Sphere, and Diasporic Politics," 206–225; Dupuy, *Prophet and Power*, 172–175.

5. Waters, "Congresswoman Waters Leads Delegation to Free Aristide from Central African Republic," press release, March 16, 2004.

6. Dupuy, *Prophet and Power*, 185.

7. Daniels' quotes come from a page on the now-defunct website Cruising Into History.

8. There are many books written on the Haitian Revolution. For a more detailed discussion and analysis of the varied objectives of the Haitian Revolution, I suggest starting with these four texts: L. Dubois, *Avengers of the New World*; Fick, *Making of Haiti*; Geggus, *Slavery, War and Revolution*; and C.L.R. James, *Black Jacobins*.

9. International Action Center, "Congresswoman Maxine Waters and Ossie Davis will speak at April 7th rally to demand restoration of democracy in Haiti," press release, April 7, 2004.

10. See Matthewson, *Proslavery Foreign Policy*; Geggus, *Haitian Revolutionary Studies*; A. Hunt, *Haiti's Influence on Antebellum America*. R. Kennedy briefly discusses the connection between the sale of the Louisiana Purchase and Haiti in *Mr. Jefferson's Lost Cause*, 176–77, 184, 229–232, 256–257.

11. Frederick Douglass, "A Trip to Haiti," *Douglass' Monthly*, May 1861, 449.

12. Refer to Moses, *Afrotopia*, and Howe, *Afrocentrism*. The U.S. North has also been a site of black liberation, yet as slaves did with Haiti, many enslaved U.S. African Americans utilized the biblical language of "bondage" or "oppression" in Egypt or Canaan to describe it.

13. Refer to Fischer, *Modernity Disavowed*.

14. Douglass, "A Trip to Haiti," May 1861, 449. My italics.

15. Ibid.

16. Ibid.

17. For more on Frederick Douglass in the black international arena, see Nwankwo, *Black Cosmopolitanism*, 114–152; and Michael, *Identity and the Failure of America*, 201–234.

18. Refer to Blight, *Frederick Douglass' Civil War*, 127–128. For more on Pan Africanism, refer to Padmore, *Pan-Africanism or Communism*; Geiss, *Pan-African Movement*; Lemelle and Kelley, eds., *Imagining Home*; and Esedebe, *Pan-Africanism: The Idea and Movement*.

19. Moses, *Creative Conflict in African American Thought*, 5.

20. Ibid., 6.

21. Belnap and Fernández, "The Architectonics of José Martí's "Our Americanism,"" 8.

22. Martí, "Our America" (1891), in *Our America*, 84–85.

23. Ibid., 93-94.

24. Plummer, "Firmin and Martí at the Intersection of Pan-Americanism and Pan-Africanism," 216.

25. Anténor Firmin, *Equality of the Human Races,* xl.

26. Refer to Ballard, "African American Protest and the Role of the Haitian Pavilion at the 1893 Chicago World's Fair," in *Multiculturalism,* ed. James Troutman, 108-124; William S. McFeely, *Frederick Douglass,* 366; Sweeney, *Frederick Douglass and the Atlantic World,* 174–182.

27. Hannibal Price, *De la Réhabilitation de la Race Noire,* iii.

28. Jenkins, *Private Lives, Proper Relations,* 14, 16.

29. Gaines, *Uplifting the Race,* xiv.

30. Ibid.

31. Hanchard, "Afro-Modernity," 248.

32. Ibid.

33. Berman, *All That Is Solid Melts into Air,* 13.

34. Lavender and Levine, eds., *Hemispheric American Studies,* 5.

35. Nwankwo, "Promises and Perils of U.S. African American Hemispherism," 189. Some recent key texts that could be grouped into the field of Hemispheric American Studies include: Gretchen Murphy, *Hemispheric Imaginings*; Nwankwo, *Black Cosmopolitanism*; Kaplan, *Anarchy of Empire in the Making of U.S. Culture*; Belnap and Fernández, *José Martí's "Our America"*; Gruesz, *Ambassadors of Culture*; Jon Smith and Deborah Cohn, eds., *Look Away*; Stephens, *Black Empire.*

36. Andrews, *Afro-Latin America, 1800-2000,* 3.

37. Douglass, "The Present Condition and Future Prospects of the Negro People," May 11, 1853, in *Frederick Douglass: Selected Speeches and Writings,* ed. P. Foner, 258.

38. Pamphile, *Haitians and African Americans,* 1.

39. Refer to Moses, *Golden Age of Black Nationalism, 1850–1925.*

40. Refer to P. Smith, *Talons of the Eagle*; LaRosa and Mora, eds., *Neighborly Adversaries*; Sheinin, ed., *Beyond the Ideal.*

41. Refer to Jean-Baptiste, *Le Fondateur devant L'Histoire*; Verna, "Haiti's Second Independence and the Promise of Pan-American Cooperation"; Dantès Bellegarde, "President Alexandre Pétion," 205–213.

42. Plummer, "Firmin and Martí," 223.

43. Much of the rich literature on Pan Americanism, which goes as far back as the late 19th century, ignores the black populations of the Caribbean and South America and often privileges Spanish- and/or Portuguese-speaking countries. As historian George Reid Andrews reveals in *Afro-Latin America,* African-descended peoples have had a major impact on the political, economic and cultural development of their societies and were often the foundation for populist regimes and racially democratic ideological movements. Refer also to Graham, ed., *Idea of Race in Latin America.* For more on coloniality, see Mignolo, *Idea of Latin America.*

44. Simón Bolívar to Francisco de Paula Santander (May 20, 1825), in Bolívar, *Selected Writings of Bolívar,* 499.

45. Refer to Fischer, *Modernity Disavowed*; Bunkley, ed., *A Sarmiento Anthology*; Andrews, *Afro-Latin America*; and Graham, *Idea of Race in Latin America,* 1–6.

46. One reporter for the *Baltimore Afro-American* asserted that President Woodrow Wilson's call for Pan Americanism was a sign that Wilson was "fishing around for allies

in case of a future war with a united Europe." Refer to "Pan Americanism," *Baltimore Afro-American*, December 25, 1915, 4.

47. *Baltimore Afro-American*, "The Effect of Pan-Americanism upon the Darker Races", January 15, 1916, 1. See also Cook, "Prejudice, Not Hitler, Greatest Threat to Pan Americanism," *Baltimore Afro-American*, September 13, 1941.

48. *Baltimore Afro-American*, "The Effect of Pan-Americanism," 1.

49. *Haiti Journal*, "Inter-American Cooperation," March 16, 1936. Attached to George A. Gordon to Sumner Welles, March 21, 1936, Records of the Department of State Relating to Internal Affairs of Haiti, 1930–1939; RG 59, General Records of U.S. Department of State; microfilm reel 69, National Archives at College Park, Md. Hereafter, National Archives at College Park abbreviated "NACP."

50. Refer to Golinger, *Bush vs. Chavez*.

51. Farmer, *The Uses of Haiti*, 41.

52. Refer to Paul Farmer, *AIDS and Accusation*, and Farmer, *The Uses of Haiti*.

53. Refer to Chris Dixon, *African America and Haiti*; Pamphile, *Haitians and African Americans*.

54. Dixon, *African America and Haiti*, 69.

55. For more information on early Haiti/U.S. relations, see Matthewson, *A Proslavery Foreign Policy*; Plummer, *Haiti and the United States*, 11–49.

56. Cuba, Jamaica, the Dominican Republic, the Bahamas and Puerto Rico were among the islands that supported tourism as early as the 1930s. Refer to Schwartz, *Pleasure Island*, 108–109. Also refer to Ramsey, "Without One Ritual Note," 7–42.

57. Holden and Zolov, eds., *Latin America and the United States*, 61. Refer also to P. Foner, ed., *Inside the Monster*.

Chapter 1. "The Spirit of the Age . . . Establish[es] a Sentiment of Universal Brotherhood": Haiti, "Santo Domingo" and Frederick Douglass at the Intersection of the United States and Black Pan Americanism

1. Perez, *Cuba and the United States*, 38–50. Refer also to the 1849 article "Annexation of Cuba" by nineteenth-century black nationalist Martin R. Delany, in *Martin R. Delany*, 160–166.

2. Jacobson, *Barbarian Virtues*, 17.

3. *Chicago Tribune*, "Frederick Douglass' Lecture Last Evening," December 30, 1871, 2.

4. Moses, *Creative Conflict in African American Thought*, 120–121.

5. For more on Washington's policy on the invasion and annexation of Mexican land, see President James K. Polk's message to the U.S. Congress, "President's Message," December 4, 1845, 4–11; U.S. Congress, Senate, Senate Document No. 337, 1846.

6. *Chicago Tribune*, "Frederick Douglass' Lecture Last Evening," December 30, 1871, 2.

7. For more on Pan Americanism, refer to Sheinin, ed., *Beyond the Ideal*; Aguilar, *Pan Americanism from Monroe to the Present*; Gilderhus, *Pan-American Visions*; Inman, *Inter-American Conferences, 1826–1954*.

8. Douglass, "The Present Condition and Future Prospects of the Negro People," May 11, 1853, in Douglass, *Frederick Douglass: Selected Speeches and Writings*, 258.

9. There is a particular need for more research on U.S. African American diplomats and their views on U.S. and international foreign policy. Refer to Skinner, *African Americans and U.S. Policy toward Africa, 1850–1924*; Jacobs, *The African Nexus*; Krenn, *Black Diplomacy*. Ebenezer Don Carlos Bassett was the first U.S. African American diplomat to Haiti. He served under President Ulysses S. Grant from 1869 to 1877. John Mercer Langston (1877–1885), George Washington Williams (1885) and John E.W. Thompson (1885–1889) were all predecessors to Frederick Douglass.

10. Jacobson, *Barbarian Virtues*, 53.

11. Stuckey, *Slave Culture*, 223.

12. E. Foner, *A Short History of Reconstruction*, 105–108, 180–198.

13. Frederick Douglass, "Reminiscences of the Antislavery Conflict as Delivered during the Lecture Season of 72 and 73," Frederick Douglass Papers, Speech, Article and Book File, microfilm reel 14, LOC. Hereafter, Frederick Douglass Papers will be abbreviated "FDP." See also "Frederick Douglass on the Fifteenth Amendment," *New York Times*, April 11, 1870, 1.

14. Douglass, "Reminiscences of the Antislavery Conflict," FDP.

15. Ibid.

16. See "Nicaraguan Canal Proposal," FDP, microfilm reel 12, Schomburg Center for Research in Black Culture, New York Public Library. Hereafter Schomburg Center will be abbreviated "SCRBC." L. Langley, *The Banana Wars*, 49–51; Jacobson, *Barbarian Virtues*; Gobat, *Confronting the American Dream*.

17. Jacobson, *Barbarian Virtues*, 41.

18. Refer to Betances, *Las Antillas para los Antillanos*; Plummer, "Firmin and Martí"; Lewis, *Main Currents in Caribbean Thought*, 271–320.

19. Blanchard, "Pan Americanism and Slavery in the Era of Latin American Independence," 15.

20. Betances quoted in Zacaïr, "Haiti on his Mind," 51.

21. Moses, *Creative Conflict in African American Thought*, 35.

22. Anténor Firmin, Haitian intellectual and statesman, noted the significance of Frederick Douglass's life as a slave to his becoming "one of the most remarkable men of color and the most engaging individual of his race in the United States." See Firmin, *Equality of the Human Races*, 208–209, 331.

23. See M. Hunt, *Ideology and U.S. Foreign Policy*; Jacobson, *Barbarian*; Paterson, Clifford, Maddock, Kisatsky and Hagan, eds., *American Foreign Relations*, vol. 1.

24. Paterson et al., *American Foreign Relations*, vol. 1, 169.

25. See Love, *Race over Empire*; Krenn, *Impact of Race on U.S. Foreign Policy*; Schueller, *U.S. Orientalisms*; M. Hunt, *Ideology and U.S. Foreign Policy*; Jacobson, *Barbarian Virtues*.

26. For more on nineteenth-century Haitian and Dominican conflicts, see Logan, *Haiti and the Dominican Republic*; Pons, *Dominican Republic: A National History*; Michel, *La Revolución Haitiana y Santo Domingo*; Fischer, *Modernity Disavowed*, 131–200.

27. San Miguel, *The Imagined Island, 77.* See also Fischer, *Modernity Disavowed,* 146–147.

28. Fischer, *Modernity Disavowed,* 151; San Miguel, *The Imagined Island, 79.*

29. Martin R. Delany also expressed his agitation over dialogues between Washington and Dominican Republic during the 1850s. Refer to Delany's address (1855) at the National Emigration Convention in Pittsburgh, Pennsylvania, titled "Political Aspect of the Colored People of the United States," in Delany, *Martin R. Delany: A Documentary Reader,* 286–287.

30. Refer to Nelson, "The Haitian Political Situation and Its Effect on the Dominican Republic, 1849–1877," 227–235.

31. For more on Spanish, British, French, Dominican and Haitian relations during Haitian invasion of Dominican Republic, see Logan, *Haiti and the Dominican Republic,* 36–41; Leger, *Haiti: Her History and Her Detractors,* 202–208. For more on William L. Cazneau, see Welles, *Naboth's Vineyard: The Dominican Republic, 1844–1924,* 146–149, 152–156.

32. Demesvar Delorme to Salomon, November 30, 1867, Papiers Diplomatique, 1850–1925, Archives Nationale, Port-au-Prince, Haiti. See also Vidas, "The Foreign Relations of Haiti," 220–221.

33. San Miguel, *Imagined Island, 72.* Jacques N. Leger, Haitian historian, asserted that "after the overthrow of Spain the Dominican Republic forgot the help that [Haiti] had given to them." See Leger, *Haiti,* 208. For more on nineteenth-century Haiti/Dominican border conflicts and Spain re-annexation, see Gándara, *Anexión y Guerra de Santo Domingo,* vol. 1, 384–385; Paulino, "Birth of a Boundary," 43–49.

34. Hauch, "Attitudes of Foreign Governments towards the Spanish Reoccupation of the Dominican Republic," 264.

35. The Haitian government helped sponsor a trip for Douglass and potential U.S. "emigrants and passengers" to Haiti in April 1861. However, the start of the U.S. Civil War postponed the voyage. See Douglass, "A Trip to Haiti," 439–442. *Douglass' Monthly* published one article by James Redpath, who was critical of Spain's occupation of the Dominican Republic. See James Redpath, "The Annexation of St. Domingo to Spain," *Douglass' Monthly,* May 1861, 460-461. For more on Redpath, see McKivigan, *Forgotten Firebrand,* and Dixon, *African America and Haiti,* 129–176.

36. Quoted from Secretary of State William Seward to Horatio J. Perry, U.S. chargé d'affaires in Madrid, Spain, in Hauch, "Attitudes of Foreign Governments," 268.

37. See Hidalgo, "Charles Sumner and the Annexation of the Dominican Republic," 51–66; Atkins and Wilson, *Dominican Republic and the United States;* Nelson, "The Haitian Political Situation," 227–235; Tansill, *United States and Santo Domingo;* Paterson et al., eds., *American Foreign Relations.*

38. Quoted in Donald, *Charles Sumner and the Rights of Man,* 443.

39. Leger, *Haiti,* 220. See also Manigat, *Leaders of Haiti, 1804–2001,* 50.

40. "Santo Domingo," no date, FDP, microfilm reel 18, SCRBC.

41. Frederick Douglass to Charles Sumner, January 6, 1871, in Douglass, *Life and Writings of Frederick Douglass,* vol. 4, 240.

42. "Santo Domingo," no date, FDP, microfilm reel 18, SCRBC.

43. Teal, *Hero of Hispaniola*, 71.

44. Douglass, *Life and Writings of Frederick Douglas,* vol. 4, 72.

45. Hamilton Fish, U.S. secretary of state, to Manuel Gautier, minister of foreign affairs of Dominican Republic, January 14, 1871, FDP, General Correspondence 1868–1877, microfilm reel 2, SCRBC.

46. Refer to "Report of the Commission of Inquiry to Santo Domingo," U.S. Senate Congressional Record, 42nd Cong., 1st sess., Executive Document no. 9, 1871, 4–285.

47. During the 1820s, U.S. African American emigration to Haiti included settlements on the Samaná peninsula. Historian Chris Dixon argued that despite "early enthusiasm" from U.S. black emigrants in Haiti, they soon experienced major problems and adjustments in their new home. For more on African American emigration to Haiti, see Dixon, *African America and Haiti.*

48. Douglass asked the U.S. American colonist, "What is the present number on the colony that settled in the vicinity of Samana Bay in 1824? Answer. From five- to six-hundred." See "Report of the Commission of Inquiry to Santo Domingo," 231. Also, see Dixon, *African America and Haiti,* 40–41, 99.

49. "Report of the Commission," 232.

50. Quoted in Welles, *Naboth's Vineyard,* 385. See also Teal, *Hero of Hispaniola,* 67.

51. "Boletin Oficial," February 19, 1870, quoted in Welles, *Naboth's Vineyard,* 385–386.

52. Fischer, *Modernity Disavowed,* 147.

53. Ebenezer Bassett to Hamilton Fish, September 1873, *Despatches from United States Ministers to Haiti, 1862–1906,* National Archives and Records Services, Washington, D.C.: 1955; See also de Vidas, "The Foreign Relations of Haiti in Hemispheric Affairs," 232.

54. Teal, *Hero of Hispaniola,* 68.

55. Ibid., 67.

56. Ebenezer Don Carlos Bassett to Frederick Douglass, Judge Burton and Benjamin Wade, March 9, 1871, FDP, General Correspondence 1868–1877, microfilm reel 2, SCRBC.

57. "Santo Domingo," FDP, microfilm reel 18, SCRBC.

58. Quoted in Novas, *Twice the Diplomat,* 70.

59. "Santo Domingo," FDP, microfilm reel 18, SCRBC.

60. Ibid.

61. *Chicago Tribune,* "Frederick Douglass' Lecture Last Evening," December 30, 1871, 2.

62. Novas, *Twice the Diplomat,* 71.

63. Moses, *Afrotopia,* 127–129.

64. Douglass briefly supported U.S. African American emigration to Haiti and Florida on the "eve" of the U.S. Civil War. See Moses, *Creative Conflict,* 40, 107–108.

65. *Chicago Tribune,* "Gen. Grant: What He Says about a Third Term," July 26, 1878, 5.

66. Douglass, *Frederick Douglass,* 177.

67. Douglass, *Life and Writings of Frederick Douglass,* vol. 5, 471.

68. "Santo Domingo," FDP, microfilm reel 18, SCRBC.

69. For an understanding of the roots of Haitian dependency, see Plummer, *Haiti and the Great Powers, 1902–1915*; Trouillot, *Haiti: State against Nation*.

70. Historian Matthew Jacobson discussed the provisions James G. Blaine and President Harrison made for the McKinley Tariff wherein the president could "punish any country that discriminated against the United States in favor of European goods by tacking prohibitive duties on that country's key exports." See Jacobson, *Barbarian Virtues*, 41.

71. Moses, *Afrotopia*, 127.

72. Quoted in Quarles, *Frederick Douglass*, 285. Antonio Maceo, Cuban rebel leader, made a significant trip to Haiti in 1879 during *La Guerra Chiquita* or Little War in Cuba. While in Haiti, he called for Haitians, particularly General Joseph Lamothe, in the spirit of Pan-Caribbean-ness, to aid Cuban rebels against Spain. See Antonio Maceo to General Joseph Lamothe, September 23, 1879, Joseph Borome Papers, box 1, folder Antonio Maceo, SCRBC; Zacaïr, "Haiti on His Mind," 47–78.

73. Douglass, *Life and Writings of Frederick Douglass*, 259.

74. Ibid.

75. Ibid.

76. Moses, *Creative Conflict*, 2.

77. Ibid., 26–27.

78. Goldstein, "Racial Loyalty in America," 475.

79. See C.H. Howard, Western Secretary of American Missionary Association to Frederick Douglass, January 9, 1872, FDP, General Correspondence, 1868–1877, microfilm reel 2, SCRBC. Editor Philip Foner noted that the National Conventions of Colored Men in St. Louis and in Columbia, South Carolina, supported annexation. See P. Foner, *Life and Writings of Frederick Douglass*, 71.

80. See Logan, *Betrayal of the Negro*, 23–47.

81. Quoted in Skinner, *African Americans and U.S. Policy*, 97.

82. Logan, *Diplomatic Relations of United States with Haiti*, 420.

83. *Les Nouvelles*, "La Question Américaine," June 12, 1889, 1. For more Haitian commentary on U.S. involvement in the Légitime coup, see also *Les Nouvelles*, December 19, 1888; January 23, 1889, 4; and April 24, 1889, 2. Additionally, see *La Voie*, "Les États-Unis et Haiti," March 22, 1890, and *La Liberté*, "La Politique du Jour," November 30, 1889, 1,5. Newspapers archived in Center for Research Libraries, Chicago.

84. Trouillot, *Haiti: State against Nation*, 69. Refer also to Plummer, *Haiti and the Great Powers*, 40–41.

85. In the Frederick Douglass Papers at the Schomburg Center for Research in Black Culture, there are a number of newspaper articles from the *Philadelphia Enquirer*, *Washington Post* and *Atlanta Journal* that discuss U.S. accusations that Douglass was unfit for the job of U.S. diplomat. See FDP, microfilm reel 11, SCRBC; Pamphile, *Haitians and African Americans*, 84–85.

86. Undated essay, FDP, microfilm reel 17, SCRBC.

87. See *Niles Weekly Register*, July 1, 1820; *Columbian Sentinel*, July 3, 1824.

88. N. Deslandes, "Une Infamie," *Le Progres: Journal Franco-Haitien*, December 22, 1888; article included in *Despatches from United States Ministers to Haiti, 1862–1906*,

microfilm reel 23 (Washington, D.C.: National Archives and Record Service, 1955), SCRBC.

89. Benjamin Harrison, *Public Papers and Addresses of Benjamin Harrison*, 7.

90. See Mahan, *Influence of Sea Power upon History*.

91. Quoted in Tyler, *Foreign Policy of James G. Blaine*, 178.

92. Price, *Rapport Adressé au Gouvernement d'Haïti*, 7.

93. N. Brown, *Black Diplomat in Haiti*, 41–42.

94. A.P. Holly, "What Hayti Has Done," *New York Age*, July 27, 1889, in FDP, microfilm reel 11, SCRBC.

95. Douglass, "Toussaint L'Ouverture," *Colored American*, July 1903, 491.

96. N. Brown, *Black Diplomat in Haiti*, 41–42.

97. Plummer, *Haiti and the United States*, 55–59.

98. N. Brown, *Black Diplomat in Haiti*, 255. My italics.

99. Refer to Jacobson, *Barbarian Virtues*; Weston, *Racism in U.S. Imperialism*.

100. Logan, *Diplomatic Relations of United States with Haiti*, 431.

101. Harrison, *Public Papers and Addresses of Benjamin Harrison*, 31.

102. Quoted in Logan, *Diplomatic Relations of the United States with Haiti*, 433.

103. Quoted in N. Brown, *Black Diplomat in Haiti*, 58. Other works documenting Frederick Douglass's involvement with Haiti's Môle St. Nicholas affair include Sears, "Frederick Douglass and the Mission to Haiti," 222–238; Himelhoch, "Frederick Douglass and Haiti's Môle St. Nicolas," 161–180.

104. Firmin, *M. Roosevelt, Président des États-Unis*, 499.

105. Ibid.

106. Ibid., 500.

107. Ibid. In subsequent years, one sees the evolution of Anténor Firmin's philosophy on inter-American affairs. In his *Lettres de Saint-Thomas* (Paris, 1910), he encouraged an Antillean federation and increased relations with the United States and with foreign investment. See also Firmin, *M. Roosevelt, Président des États-Unis*; Plummer, *Haiti and the Great Powers*; Dash, "Nineteenth-century Haiti and the Archipelago of the Americas," 44–53. Hannibal Price, Haitian ambassador to Washington, D.C., had much to say about the Môle affair in his book *The Haytian Question*. For Price, Haiti forfeited its sovereign status if it leased Môle Saint-Nicolas. Price wrote: "What is asked of the Republic of Hayti is, that she abdicate her independence ... that she become, in short, a maritime province of Uncle Sam. ...[It is an] emasculation of the little Black Republic ... and its conversion into a veritable eunuch government in the service of the United States." See Price, *The Haytian Question*, 45.

108. Douglass, "Haïti and the United States: Inside History of the Negotiations for the Môle St. Nicolas," pt.1, *North American Review* 153, no. 418 (September 1891): 341.

109. Ibid., 342.

110. In desperate need of money, former U.S. minister to Haiti Ebenezer D. Bassett accompanied Douglass to Haiti as his personal secretary. According to Christopher Teal, Bassett's connections, experience and language skills were instrumental to Douglass. During the Firmin/Gherardi negotiations, Gherardi denied Bassett access. In response to Bassett's absence, Douglass wrote that "it left me at the mercy of men [Gherardi and

his staff lieutenant] whom, I begin to think, have intentionally misrepresented me." See Teal, *Hero of Hispaniola,* 150, 153, 156.

111. Douglass, "Haïti and the United States," pt. 1, 343.

112. Ibid., 344.

113. Plummer, *Haiti and the United States,* 61.

114. Douglass, "Haïti and the United States," pt. 1, 345.

115. James G. Blaine to Benjamin Harrison, August 16, 1891, in Harrison and Blaine, *Correspondence between Benjamin Harrison and James G. Blaine,* 177.

116. Blaine to Harrison, August 27, 1891, ibid., 181.

117. Douglass, "Haïti and the United States," pt. 1, 338–339.

118. Ibid., 339–340.

119. See *La Voie,* "Au *New York Herald,"* July 18, 1891, 1.

120. Robert T. Teamoh, "Hayti Getting Better," *Boston Daily Globe,* August 19, 1890, in FDP, microfilm reel 11, SCRBC.

121. See Ewell, *Venezuela and the United States;* Linn, *Philippine War, 1899–1902;* Perez, *War of 1898.*

Chapter 2. "To Combine the Training of the Head and the Hands": The 1930 Robert R. Moton Education Commission in Haiti

1. Louis C. Lhérisson speech in honor of Moton Commission, no date, Foreign Affairs Series, box 989, Haitian Commission-Moton Commission folder; Herbert Hoover Papers, Herbert Hoover Presidential Library, West Branch, Iowa. Hereafter cited as "Hoover Papers" and "Hoover Library."

2. Cook, *Education in Haiti,* 4.

3. Lhérisson speech in honor of Moton Commission, box 989, Hoover Papers, Hoover Library.

4. Moton asked James Weldon Johnson to serve on the committee. However, Johnson respectfully declined "because of his disapproval of the character and circumstances of the President's [Hoover] request." The Moton Commission was Hoover's second appointed group, after the William Cameron Forbes Commission, an all-white committee that sought to study conditions in Haiti during the latter stages of U.S. occupation. Many politically minded U.S. African Americans believed that the predominantly black Moton Commission was a mere afterthought of Hoover's and was created only to appease U.S. African American leadership. Refer to Moton to Hoover, February 20, 1930, Foreign Affairs Series, box 989, Haitian Commission-Moton Commission folder, Hoover Papers, Hoover Library.

5. Michele Mitchell defined the U.S. black aspiring class as "workers able to save a little money as well as those who worked multiple jobs to attain class mobility" and noted that they possessed "an abiding concern with propriety—not to mention a belief that morality, thrift and hard work were essential to black progress." See Mitchell, *Righteous Propagation,* 9–10. For more information on the U.S. press and U.S. African American responses to U.S. occupation of Haiti, see Plummer, "The Afro American Response to the Occupation of Haiti, 1915–1934"; Suggs, "The Response of the African American

Press to the United States Occupation of Haiti, 1915–1934"; Blassingame, "The Press and American Intervention in Haiti and the Dominican Republic, 1904–1920."

6. Trouillot, *Haiti: State against Nation,* 103.

7. Refer to Herbert Hoover's address to the Gridiron Club, April 26, 1930, in Hoover, *Public Papers of the Presidents of the United States: Herbert Hoover, Containing the Public Messages, Speeches, and Statements of the President, 1930,* 162.

8. The Forbes Commission consisted of Henry P. Fletcher, former U.S. ambassador to Chile; Elie Vezina, described as a "student of Haitian affairs"; James Kerney, a publisher of the *Trenton (N.J.) Times;* William Allen White, a personal friend of Hoover who was active in Hoover's campaign; James C. Dunn, an official of the Latin American division of the U.S. State Department; Charles H. Marshall, former New York stockbroker; and Victor G. Heiser, a medical advisor.

9. Dantès Bellegarde testimony, March 3, 1930, President's Commission for Study and Review of Condition in Haiti, box 1074, William Allen White March 1–4, 1930, folder, Hoover Papers, Hoover Library.

10. Lhérisson is actually quoting Anténor Firmin, a former Haitian minister of foreign affairs. I do not know where the quote originated, but it probably stems from either Firmin's *Lettres de Saint-Thomas* or his *M. Roosevelt, Président des États-Unis et la République d'Haïti.*

11. Plummer, "The African American Response," 125–126.

12. Renda, *Taking Haiti,* 128.

13. *Baltimore Afro-American,* "Bullying Haiti," August 28, 1915, 4.

14. *Baltimore Afro-American,* "U.S. Not to Leave in Near Future," August 21, 1915, 1.

15. Robert Lansing, acting secretary of state, to Minister Blanchard, November 4, 1914, letter printed in appendix of Millspaugh, *Haiti under American Control, 1915–1930,* 201-202.

16. Plummer, "The African American Response," 131.

17. Ibid., 137.

18. For more on the role of U.S. banks and investors in Haiti during the occupation see Plummer, *Haiti and the United States,* 101–120; Schmidt, *U.S. Occupation of Haiti, 1915–1934;* Renda, *Taking Haiti,* 97–100; Johnson, "Self-Determining Haiti," 295-297; Prattis, "U.S. Occupation of Haiti Affected by Citizens with Investments," 1.

19. For more on L'Union Patriotique, see the Luxembourg and Victor Cauvin Haiti Collection, SRCBC; Sylvain, *Dix Années de Lutte pour la Liberté;* Pamphile, *Haitians and African Americans,* 116–120.

20. Pamphile, *Haitians and African Americans,* 111.

21. Moton quoted in Hughes and Patterson, eds., *Robert Russa Moton of Hampton and Tuskegee,* 192–194. My italics.

22. W.T.B. Williams, "Haiti," 122.

23. Trouillot, *Haiti: State against Nation,* 102.

24. Plummer, *Haiti and the United States,* 106.

25. Trouillot, *Haiti: State against Nation,* 103.

26. Plummer, *Haiti and the United States,* 118.

27. For more on Napoleon B. Marshall, see Washington Conservatory of Music Re-

cords, Moorland-Spingarn Research Center, Howard University, Washington, D.C.; Slotkin, *Lost Battalions,* 55–58.

28. Napoleon B. Marshall to Jean Price-Mars, 1929, Washington Conservatory of Music Records, Box 112–2 (Series C), Story of Haiti folder, Moorland-Spingarn Research Center, Howard University, Washington, D.C. My italics.

29. Hemenway, *Zora Neale Hurston,* 249.

30. Dash, *Haiti and the United States,* 59. Over the past few years, several scholars have reexamined Hurston's *Tell My Horse* and have found it valuable. See Nwankwo, "Insider and Outsider, Black and American," 49–77; Emery, "The Zombie In/As the Text," 327–336.

31. Undated document, President's Commission to Study and Review Conditions in Haiti (hereafter referred to as "President's Commission"), Recommendations and Suggestions folder, Hoover Papers, Hoover Library.

32. President Hoover quoted in Shannon's "U.S. Commission for the Study and Review of Conditions in Haiti," 58.

33. Herbert Hoover to Robert R. Moton, February 7, 1930, President's Commission, Robert R. Moton folder, Hoover Papers, Hoover Library.

34. Schmidt, *United States Occupation of Haiti, 1915–1934,* 210.

35. Spector, "W. Cameron Forbes in Haiti: Additional Light on the Genesis of the 'Good Neighbor' Policy," 30.

36. Shannon, "U.S. Commission for the Study and Review of Conditions," 60.

37. *New York Age,* March 8, 1930, 4.

38. Mitchell, *Righteous Propagation,* 178.

39. For more on transnational education projects between sub-Saharan Africa and the United States, and between the Caribbean and the United States, see King, *Pan-Africanism and Education,* and Guridy, *Forging Diaspora.*

40. Gaines, *Uplifting the Race,* 3, 96.

41. Ibid., 95.

42. Ackah, *Pan-Africanism: Exploring the Contradictions,* 78.

43. Wilson, *Herbert Hoover,* 52. Refer also to Hoover's *American Individualism* (New York: Doubleday-Page, 1922).

44. Dantès Bellegarde testimony, March 3, 1930, President's Commission, box 1074, William Allen White March 1–4, 1930 folder, Hoover Papers, Hoover Library. It is possible that Bellegarde's submission to the Forbes Commission may have been *Pour une Haïti Heureuse* (1927) or *L'Occupation Américaine d'Haïti* (1929). For more contemporary information on micro-lending in developing nations, see Yunus, *Banker to the Poor*; Armendàriz and Morduch, *Economics of Microfinance.*

45. According to Kenneth King, the General Education Board emphasized curricular reform "especially along industrial and domestic lines." W.E.B. Du Bois was quoted as saying "It is this board that is spending more money today in helping Negroes learn how to can vegetables than in helping them to go through college." Quoted in King's *Pan-Africanism and Education,* 35. Similar to the Phelps-Stokes Fund, the Jeanes and Slater funds helped develop public and private schools and supported traveling women teach-

ers in the rural South to encourage interest in rural industries. See also Favrot, "How the Small Rural School Can More Adequately Serve Its Community," 430–438.

46. Moton quoted in Fairclough, "Civil Rights and the Lincoln Memorial," 410–411.

47. Moton to White, March 22, 1934, box 11, folder 21, Moton Family Papers, LOC. My italics.

48. Moton to Forbes, February 21, 1930, President's Commission, box 1070, Robert R. Moton folder, Hoover Papers, Hoover Library.

49. Arthur Ruhl to Hoover, February 8, 1930, Foreign Affairs Series, box 989, Haitian Commission, Moton Commission folder, Hoover Papers, Hoover Library.

50. Cotton to Forbes, February 20, 1930, President's Commission, box 1070, Robert R. Moton folder, Hoover Papers, Hoover Library.

51. Draft of Forbes Commission report, President's Commission, box 1073, Report of Commission folder, Hoover Papers, Hoover Library.

52. Marshall, "Haitians Deny Enmity for American Negroes," 7.

53. Quoted in Pamphile, *Haitians and African Americans,* 124.

54. *Tuskegee Messenger,* "Haitian Representative Is Commencement Visitor," June 14, 1930, 1.

55. Quoted from the *St. Luke Herald* in untitled article in *New York Age,* March 15, 1930, 4.

56. Moton to James C. Dunn, April 7, 1930, Foreign Affairs Series, box 989, Haitian Commission-Moton Commission folder, Hoover Papers, Hoover Library.

57. *Le Nouvelliste,* "Arrivée de la Commission Moton," June 16, 1930, 1.

58. *Le Nouvelliste,* "Bienvenue à la Commission Moton," June 18, 1930, 1.

59. *Le Nouvelliste,* "À la Commission Moton," June 17, 1930, 1.

60. *Norfolk Journal Guide,* "Haitian Press Gives Banquet" July 12, 1930.

61. Prattis, "Moton Commissioners Visit Pineapple Factory Owned by California Company," *New York Age,* July 9, 1930.

62. *Norfolk Journal and Guide,* "Haitian President Sends Greetings to Colored Americans," July 12, 1930.

63. Prattis, "Moton Commissioners Visit Pineapple Factory," *New York Age,* July 9, 1930.

64. Louis C. Lhérisson testimony, March 8, 1930, President's Commission, box 1074, William Allen White March 7–8, 1930 folder, Hoover Papers, Hoover Library.

65. Georges N. Leger testimony, March 4, 1930, President's Commission, box 1074, William Allen White March 1–4, 1930 folder, Hoover Papers, Hoover Library.

66. Shannon, *Jean Price-Mars,* 88.

67. Verna, "Haiti's Second Independence and the Promise of Pan-American Cooperation, 1934–1956," 70–71.

68. M. Dartigue, "Rural Life and Education in Haiti," 35. See also Maurice Dartigue Papers, SCRBC; E. Dartigue, *An Outstanding Haitian.*

69. E. Dartigue, *An Outstanding Haitian,* 11–12.

70. U.S. Department of State, *Report of the United States Commission on Education in Haiti,* 63. Hereafter cited as the "Moton Commission Report."

222 · Notes to Pages 78–86

71. Trouillot, *Haiti: State against Nation*, 20–21.

72. Joseph Fénélon Geffrard to Joseph Benoit, no date, "President Commission," box 1073, Recommendations and Suggestions Submitted to Committee, October–December 1929 folder, Hoover Papers, Hoover Library.

73. *New York Age*, "Possibilities of the Moton Committee," March 22, 1930, 4.

74. *New York Age*, "Educational Needs," March 8, 1930, 4.

75. *Pittsburgh Courier*, "Odds and Ends in Haiti," July 12, 1930, 1A.

76. Moton to Hoover, July 7, 1930, Foreign Affairs Series, box 989, Countries—Haitian Commission, Moton Commission folder, Hoover Papers, Hoover Library.

77. *Pittsburgh Courier*, editorials, "Another Government Insult" and "Government in Gutter," July 26, 1930.

78. *New York Times*, "Argentinians Assail Haiti Board's Work," March 20, 1930, 6.

79. For more information on the tensions between race and national identity in Latin America, see Andrews, *Afro-Latin America;* Graham, ed., *Idea of Race in Latin America*.

80. Prattis, "Writer Says Spirit of U.S. Occupation Is Evil," 8. Prattis' series of five reports was published in a number of U.S. African American newspapers including the *Chicago Defender*. See Prattis, "America in Haiti, Big Bully or Big Brother—Which? Article 1, The American Spirit in Haiti." *Chicago Defender*, August 2, 1930, 10.

81. Moton to Walter Newton, July 30, 1930, Foreign Affairs Series, box 989, Countries—Haitian Commission, Moton Commission folder, Hoover Papers, Hoover Library.

82. William R. Castle to Walter Newton, August 8, 1930, Foreign Affairs Series, box 989, Countries—Haitian Commission, Moton Commission folder, Hoover Papers, Hoover Library.

83. Francis White to Joseph P. Cotton, January 12, 1931, Francis White Papers, box 14, Country File Haiti 1931–1933 folder, Hoover Library. (Hereafter Francis White Papers will be cited as "FWP."); Refer also to Shannon, *Jean Price-Mars*, 94.

84. Moton Commission Report, 71–72.

85. Dean B. McNealy to George Akerson, July 12, 1930, Foreign Affairs Series, box 989, Haiti Correspondence May 1930–1932 folder, Hoover Papers, Hoover Library. McNealy stated that Crouze informed him that "some of these men [U.S. employees of Service Technique] draw salaries without even being in Haiti." See also "Special Report on Education: Facts and Statistics Collected by Mr. Elie Vezina from Brothers and Sisters Having Charge of Some Schools in Port-au-Prince," undated, "President's Commission," box 1069, Education folder, Hoover Papers, Hoover Library.

86. Moton Commission Report, 73.

87. Ibid. My italics.

88. Francis White to Mr. Secretary (Probably Henry L. Stimson), February 19, 1931, FWP, box 14, Country file Haiti 1931–1933 folder, Hoover Papers, Hoover Library.

89. G. Lake Imes to Walter Newton, April 16, 1931, Foreign Affairs Series, box 989, Countries—Haitian Commission, Moton Commission folder, Hoover Papers, Hoover Library.

90. Sténio Vincent press release, December 17, 1930, Foreign Affairs Series, box 989, Haiti Correspondence May 1930–1932 folder, Hoover Papers, Hoover Library.

91. Drake, "Diaspora Studies and Pan-Africanism," 343.

Chapter 3. "We Cast in Our Lot with the Policy of Good Neighborliness": Claude Barnett, Haiti and the Business of Race

1. *New York Age,* "Haiti Would Welcome Co-operation by Negroes Says President," April 21, 1934, 3. Vincent met with Roosevelt on April 17, 1934. On July 5, 1934, Roosevelt, one of the few U.S. presidents to visit Haiti, announced the complete Haitianization of the country's army and promised U.S. military withdrawal. Henri Ch. Rosemond helped organize the luncheon for Vincent at the Harlem YMCA. At the time, he was an executive member of the League for Haitian National Independence.

2. Ibid.

3. A.L. Holsey to Claude Barnett, May 23, 1934, Claude Barnett Papers, box 203, Haiti General Correspondence, 1929–1949 folder, Chicago Historical Society. Hereafter, the Claude Barnett Papers will be abbreviated to "CBP" and the Chicago Historical Society will be "CHS." Holsey also listed himself as temporary secretary of the Haitian Afro-American Chamber of Commerce.

4. Barnett to A.L. Holsey, May 29, 1934, CBP, box 203, Haiti General Correspondence, 1929–1949 folder, CHS. Interestingly, W.E.B. Du Bois stated that he was not "interested in ordinary investment projects" in Haiti and could not be of any service to the Haitian Afro-American Chamber of Commerce. Refer to W.E.B. Du Bois to A.L. Holsey, June 14, 1934, W.E.B. Du Bois Papers, microfilm reel 42, SCRBC.

5. Léon F. Desportes to Barnett, October 22, 1934, CBP, box 203, Haiti General Correspondence, 1929–1949 folder, CHS.

6. Clamart Ricourt to Claude Barnett, March 15, 1929, CBP, box 203, Haiti General Correspondence 1929–1949, CHS. Scholar Stephen Howe notes that in the nineteenth century the term "Ethiopia" was often synonymous with "Negro" and "black African." For more on the role of Ethiopia in constructions of black identity and political and religious philosophy in U.S. African America and the Caribbean, see Howe, *Afrocentrism,* and Moses, *Afrotopia.*

7. Barnett to Ricourt, April 15, 1929, CBP, box 203, Haiti General Correspondence 1929–1949, CHS.

8. Refer also to Von-Eschen, *Race against Empire,* 164.

9. Roorda, *Dictator Next Door,* 27.

10. Webopedia Computer Dictionary. "Router." http://www.webopedia.com/TERM/r/router.html (accessed June 10, 2005).

11. Although it was a popular term for U.S. black leadership of the late-nineteenth and early-twentieth centuries, Hazel Carby challenges "race men" and argues that U.S. black leadership has typically been defined as masculine, an error that ignores the long history of black women leaders. Refer to Carby, *Race Men,* 6.

12. For more on Barnett's early life, see Hogan, *Black National News Service*, 38-55.

13. Quoted from Hogan, *Black National News Service*, 41.

14. Refer to Guridy, *Forging Diaspora*.

15. According to scholar Linda J. Evans, Barnett often edited articles and press releases, although he usually did so anonymously. Sometimes he wrote under the pseudonym Albert Anderson.

16. Linda J. Evans, "Claude A. Barnett and the Associated Negro Press," 44.

17. Von Eschen, *Race against Empire*, 15.

18. Quoted in Evans, "Claude A. Barnett and the Associated Negro Press," 48–49.

19. Refer to V. Smith, *Self Discovery and Authority in Afro-American Narrative*.

20. Hogan, *Black National News Service*, 114–115.

21. Renda, *Taking Haiti*, 120.

22. Also, Barnett served as secretary of the publicity committee of the Colored Voters Division of the Republican National Committee during Herbert Hoover's election. With regard to the promotion of U.S. black businesses in the U.S. Commerce Department, James Jackson, an ANP correspondent, was appointed Negro Business Specialist to the U.S. Commerce Department. Jackson continued to write articles for the ANP, often reporting on news from Washington and on the work he performed for the Commerce department.

23. Walker, *History of Black Business in America*, xix.

24. Ibid., 121.

25. Ibid., 219.

26. Refer to Locke, ed., "The New Negro."

27. Haynes, "A New Negro Emerging," 4.

28. *Tuskegee Messenger*, "Principal Moton in New Year's Message Urges Race to Harness Resources," January 17, 1925, 1.

29. See Suggs, "African-American Response to the U.S. Occupation of Haiti"; Plummer's "Afro-American Response to the Occupation of Haiti"; Blassingame, "Press and American Intervention in Haiti and Dominican Republic."

30. Lewis, *W.E.B. Du Bois*, 672.

31. Ibid.

32. See Shannon, *Jean Price-Mars*, 123–126, 132–135.

33. "Haiti Seeks to Free Self at Montevideo Conference," December 1933, CBP, Associated Negro Press Releases, Part 1, Series A, reel 8, SCRBC. Historian David Sheinin states that the delegation from Argentina authored a "successful resolution that denounced the interference by one state in the internal affairs of another." Refer to Sheinin, ed., *Beyond the Ideal*, 3.

34. Refer to Walter White to Jean Price-Mars, October 20, 1933, File C-329, Papers of the National Association for the Advancement of Colored People (NAACP), LOC. Hereafter, the NAACP Papers abbreviated "NP"; Memorandum from Mr. White Regarding Long Distance Telephone Talk with M. Dantès Bellegarde, October 19, 1933, NP, File C-329. See also Shannon, *Jean Price-Mars*, 132–134.

35. Associated Negro Press release, December 1933, CBP, Associated Negro Press Releases, Part 1, Series A, reel 8, SCRBC.

36. Ibid.

37. William Phillips to Franklin Roosevelt, November 28, 1933; Papers of Franklin D. Roosevelt, President's Secretary File, Diplomatic Correspondence, Haiti, Franklin D. Roosevelt Library, Hyde Park, N.Y. Hereafter, Papers of Franklin D. Roosevelt will be abbreviated "FDRP" and Franklin D. Roosevelt Library will be abbreviated "FDRL."

38. Sténio Vincent to Franklin D. Roosevelt, November 16, 1933, FDRP, President's Secretary File, Diplomatic Correspondence, Haiti, FDRL.

39. Quoted in Pamphile, *Haitians and African Americans*, 125. Walter White made this particular statement after a recent trip to U.S.-occupied Haiti. See Pamphile, *Haitians and African Americans*, 210, chapter 5, endnote 91.

40. Sténio Vincent to Franklin D. Roosevelt, September 3, 1934, FDRP, President's Secretary File, Diplomatic Correspondence, Haiti, FDRL.

41. Vincent did encounter significant opposition, particularly when he tried to extend his presidency for a third term. See "Blasts Vincent's Dictatorship in Haiti," CBP, Associated Negro Press Releases, Series A, Part 1, reel 22, SCRBC.

42. In July 1934, an Associated Negro Press release reported that "a special rate of $121.25 per person has been arranged" for those individuals "who can afford to go on a vacation to Haiti." See "Haitian Commission to Leave This Month," July 1934, CBP, Associated Negro Press Releases, Part 1, Series A, reel 9, SCRBC.

43. Haitian Afro-American Chamber of Commerce, *Official Report of the Haitian Afro-American Chamber of Commerce's Commission to Study the Commercial, Agricultural and Industrial Possibilities of the Haitian Republic* (1935), 3, SCRBC.

44. Ibid., 4–5. Although largely unsuccessful as an entrepreneurial venture but, nevertheless, rich in black nationalist symbolism, nineteenth-century U.S. African American emigration movements to Haiti in 1824 and 1859 exemplified the black republic as a space for financial renewal and independence and for the regeneration of the soul from unjust conditions in the United States. See Dixon, *African America and Haiti*, and Pamphile, *Haitians and African Americans*, 34–59.

45. See Howe, *Afrocentrism*, and Moses, *Afrotopia*. For nineteenth-century vindicationist interpretations of the black history, see Firmin, *Equality of the Human Races*; Holly, *Vindication of the Capacity of the Negro Race*; Delany, *Condition, Elevation, Emigration, and Destiny of the Colored People of the United States*; Garnet, *Past and the Present Condition*; Douglass, *Claims of the Negro*; W. Brown, *The Black Man*.

46. Haitian Afro-American Chamber of Commerce, *Official Report*, 5.

47. Trouillot, *Haiti: State against Nation*, 102.

48. Haitian Afro-American Chamber of Commerce, *Official Report*, 6, 9.

49. Joshua Cockburn served as a seaman with the British Royal Navy. He was a second mate in Liverpool, often traveling from England to Brazil, and officered several voyages to German Cameroon, West Africa, during World War I. Refer to editor Robert Hill's note in Garvey, *Marcus Garvey and Universal Negro Improvement Association Papers*, 515, note 3; Haitian Afro-American Chamber of Commerce, *Official Report*, 27.

50. Haitian Afro-American Chamber of Commerce, *Official Report*, 28–29.

51. Ibid., 32.

52. Ibid., 30; Trouillot, *Haiti,* 53–54.

53. Haitian Afro-American Chamber of Commerce, *Official Report,* 34.

54. Ibid., 24.

55. Ibid., 55.

56. Ibid., 7.

57. The Haitian Afro-American Chamber of Commerce operated in Harlem on West 138th Street, while the Haitian American Appliance Co. was on West 135th Street, and Utilites d'Haiti was on West 116th Street.

58. Alvin C. Gary to Barnett, July 16, 1935, CBP, box 203, Haiti General Correspondence, 1929–1949 folder, CHS. See also Gary to Barnett, January 24, 1935, box 203, Haiti General Correspondence, 1929–1949 folder, CHS.

59. See also Gary to Barnett, January 24, 1935. Few of the *Goodwill* magazines exist, and some are stored at the Columbus Memorial Library, Pan American Union, Washington, D.C.

60. Léon F. Desportes to Alvin C. Gary, October 22, 1935, Arthur Alfonso Schomburg Papers, reel 6, SCRBC.

61. Summary of Alfred Green's letter referred to the U.S. State Department, April 29, 1935, FDRP, Official File 162a Haiti Miscellaneous, FDRL.

62. Refer to "Colored Folk Plan Trade with Haiti," *Washington Post,* September 9, 1934, 12.

63. George A. Gordon to Sumner Welles, April 10, 1937, FDRP, Official File 162a, Haiti Miscellaneous, FDRL.

64. Plummer, *Haiti and the United States,* 140. Refer also to P. Smith, *Talons of the Eagle,* 64.

65. Ibid., 139.

66. Ibid., 140. Refer also to Lundahl, *Politics or Markets,* 113.

67. See Sumner Welles memorandum to Franklin D. Roosevelt, June 4, 1938, FDRP, Official File 162, Haiti 1935–1938, FDRL.

68. Obtaining accurate numbers on Haitian deaths remains daunting. Conservative estimates from the Dominican government report the number of deaths at less than five thousand. However, according to historian Eric Paul Roorda, it is critical that scholars take into account the number of Haitian refugees who soon died because of sickness or life-threatening wounds weeks or months after the slaughter. See Roorda, *Dictator Next Door,* 132. For more information on the Haitian massacre see Turits, *Foundations of Despotism;* Paulino, *Birth of a Boundary.*

69. Walter White to Cordell Hull, December 22, 1937, FDRP, Official File 162, Haiti 1935–1938, FDRL. See also Sumner Welles to Walter White, December 31, 1937, FDRP, Official File 162, Haiti 1935–1938, FDRL.

70. Janken, *White,* 281. See also Janken, *Rayford W. Logan,* 99.

71. Plummer, *Rising Wind,* 50–51. Refer also to B. Harris, *United States and the Italo-Ethiopian Crisis;* J. Harris, *African-American Reactions to War in Ethiopia.*

72. Roorda, *Dictator Next Door,* 128.

73. Plummer, *Haiti and the United States,* 169.

74. Elie Lescot to Edward J. Sparks, December 13, 1941, FDRP, Official File 162, Haiti

1935–1938, FDRL. See also Sumner Welles to Franklin D. Roosevelt, January 3, 1942, FDRP, Official File 162, Haiti 1942–1945, FDRL.

75. Élie Lescot to Franklin D. Roosevelt, December 3, 1942, FDRP, Personal File, 8313 Élie Lescot, FDRL.

76. Janken, *Rayford W. Logan*, 98.

77. Rayford Whittingham Logan Papers, box 9, Travel diary 1942, Caribbean folder, Manuscripts Division, LOC. Hereafter the Logan Papers will be abbreviated as "RWLP."

78. RWLP, box 3, loose material from 1942 diary, LOC.

79. Janken, *Rayford W. Logan*, 98–99.

80. RWLP, box 3, February 2, 1942, loose material from 1942 diary, LOC.

81. Refer to G. Nash, *The Crucial Era*; Sitkoff, *A New Deal for Blacks*; Kelley and Lewis, eds., *To Make Our World Anew*, 439; Blackmon, *Slavery by Another Name*.

82. Plummer, *Haiti and the United States*, 145.

83. Refer to Cordell Hull to Franklin D. Roosevelt, October 30, 1939, and March 11, 1941, FDRP, Official File 162 Haiti 1939–1941, FDRL. For more on Haiti/U.S. agricultural relations and Pan Americanism, see Verna, "Haiti's Second Independence."

84. Plummer, *Haiti and the United States*, 145 and 267 (chapter 8, endnote 24). Refer also to the "Minutes of the second meeting of Société Haïtienne-Américaine Développement Agricole Board of Directors," October 20, 1941, 838.51/Cooperative Program/26; U.S. Department of State, numerical and decimal files, NACP.

85. Plummer, *Haiti and the United States*, 146.

86. Refer to Plummer, *Rising Wind*, 3; Von Eschen, *Race against Empire*; Dudziack, *Cold War Civil Rights*.

87. Refer to "Lescot to Return to Haiti" and "Lescot Named Haitian President," March and April 1941, CBP, ANP Releases, Series A, Part 1, reel 22, SCRBC.

88. In the late 1930s and early 1940s, Barnett asked several Haitians such as Henri Ch. Rosemond, Maurice Dartigue and Joceyln M. François to be ANP correspondents. Typically, many ANP correspondents in Haiti worked for the organization for only a short period of time. The archival documents of the ANP and Claude Barnett do not include any records of the resignations or the reasoning behind them. However, the ANP often had trouble paying its correspondents, and this is one possibility for the inconsistency of Haitian correspondents.

89. September 15, 1943, CBP, box 203, Haiti General Correspondence 1929–1949 folder, CHS.

90. Barnett to Louis A. Mercier, October 27, 1943, CBP, box 203, Haiti General Correspondence 1929–1949 folder, CHS.

91. Barnett to Joseph Buteau, December 6, 1946, and January 7, 1947, CBP, box 203, Haiti General Correspondence, 1929–1949 folder, CHS. Some of the U.S. African American tourists were Earl B. Dickerson, former alderman in Chicago and a Roosevelt appointee to the Fair Employment Practice Committee, and his wife; and W. Ellis Stewart, an attorney and secretary of the Supreme Liberty Life Insurance Company, who also traveled with his wife.

92. "Rising Tide of Color in Haiti" CBP, ANP Releases, Series B, Part 1, microfilm reel 32, SCRBC.

93. Joseph Buteau to Barnett, July 12, 1946, CBP, box 203, Haiti General Correspondence 1929–1949 folder, CHS.

94. See Trouillot, *Haiti: State against Nation,* chapter 4. Within the complexities and politics of color in the Americas, Haiti is not alone. See Graham, ed., *Idea of Race in Latin America.*

95. Gaines, *Uplifting the Race,* 118.

96. Ibid.

97. Jean F. Brierre to Barnett, September 13, 1950, CBP, box 205, Haitian Tours folder, 1949–1951, CHS.

98. Barnett to Paul E. Magloire, October 17, 1950, and November 10, 1950, CBP, box 203, Haiti General Correspondence 1950 folder, CHS.

99. Claude Barnett, "A Visit to Haiti's Exposition Reveals Tropical Beauty of Black Caribbean Republic," March 27, 1950, CBP, box 205, Haitian Tours folder, 1949–1951, CHS.

100. Chester K. Gillespie to Barnett, March 9, 1951, CBP, box 203, Haitian General Correspondence 1951–1954 folder, CHS.

101. Claude Barnett, Speech given at Tuskegee Institute Founder's Day service, April 2, 1950, CBP, box 203, Haiti General Correspondence 1950 folder, CHS.

102. Etta Moten interview with James O. Plinton at Hotel Choucoune, Port-au-Prince, 1957, Sound recording, SCRBC. Moten performed the female lead in *Porgy and Bess* on Broadway and married Barnett in 1934.

103. Claude Barnett's Founder's Day speech, April 2, 1950, CBP, box 203, Haiti General Correspondence 1950 folder, CHS. Dr. Frederick Patterson was Tuskegee's president after Robert R. Moton.

104. Barnett to Paul Chetien, February 14, 1951, CBP, box 203, Haiti General Correspondence 1951–1954 folder, CHS.

105. Trouillot, *Haiti: State against Nation,* 140. UNESCO, the World Health Organization, SHADA, the United Nations, the Institute of Inter-American Affairs and the U.S. Point Four programs were particularly significant during this period.

106. ANP Press Release, April 23, 1951, CBP, box 203, Haiti Correspondence 1951–1954 folder, CHS.

107. Barnett to Blackwell Smith, May 27, 1952, CBP, box 203, Haiti Correspondence 1951–1954 folder, CHS.

108. Ibid., July 29, 1952.

109. A. J. Wakefield to Barnett, November 7, 1950, CBP, box 203, Haiti Correspondence 1950 folder, CHS.

110. "Bold New Programme or Old Imperialism: The President's 'Point Four' Still an Enigma," RWLP, box 5, LOC.

111. Walker, *History of Black Business in America,* 249.

112. I.J.K. Wells to President Magloire, May 22, 1951, CBP, box 203, Haiti Correspondence 1951–1954 folder, CHS.

113. Barnett's comments in *News of Haiti,* a newsletter published by the Haiti Tourist Information Bureau, March 15, 1951, 9. CBP, box 205, Haitian Tours, Barnett's Promotions 1949–1951 folder, CHS.

114. James O. Plinton to Barnett, July 11, 1952, CBP, box 203, Haiti Correspondence 1951–1954 folder, CHS. My italics.

115. Barnett to President Paul E. Magloire, May 10, 1952, CBP, box 203, Haiti Correspondence 1951–1954 folder, CHS. Some of these short films have been assembled in a compilation titled *Rare Black Short Subjects* (Matinee Classics, 1996).

116. Barnett to Denys Bellande, August 25, 1955, CBP, box 204, Haiti General Correspondence 1955 folder, CHS.

117. Thomas E. Weil and others, *Area Handbook for Haiti*, 61. Refer also to Service de Statistique Municipale, Bulletin de Statistique, vol. 1; Institut Haïtien de Statistique, *Bulletin Trimestriel de Statistique*; U.S. Department of Commerce, Bureau of the Census in Cooperation with the Office of the Coordinator of Inter-American Affairs, *Haiti: Summary of Biostatistics, Maps and Charts, Population, Natality and Mortality Statistics.*

118. Weil and others, *Area Handbook for Haiti*, 71.

119. For a more detailed discussion on the philosophy of black solidarity, see Shelby, *We Who Are Dark*, 1–23, 243–256.

120. Brenda Plummer documented that Willis Huggins, possibly the same individual who headed the exploratory commission of the Haitian Afro-American Chamber of Commerce, publicly chided Haile Selassie for overseeing "a corrupt and repressive regime whose medieval ignorance impeded aid efforts [anticolonial struggles by U.S. African Americans during the Italian invasion]." Refer to Plummer, *Rising Wind*, 55.

121. There were still instances of racial cooperation and correspondence between both groups, such as the proposal for an American Haitian Cultural Association and the visit of Althea Gibson, U.S. African American Wimbledon tennis champion, but these events were minimal and less focused on business transactions.

122. Plummer, *Rising Wind*, 253.

123. Barnett to Mauclair Zéphirin, March 8, 1955, CBP, box 204, Haiti General Correspondence 1955 folder, CHS.

124. Bellegarde-Smith, *Haiti: The Breached Citadel*, 94.

125. Barnett to Mauclair Zephirin, December 13, 1956, CBP, box 204, Haiti General Correspondence 1956–1957 folder, CHS.

126. Barnett to Antoine Levelt, Commander in Chief of Haitian Army, December 8, 1956, CBP, box 204, Haiti General Correspondence 1956–1957 folder, CHS.

127. Barnett to R.J. Moxon, Director of Department of Information Services, February 8, 1957, CBP, box 204, Haiti General Correspondence 1956–1957 folder, CHS.

128. Barnett to James O. Plinton, February 13, 1957, CBP, box 204, Haiti General Correspondence 1956–1957 folder, CHS.

129. Lavinia Williams to Barnett, June 5, 1957, CBP, box 204, Haiti General Correspondence 1956–1957 folder, CHS.

130. I use the phrase "relative calm" because it only reflects the experiences of the mentioned writers. General Kébreau's Military Council of Government was notorious for suppressing opposing Haitian journalists and judges. Refer to Trouillot, *Haiti: State against Nation*, 150–152.

131. Refer to Katherine Dunham's *Island Possessed*.

132. Barnett to François Duvalier, November 16, 1957, CBP, box 204, Haiti General Correspondence 1956–1957 folder, CHS.

133. Trouillot, *Haiti: State against Nation*, 193.

134. Von Eschen, *Race against Empire*, 8.

135. Fatton, *Roots of Haitian Despotism*, vii.

136. Ibid., 9. Refer also to Jennie M. Smith, *When the Hands Are Many*.

137. Walker, *History of Black Business in America*, xx, xxii.

138. Barnett to Luc E. Fouche, February 1, 1951, CBP, box 203, Haiti General Correspondence 1951–1954 folder, CHS.

Chapter 4. "What Happens in Haiti Has Repercussions which Far Transcend Haiti Itself": Walter White, Haiti and the Public Relations Campaign, 1947–1955

1. Walter White to Joseph D. Charles, September 20, 1947, NP, part 14, reel 7. In the memo, White mentions that publication of Kenneth Roberts' fictional book *Lydia Bailey* committed "irreparable harm" to Haiti's image. As a result of this book and the long line of racist literature depicting Haiti rooted in the late nineteenth century through the 1950s, the country needed a pointed public relations campaign to counter these "distortions" and images of primitivism. For more literature on perceptions of Haiti, refer to Dash's *Haiti and the United States*; Renda, *Taking Haiti*.

2. For classic and more recent interpretations of inter-American affairs, see Buell, *International Relations*; Lockey, *Pan-Americanism*; Seidel, "Progressive Pan-Americanism"; Fraser, *Ambivalent Anticolonialism*; Sheinin, ed., *Beyond the Ideal*.

3. Refer to Renda, *Taking Haiti*, 278–281.

4. Earlier, on March 31, 1947, White began to discuss modernization but he referred to the development of the Virgin Islands. He wished that the Virgin Islands attracted "tourist(s) of the right sort. . . . I do hope, however, that the islands will never attract the flashy, prejudiced type of tourists who infest places like Cuba and Bermuda." The fact that White chose to first concentrate his efforts on Haiti suggests the historical and racial significance of the republic and the potential immediate impact it wielded in the post-World War II era. White to Oscar Chapman, U.S. Department of Interior, March 31, 1947, NP, box A 659, folder Virgin Islands—1947, LOC.

5. White to Paul E. Magloire, June 9, 1950, NP, box 295, Haiti Dignitaries—1951–1954 folder, LOC.

6. Memorandum from Berend & Associates to Dumarsais Estimé, no date, NP, part 14, reel 7, LOC. *Vodou* is a religion, a way of life and complex worldview for many Haitians and non-Haitians outside of Haiti. For more information on *vodou*, refer to Cosentino, ed., *Sacred Arts of Haitian Vodou*; Deren, *Divine Horsemen*; Desmangles, *Faces of the Gods*; Métraux, *Voodoo in Haiti*.

7. The Conference of Progressives sought to rally "'independent' voters and put an end to the 'reactionary coalition' of the dominant elements in the Democratic and Republican parties in Congress." Quoted in Janken, *White*, 306, 308–310.

8. Walter White to Dumarsais Estimé, June 28, 1949, Walter White Papers, box 2,

folder 61, Yale Collection of American Literature, Beinecke Rare Book and Manuscript Library. Hereafter, Walter White Papers, Yale Collection of American Literature, and Beinecke Rare Book and Manuscript Library will be abbreviated "WWP," "YCAL" and "BRBML," respectively.

9. Brenda Plummer argued: "Westernized blacks shared the West's faith that human society naturally moves toward betterment, a notion antithetical to cultures organized around ancestor worship and celebration of tradition; . . . they instead embraced the idea that enlightened tutelage, resulting in eventual self-rule, would deliver African countries from the darkness of static, tribal societies into modern communities motivated by the desire for progress." See Plummer's *Rising Wind*, 14. For more on U.S. African American leadership and racial politics during the interwar and post-World War II period, see Anderson, *Eyes off the Prize*; and Dudziak, *Cold War Civil Rights*.

10. Walter White to Dumarsais Estimé, June 28, 1949, WWP, box 2, folder 61, YCAL, BRBML.

11. See Walter White, "Danger in Haiti," *Crisis* (July 1931), 231–232. For more on the U.S. occupation of Haiti, see Schmidt, *United States Occupation of Haiti*; Renda, *Taking Haiti*.

12. White to Estimé, June 28, 1949, WWP, box 2, folder 61, YCAL, BRBML.

13. Janken, *White*, 345.

14. Ibid., 351.

15. Ibid., 355.

16. Ibid., 442, note 74.

17. It becomes evident that White possessed a particular material focus that would indirectly aid some Haitians, particularly artists and craftsmen/women, and would directly benefit U.S. and European tourists. In his proposal, he sought to sell clothing in Saks Fifth Avenue and Macy's. Also, White wanted to nationalize Haitian cuisine in restaurants and major cities so those tourists could possess the luxury of eating authentic "native dishes" when they visited. White's plan undoubtedly sought to shape Haitian culture to suit foreign tastes.

18. For more on the Haitian art movement, refer to Rodman, *Renaissance in Haiti* and *Where Art Is Joy*.

19. White to Joseph D. Charles, September 20, 1947, NP, part 14, reel 7, LOC.

20. Trouillot, *Haiti: State against Nation*, 142. Refer also to Pierre-Charles, *L'Economie Haïtienne et Sa Voie de Développement*.

21. Ibid.

22. White to Magloire, July 25, 1950, WWP, box 4, folder 128, YCAL, BRBML.

23. Trouillot, *Haiti: State against Nation*, 22–23.

24. Ibid., 23.

25. Ibid., 67.

26. Ibid., 69.

27. Ibid., 103. Trouillot concludes that U.S. occupation also had a lasting and "accelerated" impact on Haiti's economic, military and political centralization, which signaled the beginning of the end for local economic systems.

28. Speech by Dumarsais Estimé, May 5, 1947, NP, part 14, reel 7. My italics. In 1947,

the Haitian government paid off the 1922 debt. See Plummer, *Haiti and the United States,* 163.

29. Memorandum from L'Union Patriotique to U.S. State Department, no date, NP, Group II Series A, box 295, folder Haiti General 1943–1949, LOC. Evidence shows that a small progressive group of Haitians and Haitian organizations lived and worked in Brooklyn, New York, in the 1940s. Several organizations worked in the same building at 1096 Fulton Street, in Brooklyn, including the Etoiles du Tropique Club, the Haitian Publishing Company and the Comite de Lutte Pour Une Haïtienne Democratique. Some names that frequently occur are Henri Ch. Rosemond, Lucas Premice, Maurice Bernier and Jean G. Lamothe.

30. Plummer, *Haiti and the United States,* 164.

31. Pamphile, *Haitians and African Americans,* 152.

32. Henri Ch. Rosemond to Walter White, August 9, 1944, NP, part 14, reel 7. LOC.

33. See M. Smith, "Shades of Red in a Black Republic," 183. By 1945, power within the Haitian state proved to be "colorist." According to Michel-Rolph Trouillot, *mulâtre* power was being "accused of incompetence and judged guilty by a majority of urbanites." Consequently, because of the growth of the urban center (which brought significant numbers of darker-skinned rural peasants to the cities), the strong opposition to class distinction and an anti-*vodou* campaign sponsored by the state, *noiriste* or *authentiques* power was consolidated and considered to be truly representative of those who should usurp power from *mulâtre* ruling class. Refer also to Trouillot, *Haiti: State against Nation,* 133.

34. Joseph D. Charles to Peter Hilton, June 29, 1949, WWP, box 1, folder 35, YCAL, BRBML.

35. Refer to Poppy Cannon, "Memorandum on Haiti Trip," March 19, 1953, WWP, box 10, folder 32, YCAL, BRBML.

36. "Beauty in Haiti," *Jet,* November 1956, 15.

37. White to Joseph D. Charles, September 20, 1947, NP, part 14, reel 7.

38. Trouillot, *Haiti: State against Nation,* 140.

39. Refer to Rosemond, *Truth about Haiti and the New Deal Government.*

40. "President Estimé Leads Haiti to Better Times," Walter White press release, April 20, 1950, Nelson A. Rockefeller Papers, RG 4, box 263, folder 2625, Rockefeller Archive Center.

41. Ibid.

42. Janken, *White,* 313.

43. Quoted in M. Smith, "Shades of Red in a Black Republic," 263.

44. White to Paul E. Magloire, May 18, 1950, NP, Group II Series A, box 296, General Office File, folder 1950–1954, LOC.

45. M. Smith, "Shades of Red in a Black Republic," 261–284. Refer also to Bernardin, *Général Paul Eugène Magloire.*

46. Pamphile, *Haitians and African Americans,* 156–157.

47. Haitian report, commissioned translation by Julius Weisel, August 13, 1952, WWP, box 4, folder 128, YCAL, BRBML.

48. Schwartz, *Pleasure Island,* 147.

49. Ibid., 148.

50. George M. Elsey to White, October 14, 1952, WWP, box 8a, Correspondence Concerning Haiti folder, YCAL, BRBML.

51. Trouillot, *Haiti: State against Nation,* 141.

52. Guy Laraque to Gerard de Catalogne, April 10, 1953, WWP, box 10, folder 39, YCAL, BRBML.

53. Mauclair Zéphirin to White, September 2, 1952, WWP, box 8, folder 241, YCAL, BRBML. ". . . la satisfaction de Son Excellence de noter les efforts continuels que vous dépensez en faveur du Pays, avec la collaboration de Mme. White. La Large audience que le public américain a déjà réservée à vos commentaries à la radio est un signe certain du succès de votre propaganda en faveur de notre pays qui vous compte au nombre de ses amis les plus chers." My translation.

54. Quoted in Goldberg, "Commercial Folklore and Voodoo in Haiti," 144.

55. Memorandum from Poppy Cannon to Luc E. Fouche, Haitian Secretary of State, September 6, 1951, NP, part 14, reel 7, LOC.

56. *Time,* "Bon Papa," February 22, 1954, 46. Also, see Trouillot, *Haiti: State against Nation,* 141, 236n.

57. White to John Foster Dulles, March 19, 1953, NP, Group II Series A, box 296, folder Paul Magloire, 1950–1955, LOC.

58. Cannon to Luc E. Fouche, September 17, 1951, WWP, box 10, folder 38, YCAL, BRBML.

59. Refer to Poppy Cannon memorandum, March 19, 1953, WWP, box 10, folder 32, YCAL, BRBML. Poppy suggested that Toussaint L'Ouverture's birthplace, the Amerindian caves in Dondon, and Columbus's first settlement on Hispaniola become Haitian tourist sites.

60. Latham, *Modernization as Ideology,* 5.

61. Quoted in Von Eschen, *Race against Empire,* 71.

62. Despite Haiti's economic hardships, the country during the post-occupation period and through the Élie Lescot regime (1940–1945) weathered many financial storms as well as World War II. The republic steadily increased revenues and reduced the foreign debt from 70,419,000 gourdes to 60,460,000 gourdes in 1944. See "Pan American News," *Bulletin of the Pan-American Union,* 50. In addition, during the Estimé and Magloire regimes the currency was relatively sound at five gourdes to a dollar, tourism strengthened, the Haitian Arts movement emerged and the price of coffee went up, but there were price drops in sisal and sugar as well. White was clearly impressed by the Estimé administration's relative improvement of the economic situation.

63. Refer to "Joie de Vivre en Haïti." This souvenir book is in the author's possession.

64. Harrison, "International Tourism and the Less Developed Countries," 9–10.

65. Trouillot, *Haiti: State against Nation,* 142.

66. White to Paul E. Magloire, December 28, 1953, NP, part 14, reel 7, LOC.

67. President Truman established the Point Four Program in 1949. In it he pledged the United States to "making the benefits of our scientific advances and industrial progress

available for the improvement and growth of underdeveloped areas." For more on the Point Four Program, refer to Erb's essay "Prelude to Point Four," 249.

68. Refer to Von Eschen, *Satchmo Blows Up the World.*

69. White to R.D. Muir, September 21, 1951, NP, part 14, reel 7, LOC.

70. Albert Mangones to Mr. Polutnick, July 20, 1948, NP, part 14, reel 8.

71. Ibid. Roosevelt's "Four Freedoms" included the freedoms of speech, of worship, from want and from fear.

72. See Berman, *Ideology of Philanthropy.*

73. To view a copy of that address, see U.S. Department of State, *U.S. Department of State Bulletin* 32: 273–275.

74. *Time,* "Bon Papa," February 22, 1954, 46.

75. Paul E. Magloire to White, February 26, 1955, NP, Group II Series A, box 296, Paul Magloire—1950–1955 folder, LOC. My italics.

76. ANP Press Release, March 30, 1955, WWP, box 10, folder 39, YCAL, BRBML.

77. For more information about the "golden age of Haitian tourism," read "Le Vogue Nègre" in Plummer, *Haiti and the United States,* 123–138.

78. Trouillot, *Haiti: State against Nation,* 141.

79. For more on the concept of Afro-modernity see Hanchard, "Afro-Modernity," 245–268.

80. In his biography, White emphasizes the significance of the 1921 Pan African Congress for his black internationalist perspective. He asserts that the Pan African movement "played a profound role in opening my eyes to the world implications of the race question and the interrelationship between that question and other problems of colonialism [and] imperialism . . . ." Although the Pan African Congress proved to be "a brilliant dream that fell short of translation into reality," White understood how Pan Africanism addressed a myriad of issues facing the modern world and could potentially unite emerging global markets previously hindered by European and U.S. colonialism. Refer to W. White, *A Man Called White,* 67.

81. Memorandum from White to Rockefeller, April 22, 1941, NP, part 14, reel 7, LOC.

82. Ibid. In support of White's position on the inherent racism in U.S. Pan-Americanism, Alain Locke, professor of philosophy at Howard University, gave a six-part series of lectures in Haiti in 1944 to educate and shape Haitian ideas around what Locke noted as the "common denominators" of the three Americas: Pan-Americanism and democracy. In the last public lecture, Locke astutely declared the need for a Pan American solidarity because a "hegemony of white or even fairer elements of the population cannot be made to spell real or effective democracy." See Locke, "The Negro in Three Americas," 7–18.

83. Charles, "Haiti et le Panaméricanisme," 438.

Chapter 5. "To Carry the Dance of the People Beyond": Jean-Léon Destiné, Lavinia Williams and *Danse Folklorique Haïtienne*

1. Rayford Whittingham Logan Papers, box 3, Personal diary, 1941 folder, Manuscript Division, LOC. At a luncheon with Haitian educator Maurice Dartigue, Richard Pattee and Charles Thompson, the chief of Division of Cultural Relations in the U.S. State

Department, Logan was optimistic about the development of inter-American cultural relations because Pattee and Thompson were "very liberal."

2. Robert G. Caldwell to Walter White, October 7, 1940, NP, Group II, box A 609, folder 5, General Office File Good Neighbor Policy, LOC. Refer also to Walter White to Sue Thurman, September 10, 1940; and Walter White to Nelson Rockefeller, October 4, 1940, in the aforementioned box and folder.

3. See Hanson, *Cultural-Cooperation Program*; U.S. Department of State, Office of Public Affairs, *Program of the Interdepartmental Committee on Scientific and Cultural Cooperation*; Trueblood, *U.S. Cultural Relations Program with Latin America*.

4. Frank R. Crosswaith to Walter White, March 3, 1942, NP, Group II, box A 289, LOC.

5. Refer to Pan American Good Neighbor Forum, "The Negro Pan-American of the Pan-American Good Neighbor Forum," Chicago 1943, in the Columbus Memorial Library at the Pan American Union, Washington, D.C. The Pan American Good Neighbor Forum was organized in 1937 by Edward J. Sparling, president of the Central YMCA College Fund, and by Ernst Schwarz, a former refugee from Nazi Germany.

6. Magloire and Yelvington, "Haiti and the Anthropological Imagination," 146.

7. Ibid.

8. Ibid., 132.

9. Refer to "News of Haiti," March 15, 1951, CBP, box 203, General Correspondence folder, 1951–1954, CHS. The opening of the Haiti Tourist Information Bureau, an official government agency, at Rockefeller Plaza in New York City coincided with the commencement of "Haiti Week" events.

10. Ibid.

11. For additional critical responses to U.S. Pan Americanism, see Sheinin, ed., *Beyond the Ideal*; Aguilar, *Pan Americanism*; Novoa, *La Farsa del Panamericanismo*; Martínez, *De Bolívar a Dulles*.

12. Plummer, *Haiti and the United States*, 137.

13. The March 15, 1951, issue of *News of Haiti* reports on the building of fifteen industrial centers throughout Haiti and the paving of new asphalt roads. Also, it informs readers of President Magloire's "New Deal" in Haiti, where "155 one- and two-family dwellings" were to be built in St. Martin Delmas, a suburb of Port-au-Prince. Refer to Trouillot, *Haiti: State against Nation*, 140.

14. Cuba, Jamaica, the Dominican Republic, the Bahamas and Puerto Rico were among the islands that supported tourism as early as the 1930s. See Schwartz, *Pleasure Island*, 108–109. Also see Ramsey, "Without One Ritual Note."

15. Comment made by Dr. Cary Fraser at the Association for the Study of African American Life and History Conference, October 1, 2004, Buffalo, New York.

16. Sibylle Fischer's work on the "disavowal" of Afro-Cuban art during the Age of Revolution proves to be significant to understanding the contributions of art to modernization. Fischer argues that art and its representation ". . . both visual and literary [and I would argue performative art]—is part of modernization, and to the extent that modernization makes the environment representable, it is part of an artistic process; it

is almost as if perspective were as much a quality of the world as of its representation." See Fischer, *Modernity Disavowed*, 76.

17. For more information on the "golden age of Haitian tourism," read "Le Vogue Nègre" in Plummer, *Haiti and the United States*, 123–138.

18. For more on Katherine Dunham, see Dunham, *Island Possessed*; Biemiller, *Dance*; Beckford, *Katherine Dunham*; Clark and Wilkerson, eds., *Kaiso!* Also see Terry Haman, *African Rhythm-American Dance: A Biography of Katherine Dunham* (New York: Knopf, 1974).

19. According to a 1959 souvenir book and shopping guide entitled "Joie de Vivre en Haïti," four major hotels, including the Casino International, Hôtel Castel Haiti, Hôtel Ibo Lele and Hotel Riviera, held evening dance shows, some hotels offering as many as two or three shows a night. Refer to "Joie de Vivre en Haïti." Ibo Lele is a nation of divinities remembered with a seven-mouthed pot. Shango is considered to be the god of Thunder. See Consentino, ed. *Sacred Arts of Haitian Vodou*.

20. Ramsey, "Without One Ritual Note," 11. Refer also to Ramsey, "Prohibition, Persecution, Performance," 165–179.

21. Ibid., 13.

22. Author interview with Jean-Léon Destiné, July 9, 2002, Harlem.

23. Trouillot, *Haiti: State against Nation*, 115.

24. Author interview with Destiné, July 9, 2002.

25. Dunham, *Island Possessed*, 3.

26. Ibid. My italics.

27. For a better understanding of how folk culture has been privileged in the formation of black identity, see Favor, *Authentic Blackness*.

28. Torgovnick, *Gone Primitive*, 8.

29. The influence of Lina Fussman-Mathon, or Lina Blanchet as many knew her prior to her second marriage, cannot be understated. It is critical that more research be done on her artistic career in Haiti.

30. Author interview with Destiné, July 9, 2002.

31. For more information on the events and controversies leading up to and after the National Folk Festival, see Ramsey, "Without One Ritual Note," 7–42.

32. Author interview with Destiné, July 9, 2002.

33. *Nouvelle cooperation* was a term coined by President Sténio Vincent during the post-occupation period. It designated a new independent Haiti and the formation of an egalitarian partnership between Haiti and the United States along economic, political and cultural lines. See Verna, "Haiti's Second Independence."

34. Author interview with Destiné, July 9, 2002.

35. Ibid. See also Ramsey, "Without One Ritual Note," 22–23.

36. See Berman, *Influence of the Carnegie*, and Cueto, *Missionaries of Science*.

37. Author interview with Destiné, July 9, 2002. Interestingly, during Destiné's scholarship period he picked up the name Jean. Destine's original name is Léon Destiné but he added the "Jean" since he performed a lot and he did not want the scholarship committee to hear about his extracurricular activities and possibly think that he was not fulfilling his academic duties.

38. Ibid.

39. For a better understanding of Western perceptions of Haiti and its people, see Dash, *Haiti and the United States*.

40. Destiné's opinions about U.S. African American views of Africa and black history in the Americas are valid. However, it is important to note the rich history of U.S. African American anticolonialism. Refer to the growing literature on U.S. African Americans and U.S. foreign policy in the twentieth century, such as Plummer, *Rising Wind*; Von Eshen, *Race against Empire*; Dudziak, *Cold War Civil Rights*.

41. Interview with Destiné, July 9, 2002. Paul Robeson, who played the role of Toussaint L'Ouverture in C.L.R. James's play *Black Majesty* in London in 1936, invited Destiné to perform at various events and at Communist rallies where Robeson would be speaking or performing. Destiné explained that he was unaware, initially, that Robeson was a Communist. Interestingly, Destiné's popularity began to grow in Communist circles, and he gladly accepted paying jobs and exposure whenever available.

42. *Witch Doctor*, a nine-minute short film, was given awards at the Venice and Edinburgh film festivals. The film tells the story of a *vodou* priest who expels malevolent spirits. It was produced by Ritter-Lerner-Young Associates and Unity Films.

43. Shawn, "Black Christmas." *Dance Magazine*, May 1950, 27, 29.

44. Ibid., 34.

45. Destiné assembled La Troupe Folklorique Nationale with dancers through Lina Fussman-Mathon. La Troupe Folklorique also had a fifteen-piece orchestra called Jazz des Jeunes, as well as three drummers and several singers. According to Destiné, many Haitian dance teachers were upset with him because he visited Haiti sparingly and he could recruit dancers away from Haitian teachers, possibly leaving them unemployed.

46. U.S. government officials were invited to bicentennial events. The Haitian government invited President Truman and Eleanor Roosevelt as guests to the exposition, although they did not attend; moreover, the U.S. Congress established a commission known as the "United States International Exposition for the Bicentennial of the Founding of Port-au-Prince." See Pamphile, *Haitians and African Americans*, 153.

47. See Mary McLeod Bethune to Arabella Denniston, July 29, 1949, Mary McLeod Bethune Papers, microfilm Part II, reel 3, LOC.

48. Interview with Destiné, July 9, 2002.

49. Averill, *Day for the Hunter*, 58.

50. Lavinia Williams to Roger Savain, December 2, 1952, Lavinia Williams Collection, box 2, Miscellaneous Letters folder, SCRBC. Hereafter, Lavinia Williams Collection referred to as "LWC." Roger E. Savain wrote back to Williams stating that Williams also would be "the special instructor of the National Folklore Troupe of Haiti.... In addition to that, the Department of National Education will guarantee you $50.00 a month, and it would like you to teach plastic dance only to the girls in one Lyceum and one Normal School." Refer to Roger E. Savain to Lavinia Williams, January 22, 1953, LWC, box 2, Correspondence Letters Received, 1952–1971, SCRBC.

51. Viviane Gauthier served as Lavinia Williams' assistant at the Haitian Academy of Folklore and Classic Dance in the mid-1950s.

52. *Haiti Sun,* April 21, 1957. Loose material in LWC, box 2, Miscellaneous Letters, 1952–1971, SCRBC.

53. Lois Wilcken asserted that during Magloire's presidency, Haitian intellectuals "expressed the need to temper Afro-Haitian dance with the aesthetic standards of ballet and modern dance." Refer to Wilcken, "Spirit Unbound," 116.

54. Interview with James Briggs Murray, October 1983, Sound Division, SCRBC.

55. LWC, box 1, Interview with Annette McDonald folder, SCRBC.

56. Ibid.

57. Quoted in J. Nash, "Pioneers in Negro Concert Dance," 14.

58. LWC, box 1, folder 1942–1945, SCRBC. Williams was still working for and learning from Katherine Dunham at this time.

59. Katherine Dunham to Lavinia Williams, January 17, 1946, LWC, box 10, Katherine Dunham folder, SCRBC.

60. LWC, box 1, Interview with Annette McDonald folder, SCRBC.

61. Ibid. According to Williams, she participated in *vodou* ceremonies at least once or twice a month.

62. Ibid.

63. Ibid.

64. L. Williams, "Haiti: Where I Teach and Dance." *Dance Magazine,* October 1956, 42.

65. Newspaper clipping, no date, "American Contribution to Haitian Culture: Dancer Making History as Director of Haitian Institute of Folklore and Classical Dance," LWC, box 2, Letters Received 1952–1971, SCRBC.

66. LWC, box 19, Printed Matter—Caribbean Dance folder, SCRBC. Lavinia Williams proceeded to teach Haitian folkloric dance and other Caribbean forms of dance, as well as ballet and modern dance, in Jamaica, Guyana and the Bahamas. See *Jet,* "American Teaches Haitian Dances to Jamaicans," October 2, 1958.

67. L. Williams, *Haiti Dance,* 35.

68. Ibid.

69. LWC, box 4, Régine Mont-Rosier folder, SCRBC.

70. Many of these programs were rebroadcast on Chicago radio stations, presumably because of her close relationship with Claude Barnett and his wife Etta Moten Barnett, who were based in Chicago. Moten Barnett hosted her own radio show in Chicago and sometimes broadcast from Haiti.

71. Magloire and Yelvington, "Haiti and the Anthropological Imagination," 132.

72. *Haiti Sun,* July 25, 1954. Loose material in LWC, box 2, Letters Received 1952–1971, SCRBC.

73. *Haiti Sun,* no date, LWC, box 4, Régine Mont-Rosier folder, SCRBC.

74. LWC, box 1, Interview with Annette McDonald folder, SCRBC.

75. Ibid.

76. See Hanchard, "Afro-Modernity," 245–268.

77. Trouillot, *Haiti: State against Nation,* 135–136. Trouillot also argued: "If most of the *indigéniste* writers were not *noiristes,* most *noiristes* were *indigénistes* with an eye on the worldwide *negritude* movement." Trouillot, *Haiti: State against Nation,* 32.

Chapter 6. "The Moody Republic and the Men in Her Life": François Duvalier, U.S. African Americans and Haitian Exiles, 1957–1964

1. L. Evans, "Haiti Government Aims Verbal Barrage." See also Pamphile, *Haitians and African Americans,* 167.

2. Camille Lhérisson to Oscar L. Chapman, January 17, 1959, François Duvalier Letters, Ernest Bonhomme to François Duvalier folder, SCRBC. Hereafter the François Duvalier Letters will be abbreviated to "FDL." For more on Camille Lhérisson, see the Papers of Frances R. Grant Collection, box 43, folder 44 Haiti: Haitian Study Group Fignolé and Lhérisson, and box 44 folder 3-4 Haiti: Personalities-Dr. Camille Lhérisson, 1957–1966, Special Collections and University Archives, Archibald Stevens Alexander Library, Rutgers University Libraries, New Brunswick, New Jersey.

3. Trouillot, *Haiti: State against Nation,* 143.

4. Several scholars maintain similar arguments regarding the legacy of authoritarian regimes in Haiti, particularly those rooted in the post-1804 era. See Nicholls, *From Dessalines to Duvalier*; Dupuy, "Conceptualizing the Duvalier Dictatorship"; Fatton, *Haiti's Predatory Republic.*

5. Lancelot Evans, "Haiti Government Aims Verbal Barrage."

6. *Chicago Defender,* "Duvalier and the Haitian Crisis," 10.

7. Pamphile, *Haitians and African Americans,* 168.

8. See U.S. Ambassador to Haiti Benson E.L. Timmons to U.S. Department of State, February 24, 1965, in U.S. Department of State, *Foreign Relations of the United States, Dominican Republic, Cuba, Haiti, Guyana, 1964–1968,* vol. 32, 785–786.

9. The term *cagoulars* comes from the word *cagoules,* meaning mask or ski mask. Trouillot asserts that the "name and methods" of the *cagoulars* can be linked to "European fascist organizations of the 1930s." See Trouillot, *Haiti: State against Nation,* 189.

10. Lancelot Evans, *New York Age,* "More about Haiti," March 7, 1959, 9.

11. Lancelot Evans, "The Gentleman from Haiti," *New York Age,* May 2, 1959, 9.

12. Refer to Von Eschen, *Race against Empire,* 164.

13. Haiti 1963, No. 263, 1993, "Moving Images Related to Intelligence and International Relations, 1894–2002," Records of the Central Intelligence Agency, RG 263, NACP.

14. "Observations on the Emotional Health and Attitudes of François Duvalier: Unpublished Psychiatric Evaluation Done by the Office of Medical Services," July 6, 1967, General Records of the U.S. State Department Bureau of Inter-American Affairs, Office of the Director for Caribbean Affairs, Records Relating to Haiti, 1963–1974, RG 59, box 8, Duvalier 1967 folder, NACP.

15. See Graham, ed., *Idea of Race in Latin America.*

16. Dash, *Haiti and the United States,* 106.

17. Ibid., 105.

18. "The Nation was the state. The state was Duvalier," is from Trouillot, *Haiti: State against Nation,* 196. François Duvalier, Address to the Haitian People, October 22, 1958, in "The Objective of the Duvalier Administration: A Review of the Financial Mess Inherited by President Duvalier; His Intentions for Effecting Financial Stability for Haiti; and, His Appeal to the Haitian People to Make the Necessary Sacrifices to Assist National Re-

covery" (prepared by the Haitian Department of Coordination and Information, 1958), CBP, box 204, Haiti General Correspondence 1958–1964, CHS.

19. Abbott, *Haiti,* 83–84.

20. P. Kennedy, "Haiti to Press U.S. to Oust 2 Exiles." Newspaper clipping in CBP, box 204, Haiti General Correspondence 1958–1964 folder, CHS.

21. François Duvalier, Address to the Haitian People, October 22, 1958 in "The Objective of the Duvalier Administration: CBP, box 204, Haiti General Correspondence 1958–1964 folder, CHS.

22. Interview with Roland Weiner, March 1, 2003.

23. Ibid.

24. Ibid.

25. Ibid.

26. Livingston, "Haiti Exiles in Bahamas Vow Rout of Duvalier," *Washington Post,* September 1, 1963, A12.

27. Berle, "Is Haiti Next?" 16. See also Plummer, *Rising Wind,* 273–277.

28. Burt, "Haiti," 11.

29. Plummer, *Haiti and the United States,* 180.

30. L. Langley, *United States and the Caribbean in the Twentieth Century,* 188.

31. Plummer, *Haiti and the United States,* 185.

32. Kennedy Crockett to Thomas Mann, July 17, 1964, General Records of the U.S. State Department Bureau of Inter-American Affairs, Office of the Director for Caribbean Affairs Records Relating to Haiti, 1963–1974, RG 59, POL 30–1, NACP.

33. Trouillot, *Haiti: State against Nation,* 173.

34. Unidentified newspaper clipping, June 8, 1958, CBP, box 204, Haiti General Correspondence 1958–1964, CHS.

35. Uchitelle, "Haiti Stuck with Dictator and No U.S. Aid," *Chicago Tribune,* February 14, 1965, A3.

36. Poor Haitians also fled Duvalier rule. However, many stayed in the Caribbean region, particularly in the Bahamas and the Dominican Republic.

37. Nicholls, *From Dessalines to Duvalier,* 221, 226.

38. Trouillot, *Haiti: State against Nation,* 27.

39. Averill, *Day for the Hunter,* 73.

40. See Duvalier, "The Objective of the Duvalier Administration," CBP, box 204, Haiti General Correspondence 1958–1964, CHS.

41. Averill, *Day for the Hunter,* 75.

42. Ibid., 74.

43. Ibid., 89. For more details on Duvalier and *koudyay* politics, see Averill, *Day for the Hunter,* 89–94.

44. *Chicago Daily Defender,* "Haiti's Duvalier Now Is President for Life," June 24, 1964, A3.

45. Trouillot argued that for *noiristes,* national unity meant the balance of blacks and *mulâtre* in the state government. For cultural nationalists, it meant the promise of "regeneration." And, for those on the political right, national unity was any "alliance that would block Communism." See Trouillot, *Haiti: State against Nation,* 196.

46. Trouillot, *Haiti: State against Nation,* 193.

47. Nicholls, *From Dessalines to Duvalier,* 237.

48. Trouillot, *Haiti: State against Nation,* 192. See also Nicholls, *From Dessalines to Duvalier,* 258, footnote 25.

49. Remy, "The Duvalier Phenomenon," 47–48. Duvalier advocated an elitist ideology that embraced Western civilization but also stressed the importance of African cultural retentions and connections in the Haitian peasantry. See also Duvalier's personal works: *Oeuvres Essentielles, Element d'une Doctrine; Oeuvres Essentielles, La Marche à la Présidence;* and *Bréviare d'une Révolution.*

50. François Duvalier, "Message à la Nation Haïtienne et aux Peuple de L'Amerique" April 14, 1963, FDL, SCRBC. Pan American Day, celebrated April 14, marks the date when the Pan American Union, now the Organization of American States, was established in 1890.

51. See Duvalier, "The Objective of the Duvalier Administration," CBP, box 204, Haiti General Correspondence 1958–1964 folder, CHS. For more information on L'Ouverture's plantation reforms, see C.L.R. James, *Black Jacobins,* and Dubois, *Avengers of the New World,* 238–240.

52. *New York Times,* "Haitian Exiles Form Coordination Group," May 19, 1963, 30. See also *New York Times,* "Haitian Exiles Seek Unity," January 23, 1961, 12.

53. Haitian Patriotic Alliance to Dean Rusk, December 20, 1966, General Records of the U.S. State Department Bureau of Inter-American Affairs, Office of the Director for Caribbean Affairs Records Relating to Haiti, 1963–1974, RG 59, POL 30–2, U.S.-Haitian Patriotic Alliance, 1966 folder, NACP.

54. Memorandum from Robert M. Sayre to Bundy, July 9, 1964, and July 10, 1964, U.S. Department of State, *Foreign Relations of the United States, Dominican Republic, Cuba, Haiti, Guyana, 1964–1968,* 774–775.

55. *New York Times,* "Haitian Diplomat Indicted," May 27, 1965, 3.

56. Dunham, *Island Possessed,* 172.

57. Refer to Aschenbrenner, *Katherine Dunham.*

58. "Haiti Exile Lists Grows," *New York Age,* July 18, 1959, 6.

59. Eder, "Haiti Is Defiant in Face of Reduction in U.S. Aid," *New York Times,* October 2, 1962, 17.

60. Duvalier, *Paix et Pain Pour Survivre,* 38, 41. My italics.

61. Eder, "Haiti Is Defiant," 17.

62. Abbott, *Haiti,* 108.

63. Ibid., 108–109.

64. Laguerre, "The Role of the Diaspora in Haitian Politics," 170.

65. Trouillot, *Haiti: State against Nation,* 162.

66. P. Smith, *Talons of the Eagle,* 159.

67. "Request from the Government of Haiti to the Government of the United States for Financial Assistance," FDL, box 1, Government Documents U.S./Haiti Relations folder, SCRBC.

68. François Duvalier to Dwight Eisenhower, October 8, 1959, FDL, box 1, François Duvalier Letters folder, SCRBC.

69. Dupuy, "Conceptualizing the Duvalier Dictatorship," 109. See also Péan's *Haïti, Économie Politique de la Corruption.*

70. Uchitelle, "Haiti Stuck with Dictator," A3.

71. Ibid.

72. Quoted in Streeter, "The Myth of Pan-Americanism," 172.

73. Dwight D. Eisenhower to Francois Duvalier, June 27, 1959, *Papers of Dwight David Eisenhower,* Galambos and van Ee, eds., doc. 1214. See also Duvalier to Eisenhower, June 4, 1959, *Papers of Dwight David Eisenhower,* AWF/I: Haiti; U.S. Department of State, *Foreign Relations of the United States, 1958–1960,* vol. 5, American Republics, 817–819.

74. François Duvalier to Dwight Eisenhower, July 12, 1960, FDL, FDL folder, SCRBC.

75. François Duvalier to John F. Kennedy, October 11, 1961, Records of U.S. Department of State Central File, RG 59, 838.211/2–1160, NACP.

76. P. Smith, *Talons of the Eagle,* 153. Smith argues that Latin America in the 1960s experienced a "marked acceleration in economic growth" due to the "strength of trading markets, and the stimulation of trading markets." Latin American exports missed achieving the mark set by Alliance for Progress goals by just 1 percent during the 1960s.

77. Jackson, "Haiti's Challenge to America," 31.

78. Some Haitians also stated their objections to U.S. Pan-Americanism. Roland Weiner asserted: "North Americans, for some reason, have always thought they were superior. . . . this is the reason why they never had great success in Pan-Americanism." Interview with Roland Weiner, March 1, 2003.

79. *Chicago Daily Defender,* "Haiti Gets Loan," March 26, 1964, 15.

80. The lack of U.S. aid to Haiti in comparison to support given to other nations suggests dwindling U.S. interest. However, some Haitians developed resentment towards the United States for abandoning the country financially during the mid- to late 1960s. Haitian officials such as Edouard Francisque, minister of finance, attributed it to race in addition to a lack of U.S. interest. At the same time, U.S. involvement in the Vietnam War, the souring of U.S./Haiti relations due to Duvalier's illegal re-election in 1961, Duvalier's human rights violations and his self-proclaimed lifelong dictatorship also were factors in decreased aid.

81. *Chicago Defender,* "Haiti's Poverty," April 11, 1964.

82. Ibid.

83. Pelnar, "States Rights More Evil than Communism," *Chicago Defender,* January 11, 1964.

84. *Chicago Defender,* "Haitian Dictatorship," June 27, 1961, 11.

85. Claude Barnett's ANP press release made light of Duvalier's declaration of despotism with an extremely weak article. See "Duvalier Follows Long-standing Haitian Tradition in Accepting Life Presidency," Associated Negro Press release, April 15, 1964, CBP, box 205, Racine folder, CHS.

86. Mirabeau, "Can Haiti Be Helped?" *Nation,* May 18, 1963, 417. My italics.

87. Heinl, "'Papa Doc' Uses Voodoo to 'Control' U.S. Policy," *Los Angeles Times,* July 5, 1964, 11.

88. *Chicago Defender,* "The Truth about Voodoo," June 22, 1963, 6.

89. Jules Blanchet, "An Open Letter to the Editor-in-Chief of *Time* and the *New York Herald Tribune*," July 1–2, 1957, *Le Nouvelliste*. Copy of article in CBP, box 204, Haiti General Correspondence 1956–1957, CHS.

90. Ibid.

91. Diawara, *In Search of Africa*, 7.

92. Ibid., 10.

93. Barnett to François Duvalier, November 30, 1957, CBP, box 204, Haiti General Correspondence 1956–1957 folder, CHS.

94. Barnett to Mme. Estimé, November 9, 1957, CBP, box 204, Haiti General Correspondence 1956–1957 folder, CHS.

95. Pamphile, *Haitians and African Americans*, 168–169.

96. Emmanuel Racine to Barnett, March 13, 1958, CBP, box 204, Haiti General Correspondence, 1958–1964 folder, CHS.

97. See Trouillot, *Haiti: State against Nation*, 169.

98. "Opposition Papers Sacked in Haiti," *Washington Post*, May 6, 1958, A7.

99. Barnett to Emmanuel Racine, March 24, 1961, CBP, box 204, Haiti General Correspondence 1958–1964, CHS.

100. Ibid., May 2, 1963.

101. Interview with Bernard Diederich, October 17, 2008.

102. Ibid.

103. Barnett to François Duvalier, May 9, 1964, CBP, box 204, Haiti General Correspondence 1963–1968 folder, CHS.

104. Ibid.

105. Eric F. Etienne to Barnett, April 25, 1968, CBP, box 204, folder 4, CHS.

106. *Baltimore Afro-American*, "President for Life Is Duvalier's Goal," May 16, 1964, 17.

107. Nicholls, *From Dessalines to Duvalier*, 235.

108. Guy, "Haiti: The Enigma of the Caribbean," 415–416.

109. Von Eschen, *Race against Empire*, 186.

110. Pamphile, *Haitians and African Americans*, 171–173.

Bibliography

Primary Sources

Barnett, Claude. Papers. Chicago History Museum.

Bethune, Mary McLeod. Papers. Manuscripts Division, Library of Congress, Washington, D.C.

Borome, Joseph. Papers. Schomburg Center for Research in Black Culture, New York Public Library.

Brown, Norma. *A Black Diplomat in Haiti: The Diplomatic Correspondence of U.S. Minister Frederick Douglass from Haiti, 1889–1891*. Salisbury, N.C.: Documentary Publications, 1977.

Brown, William Wells. *The Black Man: His Antecedents, His Genius, and His Achievements*. New York: Thomas Hamilton, 1863.

Cauvin, Luxembourg, and Victor, Haiti Collection. Schomburg Center for Research in Black Culture, New York Public Library.

Central Intelligence Agency. "Moving Images Related to Intelligence and International Relations, 1894–2002." Records of the Central Intelligence Agency, RG 263, National Archives at College Park, Md.

Daniels, Ronald. *Cruising into History*. http://www.cruisingintohistory.org/pdfs/article2.pdf (accessed March 15, 2003).

Dartigue, Maurice. Papers. Schomburg Center for Research in Black Culture, New York Public Library.

Douglass, Frederick. Papers. Manuscripts Division, Library of Congress, Washington, D.C.

———. Papers. Schomburg Center for Research in Black Culture, New York Public Library.

———. *The Claims of the Negro, Ethnologically Considered. An Address, Before the Literary Societies of Western Reserve College at Commencement, July 12, 1854*. Rochester, N.Y.: Lee, Mann, 1854.

———. "Haïti and the United States: Inside History of the Negotiations for the Môle St. Nicolas." Pts. 1 and 2. *North American Review* 153, no. 418 (September 1891): 337–45; no. 419 (October 1891): 450–59.

———. "Toussaint L'Ouverture." *Colored American*. July 1903.

———. "A Trip to Haiti" *Douglass' Monthly*, May 1861.

Du Bois, W.E.B. Papers. Schomburg Center for Research in Black Culture, New York Public Library.

Duvalier, François. Letters. Schomburg Center for Research in Black Culture, New York Public Library.

Eisenhower, Dwight D. Cable. "To Francois Duvalier, 27 June 1959." In *The Papers of Dwight David Eisenhower*, edited by L. Galambos and D. van Ee, doc. 1214. World Wide Web facsimile by the Dwight D. Eisenhower Memorial Commission of the print edition (Baltimore: Johns Hopkins University Press, 1996, http://www.eisenhowermemorial.org/presidentialpapers/second-term/documents/1214.cfm).

Goodman, Amy. "Randall Robinson: Aristide Says 'Tell the World It Is a Coup.'" Interview with Randall Robinson. Democracynow.org, March 1, 2004. http://www.democracynow.org/article.pl?sid=04/03/01/1929215 (accessed May 12, 2005).

Grant, Frances R. Papers. Special Collections and University Archives, Archibald Stevens Alexander Library, Rutgers University Libraries, New Brunswick, N.J.

Haitian Afro-American Chamber of Commerce. *Official Report of the Haitian Afro-American Chamber of Commerce's Commission to Study the Commercial, Agricultural and Industrial Possibilities of the Haitian Republic*. 1935. Schomburg Center for Research in Black Culture, New York Public Library.

Harrison, Benjamin. *Public Papers and Addresses of Benjamin Harrison, Twenty–third President of the United States: March 4, 1889, to March 4, 1893*. Washington, D.C.: U.S. Government Printing Office, 1893.

Harrison, Benjamin, and James G. Blaine. *The Correspondence between Benjamin Harrison and James G. Blaine, 1882–1893*. Edited by Albert T. Volwiler. Philadelphia: American Philosophical Society, 1940.

Hoover, Herbert. Papers. Herbert Hoover Presidential Library, West Branch, Iowa.

———. *Public Papers of the Presidents of the United States: Herbert Hoover, Containing the Public Messages, Speeches, and Statements of the President, 1930*. Washington, D.C.: U.S. Government Printing Office, 1976.

International Action Center. "Congresswoman Maxine Waters and Ossie Davis will speak at April 7th rally to demand restoration of democracy in Haiti." Press release. April 7, 2004. http://www.iacenter.org/Haitifiles/haiti_040704.htm (accessed February 9, 2008).

Logan, Rayford Whittingham. Papers. Manuscripts Division, Library of Congress, Washington, D.C.

Moton Family Papers. Library of Congress. Washington, D.C.

Office of the Director for Caribbean Affairs. Records Relating to Haiti, 1963–1974. "Observations on the Emotional Health and Attitudes of François Duvalier: Unpublished Psychiatric Evaluation Done by the Office of Medical Services," July 6, 1967, General Records of the U.S. State Department Bureau of Inter-American Affairs, RG 59, National Archives at College Park, Md.

National Association for the Advancement of Colored People. Papers. Library of Congress. Washington, D.C.

Papiers Diplomatique, 1850–1925. Archives Nationale, Port-au-Prince, Haiti.

Plinton, James O. Interview by Etta Moten Barnett at Hotel Choucoune, 1957. Sound Division. Schomburg Center for Research in Black Culture, New York Public Library.

Rockefeller, Nelson A. Papers. Rockefeller Archive Center, Sleepy Hollow, N.Y.

Roosevelt, Franklin D. Papers. Franklin D. Roosevelt Library. Hyde Park, N.Y.

Schomburg, Arthur Alfonso. Papers. Schomburg Center for Research in Black Culture, New York Public Library.

Union Patriotique d'Haiti. "Memoir." *Nation*, May 25, 1921.

U.S. Congress. Senate. Senate Document No. 337, 29th Cong., 1st sess. *Public Documents by Order of the Senate of the United States*, v.7. Washington, D.C.: Ritchie & Reiss, 1846.

———. *Report of the Commission of Inquiry to Santo Domingo*, 42nd Cong., 1st sess., Executive Document No. 9. Washington, D.C.: U.S. Government Printing Office, 1871.

U.S. Department of State. *Despatches from United States Ministers to Haiti, 1862–1906*. U.S. National Archives and Records Services, Washington, D.C.: 1955.

———. *Foreign Relations of the United States, Dominican Republic, Cuba, Haiti, Guyana, 1964–1968*, vol. 32. Washington, D.C.: U.S. Government Printing Office, 2005.

———. *Foreign Relations of the United States, 1958–1960*, vol. 5. Washington, D.C.: U.S. Government Printing Office, 2005.

———. *Minutes of the Second Meeting of Société Haïtienne–Américaine Développement Agricole Board of Directors*. October 1941 and November 1942, U.S Department of State, numerical and decimal files. U.S. National Archives at College Park, Md.

———. Records of the Department of State Relating to Internal Affairs of Haiti, 1930–1939; RG 59, General Records of the Department of State; microfilm reel 69, U.S. National Archives at College Park, Md.

———. Records of Department of State Central File, RG 59, 838.211/2–1160.

———. *Report of the United States Commission on Education in Haiti* (Moton Commission Report). Washington, D.C.: U.S. Government Printing Office, 1931.

Washington Conservatory of Music Records. Moorland-Spingarn Research Center, Howard University. Washington, D.C.

Waters, Maxine. "Congresswoman Waters Leads Delegation to Free Aristide from Central African Republic." Press release. March 16, 2004. http://www.house.gov/waters/ (accessed April 2, 2005).

———. "Congresswoman Maxine Waters' Statement on Kidnapping of Haitian President Aristide." Press release. March 1, 2004. http://www.house.gov/waters/ (accessed April 2, 2005).

White, Francis. Papers. Herbert Hoover Presidential Library, West Branch, Iowa.

White, Walter F. Papers. Yale Collection of American Literature, Beinecke Rare Book and Manuscript Library, New Haven, Conn.

Williams, Lavinia. Collection. Schomburg Center for Research in Black Culture, New York Public Library.

———. *Haiti Dance*. Frankfurt: Bronners Druckerei, 1959.

———. "Haiti: Where I Teach and Dance." *Dance Magazine*, October 1956, 42.

———. Interview by James Briggs Murray, October 1983. Sound Division, Schomburg Center for Research in Black Culture, New York Public Library.

Williams, W.T.B. "Haiti." *Southern Workman* 53, no. 3 (March 1924): 122.

Personal Interviews

Destiné, Jean-Léon. Interview by Millery Polyné. Harlem, New York, July 9, 2002.

Diederich, Bernard. Email interview by Millery Polyné. October 17, 2008.

Rangel, Charles. Phone interview with Millery Polyné. Staten Island, New York, November 8, 2006.

Weiner, Roland. Phone Interview by Millery Polyné. Harlem, New York, March 1, 2003.

Secondary Sources

Abbott, Elizabeth. *Haiti: The Duvaliers and Their Legacy.* New York: McGraw-Hill, 1988.

Ackah, William. *Pan-Africanism: Exploring the Contradictions.* Aldershot, England: Ashgate Publishing, 1999.

Aguilar, Alonso. *Pan Americanism from Monroe to the Present: A View from the Other Side.* New York: Monthly Review, 1969.

Alexander, Richard. "The Hell of Haiti." *Nation* 196 (1963): 98–99.

American Society of African Culture, ed. *Pan-Africanism Reconsidered.* Berkeley: University of California Press, 1962.

Anderson, Carol. *Eyes off the Prize: The United Nations and the African American Struggle for Human Rights, 1944–1955.* Cambridge: Cambridge University Press, 2003.

Andrews, George Reid. *Afro-Latin America, 1800–2000.* New York: Oxford University Press, 2004.

Antoine, Jacques C. *Jean Price-Mars and Haiti.* Washington, D.C.: Three Continents Press, 1981.

Ardao, Arturo. "Assimilation and Transformation of Positivism in Latin America." *Journal of the History of Ideas*, 24 (1963): 515–22.

———. "Mass Education in Latin America." Institute of International Education, *News Bulletin* 30, no. 7 (April 1955): 19.

Aristide, Jean-Bertrand, Noam Chomsky, Paul Farmer and Amy Goodman. *Getting Haiti Right This Time: The U.S. and the Coup.* Edited by Amy Goodman. Monroe, Maine: Common Courage Press, 2004.

Armendàriz, Beatriz, and Jonathan Morduch. *The Economics of Microfinance.* Cambridge, Mass.: MIT Press, 2005.

Aschenbrenner, Joyce. *Katherine Dunham: Reflections on the Social and Political Context of Afro-American Dance.* New York: CORD, 1981.

Atkins, G. Pope, and Larman Wilson. *The Dominican Republic and the United States: From Imperialism to Transnationalism.* Athens: University of Georgia Press, 1998.

Averill, Gage. *A Day for the Hunter, A Day for the Prey: Popular Music and Power in Haiti.* Chicago: University of Chicago Press, 1997.

Ballard, Barbara J. "African American Protest and the Role of the Haitian Pavilion at the

1893 Chicago World's Fair." In *Multiculturalism: Roots and Realities*, edited by James Troutman, 108–24. Bloomington: Indiana University Press, 2002.

Baltimore Afro-American Ledger. "Bullying Haiti." August 28, 1915.

———. "The Effect of Pan-Americanism upon the Darker Races." January 15, 1916.

———. "President for Life Is Duvalier's Goal." May 16, 1964.

———. "U.S. Not to Leave in Near Future." August 21, 1915.

———. "Pan Americanism." December 25, 1915.

Bastien, Rémy. "The Role of the Intellectual in Haitian Plural Society." In *Social and Cultural Pluralism in the Caribbean*, edited by Dorothy L. Keur et al. New York: New York Academy of the Sciences, 1960.

Beals, Carleton. "Haiti under the Gun." *Nation*, July 6, 1957.

Beckford, Ruth. *Katherine Dunham: A Biography*. New York: Marcel Dekker, 1979.

Bellegarde, Dantès. "Alexandre Pétion, a Pioneer of Pan-Americanism." Translated by Mrs. W. Geter Thomas. *Bulletin of the Pan American Union* (May 1943): 245–52.

———. "Haiti under the Rule of the United States." Translated by Rayford Logan. *Opportunity* 5, no. 12 (December 1927): 354–57.

———. "The Haitian Nation." In *The Negro in the Americas*, edited by Charles H. Wesley. Washington, D.C.: Graduate School for the Division of the Social Sciences, 1940.

———. "Haiti's Voice at the Peace Table." *Opportunity* 21, no. 4 (October 1943): 154–55.

———. "An Inter-American Economic Policy." *The Annals of the American Academy of Political and Social Science* 150 (July 1930): 186–91.

———. *L'Occupation Américaine d'Haïti: Ses Conséquences Morales et Économiques*. Port-au-Prince: Chêraquit, 1929.

———. "The Organization of Inter-American Solidarity." Translated by Mercer Cook. *Phylon* 1, no. 4 (1940): 327–35.

———. *Pour une Haïti Heureuse*. Port-au-Prince: Chêraquit, 1927.

———. "President Alexandre Pétion: Founder of Agrarian Democracy and Pioneer of Pan-Americanism." *Phylon* 2, no. 3 (1941): 205–13.

Bellegarde-Smith, Patrick. "Class Struggle in Contemporary Haitian Politics: An Interpretive Study of the Campaign of 1957." *Journal of Caribbean Studies* 2 (1981): 109–27.

———. "Dantès Bellegarde and Pan-Africanism." *Phylon* 42, no. 3 (September 1981): 233–44.

———. *Haiti: The Breached Citadel*. Boulder, Colo.: Westview Press, 1990.

———. "Haiti: Perspectives of Foreign Policy: An Essay on the International Relations of a Small State." *Caribbean Quarterly* 20, no. 3/4 (1974): 21–35.

———. *In the Shadow of Powers: Dantès Bellegarde in Haitian Social Thought*. Atlantic Highlands, N.J.: Humanities Press International, 1985.

———. "Race, Class, Ideology: Haitian Ideologies for Underdevelopment, 1806–1934." *AIMS, Occasional Papers* 32 (1982).

Belnap, Jeffrey, and Raúl Fernández. "The Architectonics of José Martí's 'Our Americanism.'" Introduction to Belnap and Fernández, *José Martí's "Our America,"* 1–26.

———, eds. *José Martí's "Our America": From National to Hemispheric Cultural Studies*. Durham, N.C.: Duke University Press, 1998.

Adolf A. "Is Haiti Next?" *Reporter* 28, no. 10 (1963): 16.

n, Edward. *The Influence of the Carnegie, Ford and Rockefeller Foundation on American Foreign Policy: The Ideology of Philanthropy.* Albany: State University of New York Press, 1983.

Berman, Marshall. *All That Is Solid Melts into Air: The Experience of Modernity.* New York: Simon and Schuster, 1982.

Bernardin, Raymond. *Général Paul Eugène Magloire: Une Biographie Politique.* Montréal: Centre International de Documentation et d'Information Haïtienne, Caribéenne et Afro-Canadienne, 2000.

Betances, Ramón Emeterio de. *Las Antillas para los Antillanos.* San Juan: Biblioteca Popular, 1975.

Biemeller, Ruth. *Dance: The Story of Katherine Dunham.* New York: Doubleday, 1969.

Bims, Hamilton. "Haiti: New Stirrings of Hope." *Ebony,* January 1973.

Blackmon, Douglas A. *Slavery by Another Name: The Re-Enslavement of Black Americans from the Civil War to World War II.* New York: Doubleday, 2008.

Blanchard, Peter, "Pan Americanism and Slavery in the Era of Latin American Independence." In Sheinin, *Beyond the Ideal,* 9–18.

Blassingame, John W. "The Press and American Intervention in Haiti and the Dominican Republic, 1904–1920." *Caribbean Studies* 9 (1969): 27–43.

Blight, David W. *Frederick Douglass' Civil War: Keeping Faith in Jubilee.* Baton Rouge: Louisiana State University Press, 1991.

Bolívar, Simón. *Selected Writings of Bolívar.* Edited by Harold A. Bierck Jr. Vol. 2. New York: Colonial Press, 1951.

Bradley, Francine. "Political Prisoners in Haiti." *New Republic,* March 27, 1935.

Brady, James P. "Haiti after Duvalier." *New Republic* 146, no. 2 (1962): 7–8.

Brown, Oral Carl. "Haitian Vodou in Relation to Negritude and Christianity: A Study in Acculturation and Applied Anthropology." PhD diss., Indiana University, 1972.

Buell, Raymond Leslie. *The American Occupation of Haiti.* New York: Foreign Policy Association, 1929.

———. *International Relations.* New York: Henry Holt, 1925.

Bunkley, Allison Williams, ed. *A Sarmiento Anthology.* Princeton, N.J.: Princeton University Press, 1976.

Burt, Al. "Haiti: Alternatives to Tyranny." *Nation* 220 (1965): 10–12.

Caldwell, Allen. "Transnational Philanthropy and African-American Education." In *Foreign Policy and the Black (Inter)National Interest,* edited by Charles P. Henry, 37-50. New York: State University of New York Press, 2000.

Carby, Hazel. *Race Men.* Cambridge, Mass.: Harvard University Press, 2000.

Catanese, Anthony V. *Haitians: Migrations and Diaspora.* Boulder, Colo.: Westview Press, 1999.

Charles, Joseph D. "Haiti et le Panaméricanisme." *Bulletin of the Pan-American Union,* 81 (1947): 438.

Chicago Daily Defender. "Duvalier and the Haitian Crisis." July 11, 1959.

———. "Haiti Gets Loan." March 26, 1964.

———. "Haitian Dictatorship." June 27, 1961.

————. "Haiti's Duvalier Now Is President for Life." June 24, 1964.

————. "Haiti's Poverty." April 11, 1964.

————. "The Truth about Voodoo." June 22, 1963.

Chicago Tribune. "Frederick Douglass' Lecture Last Evening—Geographical Position, Area, Climate, Soil, Productions, and Commercial Resources of Santo Domingo—the Government and the People—Mr. Douglass' Seven Reasons for Annexation to the United States." December 30, 1871.

————. "Gen. Grant: What He Says about a Third Term—The St. Domingo Question." July 26, 1878.

Clark, Vèvè A., and Margaret B. Wilkerson, eds. *Kaiso! Katherine Dunham: An Anthology of Writings.* Berkeley: Institute for the Study of Policy Change, University of California at Berkeley, 1978.

Cleven, N. Andrew N. "The First Panama Mission and the Congress of the United States." *Journal of Negro History* 13, no. 3 (July 1928): 225–54.

Coates, Robert. "The Art Galleries: Haiti and the Haitians." *The New Yorker,* June 29, 1946, 52.

Cobb, Martha. "Concepts of Blackness in the Poetry of Nicolás Guillén, Jacques Roumain and Langston Hughes." *College Language Association Journal* 18, no. 2 (December 1974): 262–72.

Cook, Mercer. "Dantès Bellegarde." *Phylon* 1, no. 2 (1940): 125–35.

————. *Education in Haiti.* Washington, D.C.: Federal Security Agency, 1948.

————., ed. *An Introduction to Haiti.* Washington, D.C.: Department of Cultural Affairs, Pan American Union, 1951.

————. *The Militant Black Writer in Africa and the United States.* Madison: University of Wisconsin Press, 1969.

————. "Prejudice, Not Hitler, Greatest Threat to Pan Americanism." *Baltimore Afro-American Ledger,* September 13, 1941.

————. "The Writings of Dantès Bellegarde." *Books Abroad* 25, no. 3 (1949): 292–94.

Cooper, Daniel B. "The Withdrawal of the United States from Haiti, 1928–1934." *Journal of Inter-American Affairs* 5 (1963): 83–101.

Cosentino, Donald J., ed. *Sacred Arts of Haitian Vodou.* Los Angeles: Regents of the University of California, 1995.

Cruse, Harold. *The Crisis of the Negro Intellectual: From Its Origins to the Present.* New York: William Morrow, 1967.

Cueto, Marcos. *Missionaries of Science: The Rockefeller Foundation and Latin America.* Bloomington: Indiana University Press, 1994.

Damas, Léon-Gontran. "Price-Mars: The Father of Haitianism." In *Negritude: Essays and Studies,* edited by Albert H. Berrian and Richard A. Long. Hampton, Va.: Hampton Institute Press, 1967.

Dartigue, Ester. *An Outstanding Haitian, Maurice Dartigue: The Contribution of Maurice Dartigue in the Field of Education in Haiti, the United Nations, and UNESCO.* New York: Vantage Press, 1994.

Dartigue, Maurice. "Rural Life and Education in Haiti." *Inter-American Quarterly* 3, no. 2 (1941): 30–38.

Dash, J. Michael. *Haiti and the United States: National Stereotypes and the Literary Imagination*. New York: St. Martin's, 1997.

———. *Literature and Ideology in Haiti, 1915–1961*. Totowa, N.J.: Barnes and Noble, 1981.

———. "The Marxist Counterpoint—Jacques Roumain: 1930's to 1940's." *Black Images* 2 (Spring 1973): 25–29.

———. "Nineteenth-Century Haiti and the Archipelago of the Americas: Anténor Firmin's Letters from St. Thomas." *Research in African Literatures* 35, no. 2 (Summer 2004): 44–53.

Dash, J. Michael, and Charles Arthur, eds. *Libète: An Anthology*. London: Latin American Bureau, 1999.

Dee, Bleeker. "Duvalier's Haiti: A Case Study of National Disintegration." PhD diss., University of Florida, 1967.

Deibert, Michael. *Notes from the Last Testament: The Struggle for Haiti*. New York: Seven Stories Press, 2005.

Delany, Martin R. *The Condition, Elevation, Emigration, and Destiny of the Colored People of the United States*. 1852. Reprint, Amherst, N.Y.: Humanity Books, 2004.

———. *Martin R. Delany: A Documentary Reader*. Edited by Robert S. Levine. Chapel Hill: University of North Carolina Press, 2003.

Deren, Maya. *Divine Horsemen: The Living Gods of Haiti*. New York: Thames and Hudson, 1953.

———. "Social and Ritual Dances of Haiti." *Dance Magazine*, June 1949, 5–35.

Desmangles, Leslie G. *The Faces of the Gods: Vodou and Roman Catholicism in Haiti*. Chapel Hill: University of North Carolina Press, 1992.

Diawara, Manthia. *In Search of Africa*. Cambridge, Mass.: Harvard University Press, 2000.

Dixon, Chris. *African America and Haiti: Emigrationism and Black Nationalism in the Nineteenth Century*. Westport, Conn.: Greenwood Press, 2000.

Dolkart, Andrew S., and Gretchen S. Sorin. *Touring Historic Harlem: Four Walks in Northern Manhattan*. New York: New York Landmarks Conservancy, 1997.

Donald, David. *Charles Sumner and the Rights of Man*. New York: Knopf, 1970.

Douglass, Frederick. *Frederick Douglass: Selected Speeches and Writings*. Edited by Philip S. Foner. Chicago: Lawrence Hill Books, 1999.

———. *The Life and Writings of Frederick Douglass*. Edited by Philip S. Foner. Vols. 4 and 5. New York: International Publishers, 1975.

Drake, St. Clair. "Diaspora Studies and Pan-Africanism." In *Global Dimensions of the African Diaspora*, edited by Joseph Harris. Washington, D.C.: Howard University Press, 1982.

Drake, St. Clair, and Horace R. Cayton. *Black Metropolis: A Study of Negro Life in a Northern City*. New York: Harcourt, Brace and World, 1962.

Duberman, Martin. *Paul Robeson: A Biography*. New York: New Press, 1989.

Dubois, Laurent. *Avengers of the New World: The Story of the Haitian Revolution*. Cambridge, Mass.: Harvard University Press, 2005.

Du Bois, W.E.B. *W.E.B. Du Bois: A Reader*, edited by David Leverling Lewis. New York: Henry Holt, 1995.

Dudziack, Mary. *Cold War Civil Rights: Race and the Image of American Democracy.* Princeton, N.J.: Princeton University Press, 2002.

Dunham, Katherine. *Island Possessed.* 1969. Reprint, Chicago: University of Chicago Press, 1994.

Dupuy, Alex. "Conceptualizing the Duvalier Dictatorship." *Latin American Perspectives* 15, no. 4 (Fall 1988): 105–14.

———. *The Prophet and Power: Jean-Bertrand Aristide, the International Community, and Haiti.* Lanham, Md.: Rowman and Littlefield, 2007.

Duvalier, François. *Bréviare d'une Révolution.* Port-au-Prince: Presses Nationales d'Haïti, 1967.

———. *Oeuvres Essentielles, Element d'une Doctrine.* Vol. 1. Port-au-Prince: Presses Nationales d'Haïti, 1966.

———. *Oeuvres Essentielles, La Marche à la Présidence.* Vol. 2. Port-au-Prince: Presses Nationales d'Haïti, 1966.

———. *Paix et Pain Pour Survivre.* Port-au-Prince: Imprimerie de L'État, 1962.

Eder, Richard. "Haiti Is Defiant in Face of Reduction in U.S. Aid." *New York Times,* October 2, 1962.

Emery, Amy Fass. "The Zombie In/As the Text: Zora Neale Hurston's *Tell My Horse.*" *African American Review* 39, no. 3 (Fall 2005): 327–36.

Erb, Claude. "Prelude to Point Four: The Institute of Inter-American Affairs." *Diplomatic History* 9 (Summer 1985): 249-269.

Esedebe, Peter O. *Pan-Africanism: The Idea and Movement, 1776-1963.* Washington, D.C.: Howard University Press, 1982.

Eshleman, Clayton, and Annette Smith, eds. *Aimé Césaire: The Collected Poetry.* Los Angeles: University of California Press, 1983.

Evans, Lancelot O. "Duvalier Getting Stronger." *New York Age,* May 23, 1959.

———. "The Gentleman from Haiti." *New York Age,* May 2, 1959.

———. "Haiti Government Aims Verbal Barrage at Exile for 'Shameful' Letter to 'Friends of Haiti.'" *New York Age,* January 31, 1959.

———. "The Moody Republic and the Men in Her Life." *New York Age,* January 10, 1959.

———. "More about Haiti." *New York Age,* March 7, 1959.

———. "Peasants Tell *Age*: 'We'll Die for Duvalier.'" March 7, 1959.

Evans, Linda J. "Claude A. Barnett and the Associated Negro Press." *Chicago History* 12 (Spring 1983): 44.

Ewell, Judith. *Venezuela and the United States: From Monroe's Hemisphere to Petroleum's Empire.* Athens: University of Georgia Press, 1996.

Fabre, Michel. *The Unfinished Quest of Richard Wright.* Urbana: University of Illinois Press, 1993.

Fairclough, Adam. "Civil Rights and the Lincoln Memorial: The Censored Speeches of Robert R. Moton (1922) and John Lewis (1963)." *Journal of Negro History* 82, no. 4 (Fall 1997): 408–16.

Farmer, Paul. *AIDS and Accusation: Haiti and the Geography of Blame.* Berkeley: University of California Press, 1993.

———. *The Uses of Haiti*. Monroe, Maine: Common Courage Press, 1994.

Fatton, Robert, Jr. *Haiti's Predatory Republic: The Unending Transition to Democracy*. Boulder, Colo.: Lynne Rienner, 2002.

———. *The Roots of Haitian Despotism*. Boulder, Colo.: Lynne Reinner, 2007.

Favor, J. Martin. *Authentic Blackness: The Folk in the New Negro Renaissance*. Durham, N.C.: Duke University Press, 1999.

Favrot, Leo M. "How the Small Rural School Can More Adequately Serve Its Community." *Journal of Negro Education* 5, no. 3 (July 1936): 430–38.

Fick, Carolyn. *The Making of Haiti: The Saint Domingue Revolution from Below*. Knoxville: University of Tennessee Press, 1990.

Firmin, Anténor. *The Equality of the Human Races*. 1885. Reprint, Urbana: University of Illinois Press, 2002.

———. *Lettres de Saint-Thomas: Études Sociologique, Historiques et Littéraures*. Paris: V. Giard, 1910.

———. *M. Roosevelt, Président des États-Unis et la République d'Haïti*. New York: Hamilton Bank Note Engraving and Print Co., 1905.

Fischer, Sibylle. *Modernity Disavowed: Haiti and the Culture of Slavery in the Age of Revolution*. Durham, N.C.: Duke University Press, 2004.

Foner, Eric. *A Short History of Reconstruction*. New York: Harper & Row, 1990.

Foner, Philip S., ed. *Inside the Monster: Writings on the United States and American Imperialism*. New York: Monthly Review Press, 1975.

Fordham, Monroe. "Nineteenth Century Black Thought in the United States: Some Influences of the Santo Domingo Revolution." *Journal of Black Studies* 6 (1975): 115–26.

Fowler, Carolyn. *A Knot in the Thread: The Life and Work of Jacques Roumain*. Washington, D.C.: Howard University Press, 1980.

———. "Motif Symbolism in Jacques Roumain's *Gouverneurs de la Rosée*." *College Language Association Journal* 18, no. 1 (September 1974): 44–51.

Fraser, Cary. *Ambivalent Anticolonialism: The United States and the Genesis of West Indian Independence, 1940–1964*. Westport, Conn.: Greenwood Press, 1994.

Gaillard, Roger. "Notre Ami Langston Hughes." *Le Nouvelliste*, July–August 1967.

Gaines, Kevin K. *Uplifting the Race: Black Leadership, Politics, and Culture in the Twentieth Century*. Chapel Hill: University of North Carolina Press, 1996.

Gándara, José de la. *Anexión y Guerra de Santo Domingo*. Vol. 1. Santo Domingo: Sociedad Dominicana de Bibilofilos, 1975.

Garcia-Zamor, Jean-Claude. "Papadocracy." *Caribbean Review* 2 (Spring 1970): 8–9.

Garnet, Henry Highland. *The Past and the Present Condition, and the Destiny of the Colored Race: A Discourse Delivered on the Fifteenth Anniversary of the Female Benevolent Society of Troy, New York*. Troy, N.Y.: Steam Press of J. C. Kneeland, 1848.

Garrity, Monique P. "The Assembly Industries in Haiti: Causes and Effects." *Journal of Caribbean Studies* 2 (1981): 25–37.

Garvey, Marcus. *The Marcus Garvey and Universal Negro Improvement Association Papers*. Edited by Robert A. Hill. Vol. 1, *1826–August 1919*. Berkeley: University of California Press, 1983.

Geggus, David P. *Haitian Revolutionary Studies.* Bloomington: Indiana University Press, 2002.

———. *Slavery, War and Revolution: The British Occupation of Saint Domingue, 1793–1798.* Oxford: Clarendon Press, 1982.

Geiss, Imanuel. *The Pan-African Movement: A History of Pan-Africanism in America, Europe, and Africa.* New York: Africana, 1973.

Giddens, Anthony. *The Consequences of Modernity.* Stanford: Stanford University Press, 1990.

Gilderhus, Mark T. *Pan-American Visions: Woodrow Wilson in the Western Hemisphere, 1913–1921.* Tucson: University of Arizona Press, 1986.

Gilroy, Paul. *The Black Atlantic: Modernity and Double Consciousness.* Cambridge, Mass.: Harvard University Press, 1993.

Gobat, Michel. *Confronting the American Dream: Nicaragua under U.S. Imperial Rule.* Durham, N.C.: Duke University Press, 2005.

Goldberg, Alan B. "Commercial Folklore and Voodoo in Haiti: International Tourism and Sale of Culture." Ph.D. diss., Indiana University, 1981.

Goldstein, Leslie Friedman. "Racial Loyalty in America: The Example of Frederick Douglass." *Western Political Quarterly* 28, no. 3 (September 1975): 463–76.

Golinger, Eva. *Bush vs. Chavez: Washington's War on Venezuela.* New York: Monthly Review Press, 2007.

Gordon, Lewis R. *Her Majesty's Other Children: Sketches of Racism from a Neocolonial Age.* Lantham, Md.: Rowman and Littlefield, 1997.

Graham, Richard, ed. *The Idea of Race in Latin America, 1870–1940.* Austin: University of Texas Press, 1990.

Gruesz, Kirsten Silva. *Ambassadors of Culture: The Transamerican Origins of Latino Writing.* Princeton, N.J.: Princeton University Press, 2002.

Guridy, Frank A. *Forging Diaspora: Afro-Cubans and African Americans in a World of Empire and Jim Crow.* Chapel Hill: University of North Carolina Press, 2010.

Guy, Rosa. "Haiti: The Enigma of the Caribbean." *Freedomways* 4 (Summer 1964): 413–23.

Hallward, Peter. *Damming the Flood: Haiti, Aristide, and the Politics of Containment.* New York: Verso, 2008.

Hanchard, Michael. "Afro-Modernity: Temporality, Politics, and the African Diaspora." *Public Culture* 11, no. 1 (Winter 1999): 245–68.

Hanson, Haldore E. *The Cultural-Cooperation Program, 1938–1943.* Washington, D.C.: U.S. Government Printing Office, 1944.

Hardouin, A.C. "Haiti: A Study in Regression." *Mexico Quarterly Review* 2 (1963): 77–86.

Harris, Brice, Jr. *The United States and the Italo-Ethiopian Crisis.* Stanford: Stanford University Press, 1964.

Harris, Joseph E. *African-American Reactions to War in Ethiopia, 1936–1941.* Baton Rouge: Louisiana State University Press, 1994.

Harrison, David. "International Tourism and the Less Developed Countries: The Back-

ınd." In *Tourism and Less Developed Countries*, edited by David Harrison. Lon-
Belhaven Press, 1992.

........, Charles C. "Attitudes of Foreign Governments towards the Spanish Reoccupation of the Dominican Republic." *Hispanic American Historical Review* 27, no. 2 (May
1947): 247–68.

Haynes, George E. "A New Negro Emerging." *Tuskegee Messenger*, February 13, 1926.

Heinl, Robert D., Jr. "'Papa Doc' Uses Voodoo to 'Control' U.S. Policy." *Los Angeles Times*,
July 5, 1964.

Heinl, Robert D., and Nancy G. Heinl. *Written in Blood: The Story of the Haitian People,
1492–1971*. Boston: Houghton Mifflin, 1978.

Hellwig, David J. "The Afro American and the Immigrant, 1880–1930: A Study of Black
Social Thought." Ph.D. diss., Syracuse University, 1973.

Hemenway, Robert. *Zora Neale Hurston: A Literary Biography*. Urbana: University of
Illinois Press, 1977.

Hero, Alfred O. "American Negroes and U.S. Foreign Policy, 1937–1967." *Journal of Conflict Resolution* 13 (1969): 220–51.

Herring, Hubert. "Dictatorship in Haiti." *Current History* 46 (January 1964): 34–37, 52.

Hidalgo, Dennis. "Charles Sumner and the Annexation of the Dominican Republic."
Itinerario 21, no. 1 (1997): 51–66.

Himelhoch, Myra. "Frederick Douglass and Haiti's Mole St. Nicolas." *Journal of Negro
History* 56, no. 3 (July 1971): 161–80.

Hoetink, H. *The Two Variants in Caribbean Race Relations: A Contribution to the Sociology of Segmented Societies*. Translated by Eva M. Hooykaas. London: Oxford University Press, 1962.

Hoffman, Elizabeth C. *The Rich Neighbor*. New Haven: Yale University Press, 1992.

Hofstadter, Richard. *Social Darwinism in American Thought*. New York: G. Braziller,
1959.

Hogan, Lawrence. *A Black National News Service: The Associated Negro Press and Claude
Barnett, 1919–1945*. Cranbury, N.J.: Associated University Presses, 1984.

Holden, Robert H., and Eric Zolov, eds. *Latin America and the United States: A Documentary History*. New York: Oxford University Press, 2000.

Holder, Calvin. "The Causes and Composition of West Indian Immigration to NYC,
1900–1952." *Afro Americans in New York Life and History* 11, no. 1 (January 1987):
7–27.

———. "The Rise of the West Indian Politician in New York City, 1900–1952." *Afro-Amer-
icans in New York Life and History* 4, no. 1 (January 1980): 22–42.

Holly, James T. *A Vindication of the Capacity of the Negro Race for Self-government and
Civilized Progress as Demonstrated by the Historical Events of the Haytian Revolution*.
New Haven: W.H. Stanley, 1857.

Honorat, Michel Lamartinière. *Les Dance Folklorique Haitiennes*. Port-au-Prince: Imprimerie de L'Etat, 1955.

Howe, Stephen. *Afrocentrism: Mythical Pasts and Imagined Homes*. London: Verso Press,
1999.

Hughes, Langston. "Free Jacques Roumain: A Letter from Langston Hughes." *Dynamo* 2, no. 1 (May–June 1935): 1–2.

———. *I Wonder as I Wander: An Autobiographical Journey*. New York: Rinehart, 1956.

Hughes, William Hardin, and Frederick D. Patterson, eds. *Robert Russa Moton of Hampton and Tuskegee*. Chapel Hill: University of North Carolina Press, 1956.

Hunt, Alfred N. *Haiti's Influence on Antebellum America: Slumbering Volcano in the Caribbean*. Baton Rouge: Louisiana State Press, 2006.

Hunt, Michael H. *Ideology and U.S. Foreign Policy*. New Haven: Yale University Press, 1987.

Inman, Samuel Guy. *Inter-American Conferences, 1826–1954*. Washington, D.C.: University Press, 1965.

Institut Haïtien de Statistique. *Bulletin Trimestriel de Statistique*. Issues 1–15. Port-au-Prince: L'Institut Haïtien de Statistique, 1951–1954.

Jackson, Eural Grant. "Haiti's Challenge to America." Pts. 1 and 2. *Negro History Bulletin* 21 (October 1957): 22–23 and (November 1957): 30–31.

Jacobs, Sylvia M. *The African Nexus: Black American Perspectives on the European Partition of Africa, 1880–1920*. Westport, Conn.: Greenwood Press, 1981.

Jacobson, Matthew F. *Barbarian Virtues: The United States Encounters Foreign Peoples at Home and Abroad, 1876–1917*. New York: Hill and Wang, 2000.

James, C.L.R. *The Black Jacobins: Toussaint L'Ouverture and the San Domingo Revolution*. 1938. Reprint, New York: Vintage Books, 1989.

James, Winston. *Holding Aloft the Banner of Ethiopia: Caribbean Radicalism in Early Twentieth-century America*. New York: Verso Press, 1998.

Janken, Kenneth. *Rayford W. Logan and the Dilemma of an African American Intellectual*. Amherst: University of Massachusetts Press, 1993.

———. *White: The Biography of Walter White, Mr. NAACP*. New York: New Press, 2003.

Jean-Baptiste, St. Victor. *Le Fondateur devant L'Histoire*. 1954. Reprint, Port-au-Prince: Presses Nationales d'Haiti, 2006.

Jenkins, Candice M. *Private Lives, Proper Relations: Regulating Black Intimacy*. Minneapolis: University of Minnesota Press, 2007.

Jet. "American Teaches Haitian Dances to Jamaicans." October 2, 1958.

———. "Beauty in Haiti," November 1956, 15.

Johnson, James W. *Along This Way: The Autobiography of James Weldon Johnson*. New York: Penguin Books, 1990.

———. *The Race Problem and Peace*. New York: National Association for the Advancement of Colored People Press, 1924.

———. "Self-Determining Haiti: The American Occupation." *Nation*, August 28, 1920: 236–38.

———. "What the United States Has Accomplished." *Nation*, September 4, 1920: 265–67.

———. "Self-Determining Haiti: Government Of, By, and For the National City Bank." *Nation*, September 11, 1920: 295–97.

———. "Self-Determining Haiti: The Haitian People." *Nation*, September 25, 1920: 345–47.

"Joie de Vivre en Haïti: Souvenir Book and Shopping Guide." Miami: Giltravel Publications, 1959.

Jones, Edward A. "*Phylon* Profile XX: Dantès Bellegarde, Miracle of Haiti." *Phylon* 11, no. 1 (1950): 16–22.

Joseph, Gilbert M., Catherine C. LeGrande, and Ricardo D. Salvatore, eds. *Close Encounters of Empire: Writing the Cultural History of U.S.–Latin-American Relations.* Durham, N.C.: Duke University Press, 1998.

Kaplan, Amy. *The Anarchy of Empire in the Making of U.S. Culture.* Cambridge, Mass.: Harvard University Press, 2002.

Kelley, Robin D.G., *Freedom Dreams: The Black Radical Imagination.* Boston: Beacon Press, 2002.

Kelley, Robin D.G., and Earl Lewis, eds. *To Make Our World Anew: A History of African Americans.* New York: Oxford University, 2000.

Kennedy, Paul. "Haiti to Press U.S. to Oust Two Exiles." *New York Times,* August 3, 1958.

Kennedy, Roger. *Mr. Jefferson's Lost Cause: Land, Farmers, Slavery and the Louisiana Purchase.* New York: Oxford University Press, 2004.

King, Kenneth. *Pan-Africanism and Education: A Study of Race Philanthropy and Education in the Southern States of America and East Africa.* Oxford: Clarendon Press, 1971.

Kirby, John B. *Black Americans in the Roosevelt Era: Liberalism and Race.* Knoxville: University of Tennessee Press, 1992.

Kirkland, Frank. "Modernity and Intellectual Life in Black." *Philosophical Forum* 24, nos. 1–3 (1992–1993): 136–65.

Kisseloff, Jeff. *You Must Remember This: An Oral History of Manhattan from the 1890s to World War II.* New York: Schoken Books, 1989.

Krenn, Michael L. *Black Diplomacy: African Americans and the State Department, 1945–1969.* New York: M. E. Sharpe, 1998.

———. *The Impact of Race on U.S. Foreign Policy: A Reader.* New York: Routledge, 1999.

Lacerte, Robert K. "Xenophobia and Economic Decline: The Haitian Case, 1820–1843." *Americas* 37, no. 4 (April 1981): 507–9, 512–15.

Laguerre, Michel S. *The Complete Haitiana: A Bibliographic Guide to the Scholarly Literature, 1900–1980.* 2 vols. Millwood, N.Y.: Kraus International, 1982.

———. "Homeland Political Crisis, the Virtual Diasporic Public Sphere, and Diasporic Politics." *Journal of Latin American Anthropology* 10, no. 1 (April 2005): 206–25.

———. "The Role of the Diaspora in Haitian Politics." In *Haiti Renewed: Political and Economic Prospects,* edited by Robert I. Rotberg. Washington, D.C.: Brooking Institution Press and World Peace Foundation, 1997.

La Liberté. "La Politique du Jour," November 30, 1889.

Langley, J. Ayo. "Pan-Africanism in Paris, 1924–1936." *Journal of Modern African Studies* 7, no. 1 (April 1969): 69–94.

Langley, Lester D. *The Banana Wars: United States Intervention in the Caribbean, 1898–1934.* New York: Scholarly Resources, 2002.

———. *The United States and the Caribbean in the Twentieth Century*. Athens: University of Georgia Press, 1985.

LaRosa, Michael, and Frank O. Mora, eds. *Neighborly Adversaries: Readings in U.S.-Latin-American Relations*. Lanham, Md.: Rowman and Littlefield, 1999.

Latham, Michael E. *Modernization as Ideology: American Social Science and Nation Building in the Kennedy Era*. Chapel Hill: University of North Carolina Press, 2000.

Latortue, Gérard R. "Chairman Duvalier." *Caribbean Review* 2 (Spring 1970): 9–10.

———. "Haiti: Chaotic and Corrupt." *Nation*, November 21, 1966, 539–41.

La Voie. "Les États-Unis et Haiti." March 22, 1890.

———. "Au *New York Herald*." July 18, 1891.

Leger, Jacques N. *Haiti: Her History and Her Detractors*. 1907. Reprint, Westport, Conn.: Negro University Press, 1970.

———. "Tyranny in Haiti." *Current History* 51 (1966): 349–53.

Lemelle, Sidney, and Robin D. G. Kelley, eds. *Imagining Home: Class, Culture, and Nationalism in the African Diaspora*. New York: Verso, 1994.

Le Nouvelliste. "À la Commission Moton." June 17, 1930.

———. "Arrivée de la Commission Moton." June 16, 1930.

———. "Bienvenue à la Commission Moton." June 18, 1930.

———. "Interview de M. Jacques Roumain." March 18, 1930.

Leonard, Thomas, "The New Pan-Americanism in U.S.-Central American Relations, 1933–1954." In Sheinin, *Beyond the Ideal*, 95–114.

Les Nouvelles. "La Question Américaine." June 12, 1889.

Levender, Caroline F., and Robert S. Levine, eds. *Hemispheric American Studies*. New Brunswick, N.J.: Rutgers University Press, 2008.

Lewis, David Levering. *W.E.B. Du Bois: The Fight for Equality and the American Century, 1919–1963*. New York: Henry Holt, 2000.

———. *When Harlem Was in Vogue*. New York: Knopf, 1981.

Lewis, Gordon K. *Main Currents in Caribbean Thought: The Historical Evolution of Caribbean Society in its Ideological Aspects, 1492–1900*. Baltimore: Johns Hopkins University Press, 1983.

Linn, Brian McAllister. *The Philippine War, 1899–1902*. Lawrence: University Press of Kansas, 2002.

Livingston, Carl. "Haiti Exiles in Bahamas Vow Rout of Duvalier." *Washington Post*, September 1, 1963.

Locke, Alain. "Jacques Roumain." *Opportunity* 12 (May 1935): 134–35.

———. "Jacques Roumain." *New Masses*, May 22, 1945.

———. "The Negro in Three Americas." *Journal of Negro Education* 13 (Winter 1944): 7–18.

———. "The New Negro." In *The New Negro*, edited by Alain Locke. 1925. Reprint, New York: Atheneum, 1977.

Lockey, Joseph Byrne. *Pan-Americanism: Its Beginnings*. New York: MacMillan, 1920.

Logan, Rayford W. *The Betrayal of the Negro: From Rutherford B. Hayes to Woodrow Wilson*. New York: Collier Books, 1965.

———. *The Diplomatic Relations of the United States with Haiti, 1776–1891*. Chapel Hill: University of North Carolina Press, 1941.

———. "Education in Haiti." *Journal of Negro History* 15, no. 4 (October 1930): 401–60.

———. *Haiti and the Dominican Republic*. New York: Oxford University Press, 1968.

———. "The Historical Aspects of Pan-Africanism, 1900–1945." In *Pan-Africanism Reconsidered*, edited by the American Society of African Culture. Berkeley and Los Angeles: University of California Press, 1962.

Lomax, Louis E. "Eight Man Invasion." *Nation*, August 30, 1958, 89–91.

Love, Eric T. *Race over Empire: Racism and U.S. Imperialism, 1865–1900*. Chapel Hill: University of North Carolina Press, 2004.

Lundahl, Mats. "A Note on Haitian Migration to Cuba, 1890–1934." *Cuban Studies* 12 (1982): 22–36.

———. "Papa Doc: Innovator in the Predatory State." *Scandia* 50 (1984): 39–78.

———. *Politics or Markets: Essays on Haitian Underdevelopment*. New York: Routledge, 1992.

MacCorkle, William A. *The Monroe Doctrine in Its Relation to the Republic of Haiti*. New York: Neale Publishing, 1915.

MacLeod, Murdo J. "The Haitian Novel of Social Protest." *Journal of Inter-American Studies* 4, no. 2 (April 1962): 207–21.

Magloire, Gérarde, and Kevin A. Yelvington. "Haiti and the Anthropological Imagination." *Gradhiva* 1 (2005): 127–52.

Mahan, Alfred T. *The Influence of Sea Power upon History, 1660–1783*. 1890. Reprint, New York: Pelican Publishing, 2003.

Makonnen, Ras. *Pan-Africanism from Within*. Recorded and edited by Kenneth King Nairobi. London: Oxford University Press, 1973.

Manigat, Max. *Leaders of Haiti, 1804–2001: Historical Overview*. Coconut Creek, Fla.: Educa Vision, 2005.

Marshall, Napoleon B. "Haitians Deny Enmity for American Negroes." *New York Age*. March 8, 1930.

Martí, José. *Our America: Writings on Latin America and the Struggle for Cuban Independence*, edited and with an introduction by Philip S. Foner and translated by Elinor Randall. New York: Monthly Review Press, 1977.

Martin, Wendy. "'Remembering the Jungle': Josephine Baker and the Modernist Parody." In *Prehistories of the Future: The Primitivist Project and the Culture of Modernism*, edited by Elazar Barkan and Ronald Bush. Stanford: Stanford University Press, 1995.

Martínez, Ricardo A. *De Bolívar a Dulles: El Panamericanismo Doctrina y Practica Imperialista*. Mexico City: Editorial América Nueva, 1959.

Mathieson, Alister, and Geoffrey Wall, eds. *Tourism: Economic, Physical and Social Impacts*. London: Longman Scientific and Technical, 1987.

Matthewson, Tim. *A Proslavery Foreign Policy: Haitian-American Relations during the Early Republic*. Westport, Conn.: Praeger Publishers, 2003.

Mazrui, Ali A. "From Social Darwinism to Current Theories of Modernization." *World Politics* 21, no. 1 (October 1968): 69–83.

McFeely, William S. *Frederick Douglass*. New York: W. W. Norton, 1995.

McKivigan, John R. *Forgotten Firebrand: James Redpath and the Making of Nineteenth-Century America*. Ithaca: Cornell University Press, 2008.

Métraux, Alfred. *Voodoo in Haiti*. New York: Oxford University Press, 1959.

Mettler, Barbara. "Modern Dance: Art or Show Business." *Dance Observer*, May 1952, 68.

Michael, John. *Identity and the Failure of America: From Thomas Jefferson to the War on Terror*. Minneapolis: University of Minnesota Press, 2008.

Michel, Emilio Cordero. *La Revolución Haitiana y Santo Domingo*. Santo Domingo: Editora Nacional, 1968.

Mignolo, Walter D. *The Idea of Latin America*. Malden, Mass.: Blackwell Publishing, 2005.

Millspaugh, Arthur. *Haiti under American Control, 1915–1930*. Boston: World Peace Foundation, 1931.

Mintz, Sidney W. *Caribbean Transformations*. Baltimore: Johns Hopkins University Press, 1983.

Mirabeau, Roch L. "Can Haiti Be Helped?" *Nation*, May 18, 1963: 416–18.

Mitchell, Michele. *Righteous Propagation: African Americans and the Politics of Racial Destiny after Reconstruction*. Chapel Hill: University of North Carolina Press, 2004.

Montague, Ludwell Lee. *Haiti and the United States, 1714–1938*. Durham, N.C.: Duke University Press, 1940.

Morris, Joe A. *Nelson A. Rockefeller: A Biography*. New York: Harper and Brothers, 1960.

Morrison, Allan. "The Secret Papers of Franklin D. Roosevelt." *Negro Digest*, January 9, 1951.

Moses, Wilson J. *Afrotopia: The Roots of African American Popular History*. Cambridge: Cambridge University Press, 1998.

———. *Creative Conflict in African American Thought: Frederick Douglass, Alexander Crummell, Booker T. Washington, W.E.B. Du Bois, and Marcus Garvey*. New York: Cambridge University Press, 2004.

———. *The Golden Age of Black Nationalism, 1850–1925*. New York: Oxford University Press, 1988.

Murphy, Gretchen. *Hemispheric Imaginings: The Monroe Doctrine and Narratives of U.S. Empire*. Durham, N.C.: Duke University Press, 2005.

Myers, Gerald E., and Stephanie Reinhart, eds. *African American Genius in Modern Dance*. New York: American Dance Festival, 1993.

———, eds. *American Dance Festival: The Black Tradition in American Modern Dance*. New York: American Dance Festival, 1988.

Nash, Gerald D. *The Crucial Era: The Great Depression and World War II, 1929–1945*. New York: St. Martin's, 1992.

Nash, Joe. "Pioneers in Negro Concert Dance: 1931–1937." In Myers and Reinhart, *American Dance Festival*.

Nelson, William Javier. "The Haitian Political Situation and Its Effect on the Dominican Republic, 1849–1877." *Americas* 45, no. 2 (October 1988): 227–35.

New York Age. "Educational Needs." March 8, 1930.

———. "Government in Gutter." July 26, 1930.

———. "Haiti Exile Lists Grows." July 18, 1959.

———. "Haiti Would Welcome Co-operation by Negroes Says President." April 21, 1934.

———. "Possibilities of the Moton Committee." March 22, 1930.

New York Amsterdam News. "Haiti Prez Chafes at U.S. Aid." January 13, 1962.

New York Times. "Argentinians Assail Haiti Board's Work." March 20, 1930.

———. "Frederick Douglass on the Fifteenth Amendment." April 11, 1870.

———. "Haitian Exiles Form Coordination Group." May 19, 1963.

———. "Haitian Exiles Seek Unity." January 23, 1961.

———. "Haitian Diplomat Indicted." May 27, 1965.

Nicholls, David. "Biology and Politics in Haiti." *Race* 13 (1971): 203–14.

———. *From Dessalines to Duvalier: Race, Colour and National Independence in Haiti.* Cambridge: Cambridge University Press, 1979.

———. "A Work of Combat: Mulatto Historians and the Haitian Past, 1847–1867." *Journal of Inter-American Studies and World Affairs* 16, no. 1 (February 1975): 15–38.

Nichols, Charles, ed. *Arna Bontemps—Langston Hughes Letters, 1925–1967.* New York: Dodd, Mead, 1980.

Norfolk Journal Guide. "Haitian President Sends Greetings to Colored Americans." July 12, 1930.

———. "Haitian Press Gives Banquet." July 12, 1930.

Novas, Jose C. *Twice the Diplomat: Frederick Douglass's Assignments to the Island of Santo Domingo.* New York: Vantage Press, 2001.

Novoa, Ezequiel Ramírez. *La Farsa del Panamericanismo y la Unidad Indoamerica.* Buenos Aires: Editorial Indoamerica, 1955.

Nwankwo, Ifeoma K. *Black Cosmopolitanism: Racial Consciousness and Transnational Identity in the Nineteenth-Century Americas.* Philadelphia: University of Pennsylvania Press, 2005.

———. "Insider and Outsider, Black and American: Rethinking Zora Neale Hurston's Caribbean Ethnography." *Radical History Review* 87 (Fall 2003): 49–77.

———. "The Promises and Perils of U.S. African American Hemispherism: Latin American in Martin Delany's *Blake* and Gayl Jones's *Mosquito*." In *Hemispheric American Studies*, edited by Caroline F. Lavender and Robert S. Levine. New Brunswick, N.J.: Rutgers University Press, 2008.

Oichere, Boniface I. "Dr. Francois Duvalier: High Priest and President of Haiti: 1957–1971." *Black Academy Review* 2, no. 3 (1971): 42–64.

Omi, Michael, and Howard Winant. *Racial Formation in the United States: From the 1960s to the 1990s.* New York: Routledge, 1994.

Osofsky, Gilbert. *Harlem: The Making of a Ghetto; Negro New York, 1890–1930.* New York: Harper and Row, 1971.

Padmore, George. *Pan-Africanism or Communism.* Garden City, N.Y.: Anchor Books, 1972.

Pamphile, Léon D. "America's Policy-making in Haitian Education, 1915–1934." *J* *of Negro Education* 54, no. 1 (Winter 1985): 99–108.

———. *Haitians and African Americans: A Heritage of Tragedy and Hope.* Gainesville: University Press of Florida, 2001.

Pan-American Good Neighbor Forum. "The Negro Pan-American of the Pan-American Good Neighbor Forum." Pamphlet. Chicago, 1943. In the collection of Columbus Memorial Library at the Pan American Union, Washington, D.C.

Pan-American Union. "Pan American News." *Bulletin of the Pan-American Union* 80, no. 1 (January 1946): 50.

Paterson, Thomas G., J. Garry Clifford, Shane J. Maddock, Deborah Kisatsky and Kenneth Hagan, eds. *American Foreign Relations: A History.* Vol. 1, *To 1920.* Boston: Houghton Mifflin, 2005.

Paul, Max. "Racial Ideology and Political Development: The Cases of Haiti and Bermuda." *Sociologus* 32 (1982): 64–80.

Paulino, Edward Ramon. "Birth of a Boundary: Blood, Cement, and Prejudice and the Making of the Dominican-Haiti Border, 1937–1961." PhD diss., Michigan State University, 2001.

Péan, Leslie J.R. *Haïti, Économie Politique de la Corruption: Ensauvagement Macoute et Ses Conséquences.* Vol. 4. Paris: Maisonneuve et Larose, 2007.

Pelnar, Alfred W. "States Rights More Evil than Communism." *Chicago Defender*, January 11, 1964.

Perez, Louis A., Jr. *Cuba and the United States: Ties of Singular Intimacy.* Athens: University of Georgia Press, 2003.

———. *The War of 1898: The United States and Cuba in History and Historiography.* Chapel Hill: University of North Carolina Press, 1998.

Pierre-Charles, Gérard. *L'Economie Haïtienne et Sa Voie de Développement.* Paris: Editions G. P. Maisonneuve et Larose, 1967.

Pittsburgh Courier. "Another Government Insult." July 26, 1930.

———. "Odds and Ends in Haiti," July 12, 1930.

Plummer, Brenda G. "The Afro-American Response to the Occupation of Haiti, 1915–1934." *Phylon* 43, no. 2 (June 1982): 125–43.

———. "Firmin and Martí at the Intersection of Pan-Americanism and Pan-Africanism." In Belnap and Fernández, *José Martí's "Our America,"* 210–27.

———. *Haiti and the Great Powers, 1902–1915.* Baton Rouge: Louisiana State Press, 1988.

———. *Haiti and the United States: The Psychological Moment.* Athens: University of Georgia, 1992.

———. *Rising Wind: Black Americans and U.S. Foreign Affairs, 1935–1960.* Chapel Hill: University of North Carolina Press, 1996.

Polk, James K. "President's Message." *Congressional Globe*, 29th Cong., 1st sess., December 4, 1845.

Pons, Frank Moya. *The Dominican Republic: A National History.* Princeton, N.J.: Markus Weiner, 1998.

Porter, Eric. *What Is This Thing Called Jazz? African American Musicians as Artists, Critics, and Activists.* Berkeley: University of California Press, 2002.

Prattis, P.L. "Moton Commissioners Visit Pineapple Factory Owned by California Company." *New York Age*, July 9, 1930.

———. "U.S. Occupation of Haiti Affected by Citizens with Investments." *Norfolk Journal and Guide*, August 2, 1930.

———. "Writer Says Spirit of U.S. Occupation Is Evil." *Norfolk Journal and Guide*, July 26, 1930.

Price, Hannibal. *De la Réhabilitation de la Race Noire par la République d'Haïti*. Port-au-Prince: Imprimerie J. Verrollot, 1900.

———. *The Haytian Question*. New York: Imprimerie Française L. Weiss & Co., 1891.

———. *Rapport Adressé au Gouvernement d'Haïti sur la Conférence Internationale Américaine de Washington*. New York: Imprimerie Française L. Weiss & Co., 1890.

Price-Mars, Jean. *So Spoke the Uncle*. Translated by Magdaline W. Shannon. Washington, D.C.: Three Continents Press, 1983.

Quarles, Benjamin. *Frederick Douglass*. New York: Atheneum, 1964.

Quintanilla, Luis. *Pan Americanism and Democracy*. Boston: Boston University Press, 1952.

Ramsey, Kate. "Prohibition, Persecution, Performance: Anthropology and the Penalization of Vodou in Mid-20th Century Haiti." *Gradhiva* 1 (2005): 165–79.

———. "Without One Ritual Note: Folklore Performance and the Haitian State, 1935–1946." *Radical History Review* 84 (Fall 2002): 7–42.

Redpath, James. "The Annexation of St. Domingo to Spain." *Douglass' Monthly*, May 1861: 460–61.

Remy, Anseleme. "The Duvalier Phenomena." *Caribbean Studies* 14, no.2 (1974): 38–65.

Renda, Mary A. *Taking Haiti: Military Occupation and the Culture of U.S. Imperialism, 1915–1940*. Chapel Hill: University of North Carolina Press, 2001.

Richter, Linda K. "Political Instability and Tourism in the Third World." In *Tourism and the Less Developed Countries*, edited by David Harrison. New York: Belhaven Press, 1992.

Robinson, Cedric. *Black Marxism*. Chapel Hill: University of North Carolina Press, 2000.

Robinson, Randall. *An Unbroken Agony: Haiti, from Revolution to the Kidnapping of a President*. New York: Basic Civitas Books, 2007.

Rodman, Selden. *Renaissance in Haiti: Popular Painters in the Black Republic*. New York: Pellegrini and Cadulhany, 1948.

———. *Where Art Is Joy: Haitian Art, the First Forty Years*. New York: Ruggles de Latour, 1988.

Roorda, Eric Paul. *The Dictator Next Door: The Good Neighbor Policy and the Trujillo Regime in the Dominican Republic, 1930–1945*. Durham, N.C.: Duke University Press, 1998.

Rosemond, Henri Ch. *The Truth about Haiti and the New Deal Government*. Brooklyn, N.Y.: Haitian Publishing, 1950.

Rotberg, Robert I. *Haiti: The Politics of Squalor*. Boston: Houghton Mifflin, 1971

Rubin, Vera, and Richard P. Schaedel, eds. *The Haitian Potential: Research and Resources of Haiti*. New York: Teachers College Press, 1975.

Salisbury, Richard V. "Hispanismo versus Pan Americanism: Spanish efforts to Counter U.S. Influence in Latin American before 1930." In Sheinin, *Beyond the Ideal*, 67–78.

San Miguel, Pedro L. *The Imagined Island: History, Identity and Utopia in Hispaniola.* Chapel Hill: University of North Carolina Press, 2005.

Schmidt, Hans. *The United States Occupation of Haiti, 1915–1934.* New Brunswick, N.J.: Rutgers University Press, 1971.

Schueller, Malini Johar. *U.S. Orientalisms: Race, Nation and Gender in Literature, 1790–1890.* Ann Arbor: University of Michigan Press, 2001.

Schwartz, Rosalie. *Pleasure Island: Tourism and Temptation in Cuba.* Lincoln: University of Nebraska Press, 1997.

Sears, Louis Martin. "Frederick Douglass and the Mission to Haiti, 1889–1891." *Hispanic American Historical Review* 21, no. 2 (May 1941): 222–38.

Seidel, Robert. "Progressive Pan-Americanism." Ph.D. diss., Cornell University, 1975.

Service de Statistique Municipale. *Bulletin de Statistique.* Vol. 1. Port-au-Prince: Imprimerie de L'État, 1943.

Shannon, Magdaline W. *Jean Price-Mars, the Haitian Elite and the American Occupation, 1915–1934.* New York: St. Martin's, 1996.

———. "The U.S. Commission for the Study and Review of Conditions in Haiti and Its Relationship to President Hoover's Latin American Policy." *Caribbean Studies* 15, no. 4 (January 1976): 53–72.

Shapiro, Herbert. *White Violence and Black Response: From Reconstruction to Montgomery.* Amherst: University of Massachusetts Press, 1988.

Shawn, Ted. "Black Christmas." *Dance Magazine*, May 1950, 27–29.

Sheinin, David, ed. *Beyond the Ideal: Pan Americanism in Inter-American Affairs.* Westport, Conn.: Praeger, 2000.

Shelby, Tommie. *We Who Are Dark: The Philosophical Foundations of Black Solidarity.* Cambridge, Mass.: Harvard University Press, 2007.

Sherman, George. "Nonintervention: A Shield for 'Papa Doc.'" *Reporter*, June 20, 1963, 27–29.

Singer, Marshall R. *Weak States in World of Powers: The Dynamics of International Relationships.* New York: Free Press, 1972.

Sitkoff, Harvard. *A New Deal for Blacks: The Emergence of Civil Rights as a National Issue.* New York: Oxford University Press, 1978.

Skinner, Elliot P. *African Americans and U.S. Policy toward Africa, 1850–1924: In Defense of Black Nationality.* Washington, D.C.: Howard University Press, 1992.

———. "The Dialectic between Diasporas and Homelands." In *Global Dimensions in the African Diaspora*, by Joseph E. Harris. Washington, D.C.: Howard University Press, 1982.

Slotkin, Richard. *Lost Battalions: The Great War and the Crisis of American Nationality.* New York: Henry Holt, 2005.

Smith, Jennie M. *When the Hands Are Many: Community Organization and Social Change in Rural Haiti.* Ithaca: Cornell University Press, 2001.

Smith, Jon, and Deborah Cohn, eds. *Look Away: The U.S. South in New World Studies.* Durham, N.C.: Duke University Press, 2004.

Smith, Matthew J. "Shades of Red in a Black Republic: Radicalism, Black Consciousness, and Social Conflict in Postoccupation Haiti, 1934–1957." Ph.D. diss., University of Florida, 2002.

Smith, Peter H. *Talons of the Eagle: Dynamics of U.S.-Latin American Relations*. New York: Oxford University Press, 2000.

Smith, Valerie. *Self Discovery and Authority in Afro-American Narrative*. Cambridge, Mass.: Harvard University Press, 1987.

Sommers, Jeffrey. "Haiti and the Hemispheric Imperative to Invest: *The Bulletin of the Pan American Union*." *Journal of Haitian Studies* 9, no. 1 (Spring 2003): 68–94.

Spector, Robert M. *W. Cameron Forbes and the Hoover Commissions to Haiti (1930)*. Latham, Md.: University Press of America, 1985.

———. "W. Cameron Forbes in Haiti: Additional Light on the Genesis of the 'Good Neighbor' Policy." *Caribbean Studies* 6, vol. 2 (July 1966): 28–45.

Stephens, Michelle Ann. *Black Empire: The Masculine Global Imaginary of Caribbean Intellectuals, 1914–1962*. Durham, N.C.: Duke University Press, 2005.

Stovall, Tyler. *Paris Noir: African Americans in the City of Light*. New York: Houghton Mifflin, 1996.

Streeter, Stephen M. "The Myth of Pan-Americanism: U.S. Policy toward Latin American during the Cold War, 1954–1963." In Sheinin, *Beyond the Ideal*, 167–182.

Stuckey, Sterling. *Slave Culture: Nationalist Theory and the Foundations of Black America*. New York: Oxford University Press, 1987.

Suggs, Henry L. "African-American Response to the U.S. Occupation of Haiti." *Journal of Negro History* 73 (Fall–Winter 1988): 33–45.

Sweeney, Fionnghuala. *Frederick Douglass and the Atlantic World*. Liverpool University Press, 2007.

Sylvain, Georges. *Dix Années de Lutte pour la Liberté*. Port-au-Prince: Henri Deschamps, 1950.

Szulc, Ted. "Beautiful, Cruel, Explosive—Haiti." *New York Times Magazine*, June 9, 1963.

Tansill, Charles C. *The United States and Santo Domingo*. Baltimore: Johns Hopkins Press, 1938.

Teal, Christopher. *Hero of Hispaniola: America's First Black Diplomat, Ebenezer D. Bassett*. Westport, Conn.: Praeger, 2008.

Time. "Bon Papa." February 22, 1954.

Torgovnick, Marianna. *Gone Primitive: Savage Intellects, Modern Lives*. University of Chicago Press, 1990.

Trouillot, Michel-Rolph. *Haiti: State against Nation; The Origins and Legacy of Duvalierism*. New York: Monthly Review Press, 1990.

Trueblood, Edward Gatewood. *The U.S. Cultural Relations Program with Latin America: The Formative Years*. Gainesville, Fla.: Felicity Press, 1977.

Turits, Richard Lee. *Foundations of Despotism: Peasants, the Trujillo Regime and Modernity in Dominican History*. Stanford: Stanford University, 2004.

Tuskegee Messenger. "Haitian Representative Is Commencement Visitor." June 14, 1930.

———. "Principal Moton in New Year's Message Urges Race to Harness Resources." January 17, 1925.

Tyler, Alice F. *The Foreign Policy of James G. Blaine.* Minneapolis: University of Minnesota Press, 1927.

Uchitelle, Louis. "Haiti Stuck with Dictator and No U.S. Aid." *Chicago Tribune,* February 14, 1965.

U.S. Department of Commerce, Bureau of the Census in Cooperation with the Office of the Coordinator of Inter-American Affairs. *Haiti: Summary of Biostatistics, Maps and Charts, Population, Natality and Mortality Statistics.* Washington, D.C.: U.S. Government Printing Office, 1945.

U.S. Department of State. *U.S. Department of State Bulletin* 32 (February 14, 1955): 273–75.

U.S. Department of State, Office of Public Affairs. *The Program of the Interdepartmental Committee on Scientific and Cultural Cooperation.* Washington, D.C.: U.S. Government Printing Office, 1944.

Vandenbosch, Amry. "The Small States in International Politics and Organization." *Journal of Politics* 26, no. 2 (May 1964): 293–312.

Verna, Chantalle F. "Haiti's Second Independence and the Promise of Pan-American Cooperation, 1934–1956." Ph.D. diss., Michigan State University, 2005.

de Vidas, Albert. "The Foreign Relations of Haiti in Hemispheric Affairs from Independence to Occupation, 1804–1915." PhD diss., New York University, 1971.

Von Eschen, Penny. *Race against Empire: Black Americans and Anticolonialism.* Ithaca: Cornell University Press, 1997.

———. *Satchmo Blows Up the World: Jazz Ambassadors Play the Cold War.* Cambridge, Mass.: Harvard University Press, 2004.

Walker, Juliet E.K. *The History of Black Business in America: Capitalism, Race, Entrepreneurship.* New York: MacMillan Library Reference, 1998.

Washington Post. "Colored Folk Plan Trade with Haiti." September 9, 1934.

———. "Opposition Papers Sacked in Haiti," May 6, 1958.

Weil, Thomas E., et al. *Area Handbook for Haiti.* Washington, D.C.: U.S. Government Printing Office, 1973.

Welles, Sumner. *Naboth's Vineyard: The Dominican Republic, 1844–1924.* New York: Arno Press, 1972.

Weston, Rubin F. *Racism in U.S. Imperialism: The Influence of Racial Assumptions on American Foreign Policy.* Columbia: University of South Carolina Press, 1972.

White, Deborah Gray. *Too Heavy A Load: Black Women in Defense of Themselves, 1894–1994.* New York: W. W. Norton, 1999.

White, Walter F. *A Man Called White.* New York: Arno Press, 1954.

Wilcken, Lois E. "Spirit Unbound: New Approaches to the Performance of Haitian Folklore." In *Caribbean Dance from Abakuá to Zouk: How Movement Shapes Identity,* edited by Susanna Sloat. Gainesville: University Press of Florida, 2002.

Wilson, Joan H. *Herbert Hoover: Forgotten Progressive.* Boston: Little, Brown, 1975.

Yunus, Muhammad. *Banker to the Poor: Micro-lending and the Battle against World Poverty*. New York: Public Affairs, 2003.

Zacaïr, Philippe. "Haiti on His Mind: Antonio Maceo and Caribbeanness." *Caribbean Studies* 33, no. 1 (2005): 47–78.

Zoumaras, Thomas. "The Path to Panamericanism: Eisenhower's Foreign Economic Policy toward Latin America." Ph.D. diss., University of Connecticut, 1987.

Index

Abbott, Elizabeth, 195

Adam, J. Joseph, 62

Africa: Claude Barnett and, 122, 129; Joshua Cockburn in, 225n49; and colonialism and anticolonialism, 31, 39, 43, 54, 109, 113, 114, 165; cultural influence of, 163, 166; education in, 67; Haitians in, 190, 196, 206; as homeland, 177; independence in, 184, 185, 207; literary depictions of, 186; NAACP and, 132; New Negro interests in, 95; and race, 165; and self-determination, 122; U.S. African Americans and, 43, 113, 114, 148, 207; U.S. anti-Communism programs in, 148; and World War II, 113

African America and Haiti (Dixon), 16

African American press, U.S.: 19th-century, 95; and Africa, 207; and class, 95; components of, 94; development of, 95; focuses of, 95; and Haiti, 60–61, 96, 99–100, 181, 183, 199, 201, 204–5; and Hoover administration, 80; impact of, 95–96; international coverage by, 96; and Moton Commission, 76, 80; treatment of independent black nations by, 125; and U.S. expansion, 60; and U.S. occupation of Haiti, 57; and World War I, 60. *See also* Associated Negro Press (ANP)

African Americans (non-U.S.): Afro-Caribbeans, 132; Afro-Cubans, 10; Afro-Latin Americans, 15, 132; and anticolonialism, 122; and collective action, 15; definitions of, xv; and discrimination, xv, 19; and Haiti, 3, 12–13; impact of, 211n43; intellectual and cultural exchanges among, xv; and migration, xv; and Pan Americanism, 10; perceptions of, 65; scholarship on, 17; and

slavery, xv, 10, 31; United Nations and, 134; U.S. African Americans and, 55

African Americans, U.S.: and African culture, 166; and Afro-Modernity, 15; and anticolonialism, 23–24, 113, 114, 184, 185, 237n40; and class, 115, 218n5; and Cold War, 142, 149, 152, 200–201, 206, 207; and color politics, 116–17; Communist depictions of, 148; and dance, 170, 178; definition of, xv; depictions of, in film, 122–23; Jean-Léon Destiné on, 166; as diplomats, 21, 27, 38, 52, 53, 213n9; and Dominican Republic, 43; and Forbes Commission, 67; and Fourteenth Amendment, 70; and Haiti, as symbol, 88; and Haitian exiles, 194, 196, 206; and Haitian government and leaders, 102, 181–83, 185, 186, 196, 201, 206; and Haitian Revolution, 4, 5, 11, 80, 123, 129; and killings on Haiti/Dominican Republic border, 109; middle class, 98, 115; and Moton Commission, 218n4; and nationalism, 8, 16, 26, 204; and Pan Americanism, 8–9, 10–11, 13, 15, 19, 23, 30–31, 48, 60, 80, 87, 110, 152, 182; and poverty, 58; and race, 13, 16, 62, 114, 118; and racial uplift, 14, 66, 87, 92, 98, 182; scholarship on, 16, 60, 213n9, 218n5, 237n40; and self-determination, 86, 97; self-perceptions of, 65; and slavery, xv, 5, 210n12; use of *Ethiopia* by, 223n4; and U.S. foreign policy, 54, 55, 82; and U.S. government, 3, 9, 66; and U.S. mainstream press, 202; and U.S. occupation of Haiti, 59, 60, 61–62, 101; and U.S. Reconstruction, 27, 35; and world wars, 95, 109, 113, 115, 152. *See also* Elites, U.S. African American

and Charles Sumner, 35; as symbol, 4, 5, 6, 12–13, 88, 93, 103, 120, 129, 131–32, 152, 165, 184–85, 186, 201, 225n44; taxes in, 56, 64, 68–69; *Time* magazine on, 150; and United States, 7, 20, 163; and U.S. expansion, 45–46; U.S. mainstream press coverage of, 186, 188, 201–2; U.S. ministers to, 36; and U.S. Navy, 49, 50; U.S. recognition of (1862), 5, 21; U.S. whites and, 6–7; violence in, 13, 64, 66, 67, 85, 91, 109; and wealth, 20, 48; and World War II, 111, 114. *See also* Douglass, Frederick: as U.S. minister to Haiti

—economy of: 19th-century, 138; and 1956 general strike, 126, 127; and anticommunism, 121; and arts, 177; and banking, 96; and business creation, 99; and capital, 109, 129; and class, 120; and commercial ventures, 92–93; and cultural exchange, 176; and currency, 233n62; and debt, 109, 126, 138, 145, 198, 231n28, 233n62; and deficits, 197; and dependence on foreign countries, 51, 59, 63, 138; and development and modernization, 12, 119, 121, 151; and diversification, 146; Frederick Douglass and, 48, 51; during Duvalier regime, 181, 182; and economic disadvantages, 147; during Estimé administration, 181, 233n62; and foreign aid, 87, 108, 111, 121, 140, 145, 147, 148, 181, 182, 189, 194–95, 196–98, 199–200, 242n80; and foreign businesses, 119, 147; and foreign organizations, 104, 120; and foreign philanthropy, 149; Fourth Pan African Congress and, 99; during Great Depression, 104; and Hurricane Hazel, 124; and industry, 99; and infrastructure and internal improvements, 96, 143, 144, 145, 151, 200; and investment, 87, 88, 89, 93, 96–97, 111–12, 119, 128, 151, 156; and joint business ventures, 107; during Lescot administration, 233n62; L'Union Patriotique Haïtienne and, 139; during Magloire administration, 126, 143, 145, 181, 233n62; merchants and, 107; and politics, 109, 126–27, 145, 180; post-U.S. occupation, 104, 111, 120, 138; and public relations campaign, 140–41, 144–45, 147, 151; and race, 119, 122; and racial solidarity, 121–22; revenues of, 233n62; scholarship on, 104, 121, 139; and self-determination, 121, 182;

and shipping industry, 104–5; and social issues, 119; and standard of living, 124–25; and tariffs, 105, 138; and trade, 14, 45, 48, 51, 56, 57–58, 63, 93, 97, 99, 108, 137, 138; and transnational businesses, 129; U.S. African Americans and, 60; U.S. dominance of, 102, 198; U.S. economic intervention in, 20; U.S. elites and, 136; U.S. merchants and, 45, 105; during U.S. occupation, 63, 64, 99–102, 120, 137, 138; Walter White and, 133, 134, 152; and World War II, 109, 111, 113, 233n62. *See also* Agriculture, Haitian; Tourism, in Haiti

—education in: Mary McLeod Bethune and, 167; Catholic Church and, 76, 77; and class, 76, 77, 78; curricula for, 76, 77; curriculum for, 59; and development, 78; Duvalier regime and, 190; French influences in, 59; funding of, 76; government expenditures on, 56; Harding administration and, 62–63; and industrial education, 87; institutions for, 165; languages for, 76–77; Ministry of Agriculture and, 75; Ministry of Education and, 59; and national public school system, 76; quality of, 76; reform of, 14; U.S. African Americans and, 80; U.S. schools for, 72, 76, 77; Walter White and, 133. *See also* Moton Commission

—occupation of (1915–1934): beginning of, 19; end of, 89; and Executive Accord of August 1933, 99, 100; Forbes Commission and, 58, 67; and formation of L'Union Patriotique Haïtienne, 139; and Haitian culture, 160–61, 176; and Haitian economy, 57, 63, 64, 99–102, 120, 137, 138, 201; Haitian leadership and, 96; Harding administration and, 62–63; Herbert Hoover and, 102; and internal improvements, 63; latter stages of, 22; legacy of, 157, 231n27; opposition to, 55, 57, 61–62, 111; and paternalism, 91; and political affairs, 120; press and, 101; Franklin Roosevelt and, 102, 223n1; scholarship on, 21; significance of, 120; U.S. African Americans and, 59, 60–61, 62, 75, 96, 99, 101, 111; and U.S. control of Haitian treasury, 135; U.S. perceptions during, 157; violence during, 135; Walter White and, 135, 225n39; white U.S. investors and, 96. *See also* Moton Commission

Puerto Rico, 30, 54, 121, 143, 212n56, 235n14
Punta del Este conference, 198–99

Quisqueya (airline), 119

Race: and anti-imperial protests, 64–65; and
class, 10, 18, 64; and discrimination, 19,
28, 74; and education, 67; Europeans and,
10; Frederick Douglass and, 6–7, 9, 22, 27,
38–39; Haitians and, 11, 16; and legislation, 27, 28; and Pan Americanism, 17,
18–20, 24; and slavery, xv, 5, 6, 18, 26; and
socioeconomic inequality, 17; U.S. African
Americans and, 11, 13, 16, 19; and U.S.
exceptionalism, 31; and U.S. expansion, 22,
27, 28, 29, 38–39; and U.S. foreign policy,
17; U.S. government and, 24; and violence,
28, 70, 85
Racial progress/racial uplift: and African
American press, 91; Claude Barnett and,
91, 97, 115, 205; and business ventures in
Haiti, 118; and capitalist development, 128;
and class, 14, 68; and collaboration, 8, 21,
59; and commercial ventures, 92–93; components of, 59; and Duvalier regime, 186;
Frederick Douglass and, 8, 9, 27, 41, 42, 43;
and education, 68, 75; Haitian Afro-American Chamber of Commerce Commission
and, 103, 105; and Haitian public relations
campaign, 132, 151; and Haitian Revolution,
87–88; Haitians and, 92; ideology of, 68;
international, 88, 92; and Moton Commission, 59; and Pan Americanism, 42; and
propagandistic cinema, 123; scholarship on,
231n9; U.S. African Americans and, 14, 87,
92, 98, 182; and U.S. expansion, 27, 41, 42,
43; whites and, 14
Racine, Emmanuel, 126, 203, 204
Ramsey, Kate, 160–61
Rangel, Charles, 209n4 (introduction)
Rare Black Short Subjects (film), 229n115
RCA Communications, 147
Reader's Digest (magazine), 141
Reconstruction, U.S.: black self-determination
and self-help during, 97; Frederick Douglass during, 27, 28, 36; education during,
106; end of, 40, 43
Red Cross, 116

Redd, George, 150
Redpath, James, 34, 214n35
Reed, E. C., 45
Renda, Mary A., 61
Republicans and Republican Party: Claude
Barnett and, 97; Frederick Douglass and, 35;
Robert R. Moton and, 69; National Com-
mittee of, 224n22; Progressives and, 230n7;
Radical, 28, 35, 53–54; and U.S. occupation
of Haiti, 62
Ricourt, Clamart, 91, 96
Ritter-Lerne-Young Associates, 237n42
Robert R. Moton Commission. *See* Moton
Commission
Roberts, Kenneth, 230n1
Robeson, Paul, 146, 153, 166, 237n41
Robinson, Randall, 1–2, 209n4 (introduction)
Rockefeller, Nelson: and Institute of Inter-
American Affairs, 111, 112, 114, 115, 126; and
Rayford W. Logan, 112; and Walter White,
135, 152, 154
Rockefeller Foundation, 137, 155, 164
Rodman, Selden, 137
Roorda, Eric Paul, 226n68
Roosevelt, Eleanor, 135, 136, 237n46
Roosevelt, Franklin D.: appointments by,
227n91; and Four Freedoms, 149, 234n71;
and Good Neighbor Policy, 22, 67, 101, 106,
112, 126, 156, 164; and Haiti, 100–101, 102,
110, 223n1; and New Deal, 95; and Sténio
Vincent, 89, 223n1; and Walter White, 110
Roosevelt, Theodore, 55
Rosemond, Henri Ch., 107, 140, 141, 223n1,
227n88, 232n29
Rosemond, Ludovic, 107
Rosenwald Foundation, 137
Roumain, Jacques, 148
Roy, Eugène, 75, 76, 82
Ruhl, Arthur, 72
Russell, John H., 57, 67
Russia, 100, 141, 177. *See also* Soviet Union
Russwurm, John B., 6
Rustin, Bayard, 207

Saget, Nissage, 36, 37, 38
Saint-Domingue. *See* Haiti
Saint-Marc, Haiti, 76, 105, 161
Saks Fifth Avenue, 231n17

26–27, 49, 50, 51; and Moton Commission, 72, 80, 83, 86; and Pan Americanism, 52; and Service Technique L'Agriculture, 82; John H. Smyth and, 44; and U.S.-Haitian trade balance, 108; and R. R. Wright trip to Haiti, 108

Stephens, Alexander, 28

Stephens, Michelle Ann, 211n35

Stevens, Johnnie, 4–5

Stewart, W. Ellis, 227n91

Still, William Grant, 166

Stimson, Henry, 86

St. Louis, Mo., 39, 216n79

St. Louis Exposition, 77

St. Luke Herald (newspaper), 74

Stormy Weather (film), 171

Sumner, Charles, 28, 34, 35

Supreme Court, U.S., 43

Supreme Liberty Life Insurance Company, 227n91

Sutton Art Theater, 166

Tamaris, Helen, 174

Teacher's College, Columbia University, 78–79

Teal, Christopher, 36, 38, 217n110

Tell My Horse (Hurston), 65–66, 220n30

Tennessee, 149

Texas, 39, 40

Thirteenth Amendment. U.S., 35, 38

Thompson, Charles, 234n1

Thompson, John E. W., 213n9

Ti-Marcel, 168

Time (magazine), 150, 202

Ti-Roro, 168

Tobias, Channing, 136

Tonton-makout and *cagoulars,* 181, 183, 239n9

Torgovnick, Marianna, 162

Touré, Sekou, 189

Tourism, Caribbean, 212n56, 230n4, 235n14

Tourism, in Haiti: and arts and culture, 23, 109, 117, 119, 137, 141, 147, 151, 155, 158, 160, 165, 168, 173, 174, 176, 178, 231n17, 233n62; Claude Barnett and, 117, 120, 121, 124, 127, 128, 130, 181; critical assessments of, 24, 130; and development, 14, 93, 109, 120, 133, 146; and general strike, 127; growth of, 117, 119, 143, 145, 233n62; Haitian government and, 23, 130, 136–37, 141, 143, 144–45, 147;

impact of, 117, 146–47, 151, 165; and internal improvements, 141; joint advisory board for, 134; and modernization theory, 146, 147, 151; and perceptions of Haiti, 155, 157;; U.S. African Americans and, 4, 23, 93, 109, 119, 120, 121, 147, 181, 227n91; U.S. promotion of, 4; Poppy Cannon White and, 144–46; Walter White and, 132, 134, 136, 140–42, 143, 144–45, 151, 230n4, 231n17

Toussaint L'Ouverture, François Dominique: Claude Barnett and, 123; birthplace of, 233n59; Frederick Douglass and, 48; dramatic depictions of, 237n41; Katherine Dunham and, 128; as Haitian head of state, 32, 192–93; Moton Commission and, 103; and peasantry, 103, 128; as revolutionary, 32, 103; and slavery, 32; U.S. African Americans and, 13. See also College of Toussaint L'Ouverture

Trade goods: bananas, 105; Barbancourt Haitian rum, 136, 147; bauxite, 198; cacao, 124, 138; clothing, 147; coffee, 41, 48, 57, 64, 89, 105, 108, 109, 113, 124, 138, 188, 198, 233n62; cotton, 89; duty-free, 147; European, 216n70; glassware, 147; gunpowder, 33; handcrafts, 147; industrial alcohol, 145; jewelry, 147; leather items, 105; livestock, 33; logwood, 105, 138; perfumes, 147; pineapple, 76; poultry, 106; rubber, 112, 113, 114; rum, 105, 188; salt, 146; sisal, 76, 105, 113, 233n62; soap, 105; sugar, 41, 64, 105, 112, 113, 233n62; and tariffs, 216n70; tobacco, 105; U.S., 216n70; wheat, 198; during World War II, 113

Treasury, U.S., 198

Treaty of Basilea, 32

Trenton (N.J.) Times (newspaper), 219n8

Trinidad and Tobago, 20

"Trip to Haiti, A" (Douglass), 5–7

Troubled Island (Still, opera), 166

Trouillot, Michel-Rolph: on authoritarian government in Haiti, 180, 181; on *cagoulars,* 239n9; on color politics, 178–79, 232n33, 238n77, 240n45; on Haitian diaspora, 196; on Haitian economy, 104, 137; on Haitian national unity, 240n45; on Haiti in the 1940s and 1950s, 120, 121; on legacy of U.S. occupation, 231n27; on religion and class in Haiti, 161